COMPELLING CRIMINAL
JUSTICE COMMUNICATIONS

COMPELLING CRIMINAL JUSTICE COMMUNICATIONS

SHANNA R. VAN SLYKE

NEW YORK OXFORD
OXFORD UNIVERSITY PRESS

Oxford University Press is a department of the University of Oxford.
It furthers the University's objective of excellence in research, scholarship,
and education by publishing worldwide. Oxford is a registered trade mark of
Oxford University Press in the UK and certain other countries.

Published in the United States of America by Oxford University Press
198 Madison Avenue, New York, NY 10016, United States of America.

Library of Congress Cataloging-in-Publication Data
Names: Van Slyke, Shanna, author.
Title: Compelling criminal justice communications / Shanna Van Slyke.
Description: New York : Oxford University Press, [2020] |
    Includes bibliographical references and index. | Summary:
    "The primary aim of this proposed book is to motivate and assist
    criminal justice students to produce compelling written and oral
    communications. Strong communication skills are critical to success
    both as a criminal justice student and as a criminal justice professional.
    The text provides comprehensive coverage of the concrete principles
    involved in the production of compelling writings and briefings about
    crime, accompanied by both end-of-chapter review and writing exercises.
    The contents include broad coverage and consideration of academic as well
    as professional communications"—Provided by publisher.
Identifiers: LCCN 2019033688 (print) | LCCN 2019033689 (ebook) | ISBN
    9780190848026 (paperback) | ISBN 9780190848033 (ebk) | ISBN 9780190084387 (ebk)
Subjects: LCSH: Criminal justice, Administration of—Study and teaching—
    United States. | Business communication—Study and teaching—United States.
Classification: LCC HV9950 .V37 2020 (print) | LCC HV9950 (ebook) | DDC
    808.06/6364—dc23
LC record available at https://lccn.loc.gov/2019033688
LC ebook record available at https://lccn.loc.gov/2019033689

Printing number: 9 8 7 6 5 4 3 2 1
Printed by Sheridan Books, Inc., United States of America

For my children: Lily Belle, Haven Leigh, Jackson Charlie, and Devin Beau.
My world became an even better place the days they were born.
I am already proud of them, and think they will enjoy reading this book
when they get old enough.

BRIEF TABLE OF CONTENTS

DETAILED TABLE OF CONTENTS

PREFACE

This book is about how to produce effective written and oral communications about crime and criminal justice. The overarching premise is that an effective criminal justice communication is one that is *compelling*. Compelling communications have the power to convince. For criminal justice students, this means creating an impression of a dedicated and knowledgeable student, one who knows the material and is willing and able to follow instructions. This is the type of student who earns high grades and for whom instructors are willing to serve as references and write letters of recommendation. For criminal justice professionals, effective communication creates an impression of competence, professionalism, and credibility; inspires trust and confidence; fosters cooperation and compliance; and ultimately facilitates effective and efficient criminal justice system operation.

PREMISE AND IMPETUS

Communication is ubiquitous in the study and practice of criminal justice and related fields. Writing does not occur only in English courses, nor are presentations limited to oral communications courses. Instead, contemporary higher education stresses the importance of communication skills throughout the curriculum. Writing and presentations are also a major component in the daily routines of criminal justice professionals—whether they work in policing, courts, or corrections. Thus, starting when we are students and continuing throughout our careers, we will be writing and presenting, and effective communication skills have a strong and positive impact on career success.

Because communication is so common and consequential from college to career, it is worth the effort to do our best at it. What we learn as a student will be useful throughout our careers—not just while we are students, and certainly not just in the class in which we have the writing or public speaking assignment. In the long term, even a paper that is substantively unrelated to our major teaches us and provides experience sharpening relevant communication skills, such as organizing and expressing ideas, undertaking research and thinking critically about evidence, budgeting our time and handling our anxiety, and recognizing our communication strengths and weaknesses. Each paper and presentation we develop, therefore, adds to our continually expanding repertoire of communication skills. Even when we do not learn a new skill, we are practicing and thereby sharpening our existing skills as we undertake more and more communications assignments.

In seeking to elevate the quality of criminal justice communications, this book makes an important assumption: Every single one of us can become a better communicator. No one, in other words, is a perfect communicator. Thus, this book is not just for poor communicators. Rather, as our awareness and experience accumulate, an already strong communicator can become even stronger.

GOAL AND STRUCTURE

Criminal justice students and professionals who are committed to being the best they can be—as well as criminal justice instructors dedicated to improving their students' communication skills—will love this book. The reason they will love it is because this book's primary goal is to provide actionable guidelines for producing effective criminal justice communications. This book not only identifies the features of effective communication, in other words, but it also illustrates exactly how to achieve them.

The heart of this book lies in the middle nine chapters, each one devoted to one of the following principles of effective criminal justice communication: professionalism, responsiveness, organization, logic, evidence, completeness, correctness, clarity, and conciseness. Each principle is then broken down into specific guidelines before being applied to two concrete communication assignments, one for students and one for professionals working in in the field. Prior to the principles is the introduction, which makes a case for the importance of compelling criminal justice communications, contrasts criminal justice communications with other types of communications, and outlines the six stages involved in producing effective criminal justice communications. Following the principles is a chapter on how to prepare and deliver compelling PowerPoint presentations, which draws on research about how to maximize audience attention, comprehension, and retention. At the end of the book are three appendices covering processes involved in producing effective communications: researching, formatting in American Psychological Association (APA) style, and editing.

The eleven chapters end with a set of exercises that are explicitly linked to the chapter's learning objectives. All chapters have matching and writing exercises. Matching questions are the most basic exercises and are designed to gauge proficiency in recognizing relevant terminology. The writing exercises involve describing and demonstrating how to produce effective communications. Most chapters also have multiple choice questions, which help us distinguish between effective and ineffective techniques and communications. And the nine principles chapters also contain editing exercises, which challenge us to detect and correct flawed communications. Answers to these exercises are provided at the end of the text, while instructors can find additional exercises, recommended 16-week and 8-week schedules, and grading rubrics for papers and presentations in the instructor's manual.

AUDIENCE AND USAGE

This book has been designed to meet the needs of multiple audiences. The primary audience is undergraduate students majoring in criminal justice, criminology, or related disciplines (e.g., cybersecurity, criminal intelligence analysis, homeland security). This book can serve as the primary text in lower-level courses and as a supplemental text in upper-level courses. These students should read all chapters and appendices; but it would be too much to complete all of the exercises that have students construct their own writings and presentations. Instead, instructors can pick and choose which exercises best fit the course purpose and student needs.

There are two secondary audiences: graduate students and criminal justice professionals. This book can serve as a supplemental text in a course at the beginning of a graduate program and as a self-paced refresher text for graduate students and criminal justice professionals. Members of this audience would likely find it useful to pick and choose particular segments of this book, such as those that address their communication weaknesses or that cover specific communications relevant to their current or intended job duties.

ACKNOWLEDGMENTS

I would like to thank the reviewers for their suggestions throughout the development of the book.

Amy S. Vanderford, University of Mississippi
Connie M. Koski, Longwood University
Milton C. Hill, Stephen F. Austin State University
William P. DeFeo, Western Connecticut State University
Gregory W. Bridgeman, Lake Sumter State College
Julie Campbell, University of Nebraska at Kearney
Julie Coon, Roger Williams University
C Nana Derby, Virginia State University
George R. Franks, Stephen F. Austin State University
William Mixon, Columbus State University
Sheryl Sunia, Hawaii Pacific University

Introduction

After reading this chapter, you will be able to

1. Recognize terminology relevant to compelling criminal justice communication.
2. Argue for the importance of effective communication skills in the study and practice of criminal justice.
3. Contrast technical communication with other types of communication.
4. Describe the special challenges involved in criminal justice communication.
5. Outline the nine principles of compelling criminal justice communication.
6. Outline the six stages of the communication process.
7. Exhibit effective note-taking strategies.
8. Demonstrate awareness of effective interview and interrogation practices.

Without credible communication, and a lot of it, the hearts and minds of others are never captured.

–JOHN P. KOTTER

Look closely: "SHOPLIFTERS WILL BE PROSTITUTED," "GO SLOW ACCIDENT PORN AREA" (Cliff, 2017), and "VIOLATORS WILL BE TOWED AND FIND $50" (Chi, 2017). These are real signs. The errors were not caught and corrected before these signs were posted in public. Let them make you laugh but also to serve as a reminder of why using all capital letters is unwise. It is harder to catch such typos in our own work, as we tend to see what we intend (and which looks similar to what we intend) rather than what is actually there.

Not all typos and communication blunders are funny or harmless, though. University of Missouri–Columbia basketball fans were panicked when, during a game, police officers in the audience tweeted, "Okay but can we talk about how @MizzouHoops is so good it's criminal. About to be a homicide at Mizzou Arena. #MIZ" (Jost, 2017). And a national CNN news headline read, "Police: Manhunt Marred by Poor Communication" (CNN.com, 2005). It continued: "Atlanta's police chief Friday said last week's deadly courthouse shooting and the subsequent manhunt for a suspect points to the need for improvements in communications and leadership protocol during emergencies." Much about this tragedy was avoidable, it was learned. Among other problems, the police chief identified "using 'plain talk' rather than codes, which are different from agency to agency."

These examples illustrate not only the diversity of communication problems that are possible but also the varying seriousness of communication problems. As we will see in later chapters, errors in our written and spoken words can profoundly and irreversibly impact the lives of others. As a current or aspiring criminal justice professional, it is therefore imperative that we commit to being a consistently strong communicator. We need to be motivated—to appreciate the need for expending additional effort to construct higher quality communications. And we need the knowledge and skills to translate our motivation into reality. This book is one step in that direction.

This chapter's purpose is to pave the way for our study of how to produce successful criminal justice communications. We start by take a closer look at the role and importance of formal communication in both the study and the practice of criminal justice. Having established its prominence and impact, we turn to reflecting on what it means to communicate. We will then move into considering what criminal justice communication involves and how it differs from other forms of communication. Doing so helps us recognize how some strategies that work in other fields and applications are not going to work for us in our field. Next, this chapter introduces nine principles, which are the hallmark traits of compelling criminal justice communications and the topics of the next nine chapters. Finally, before leaving this chapter, we look at the six-step process involved in creating compelling criminal justice communications. Understanding and following these six steps can empower us with the confidence and control to become the creators of consistently strong communications.

IMPORTANCE OF COMMUNICATION IN CRIMINAL JUSTICE

Communication skills are a critical component in the successful study and practice of criminal justice. Like students in other majors, criminal justice students need to be effective communicators to earn good grades, maintain a high GPA, and graduate. Writing and public speaking are not limited to English and oral communications courses. Thus, writing and presenting are not obstacles that we can "get out of the way" early in our education. When we learn how to write and present in English and oral communication courses, we need to take those lessons seriously so that we can apply that knowledge as we move through college and from college to career. Students, especially those in smaller colleges with low student–teacher ratios, should expect papers and presentations throughout their experience in higher education—reflecting widespread acceptance of the need for "writing across the curriculum" in colleges and universities throughout the United States.

Those who aspire to join the ranks of criminal justice professionals, moreover, will need to be able to communicate effectively to request recommendation letters, prepare job application materials, and participate in job interviews. Twenty-first century employers consistently cite written and verbal communication skills among the top qualities they look for when making hiring decisions, along with leadership and teamwork abilities, problem-solving skills, and a strong work ethic (Bortz, 2018; Klazema, 2018; National Association of Colleges and Employers, 2016). Communication skills are the most frequently mentioned as necessary in crime analyst job advertisements (Corkhill, Conow, Ashton, & East, 2015). Some potential employers will want to see writing samples (Doyle, 2018), and some immediately dismiss any applicant whose cover letter contains typos (Smith & Cain, 2016). At the same time, however, a substantial portion of the 64,000 interviewed managers reported that recent college graduates are deficient in writing skills (44 percent), problem-solving skills and critical thinking (60 percent), and attention to detail (56 percent; Klazema, 2018). All of this suggests that people who want to be successful in the study and/or practice of criminal justice need to be learn how to write and speak effectively during college and that they will need those skills to land a criminal justice career.

Once employed in the criminal justice system, furthermore—whether it be a career in policing, intelligence, courts, or corrections—communication will be a critical part of one's daily routine. It is not only that criminal justice practitioners spend a lot of time writing and speaking but also that writing and speaking are necessary for success:

- "While the vast majority of [police] officers do not enjoy writing reports, it is central to their success and effectiveness as an officer. Skillful writing teaches them how to form good arguments and think critically about investigations and evidence. Focusing on critical thinking and writing will enable officers to form good arguments and it will make them better, more well-rounded and effective officers" (DuFour, 2018).
- "Analysts must have strong communication and analytical skills as well as great writing ability. They need to be able to locate and interpret data and must be able to repackage and present it in a way that can be easily understood by others" (Roufa, 2018).
- "Lawyers must be orally articulate, have good written communication skills, and also be good listeners. In order to argue convincingly in the courtroom before juries and judges, good public speaking skills are essential. . . . Lawyers must also be able to write clearly, persuasively, and concisely, as they must produce a variety of legal documents. But it's not all about projection. To be able to analyze what clients tell them or follow a complex testimony, a lawyer must have good listening skills" (Gymer, 2018).
- "Successful correctional officers carry certain traits that allow them to be who they are and how they do their job whether innate or learned. . . . It's no secret communication is key to successfully doing this job. Learn how to communicate effectively and learn to write reports that are clear and concise and record documentation in an appropriate manner. Communicate with your peers, whether good or bad in nature, and do so directly but diplomatically" (Fox, 2015).

The bottom line is that ineffective communications can hurt not only your job performance but also the reputation of your agency and the effectiveness and efficiency of the criminal justice system.

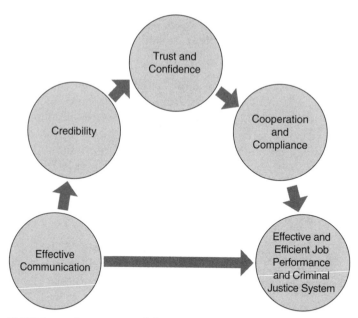

FIGURE 1.1   Importance of Communication in Criminal Justice

Figure 1.1 illustrates communication's impact on a number of important outcomes. First, note the direct impact of communication on effectiveness. This relationship reflects such occurrences as how mistaken information in arrest and search warrants can lead to suppressed evidence, lost cases, and criminals remaining free; and how unclear jury instructions and expert witness testimony can confuse juries, leading to misunderstandings and miscarriages of justice. Chapter 8 presents many actual examples of these situations. Beyond that direct effect is the way communications affect credibility. When we are perceived as credible, we are seen as possessing both competence and integrity, and people tend to trust us more; they will be confident that we know the right thing to do and will do the right thing. As Chapter 2 will address in more detail, trust and confidence lead to cooperation and compliance—which, in turn, yield a more effective and efficient criminal justice system.

Effective criminal justice communications, above all else, are compelling. A **compelling** communication is powerful. Compelling communications are powerful in their ability to foster credibility and, in turn, generate positive outcomes. **Credibility** refers to believability, and compelling communications inspire our audience to trust us and have confidence in what we say and do. Once we master the science of creating compelling communications, we become a more powerful and successful criminal justice student and practitioner.

THE COMMUNICATION PROCESS

As shown in Figure 1.2, communication requires a sender, an encoding process, a message, a decoding process, and a receiver (Kirk, 2012). The message is the information that sender wants to share (e.g., an agency's new whistleblower procedure). The sender is the communicator, the person who is trying to share information (e.g., a compliance officer). Encoding is the process whereby the sender figures out how best to transmit

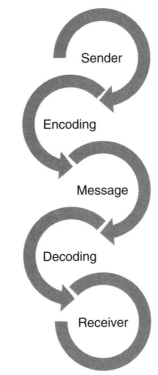

FIGURE 1.2   How Communication Works
Source: Kirk (2012)

the message (e.g., a memo emailed to all employees, a presentation during a mandatory meeting with a handout showing a diagram of the new process). Decoding is the process whereby the receiver interprets the message (e.g., downloading and reading the memo, paying attention during the presentation, and examining the handout). And the receiver is the person or people comprising the sender's audience (e.g., all agency employees). The communication process is judged a success by whether the receiver decodes the message accurately, without any misunderstanding, misinterpretation, or missing pieces.

Figure 1.2 makes the point that communication is a process; it is not merely the simple act of writing or saying words and then being done. Rather, it is the creation, transmission, and reception of the message. In this process, the communication burden is on the sender, and the sender does not satisfy this burden until the receiver accurately comprehends the complete message. Thus, we need to make every reasonable effort to communicate our message in a way that is best designed to facilitate the receiver's accurate understanding. As senders, in other words, our encoding process should maximize the likelihood of proper decoding.

Multiple factors can affect the likelihood that the message will be decoded properly, such as the complexity of the message, the length of the message, the receiver's ability to pay attention, the receiver's willingness to pay attention, the receiver's intelligence level, and the sender and receiver's shared understanding of the words used. When we talk about how to produce effective communications to generate a successful communication, we are really talking about how to reduce the factors that interfere with and increase the factors that facilitate the exchange of information. We do not have complete control over all of these factors, but we do have some level of control over many of them. While we cannot change the complexity of the point of the message, for example, we can do our best to present a complicated point as simply as possible. Although we cannot choose only highly intelligent people to be in our audience, we can use language that just about everyone would understand. We have no choice sometimes about confronting a hostile or skeptical audience, but we can present our message in a way that makes it more palatable. To the extent that we can demand as little effort on the part of the receiver as possible, moreover, we can increase the likelihood that our message will be received accurately.

SPECIAL CHALLENGES IN CRIMINAL JUSTICE COMMUNICATIONS

Satisfying our communication burden often involves overcoming obstacles that are common in criminal justice more so than in other fields. Some of these challenges do not become apparent until we move from college to our career, and others exist at both points but in different forms.

One challenge is that criminal justice communications are *consequential*. As a student (in any major), the quality of our communications determines grades, which in turn affect our GPA, graduation, and possible awards. Students and others who write for publication soon learn how much work it takes to create publication-worthy papers—processes some refer to as "writing for rejection" because of how much more common it is to have a paper be rejected than accepted for publication in peer-reviewed journals. As a practitioner, the stakes could not be higher. Lives literally depend on criminal justice practitioners. Communication affects the wining or losing of cases, negotiations of hostage release, notifications to community members, instructions to a death penalty jury, and so on. With such significant potential repercussions, criminal justice communications are understandably incredibly intense and stressful. Yet we cannot allow this pressure to affect the quality of our communications—including the professional, evidence-based manner in which they are presented.

A second challenge is *conflict of interest*. When we have a conflict of interest, we have competing concerns that we must balance, such as the desire to finish a report and the competing desire to do our best on the report. The field of criminal justice is rife with conflicts of interest; hence, the widespread emphasis on ethics, integrity, and accountability in the criminal justice system and in other institutions. Students learn early on that we often need to decide between doing what is easiest or quickest and what is best or right. Professionals continue to struggle with conflict of interest, such as the desire to be open, honest, and informative and the competing need to keep information classified to protect ongoing investigations, witnesses, and victims.

A third challenge is the *sensitivity* of the subject matter. We deal with some tough issues. Students sometimes struggle with their emotions when they research and report on topics such as domestic violence, rape, human trafficking, elder abuse, hate crime, and terrorism. They learn to take care not to offend people with strong opposing viewpoints on or traumatic personal experiences with such sensitive and controversial matters. Moving into the practice of criminal justice presents even more vivid and emotional situations, such as communicating with rape and domestic violence victims and parents of missing or murdered children; responding to hate crimes and explaining them to a racially and ethnically diverse community; and disciplining and firing employees and handling conflicts between colleagues.

A fourth challenge is the *urgency* of some of these communication scenarios. Despite how important and sensitive some situations may be, we have to act quickly—without the benefit of sufficient time to research, draft, get feedback, and improve. Students are used to having sufficient time, such as an entire semester to write a term paper. Although some assignments provide for less time, such as test essay questions and term papers in accelerated courses, college communication assignments generally do not have the sense of tension that criminal justice practitioners experience. Yet urgency is not just about time. It is also about pressure and seriousness of the situation. Thus, some urgent criminal justice field communications are strategic and operational briefings (e.g., in response to a school shooting or high-speed car chase), a crime in progress (e.g., domestic violence, bar fight, intoxicated driver), and Amber Alerts.

A fifth challenge is *complexity*. In both the study and practice of criminal justice, we will need to delve into highly complicated, nuanced material. To address cybercrimes and other technology offenses, for example, contemporary law enforcement officials and forensic investigators are trained in computer science, digital forensics, and information assurance. Evidence and courtroom testimony may deal with psychology, statistics, chemistry, biology, engineering, neuroscience, and accounting. Although experts can analyze the evidence and testify in court, attorneys need to know enough to identify where such expertise is needed and to question those experts during direct examination and cross-examination. The complex nature of much of the information we need to communicate can make encoding and decoding especially difficult.

Despite all of these challenges, criminal justice communicators must maintain their credibility. They cannot succumb to the pressure, the fear, the conflicts, the urgency, or the confusion and either fail to produce anything at all or to produce ineffective communications. This is not to say that the daily routine of the average criminal justice practitioner is fraught with these challenges. Rather, these challenges are covered here to prepare you for what you might encounter. Additionally, these challenges are discussed as a way of recognizing how much poise and professionalism our criminal justice practitioners demonstrate when they do overcome these challenges to protect the community and execute their jobs effectively. These challenges are not reasons to produce inferior communications, in other words. They can be overcome, and professionals do overcome them. Just be prepared.

CRIMINAL JUSTICE COMMUNICATION AS TECHNICAL COMMUNICATION

Despite the emotionalization, intensity, and high stakes involved, criminal justice communication is a form of technical communication, which may strike some people as rather dry and mechanical. **Technical communication** is "the process of finding and using information and sharing meaning" (Markel, 2012, p. 4). What we are trying to do is convey, or impart, information using formal channels of communication such as documents, instructions, reports, and briefings. This might sound painfully obvious, but this definition sets criminal justice communications apart from other forms of communication. To emphasize the distinctiveness of technical communication, let us look briefly at what technical communication is *not*.

First, some communications are *opinionated*. Diaries, journals, opinion papers, and reflective essays are examples of personal communications. Here, senders are talking about themselves—experiences, feelings, intuitions, passions, preferences, attitudes, and so on. Technical communication, on the other hand, is decidedly impersonal. Even a report describing, for example, what a police officer personally encountered during a traffic stop will not be about whether the officer was scared, offended, confused, and so on (even if the officer believes knowing this information would create a fuller account of the incident). It would not explain the officer's decision to ticket the driver by recalling past instances when the officer decided not to ticket drivers and how those drivers were pulled over a week later for the same traffic offense (even though these experiences might be the reason the officer decided to ticket rather than warn a particular driver). Rather, such a report would be an objective recitation of events, people, places, and times. In technical communication, then, we are not talking about ourselves.

Second, some communications are *dramatic*. Technical communications, including criminal justice communications, are not for entertainment or dramatic purposes. Technical communicators do not exaggerate or otherwise sensationalize. They are not trying to be artistic or poetic; and they do not try to sway the audience using emotional appeals or by inspiring fear, sadness, anger, pity, or compassion. We do not want to frighten or trick a judge into issuing a search warrant; instead, we want to demonstrate probable cause so that the judge approves the search based on a dispassionate, critical analysis of our application. Criminal justice communicators either aim to inform in a nonjudgmental, purely descriptive manner (e.g., incident reports), or they seek to persuade via logic and evidence (e.g., search warrant affidavits).

NINE PRINCIPLES OF EFFECTIVE CRIMINAL JUSTICE COMMUNICATION

The previous section gave us an idea of what technical, criminal justice communication is *not*. This section tells us what technical, criminal justice communication *is*. It is the embodiment of the following nine principles:

1. **Professionalism**: Consistent exhibiting of certain personal characteristics in addition to technical competence that inspires trust (Wiersma, 2010–2011).
2. **Responsiveness**: Directly addressing its objective, adhering to all parameters, and tailored to the audience(s).
3. **Organization**: Arrangement of information in a manner that will best help the communication achieve its purpose.
4. **Logic**: The reasoning process used to justify claims and reach conclusions; a conclusion is logical when it is supported by adequate reasoning.
5. **Evidence**: Proof; something that is used to justify a claim.
6. **Completeness**: Thorough, containing all pertinent parts and information.

7. **Correctness**: Free from error in terms of both the truth/accuracy of the information itself and the proper presentation of the information.
8. **Clarity**: Straightforward, unambiguous, and therefore able to be understood.
9. **Conciseness**: Using as few simple words as possible to make a point.

The next nine chapters cover these principles in detail, describing how to achieve them and presenting examples of communications in the study and practice of criminal justice communications that exemplify the importance of these principles.

SIX STAGES FOR PRODUCING EFFECTIVE CRIMINAL JUSTICE COMMUNICATIONS

It is difficult to conceive of a situation wherein practicing more or harder could cause someone to do worse. The popularity of the adage "practice makes perfect" speaks to the common consensus that the harder we practice, the better we do. Although there likely are exceptions to this pattern (e.g., "phenoms"), most people need to practice and prepare to deliver successful performances. This pattern holds true with regard to communication as much as it does to sports. All else equal, the more effort we put into a communication, the better that communication will be.

Constantly striving to be better, moreover, is a distinguishing characteristic of a professional (a topic to which we will turn in Chapter 2). Being a strong criminal justice communicator is not about doing the bare minimum. It is about constantly demanding excellence of ourselves and exceeding other people's expectations. Thus, even if they are already high-performing, professionals will keep finding ways to improve.

From this we can conclude that producing an effective criminal justice communication should be not treated as an in-and-out kind of an operation. Instead, we need to prepare and practice, thus treating the development of communications as a process. To this effect, Figure 1.3 presents six stages we can use to develop and deliver our very best papers and presentations.

Sometimes, these stages will stretch out over months. Other times, they will occur within a day or two. Some people might like to follow these steps precisely—never, say, going back to collecting information after they have started drafting. Others might prefer a more back and forth, relaxed progression. This is not a problem. The process we use needs to work for us given our individual strengths and weaknesses as well as the time

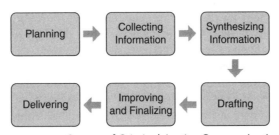

FIGURE 1.3   Stages of Criminal Justice Communication

and other resources we have available. So, we should consider Figure 1.3 a general approach; it does not claim to be the exclusive route to a high-quality paper or presentation. We need to be flexible with our process, ultimately settling on one that suits our needs for the communication at hand.

But the basic idea—that creating effective communications involves a progression of learning, thinking, organizing, and refining designed to maximize the likelihood that our audience will receive our message—should apply in any context. If criminal justice communication were merely a matter of moving ideas from our head to paper, we probably would not need to do so much work. But getting ideas from our head to paper is just one part of the communication task: We also need to get informed ideas into our head, and then we will need to get those ideas into the heads of others. Achieving effective communication is difficult, but breaking it up into smaller stages can help make it manageable and less intimidating.

Planning

The first stage is planning, which starts with determining (and, as needed, clarifying) the communication's objective(s), parameters, and audience(s) (see Chapter 3). Once we have a firm understanding of what needs to be accomplished, we should lay out exactly how we will proceed from Stage 1 to Stage 6, including setting milestones with deadlines. Use a calendar and work backward from the final deadline for the communication, plotting when you need to complete each stage. Try to leave some room for unexpected life events, such as needing to work overtime, flight delays when traveling, car trouble, technical problems, and you or your family members getting sick.

Part of planning a group project is deciding how and when the group will communicate, who the leader and secretary will be, and what the expectations are for the group's performance. Make sure every group member has the rest of the group's names, phone numbers, and email addresses. If you are working in a group, divide the project into separate tasks for each group member, giving each person deadlines and putting all of this in writing. To keep it in writing, either make these decisions online, such as via email, or use email to confirm decisions made during a face-to-face meeting or conference call. One person should serve as the group "secretary," and this person can email all group members after the meeting to document all the decisions that were made. Address any confusion or objections immediately so that everyone is on the same page moving forward.

Collecting Information

The second stage is collecting information. Here, start by deciding what information is needed and where (see Chapter 6 and Appendix B). Then, develop a plan for acquiring the needed information. Remember to collect full bibliographic information for each source you collect. If you conduct interviews, record the time, date, and person's full name. At this stage, give yourself time to troubleshoot events such as a library book already being checked out by someone else and your institution not having a subscription to the journal you need. You might need to find another way to obtain some forms of information, such as purchasing a particularly important book or requesting an interlibrary loan. Before moving on to the next stage, be sure to critically evaluate your evidence. Avoid sources of dubious credibility, and compensate for flawed sources by using multiple sources.

Groups might want to use an **annotated bibliography** at this stage, which is a References list that contains a brief summary of the source directly under the source's bibliographic information. The sources can be divided across group members, with each person being assigned some subset of the total sources. Each person can email his or her source notes to the rest of the group, and one person can be designated to compile all the source notes into a single annotated bibliography.

Synthesizing Information

Synthesizing information is the third stage, which involves studying and making sense of all the information you have collected, and then figuring out how to put all the pieces together to form a coherent whole. You do not want to rush this stage. It can take some time to read your sources carefully so that you understand them. Students might need to bring some sources to their instructor for help understanding complicated passages, such as theoretical or methodological details. Once you have reviewed all of your sources, you are ready to organize and outline your communication (see Chapter 4). The organizational structure you choose should be the one that best reflects the communication's objective and will best facilitate the audience's ability to understand the communication. In your outline, indicate where you are using each piece of evidence. If you see any evidence gaps, then you need to conduct additional research to fill in those gaps.

When working in a group, make sure each person sees, agrees to, and has a copy of the outline. You can use the outline to assign tasks to different group members, such as by inserting peoples' names or initials by each major section along with a deadline and estimated length (number of paragraphs or pages for written communications and number of minutes for oral communications). By this point, if not sooner, it is wise to address any problems with particular group members that you are experiencing. Try addressing them as a group first and, if that does not work, then contact the instructor. Sometimes, groupwork problems (e.g., lack of responsiveness or poor-quality work on the part of a particular individual) can be resolved simply by copying the instructor on all group emails. Employees, unlike students, will probably have to troubleshoot these problems on their own.

Drafting

The fourth stage is drafting. This is when you produce the first full iteration of the communication. Even if the communication will be delivered orally, you should write it up. Although it is no secret that many people skip the drafting stage, there are numerous benefits to drafting before writing the final version.

First, drafting helps us get started. Waiting for inspiration is a common reason why people procrastinate on writing assignments: We want to wait until we have a great idea. Then, once we start writing, we start fiddling with words and commas, and the next thing we know, we have lost our train of thought and are running out of time. But drafting is about getting ideas down, quickly in fact—not about writing well. This is not the time to worry about grammar and formatting; instead, just get the ideas and information on paper. Strong writers will end up deleting a significant portion of what they write in a first draft (sometimes 80 percent or more), so it is inefficient to worry about writing mechanics at this point.

Second, drafting pushes us to think and develop our ideas clearly. You have probably heard people say that the best way to learn something is to try teaching it to someone else. There are at least two elements of truth in this saying. On the one hand, if you have trouble expressing your thoughts in writing, then you probably need to do some additional thinking. If you cannot explain how a piece of evidence supports your claim, for example, then you should reevaluate your claim and/or the evidence you are offering to support it. You might need to do some more research until you have a better handle on the topic. On the other hand, if you cannot understand a point that a group member is trying to make in a section of the draft, then you can ask that member to clarify. Your inability to understand is a warning sign that others reading the paper also would have trouble understanding, which is a situation we want to prevent.

Third, drafting paces us and keeps us on schedule. This is especially important in preventing last-minute problems in group work. If group members are each assigned to write a section, and those sections are due the day before the final paper's deadline, then you probably would not have time to deal with a group member who submits nothing or something of poor quality. But having the draft due well ahead of the final paper's deadline can give you flexibility in how to handle such a problem, such as asking the instructor for assistance or even assigning the section to another group member and ejecting the nonperforming group member from the group.

Fourth, drafting helps us write ethically. As we move from outline to draft, we should take care to bring in-text citations and references with us. In the draft, clearly indicate source ideas, information, and words. Especially when we start running out of time as the deadline approaches, relocating sources and making sure we used quotation marks whenever we used exact source language can seem tedious and thus get skipped, which is a source of plagiarism (albeit unintentional) and associated penalties.

And fifth, drafting reveals any length deficits or surpluses. You might see that your paper or presentation is far too short or long given the parameters. Or maybe a section or two are overly long or short. These situations are better realized at the drafting stage than later. You want to ensure that you meet any length requirements but also that you devote the most time to the most important points, and drafting can help you meet these conditions.

Improving and Finalizing

The fifth stage is improving and finalizing, which involves critically evaluating your own work and then reworking it to make it as good as it can be. Expect to go through multiple drafts at this stage. Appendix C goes into detail about this process, including strategies to identify flaws and specific questions to ask as you review, revise, and proofread your draft. The general idea is that you begin with the big issues: purpose, content, and structure. Once you have these major issues set, then you are ready to look at other issues, including tone, diction, clarity, conciseness, and writing mechanics. The saying that people are silly to polish knobs on the Titanic is an apt way to convey the inefficiency and pointlessness of looking at the little things before the big things. If, for example, you will be removing an entire paragraph when you eventually realize that it contributes nothing to the paper, it would be a waste to have spent your valuable time perfecting the writing mechanics in that paragraph.

If the communication is a group assignment, then this stage has an added concern: uniformity. One of the major hurdles to having different people write different parts of a paper is that the result is often disjointed. Readers can tell when the paper shifts from one author to another author, because the writing is so different. Try to smooth out any disjointedness to create a flowing, coherent whole. Things some writers do differently involve use of capitalization and hyphens, tone (some formal, some informal), format of in-text citations and frequency and length of direct quotations, and use of transitions. One section might stand out from the rest due to heavy use of lengthy quotes, for example, while another section might be overly casual, containing many personal words and contractions. Maintaining a professional communication style and consistently using proper writing mechanics will resolve much of this problem.

As you near the end of this stage, try not to think in terms of whose section is whose but of all group members sharing authorship for the entire communication. Spend the time to perfect the document so that all of you are proud of the entire work. After all, most instructors grade group projects by giving the entire group the same grade—not by giving each group member a separate grade based only on that member's contributions.

Delivering

Delivering is the sixth and final stage. At this point, you are done writing, revising, and editing. This stage plays out differently for papers than for presentations.

Papers

With a paper, this stage is about logistics. You are beyond the point of changing around or adding words, and you are ready to submit.

HARD COPY. If the paper is due in hard copy, then what you have left is getting it from your computer into the hand of the person who assigned it to you (e.g., teacher, boss). At a minimum, this involves printing and binding the paper.

Most of us have a computer, but most students probably do not have a printer. If you have your own printer, then you need to make sure you have paper, ink, and no connection problems between your printer and computer. Wireless connections are predictably problematic, so leave yourself time to troubleshoot, such as turning your printer and computer off and then on again. If you do not have your own printer, then you need to save yourself time to get to a computer lab or print shop. Make sure you bring your paper with you more than one way, such as a flash drive and emailing it to yourself as an attachment. At a computer lab or print shop, you might encounter a wait for a computer, malfunctioning computers and/or printers, or an inaccessible computer lab (e.g., under construction or in use for a class).

Whether you are using your own printer or someone else's, you will need to bind your paper. Most often, a single staple in the upper left-hand corner will suffice. Some professors require different types of bindings, and some papers are so long that traditional staplers will not work; so it is important for you to know these requirements and be prepared to meet them. Do not assume a computer lab will have a suitable working stapler and staples. It looks unprofessional to rush into your instructor or boss's office to do your stapling right before a deadline—and they might not even have a working stapler with staples.

SOFT COPY. If the paper is due in soft copy (i.e., electronically), then your concerns are about software compatibility and Internet connection.

If you used software other than Microsoft Word, you might need some time to check and fix formatting as you convert your document into Microsoft. Most instructors require papers to be typed in Word, and using other programs can create two problems. First, converting from another program to Word can alter formatting, which means your document will look like you formatted it incorrectly. Second, if you do not convert to Word, then your audience might not be able to read it. For students, this could mean a grade of 0 percent. For employees, this could mean a reprimand, demotion, or termination. At the very least, submitting in the wrong format is indicative of a lack of concern with rules and requirements.

Beyond software incompatibility, you need to know exactly where and how to submit. Some papers need to be emailed directly to a person, while others should be uploaded to a website or submitted to a drop box. Give your file an informative and professional name so that it is easily recognizable for what it is. Finally, anticipate Internet connectivity problems and last-minute setbacks, such as getting a phone call in the minutes leading up to the deadline.

The bottom line is that you should give yourself sufficient time to deal with these possibilities. You spent a lot of time and effort writing a solid paper, and dropping the ball at the delivery stage can create a negative first impression of the seriousness with which you approached the assignment. Instead, play it safe. If your paper is due in hard copy, then have it completely ready to submit before you go to bed the night before it is due. If your paper is due electronically, then submit it hours if not the day before the deadline.

Presentations

When the communication is oral rather than written, you have much more than logistics left at this stage. In this case, the delivery stage involves such considerations as knowing the size and layout of the room where you will present, getting your visual aid(s) to the proper location, wearing an appropriate outfit, anticipating questions from the audience, and being mentally prepared to deliver a high-quality presentation. Chapter 11 will cover presentations in detail. For now, it is important to realize that the communication being oral rather than written does not mean that you should spend any less time or that you should skip any of these six stages. It is just as important for a presentation as for a paper to be professional and responsive to its objective, parameters, and audience. Likewise, presentations need to be organized, logical, evidence-based, complete, and correct as well as clear and concise.

APPLICATIONS

Compelling criminal justice communication is about more than putting our ideas into words. It is also about listening. We need to be active listeners, paying close attention—often noting more than what is explicitly stated—and collecting information to use later. Along these lines, this chapter turns to two forms of communications that revolve around effective listening and that play a prominent role in the study and practice of criminal justice: (1) notes and (2) interviews and interrogations.

Notes

Note-taking is one of the most important and yet undervalued skill sets possessed by successful students. For at least four reasons, we should take notes as we complete assigned readings and listen to the professor talk (among other situations, such as during advising appointments).

First, taking notes can help us focus and keep our attention on what we are hearing, reading, or otherwise observing. Active note-taking can prevent us from falling asleep or getting distracted. Some people are less prone to get bored or antsy when they have something to occupy their hands. Second, taking notes can also push us to think about, truly learn, and then later be able to recall the material accurately and in sufficient detail. We spend more time with each idea when we write it out, which facilitates memory. And we can push ourselves to get a solid grasp of the material when we phrase and organize it in our own way. Third, taking notes can make us look sincere and professional. People who take notes give the impression that what they are hearing or reading is important to them—that they care. And fourth, note-taking is a safety precaution. It is better to have taken notes and not needed them to have needed notes but not have taken them.

Of course, we might take notes but miss something important, such that our notes do not do a perfect job of helping us pass a test. But some gaps here and there should not be interpreted as meaning that note-taking is useless. In short, it just makes sense to take notes. Here, we look at some strategies for taking reading notes and lecture notes.

The Cornell Note-Taking System

There are many ways to take notes. One of the most popular and effective ways is the Cornell system. As illustrated in Figure 1.4, the Cornell system involves dividing the paper on which we will take notes into three major sections: (1) lecture note area, (2) questions and cues area, and (3) summary area.

With note pages formatted consistent with Figure 1.4, the Cornell note-taking proceeds in five basic steps:

1. Take notes during the lecture in the lecture note area. Avoid long sentences. Use abbreviations (e.g., "&" for "and," "CJ" for "criminal justice," "Δ" for "defendant"). Separate ideas with blank lines and/or headings, and indicate how information connects using bullet lists, numbering, and indenting wherever appropriate.
2. Articulate review questions, writing them in the questions and cues area. As soon as possible after the lecture, review your lecture notes to extract the major ideas and most important information. Create a little practice quiz for yourself. Perform this step as soon as possible after the lecture, while the material is still fresh in your mind.
3. Quiz yourself on your reviews. Hide the lecture note area, and try to answer the questions you wrote in the questions and cues area. Do this aloud and in your own words. Then, check your answers by looking at the lecture note area.
4. Summarize the notes in the summary area. Reflect on the material, extracting from your lecture notes the main ideas. Use your own words.
5. Study your notes frequently. Go over your notes at least weekly to keep the material fresh and help you commit it to memory.

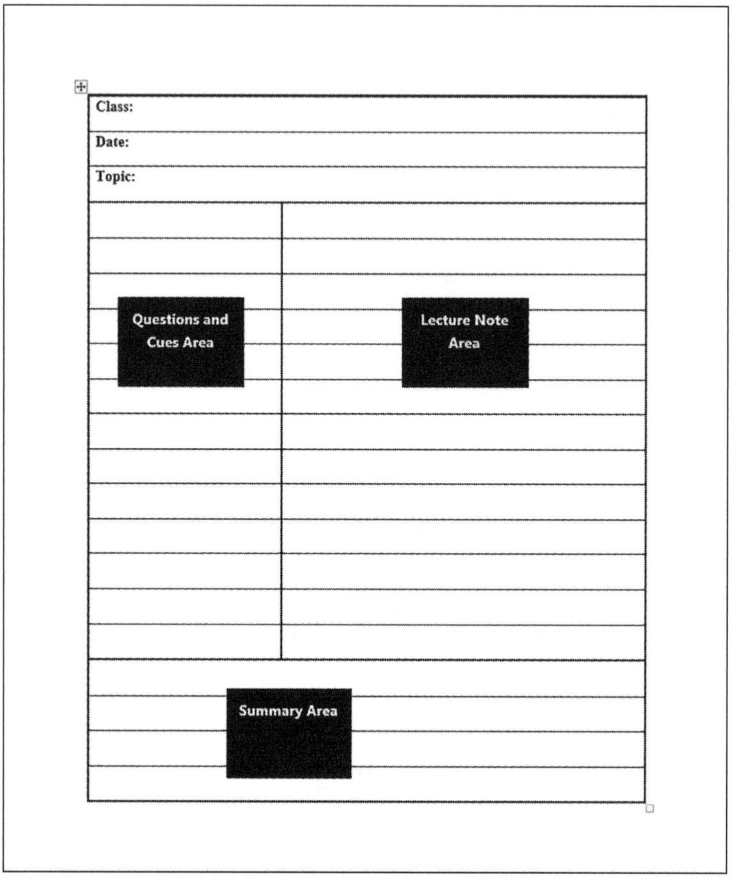

Class:

Date:

Topic:

Questions and
Cues Area

Lecture Note
Area

Summary Area

FIGURE 1.4 Cornell Note-Taking

This system can easily be used for lecture or reading notes. We can write or type. And we can make adjustments to these five steps to suit our individual learning needs.

Best Practices

What follows is a list of best practices for taking reading and lecture notes:

1. **Set yourself up for success.** For readings, give yourself time to read and take notes as well as a quiet place so you can concentrate. For lectures, come to class alert and with the necessary note-taking items (e.g., paper, pens), and then sit where you can see and hear easily.

2. **Read before coming to class.** If a lecture is going to cover a particular chapter, for instance, read that chapter before the lecture. Doing so will help you follow along with the lecture and distinguish between more and less important material.

3. **Record more than just what the instructor writes.** Do not write down only what the instructor writes on the board or shows on PowerPoint slides. Try to capture

everything important, where important means what will be on the test as well as other material that might help you understand or recall test material.

4. **Use a note-taking system that works for you,** such as the Cornell system. The Cornell system can be adapted to your learning styles as well as other relevant factors such as the complexity of the material.

5. **Take notes that you will be able to decipher later.** Do not write so messy that you cannot read your notes later or use abbreviations that you will not later be able to understand.

6. **Ask questions.** Do not be afraid to ask your instructor to repeat or clarify material.

7. **Use your notes.** While notes are not entirely worthless if we never look at them again after taking them, notes are much more effective the more we use them.

8. **Keep your notes.** It can be a good idea to keep your notes even after the class ends, especially for classes in your major. You might need this information later in the curriculum or your career.

Interviews and Interrogations

When investigating a crime, police ask people questions in two general circumstances: interviews and interrogations. When the person being questioned is not a suspect, the question and answer session is called an **interview**. And when the person being questioned is a suspect, the question and answer session is called an **interrogation**. Table 1.1 distinguishes between these two law enforcement activities.

As shown in Table 1.1, there are some important differences between interviews and interrogations. Moreover, case complexity differs across investigations, and some techniques work well with some interviewees but poorly with others. Some cases begin with clear evidence of who committed the crime, for example, whereas it is unclear in other cases whether or not a crime even happened. One case might have video evidence of the person who robbed a store, while another case might have several witnesses that each identify a different person as the robber. In some cases, it is clear who the relevant

TABLE 1.1 Interviews Versus Interrogations

Interviewing	Interrogating
Exploratory	**Accusatory**
• Earlier in the investigation	• Later in the investigation
• Intended to learn more about the crime and/or suspect(s)	• Intended to elicit a confession or other incriminating evidence
• Used with victims and witnesses	• Used with suspects
• Simple, broad questions	• Specific, narrow questions
Conversational	**Confrontational**
• Interviewee is free to leave	• Suspect is not free to leave
• Informal settings	• Format setting
• Casual tone	• Formal tone
	• Triggers *Miranda v. Arizona* (1966) and related constitutional concerns

Sources: Grubb and Hamby (2019); Wallace and Roberson (2013)

TABLE 1.2   The Cognitive Interviewing (CI) Approach

Social Dynamics	Memory and Cognition	Communications
• Rapport • Active witness participation	• Context reinstatement • Limited mental resources • Witness-compatible questioning • Multiple and varied retrieval • Minimal guessing • Minimal constructive recall	• Extensive, detailed responses • Nonverbal output

Source: Fisher, Ross, and Cahill (2010)

witnesses are; but in other cases, there might seem to be no witnesses. Some interviews might be rushed, furthermore, with the goal of preventing harm to the captive victim, where other interviews might not have such critical time constraints. As a consequence, there is no "silver bullet" set of strategies that ensures successful interviews and interrogations across all investigations.

Interviews

The purpose of the interview is to gain as much relevant and credible information as possible. Decades of research on effective police interviewing techniques have reported that the cognitive interviewing (CI) approach consistently yields a higher quantity and quality of information than other approaches to interviewing witnesses (Schreiber Compo, Hyman Gregory, & Fisher, 2012). As shown in Table 1.2, the CI approach centers on three broad psychological processes: social dynamics, memory and cognition, and communications.

In terms of social dynamics, the interviewer's goal is to build rapport by establishing an open and trusting information so that the witness feels comfortable sharing as many (sometimes personal) details as possible (Fisher, Ross, & Cahill, 2010). The witness should do most of the talking. To accomplish this objective of active witness participation, officers are advised to avoid interrupting and asking many questions having short answers. Officers also are advised to invite the witness to talk as much as possible.

In terms of memory and cognition, the interviewer's goal is to reduce unnecessary cognitive demands for both the witness and the interviewer (Fisher et al., 2010). Strategies for reducing cognitive demands include mentally recreating the event, asking few open-ended questions, avoiding asking questions while the witness is thinking, encouraging the witness to concentrate (e.g., closing their eyes, looking at the floor), avoiding using a standardized checklist of questions for all witnesses in a case, asking questions related to what the witness is thinking about at the time, asking the witness to cover the event more than once in an interview, and interviewing the same interview more than once.

To elicit more detailed information, furthermore, Fisher et al. (2010) suggest using more than one approach to question the witness about the same event, such as asking a witness "to describe what he/she saw and then to describe what he/she heard or felt" (p. 60). To guard against false information, interviewers should explicitly instruct the witness not to guess and to take care not to lead the witness into constructing memories. In the case of leading witnesses, interviewers should be sensitive to verbal and nonverbal signals (e.g., paying increased attention in response to something the witness says) as well as avoiding sharing information/evidence with the witness.

With regard to communication, the CI approach emphasizes the need to gather as much information as possible, which involves discouraging witnesses from withholding information as well as being attuned to nonverbal communications methods and messages (Fisher et al., 2010). Witnesses should be encouraged "to report everything they think about, whether it is trivial, out of chronological order or even if it contradicts a statement made earlier" (p. 61). Also, be open to nonverbal communication channels, as some information (e.g., how a suspect looks) can be expressed better using channels other than spoken words (e.g., a drawing of the suspect).

Of the many CI components outlined in Table 1.2 and described above, research has identified three that are most effective: context reinstatement, focused concentration, and explicit instructions (Schreiber Compo et al., 2012). Additionally, recent research has found that category clustering recall (CCR) is more effective than other recall methods (Paulo, Albuquerque, Vitorino, & Bull, 2017; Thorley, 2018). In contrast to free recall, wherein a witness recounts events as they remember them, CCR involves witnesses focusing on one topic at a time (e.g., what the witness knows about the suspect, and then what the witness knows about the victim). An overarching theme is that interviewers should remain flexible (Fisher et al., 2010). The need for flexibility relates back to the variability noted earlier across and within investigations: Because there is no silver bullet, the interviewer needs to be attentive and responsive to what does and does not work in a particular interview.

The CI approach is not effortless; rather, it requires close attention and an ability to improvise and is facilitated by at least three forms of preparation. First, learn as much as possible about the case, including about the witness. Grubb and Hemby (2019) suggest reviewing the following sources of case information: the incident report, crime-scene photos, notes from other interviews, and other case information that could help you determine when the witness might be lying.

Second, choose a time and place for the interview that will best help you implement the components of CI, such as concentration and long, detailed responses. There is a trade-off here: In general, the more formal the setting, the more the witness can concentrate but the less comfortable the witness will be. The less formal the setting, the less the witness can concentrate but the more comfortable the witness will be (Grubb & Hemby, 2019).

And third, be aware of your options for phrasing questions. A fundamental distinction is between close-ended and open-ended questions. *Close-ended questions* involve shorter answers and limited response options. Examples are yes/no questions, questions about what day of the week something occurred, and questions about where someone is currently employed. In contrast, *open-ended questions* involve longer answers without clear limitations on the depth or breadth of the response. "How do you know about John Doe?" and "Will you walk me through what you did yesterday?" are examples of an open-ended question. Clearly, open-ended questions are more consistent than close-ended questions with the CI principle of eliciting detailed responses. Closed questions can be effective, however, when they are used at the end of a line of questioning, after open and probing questions; in contrast, closed questions are ineffective when they are used at other points in an interview (Oxburgh, Myklebust, & Grant, 2010).

Building off the distinctions in relative effectiveness of open- and close-ended questions, Oxburgh and associates (2010) differentiated between interviewing questions that are productive/appropriate and those that are unproductive/risky/inappropriate. Their classification scheme is summarized in Table 1.3, which identifies broad forms of productive/appropriate questions and then lists more specific questioning techniques.

TABLE 1.3   Interview Question Types

Productive or Appropriate	Unproductive, Risky, or Inappropriate
Open	Closed
EX: TED, 5WH	EX: Yes/no, specific
Probing	Echo
EX: 5WH, specific, parameter, clarification	EX: Parroting, paraphrasing
Facilitative	Leading
EX: Encouragement, acknowledgment	EX: Suggestive
Appropriate Closed	Multiple
	EX: Marathon
	Forced Choice
	EX: Option posing
	Opinion/Statement
	Hypothetical

Source: Oxburgh, Myklebust, and Grant (2010, p. 53)
Note. TED = "tell," "explain," or "describe"; 5WH = "what," "when," "where," "who," "why" and "how."

The left side of Table 1.3 begins with open-ended questions. Here, **TED questions** are those that ask the witness to "tell," "explain," or "describe" something, and the **5WH questions** ask witnesses "what," "when," "where," "who," "why" and "how." Note that 5WH questions can be used both as open-ended and as close-ended. Probing questions are follow-up questions designed to elicit additional information that is more particular (specific), focused (parameter), or clear (clarification). "Can you recall what you did between the hours of 9:00 and 11:00 p.m. last night?" is an example of a parameter probe. Some facilitative questions are used to motivate the witness to provide information (encouragement), while others are used to express recognition and/or appreciation for information already provided (acknowledgment). In either case, facilitative questions can make the witness more comfortable sharing information.

The right side of Table 1.3 is a collection of questioning techniques to be avoided:

- A type of follow-up question, *echo questions*, repeat essentially verbatim (i.e., parroting) or in slightly different form (i.e., paraphrasing) that which the witness already has said, which can create the impression that the interviewer does not believe it.
- *Suggestive questions* are biased. They lead the witness to a particular response, such as saying they actually witnessed a mugging when in reality, they only saw one person running away from another person and the latter person shouting that he had been mugged. Another form of bias is when the interviewer injects the interview with statements of that interviewer's opinions.
- Asking multiple questions at the same time can not only be cognitively demanding but also reduce the amount of information elicited. A form of this is *marathon questioning*, wherein the interviewer asks a series of questions without giving the witness time to answer each one.

- *Forced-choice questions* ask the witness to choose between listed options and are particularly ineffective when the list is incomplete, has overlap between options, and/or creates a false dilemma (e.g., "Did you two break up, or were you still friends?").
- *Hypothetical questions* ask the witness to speculate on events, engaging in what if questions instead of recalling what did happen (e.g., "While you were in the restroom, do you think it's possible that he slipped something into her drink?").

Interrogations

Although this discussion has focused on witness interviews, much of the information presented here is equally applicable to interrogations. As such, this discussion of interrogations will be somewhat brief, emphasizing some considerations that are particularly relevant to interrogations but not to interviews.

To begin, recall that where interviews are conducted with witnesses and victims, interrogations are conducted with a person who has been identified as a possible suspect. Thus, the police enter the interrogation room with the belief that the person to be questioned is guilty, and the goal is to elicit as much incriminating information as possible. While a complete confession is the strongest form of incriminating evidence that can emerge from an interrogation, complete confessions are probably less common than other forms of incriminating evidence (e.g., inconsistencies, lack of alibi, motive).

Unlike witness (and victim) interviews, suspect interrogations trigger important legal safeguards. The difference is rooted in the conversational nature of interviews compared with the confrontational, potentially coercive nature of interrogations. First, suspects have a right to counsel during an interrogation (*Escobedo v. Illinois*, 1964). Second, suspects must be informed of their rights prior to being questioned by the police (*Miranda v. Arizona*, 1966). Figure 1.5 is an example of a *Miranda* warning card carried by police officers.

In addition to the aforementioned procedural protections, interrogators must refrain from coercive threats and bribery (Wallace & Roberson, 2013). Under some

---

Miranda Warning

1. You have the right to remain silent.
2. Anything you say can and will be used against you in a court of law.
3. You have the right to talk to a lawyer and have him present with you while you are being questioned.
4. If you cannot afford to hire a lawyer, one will be appointed to represent you before any questioning, if you wish.
5. You can decide at any time to exercise these rights and not answer any questions or make any statements.

Waiver

Do you understand each of these rights I have explained to you?
Having these rights in mind, do you wish to talk to us now?

FIGURE 1.5 Miranda Warning Card

circumstances, interrogators may employ trickery, deception, and even psychological manipulation (Grubb & Hemby, 2019).

Because of the divergent nature and purpose of interviews and interrogations, some techniques are used with the latter but not the former. Accordingly, Wallace and Roberson (2013, pp. 141–142) distinguished between three popular police interrogation techniques:

1. **Factual technique:** The interrogator presents the evidence incriminating the suspect, concluding that it is a given that the suspect committed the crime and therefore is in the suspect's best interest to confess. The interrogator remains professional, businesslike, and emotionless.
2. **Sympathetic technique:** The interrogator acts like they understand the suspect's actions or position. The interrogator acts kind, gentle, and friendly.
3. **Face-saving (or justification) technique:** The interrogator implies that what the suspect did is completely natural, that anyone in the same situation would have done the same thing.

Regardless of which technique is used, most interrogations are conducted by two officers, with one officer serving as the primary interrogator and the other officer serving primarily as witness and recorder (Wallace & Roberson, 2013). Some interrogations might call for a change from one to another technique. Likewise, with some suspects, the officers might need to switch which one of them is the primary interrogator (Wallace & Roberson, 2013).

Best Practices

To summarize, the main goal of police interviews and interrogations is to elicit as much credible information as possible. In contrast to interviews, an interrogation has a narrower focus and confrontational nature typically intended to elicit a confession or other incriminating information. Despite these differences, the following list of best practices generally applies to both interviews and interrogations:

1. **Set yourself up for success.** Prepare for the interview, learning as much as you can about the case before you start the interview.
2. **Develop rapport,** creating an open and trusting environment and encouraging their active participation.
3. **Take notes.** If you cannot write during the interview, write down as much as you can remember as soon as possible afterward.
4. **Make recalling and relating information accurately as effortless as possible.** Reduce cognitive demands wherever possible. Use multiple and varied recall methods, with emphasis on CCR. Mentally recreate the event.
5. **Ask productive, appropriate questions, such as TED and 5WH questions.** Minimize guessing and constructive recall, and encourage lengthy, detailed responses.
6. **Let the interviewee/suspect do most of the talking.** Prefer open- to-close-ended questions, and give time for lengthy responses. Ask probing questions. Do not ask the next question until the person has finished answering the last question.
7. **Be alert and flexible.** Consider nonverbal forms of communication. Remain flexible, adapting to the witness/suspect as the interaction unfolds.

8. **Adhere to relevant legal and ethical principles.** Be especially mindful of legal protections for suspects during interrogations, including when to read the Miranda warning.

EXERCISES
Matching
These exercises are designed to assess Chapter 1 Learning Objective 1 (see Box 1.1). Match each numbered statement to the lowercase letter corresponding to the key word it defines. Each key word will be used only once.

1. The consistent exhibiting of certain personal characteristics in addition to technical competence that inspires trust
2. The police questioning of a person who is not a crime suspect
3. The reasoning process used to justify claims and reach conclusions; a conclusion is logical when it is supported by adequate reasoning
4. Powerful
5. Free from error in terms of both the truth/accuracy of the information itself and the proper presentation of the information
6. Arrangement of information in the manner most likely to achieve its purpose
7. The process of finding, using, and sharing information
8. Questions asking a person to tell, explain, and describe
9. The police questioning of a person who is a crime suspect
10. Straightforward, unambiguous, and therefore able to be understood
11. A References list with a brief summary for each source
12. Using as few simple words as possible to make a point
13. Believability; inspiring trust and confidence
14. Thorough, containing all pertinent parts and information
15. Questions asking a person what, when, where, who, why, and how
16. Proof; that which is used to justify a claim

a. 5WH questions	i. evidence
b. annotated bibliography	j. interrogation
c. clarity	k. interview
d. compelling	l. logic
e. completeness	m. organization
f. conciseness	n. professionalism
g. correctness	o. technical communication
h. credibility	p. TED questions

Writing
These writing exercises are designed to assess Chapter 1 Learning Objectives 2–8 (see Box 1.1).

1. Argue for the importance of effective communication skills in the study and practice of criminal justice.
2. Contrast technical communication with other types of communication.

3. Describe the special challenges involved in criminal justice communications.
4. Outline the nine principles of compelling criminal justice communication.
5. Outline the six stages of the communication process.
6. Use the Cornell note-taking system for the next class lecture. Use the note page format, and follow the five steps.
7. Create a brief training manual for rookie police officers, highlighting what to do and what not to do during interviews. End the manual with some additional tips for interrogations.

REFERENCES

Bortz, Daniel. (2018). Skills employers look for in college graduates: Highlight these abilities to help yourself land a job. *Monster*. Retrieved from https://www.monster.com/career-advice/article/5-skills-employers-want-in-new-grads-and-arent-finding

Chi, Clifford. (2017, June 29). 20 of the worst typos, grammatical errors, & spelling mistakes we've ever seen. *HubSpot*. Retrieved from https://blog.hubspot.com/marketing/14-worst-typos-ever

Cliff, Martha. (2017, January 13). "Illegally parked cars will be fine": Hilarious photos capture the VERY unfortunate spelling mistakes that gives signs a whole new meaning. *DailyMail.com*. Retrieved from https://www.dailymail.co.uk/femail/article-4113368/Illegally-parked-cars-fine-Hilarious-photos-capture-unfortunate-spelling-mistakes-signs-new-meaning.html

Corkhill, Jeffrey D., Teresa Kasprzyk Cunow, Elisabeth Ashton, & Amanda East. (2015). Attributes of an analyst: What we can learn from the intelligence analysts job description. Edith Cowan University Research Online, Australian Security and Intelligence Conference, *The Proceedings of the 8th Australian Security and Intelligence Conference* (pp. 36–42). Retrieved from https://ro.ecu.edu.au/cgi/viewcontent.cgi?referer=https://www.google.com/&httpsredir=1&article=1041&context=asi

CNN.com. (2005, March 18). Police: Manhunt marred by poor communication. *CNN.com*. Retrieved from http://www.cnn.com/2005/US/03/18/atlanta.shooting/index.html

DuFour, Scot. (2018, March 12). Mastering essential police skills: Critical thinking and writing. *In Public Safety*. Retrieved from https://inpublicsafety.com/2018/03/mastering-essential-police-skills-critical-thinking-and-writing/

Doyle, Alison. (2018, August 13). What to give an employer when they need a writing sample. *The Balance Careers*. Retrieved from https://www.thebalancecareers.com/writing-samples-for-job-applications-and-interviews-2061594

Escobedo v. Illinois, 378 U.S. 478 (1964).

Fisher, Ronald P., Ross, Stephen J., & Cahill, Brian S. (2010). Interviewing witnesses and victims. In P. A. Granhag (Ed.), *Forensic psychology in context: Nordic and international approaches* (pp. 56–74). Cullompton, UK: Willan Publishing.

Fox, Harriet. (2015, July 21). 8 skills of successful correctional officers. CorrectionsOne.com. Retrieved from https://www.correctionsone.com/corrections/articles/8685690-8-skills-of-successful-correctional-officers/

Grubb, Robert E., & Hemby, K. Virginia. (2019). *Effective communication in criminal justice*. Thousand Oaks, CA: SAGE.

Gymer, Sofia. (2018, February 9). 7 qualities every good lawyer should have. AllAboutLaw.co.uk. Retrieved from https://www.allaboutlaw.co.uk/stage/becoming-a-lawyer/7-qualities-every-good-lawyer-should-have

Jost, Ashley. (2017, November 15). "Poor judgment:" Mizzou police tweets during basketball game backfire. *St. Louis Post-Dispatch*. Retrieved from https://www.stltoday.com/news/local/education/notes-from-campus/poor-judgment-mizzou-police-tweets-during-basketball-game-backfire/article_d8ae0c0d-b9ca-53d4-8596-766c477e2207.html

Kirk, Andy. (2012). *Data visualization: A successful design process*. Birmingham, UK: Packt Publishing Ltd.

Markel, Mike. (2012). *Technical communications* (10th ed.). Boston, MA: Bedford/St. Martin's.

Miranda v. Arizona, 384 U.S. 436 (1966).

National Association of Colleges and Employers (NACE). (2016). *Job outlook 2016: The attributes employers want to see on new college graduates' resumes*. NACE Center for Career Development and Talen Acquisition. Retrieved from http://www.naceweb.org/career-development/trends-and-predictions/job-outlook-2016-attributes-employers-want-to-see-on-new-college-graduates-resumes/

Oxburgh, Gavin E., Myklebust, Trond, & Grant, Tim. (2010). The question of question types in police interviews: A review of the literature from a psychological and linguistic perspective. *International Journal of Speech, Language and the Law, 17*(1), 45–66.

Paulo, Rui M., Albuquerque, Pedro B., Vitorino, Fabiana, & Bull, Ray. (2017). Enhancing the cognitive interview with an alternative procedure to witness-compatible questioning: Category clustering recall. *Psychology, Crime and Law, 23*(10), 967–982.

Roufa, Timothy. (2018, June 19). What does a crime analyst do? Learn about the salary, required skills, & more. *The Balance Careers*. Retrieved from https://www.thebalancecareers.com/crime-analyst-career -profile -974846

Schreiber Compo, Nadja, Hyman Gregory, Amy, and Fisher, Ronald. (2012). Interviewing behaviors in police investigators: A field study of a current U.S. sample. *Psychology, Crime and Law, 4*, 359–375.

Smith, Jacquelyn, & Áine Cain. (August 30, 2016). 9 cover letter mistakes that will annoy any hiring manager. *Business Insider*. Retrieved from https://www.businessinsider.com/things-that-will-ruin-your-cover-letter-mistakes-2016-8

Thorley, Craig. (2018). Enhancing individual and collaborative eyewitness memory with category clustering recall. *Memory, 26*, 1128–1139. doi:10.1080/09658211.2018.1432058

Wallace, Harvey, & Roberson, Cliff. (2013). *Written and interpersonal communication: Methods for law enforcement* (5th ed.). Upper Saddle River, NJ: Pearson.

Wiersma, Bill. (2010–2011). *The power of professionalism: The seven mind-sets that drive performance and build trust*. Los Altos, CA: Ravel Media.

CHAPTER 2

Principle 1: Professionalism

BOX 2.1   **Learning Objectives**

After reading this chapter, you will be able to

1. Recognize terminology relevant to professional communications.
2. Argue for the importance of professionalism in criminal justice communications.
3. Distinguish between professional and unprofessional communications.
4. Outline strategies for professional communication as a criminal justice student and professional.
5. Rewrite unprofessional phrases and sentences to make them professional.
6. Construct professional job application materials.
7. Draft professional performance evaluation reviews.

Professionalism is unique; it's the ladder upon which all other organizational virtues mount.

—BILL WIERSMA

Judge Rosemarie Aquilina was soundly rebuked for her sentencing of Larry Nassar, the former Olympic doctor who sexually abused hundreds of young female athletes. She sentenced him to 40–175 years in prison saying, "Our Constitution does not allow for cruel and unusual punishment. If it did," continued Judge Aquilina, "I have to say, I might allow what we did to all of these beautiful souls—these young women in their childhood—I would allow someone or many people to do to him what he did to others" (Gowen, 2018).

The problem here is not the lengthy prison sentence Judge Aquilina gave the defendant, but the way she communicated that sentence. Judge Aquilina stepped out of her role as an objective and impartial professional when she made this case about her—her sympathy for the victims and her revulsion for the defendant. As Anne Gowen (2018), practicing attorney for over 17 years explains, "all of us who depend on the criminal justice system's being fair—and in the end, that really is all of us—need to be able to rely on the judiciary's administering justice consistently and predictably, based on laws rather than on judges' emotional reactions to particular sets of facts."

This case is illustrative of a broader concern: the importance not just of what we do but of how we do it; our attitude and demeanor, our way of interacting with information and with others, and our reactions to pressure such as difficult co-workers and impending deadlines—our "bedside manner," so to speak. The manner in which we deliver news is at least as important as the news we deliver. To be compelling criminal justice communicators, we will need to adopt and maintain a professional manner.

Professionalism means consistently exhibiting certain personal characteristics in addition to technical competence that inspires trust (Wiersma, 2010–2011). Technical competence makes one an expert, Wiersma continues, but *expert* is not synonymous with *professional*: There can be unprofessional experts, but a professional inspires trust on the basis of attitude and action. Professionals are reliable; they get the job done, make decisions and perform tasks that benefit their organization, do not get emotional when they get critical feedback or lose their composure when the stakes are high, strive to become and do better, and they value and work well with others. Criminal justice students should strive to make professionalism a habit so that professionalism is ingrained before they begin working in the criminal justice system. And people working in the criminal justice system, moreover, are expected to exhibit professionalism in all interactions with members of the public.

Professionalism is linked to perceived fairness and legitimacy, trust, confidence, cooperation, and compliance (Tyler, 2003; Tyler, Goff, & MacCoun, 2015). When police and other agents of the criminal justice system act professionally, citizens have more favorable impressions of the criminal justice system and its agents. Professionalism thus enhances trust and legitimacy. Citizens who are more trustful of the criminal justice system and its agents, in turn, are more likely to report crimes, comply with directives, and follow laws. The net effect of professionalism, then, is a more effective and efficient criminal justice system. Thus, professionalism is not just a short-term strategy for getting a job and earning promotions; it is also an efficient approach to effectuating social order and crime control.

Where professionals are seen as knowledgeable, fair, and trustworthy, people who are unprofessional may be regarded as incompetent, biased, and untrustworthy. Like Judge Aquilina, they might draw censure. We trust professionals to make the right decisions, but we do not trust non-professionals to make the right decisions. If we are treated fairly and respectfully, we will probably assume that others are treated fairly and respectfully. Conversely, if we are treated poorly, we may believe we were singled out for poor treatment by an unfair and discriminatory system or perhaps that everyone is treated like dirt by an unjust and corrupt system. Here, there is some truth to the adage that "a rotten apple spoils the bunch": A single negative encounter can tarnish perceptions of an entire police force, legal practice, judiciary, correctional workforce, or criminal justice system. By maintaining professionalism—even in heated situations with hostile people—we give citizens a powerful reason to trust us and the system.

This chapter outlines three guidelines for developing professional communications, and then it describes two forms of communications wherein professionalism is particularly important. After reading this chapter, you should have a solid understanding of why professionalism is important as well as clear guidance for producing professional communications.

BOX 2.2	Credibility Connection

Use communication as an opportunity to demonstrate your credibility by imbuing your writing with logic, evidence, and professionalism.

GUIDELINES

Follow these guidelines to develop a professional communication:

1. Adopt an assertive communication style.
2. Adhere to the strictest standards of integrity and ethics.
3. Maintain an appropriate level of formality.

Adopt an Assertive Communication Style

The major communication styles are assertive, aggressive, and passive. As indicated in Figure 2.1, the assertive style lies between aggressive and passive on a continuum of communication styles. Table 2.1 compares the three major communication styles.

The **assertive communication style** involves being forthright about your purpose without being antagonistic or evasive. Assertive communications are imbued with confidence. Consequently, they inspire respect, trust, and cooperation. Whether written or verbal, assertiveness involves being open and honest, direct, and respectful. Assertive speakers articulate their points and perspectives clearly, without obfuscation or equivocation, but they are also attentive to other points and respectful of other perspectives. In just about any situation, assertive is the most effective and efficient communication style.

Adhere to the Strictest Standards of Integrity and Ethics

Ethics is a crucial part of professionalism. **Ethics** relates to moral standards governing decisions and actions. Where capability refers to what people *can* do, morality refers to what people *should* do. When presented with a choice, the ethical option is the most moral option; it is what should be done even when something else easier could be done.

People might have their own personal standards of morality, and people also might be subject to organizational standards of the morality of ethics. In the first case, we can liken ethics with **integrity**: People with integrity hold moral principles that are reflected in their words and behavior. Someone with integrity does what that person says they will do. Someone does the right thing because it is the right thing—not because they are fearful of getting caught. People with integrity take responsibility for their actions; they do not engage in deception or blame.

FIGURE 2.1 Major Communication Styles

TABLE 2.1   Comparison of Communication Styles

	Passive	Assertive	Aggressive
Motto	"Others have more rights than I."	"I have rights and so do others."	"I've got rights, but you don't."
Characteristics	Indirect, always agrees, does not speak up, hesitant	Active listener, checks on others' feelings, proactive, flexible	Poor listener, close-minded, interrupts, monopolizes
Orientations	Apologetic, trusting of others (but not of self), self-conscious	Nonjudgmental, trusting, confident, self-aware	Know-it-all attitude, trusting of self (but not of others), self-oriented
Approaches	Often asks permission, lacks initiative, defers to others	Action- and goal-oriented, firm, realistic, fair, consistent	Goal-oriented, bossy, overpowering, bullying, patronizing
Verbal Cues	"You should do it," "I can't …," "I'll try."	"I choose to …," "What are our options?"	"You must …," "Don't ask; just do it."
Nonverbal Cues	Downcast eyes, slumped posture, fidgety, lacks facial animation	Direct eye contact, relaxed posture, attentive, natural gestures	Squints eyes, glares, and stares; rigid posture, points finger, frowns
Voice and Speech	Low volume, fast speech when anxious and slow when doubtful	Moderate volume, varied rate of speech	Loud volume, fast and slipped speech
Problem-Solving	Avoids and ignores, withdraws, avoids taking a side, agrees externally but disagrees internally	Negotiates and compromises, confronts problems promptly, does not bottle up negative feelings	Threatens and attacks, operates on an I-win/you-lose basis, causes and exacerbates problems
Feels	Powerless, dependent, insecure, loss of self-esteem	Motivation, enthusiasm, security, self-esteem	Hostility and anger, frustration and impatience
Effects on Others	Dislike, contempt, irritation, sense of being overwhelmed and the only one who cares	Sense of being valued, understood, connected, and respected; satisfaction, security, cooperation	Alienation, ill-health, fear, insecurity, resentment, resistance, defiance, lying, counteraggression

Source: Sherman (n.d.)

In the second case, ethics are expressed in **ethical codes of conduct**, which are rules for ethical decision-making and behavior prescribed by an organization for members to follow. Members are expected to know and follow their organization's ethics code, and they can be ejected from the organization if they are caught deviating from the ethical code. In many cases, people with integrity could probably conform to organizational ethical codes without ever having read them, simply because both ethical codes and integrity reflect socially accepted values such as truth and justice. The study and practice of criminal justice presents abundant ethical dilemmas and opportunities to exhibit integrity.

Ethics and Integrity in School

Like the study of any other academic discipline, students of criminal justice must follow academic honesty codes (also called academic integrity policies). Such codes apply to all students at the institution and prohibit academic offenses such as lying, cheating,

TABLE 2.2   Examples of Academic Ethical Violations

Lying	Cheating	Plagiarism
Saying that you did not understand the rules, and that is why you broke them when you really did understand the rules but just did not follow them	Getting (or giving) test questions from a student in an earlier section of the same course	Copying and pasting from a source into one's own paper and providing an in-text citation and Reference-list entry but not using quotation marks to indicate the source's exact words
Claiming that your computer crashed, causing you to lose a term paper, when you really had not written the paper	Working with other students to complete a homework assignment	Getting ideas from a source but not crediting that source via in-text citation and Reference-list entry
Telling the professor that you were sick when you had really just overslept	Using notes to complete a closed-book test	Using portions of a paper written for one course in another course (i.e., self-plagiarism)

stealing, and plagiarism. Students who deviate from their institution's code of academic integrity are considered to be in violation of the code and thus are subject to a variety of penalties, ranging from a grade of "0" on the assignment or a grade of "F" in the course to suspension or expulsion.

Lying involves fabrications, misrepresentations, and omissions of material facts. **Cheating** involves giving or getting unauthorized assistance in the completion of graded work. A form of stealing, **plagiarism** involves failing to acknowledge properly the source of information—whether intentional or unintentional. Table 2.2 further distinguishes between these academic offenses.

Plagiarism is probably the academic violation about which we hear the most. Most professors include a statement on plagiarism—what it means and how it will be handled—in their syllabi. For student writers, the best course of action is to use the broadest definition of plagiarism possible in your own writing and to err on the side of citing too much. A helpful way to approach ethical writing is the notion of an implicit contract between authors and the audience, whereby the audience will assume—unless otherwise noted using established conventions (e.g., quotation marks, in-text citations)—that all ideas and words are the author's own and have been written for one and only one purpose: for the present audience (Roig, 2015). Drawing from this notion of an implicit contract, some specific guidelines for avoiding plagiarism include the following (Harris, 2017; Roig, 2015):

1. Indicate the source of any idea, words, images, or other text or non-text material by providing an in-text citation and corresponding entry in the References. Put differently, "If the information came from outside your own head, cite the source" (Harris, 2017, p. 104).

BOX 2.3	Plagiarism Pointer

Plagiarism calls one's character into question. *Intentional* plagiarism signals ineptitude and a lack of integrity. *Unintentional* plagiarism suggests incompetence and ignorance. The bottom line is that whether intentional or unintentional, plagiarism is a sign of an untrustworthy person.

2. Indicate the exact words from a source by enclosing them in quotation marks (or using block indentation for longer quotes) and providing an in-text citation and corresponding entry in the References. This rule applies whether you quote a phrase, a sentence, or more.

3. Source material does not become your own when you substitute some words for others, reorganize the order of words in a sentence, or put sentences in a different order. Making such superficial alterations is considered **mosaic plagiarism** when you claim the ideas and words as your own, and it is called **inappropriate paraphrasing** when you claim the words as your own but give credit to the source for the ideas. Both mosaic plagiarism and inappropriate paraphrasing are unethical writing practices (see Table 2.3).

4. Do not reuse your own work, either in part or in whole, such as submitting the same paper in two courses or using part of a paper written in one course for a discussion post in another course, without the express permission of both instructors. Doing this is called **self-plagiarism**, and it is just as serious as plagiarism, lying, and cheating.

5. Citing a source means that you have read the entire source. Do not read only an article's abstract, for instance, but then cite the full-text version of the article. Either read and cite the abstract, or read and cite the full-text version.

6. Citing a source means that it is truly your source of the information. For example, do not cite primary versions when you have only read secondary versions, nor should you cite the original work after only reading an encyclopedia summary of that work.

Remember that plagiarism can be intentional or unintentional. The best safeguard against unintentional plagiarism is to know all the rules about plagiarism.

Group work can present some additional challenges in terms of ethical writing. How, for example, should we deal with a group member who contributes nothing but expects their name to go on the final paper? And is everyone in the group guilty of plagiarism if one of the group mates plagiarized in their section?

TABLE 2.3   Examples of Unacceptable and Acceptable Use of Source Text

Original Text	Unacceptable Use	Acceptable Use
The evidence handling process was complex.	*Mosaic plagiarism*: The process for handling evidence was complicated.	The many steps involved in evidence handling make it complicated (Durden, 2012).
		Handling evidence is far from simple (Durden, 2012).
There were three steps. First, the evidence was collected. Second, the evidence was transported. Third, the evidence was analyzed.	*Inappropriate paraphrasing*: According to Durden (2012), three steps occurred. The first step was collecting the evidence. The second step was transporting the evidence. The third step was analyzing the evidence.	The three steps in handling the evidence were collection, transportation, and analysis (Durden, 2012).
		Durden (2012) outlined three steps in how the evidence was handled: (1) collection, (2) transportation, and (3) analysis.

To answer the first question, all authors should be listed. Authors are people who contributed substantially to the written work. People who did not contribute as authors should not be listed as such. Merely being in a group does not make someone an author.

The answer to the second question is, unfortunately, yes. This is because all people listed as authors should have read and agreed to all content prior to submitting it. All authors should take equal responsibility for the final product. Be wary of a group member who produces nothing until the night before the paper is due, especially when that member's writing is of better quality than you have ever seen from them. If you are concerned about a group member plagiarizing, contact your instructor immediately. Do not wait until the instructor assigns a penalty for plagiarism to bring the matter to the instructor's attention.

Ethics and Integrity in the Workforce

While criminal justice students do not tend to have ethical challenges unique to them, criminal justice employees frequently do encounter varied and unique ethical dilemmas. An **ethical dilemma** is a choice between options having moral implications. To illustrate, imagine two people are about to fall off a roof, and you can only save one: Which person would it be? Suppose one of these people is a mentally and physically handicapped child and the other is a brilliant scientist on the brink of curing cancer. Saving the child means protecting the more vulnerable person, while saving the scientist could benefit humanity. The choice is not clear-cut; it is not immediately (or even eventually) clear which is the "right" decision. Considered separately, we would probably all agree that saving the child is a moral thing to do. Likewise, we would probably all agree that saving the scientist is a moral thing to do. But, if we can only choose one of these options, which one is more moral?

Table 2.4 presents five approaches for resulting such ethical dilemmas. Without going into too much into detail on these approaches to ethical decision-making, the general starting point is to identify what the options are. Once we have identified the options, we can use one or more ethical approaches to choose the one most ethical option.

TABLE 2.4   Approaches to Resolving Ethical Dilemmas

Approach	Description
The Common Good Approach	The most ethical option is the one that best advances the common good. The least ethical option is the one that least advances the common good.
The Fairness (or Justice) Approach	The most ethical option is the one that treats morally equal people the most fairly. The least ethical option is the one that treats morally equal people the most unfairly.
The Rights Approach	The most ethical option best respects the moral rights of everyone. The least ethical option constitutes the most serious violations of individuals' moral rights.
The Utilitarian Approach	The most ethical option creates the greatest benefits and least harm. The least ethical option creates the most harm and the least benefits.
The Virtue Approach	The most ethical option is the one most in harmony with moral ideals for our own behavior. The least ethical option is the least in harmony with moral ideals for our own behavior.

Source: Meeler (n.d.)

TABLE 2.5   Unethical Behaviors by Criminal Justice System Agents

Phenomena	Examples
Abuse of Power	Threatening a suspect with physical harm if he does not confess
Conflict of Interest	Failing to disclose a conflict of interest regarding a family member charged with a crime
Corruption	Sharing privileged information between defense and prosecution to expedite the process
Deception	Omitting from an arrest report the use of excessive force
Defense Counsel Misconduct	Misrepresenting facts to the court
Discrimination	Asking a qualified individual about disabilities in a job interview
Judicial Misconduct	Advertising one's status as a judge to avoid getting a speeding ticket
Perjury	Lying on the stand to help gain a conviction
Prosecutorial Misconduct	Withholding exculpatory evidence during discovery

Source: Roberson and Mire (2010)

Not only do criminal justice system agents face such ethical dilemmas routinely, but they also are often in a position of insufficient information. They might not know, for example, what the possible consequences are for a given course of action. And yet, despite not having such information, criminal justice system agents must act; they cannot delay action until they have all the relevant information needed to arrive at a fully informed decision. Table 2.5 presents some situations involving the intersection of ethics and communication in the criminal justice system.

Before leaving the topic of ethics, the inextricable link between ethics and integrity, professionalism and effectiveness in the field of criminal justice bears reiteration. One cannot be professional without valuing and possessing integrity and consistently exhibiting ethical behavior. And one cannot be truly effective without inspiring trust and confidence by maintaining professionalism.

Maintain an Appropriate Level of Formality

Recall that criminal justice communications are formal communications. Formal language is appropriate for serious situations as well as when we do not know our audience or have a professional (rather than a personal) relationship with our audience. Two dimensions of formal communication style are covered here: (1) tone and (2) diction.

Tone

In communication, **tone** means attitude: your attitude toward the subject and the communication task itself. Criminal justice communications generally should convey an attitude of dispassionate concern. That is, we care—we care a lot—but in a professional sense, not in a personal sense. Yet we recognize that much of what we do and say is very personal to others, such as crime victims, suspects, and witnesses and their families. We do not want to ignore or dismiss peoples' legitimate emotions. Indeed, our skill set should include sympathy, empathy, patience, and understanding. But in our formal communications, we need to assume and maintain a formal to moderately formal communication style. We can do so by taking the approaches presented in Table 2.6.

TABLE 2.6   Appropriately Formal Tone

Approach	Meaning
Prefer objective to subjective	Focus on the facts and your job/assignment
	Be careful not to base decisions on intuition, hunches, and other unmeasurable factors
	Avoid personal opinions, biases, and expectations
Prefer logical to emotional	Make decisions based on evidence and logic
	Recognize when emotions are involved; do not discount the power of emotions over logic
	Avoid letting emotions overshadow evidence and logic
Prefer serious to humorous	Act sincere and attentive
	Avoid jokes and attempts at being funny
	Take your time; do not appear to be in a hurry
Prefer impersonal to intimate	Act dignified and respectful
	Avoid being overly familiar, casual, and chatty
	Set aside your own opinions and experiences unless they are solicited

Diction

Diction refers to word choice. Like tone, we want our choice of words to give the impression that we are professionals. To match the professional tone we seek to project, moreover, our words should be objective, logical, and impersonal. Recall that many aspects of word choice are covered elsewhere in this text, particularly in the chapters on correct and clear writing (Chapters 8 and 9, respectively). Here, we will consider four matters involving diction that are not covered elsewhere: (1) personal words, (2) contractions, (3) colloquialisms, and (4) loaded terms.

PERSONAL WORDS. **Personal words** refer to the following personal pronouns: I, me, my, mine, you, yours, we, us, our, and ours. Unless a specific communication necessitates the use of personal pronouns, we should not exhibit a personal attitude by using them. From this it follows that we should refrain from personal expressions, beliefs, mottos, and so on that make use of personal words, such as the following:

- I discovered . . .
- She told me . . .
- You should . . .
- We have . . .
- Our neighborhood . . .
- This teaches us . . .

An example of a communication that necessitates personal pronouns are some reports, wherein a police officer might note when and why the officer arrived to the scene. But most written academic and legal communications should avoid personal words.

In academic writing, for example, we often want to come across as objective, and one way to accomplish that is to leave ourselves out of our writing. Where we are "in our writing" when we use personal pronouns, we are "out of our writing" when we avoid personal pronouns. Sometimes, avoiding personal words creates tension when we also try to prefer the active to the passive voice. Consider these two sentences:

- Active voice 1: "I surveyed 1,000 American adults."
- Passive voice: "One thousand American adults were surveyed."

The difference is that active voice leads with the subject—the agent causing the action—whereas passive voice leads with the object—the recipient of the action. It can be tricky both to avoid personal words and to use active voice, but consider these alternatives:

- Active voice 2: "This article reports on a survey of 1,000 American adults."
- Active voice 3: "A survey of 1,000 American adults found that. . . ."

The solution illustrated in the third example of active voice avoids personal words, retains active voice, and exhibits conciseness. It does so by combining the sentence in question with another piece of information. This makes the third active voice example the superior solution. It takes some thinking and tinkering to solve one writing problem without creating another writing problem, but the end result is worth the effort.

CONTRACTIONS. **Contractions** are when multiple words are joined together with an apostrophe and by abbreviating one of the words, such as the following:

- don't (for "do not")
- he's (for "he is")
- it's (for "it is")
- isn't (for "is not")
- shouldn't (for "should not")
- would've (for "would have")

Unless quoting, avoid contractions in most criminal justice communications. Contractions can be easily avoided by writing out the words. For example, change "can't" to "cannot." All you need to do to avoid contractions, then, is to review your complete draft, looking for any contractions, and then replacing any contractions you find with the written-out version of the words.

COLLOQUIALISMS. **Colloquialisms** are informal expressions. Sometimes, they make use of contractions. Though just about anyone will understand the expression, the problem with colloquialisms is their informality. They imply a casual attitude that clashes with and thus chips away at the aura of professionalism we are trying to project in our communications. Common colloquialisms include

- Ain't
- Gonna
- Freak out
- Have a good one
- No problem
- Wanna
- What's up?
- Ya'll

Colloquialisms are such a prominent feature of conversation that we often use them inadvertently. Thus, one route to avoiding colloquialisms is to be cognizant of their undesirability in formal, professional communication. Another route is training ourselves to avoid them. In written communications, a third route is to review our draft closely, looking for any colloquialisms. If we find one, we should replace it with more formal language. For example, we can change "No problem" to "You are welcome" and "Have a good one" to "Have a nice day."

LOADED TERMS. A thesaurus contains synonyms, or words with the same meaning. Often, however, the words do not have exactly the same meaning. A case in point is **loaded terms**, which have similar dictionary definition but—instead of being a neutral—possess either a positive or negative connotation. Professional writing uses neutral terms, not loaded terms.

When we use loaded terms, we inject our opinions, perspectives, and perhaps even biases into our communications. As a result, our communication moves from being objective to subjective. Loaded terms generally are used when the communicator has an agenda. If we want increased law enforcement attention on some crime problem, we might refer to that crime problem as an "epidemic" or "scourge"; if, on the other hand, we want more compassionate treatment, we instead might refer to the problem as an "tragedy" or a "plight." Table 2.7 contains more examples of loaded terminology.

In criminal justice communications, loaded terms are relevant both when we are the sender and when we are the receiver. As a sender, and similar to colloquialisms, perhaps the best way to avoid loaded terms is to be aware of their existence and to train ourselves not to use them. We can also review a draft, looking for and replacing any loaded terms. As a receiver, we can look for loaded terms in other people's communications. Loaded terms can be used as clues regarding the sender's stance on an issue. Someone might claim to be impartial but then use loaded terms in such a way as to make obvious which side of an issue that person really supports.

TABLE 2.7   Loaded Terms

Neutral Term	Positive Connotation	Negative Connotation
Assertive	confident, self-assured, decisive	arrogant, cocky, pushy
Criminal	offender, deviant, delinquent	predator, monster, animal, villain
Different	unique, special, one of a kind, rare	peculiar, odd, irregular
Economical	thrifty, frugal, efficient, prudent	stingy, miserly, close-fisted, tight
Energetic	active, dynamic, vigorous	aggressive, forcible, violent
Shy	modest, cautious, circumspect	mousy, afraid, nervous, timid
Questioning	interested, inquisitive, analytical	nosy, meddlesome, snooping
Selective	meticulous, careful, fastidious	picky, critical, fussy
Smell	aroma, scent, perfume	odor, stench, stink
Tenacious	steadfast, strong-willed, persistent	stubborn, ornery, unreasonable

APPLICATIONS

Here, we look at two forms of criminal justice communications related to job acquisition and advancement: (1) job application materials and (2) performance evaluation reviews. Nonprofessional jobs, such as working in restaurants and clothing stores, often use an application form, where applicants fill out a document with their personal and job experiences. But professional jobs in the criminal justice system typically use a more involved process. Many professional jobs, moreover, have periodic employee evaluations, which are conducted and written by supervisors who assess their employees' job performance.

Job Application Materials

This section looks at the written communications associated with applying for a professional job in the criminal justice system. The two most common job application materials are the cover letter and résumé. A **cover letter** is a letter written by an applicant to the organization to which one is applying, which expresses the applicant's interest in and suitability for a job. A **résumé** is a document listing a job applicant's education, skills, and employment history. Many professional jobs will require at least these two documents.

Although it can be tempting to have one standard cover letter and one standard résumé that you use to apply to several jobs, it is more effective to write these materials anew for each job to which you apply. This way, you can tailor the documents to the specifics of the job to which you are applying. Tailoring the documents helps the person reviewing your application materials see how well suited to the job you are in addition to showing that you are interested enough to resist using boilerplate materials for your application.

Cover Letters

Your goal in writing this letter is to sell yourself—to make the employer believe that you are the best person for the job. Use the cover letter as an opportunity to make a strong, favorable, and memorable first impression. Show that you understand what the job entails, and that you possess the necessary skills for the position. Also, demonstrate with your writing that you are a professional, effective communicator. Table 2.8 shows the contents and organization of a cover letter.

In your cover letter, do not merely repeat the same material that is in your résumé; instead, share information that is not in your résumé, such as concern for detail and organizational skills. The education paragraph should make an argument about how your educational experiences have prepared you for the job, while the employment paragraph should make an argument about how your employment background has prepared you for the job. Take these arguments beyond formal accomplishments (e.g., courses taken, jobs held) to informal experiences and personal and professional development. Consider information such as what you have learned in previous positions, your approach to complicated tasks, and your ability to collaborate with and/or lead others on projects.

With regard to layout, cover letters generally should not exceed one page. Four paragraphs should easily fit onto one page, without having to shrink the font or narrow the margins. Left-align all content, single space, and insert one blank line space between each

TABLE 2.8   Contents and Structure of a Cover Letter

Part	Specific Contents
Basic Information	• Provide your contact information • Include the date on which you apply • Provide the addressee's name and contact information
Salutation	• Start with "Dear" addressee title and last name
Introduction Paragraph	• Describe how you learned about the job • Identify the position for which you are applying and any key skills listed in the job ad • State your desire to be considered for the position • Give a brief overview of the rest of the letter
Education Paragraph*	• List college attended, years, and GPA • Identify courses relevant to the job • Identify additional academic experiences and skills relevant to the job, such as certifications, hardware and software proficiency, notable writing and presentation experiences, data analysis training, leadership and collaboration experiences, and extracurricular activities
Employment Paragraph*	• Present relevant positions held • List relevant experiences and skills gained through past and present positions
Conclusion Paragraph	• Refer to your resume • Request an interview • Provide your phone number and email address
Closing	• "Sincerely" your full name typed and signed
Enclosure Note	• "Enclosure" and the number of enclosures

*The order of these paragraphs should be determined by which one is stronger: If your educational background is stronger, then place it first; however, if your employment background is stronger, then place it first. If they are equally strong (or weak), then just be sure to use the same order in your letter as in your resume.
Source: Markel (2012)

part of the letter. Give yourself some extra space between the closing ("Sincerely") and your typed, full name so that you have space to sign your name. Print your letter, sign your letter, and then scan the letter into your computer. Most employers expect online submission of application materials, but double-check the job ad's instructions to make sure you comply.

Résumés

While the cover letter should provide the big picture, the résumé should provide the details. Not only does it outline your educational and employment background, but also it should represent a timeline of your professional experiences that are relevant to the position you seek in the organization. Table 2.9 presents the contents and structure of a résumé.

The résumé serves as a detailed timeline, telling the story of how you got from the point of college freshman to the point of being the best candidate for the position. As a timeline, one feature of an effective résumé is a lack of interruptions. For example, if you say you attended University A from 2010 to 2012 and University B from 2014 to 2016, then the logical question arises: What were you doing from 2012 to 2014? Try to avoid timeline gaps and, when gaps are unavoidable (i.e., they are the truth), address them directly. Perhaps, for example, you were taking care of a sick relative, raising children, or

TABLE 2.9   Contents and Structure of a Résumé

Part	Specific Contents
Contact Information	• Provide your name and current, complete contact information (postal address, phone number[s], and email address)
Objectives (or Summary)	• Present either a Statement of Objectives or a Summary of Qualifications • Consider a Statement of Objectives if you are new to the field and do not have particularly impressive qualifications, and then draw from the job advertisement to formulate and express your objectives • Consider a Summary of Qualifications if you have an impressive collection of qualifications, and then select approximately three to four relevant skills or accomplishments • Be specific
Education*	• Identify your highest degree earned along with your major, institution, institution location, GPA, and date of graduation • Identify any other post-high school academic institutions attended, from most to least recent, with degree (if earned), major institution name and location, and date of graduation (or years attended) • List relevant coursework • List and briefly describe any special accomplishments (e.g., major research projects, work on funded projects) • List any honors and awards
Employment*	• Identify each job you have had—your position or title, the organization's name and location, and employment dates—and provide a 2–3-line description of your duties and accomplishments • Present more information for particularly relevant jobs, addressing topics such as skills used, equipment used, money involved, personnel supervision, client interaction
Other	• Present other relevant material, such as community service, career-related hobbies, sports, student organizations, military languages, and additional languages in one or more other sections • Title this section in a way that reflects its contents
References	• Put only "Available upon request"; this material should be a separate document from your résumé

*Most students and recent graduates should cover education first, while people with more extensive professional employment experience should cover employment first. Use the same order for the résumé as you use in your cover letter.
Source: Markel (2012)

earning money so you could complete your college degree. Timeline gaps in education and employment warrant justification.

Résumé layout has received a good deal of attention. There is a widely held belief, for example, that a résumé must not exceed one page. But this is not entirely true. If you have considerable relevant educational and/or employment experiences, then it is better to include that information and go over one page than to exclude that information merely to avoid exceeding one page. Strict adherence to the one-page principle, moreover, can make it difficult for the reader to locate particular information, such as when sections are not separated by blank line spaces. That said, do not make your résumé long for the sole purpose of creating the impression that you have extensive expertise and credentials. In addition, if your material spills over one page by just a couple lines, then figure out how to condense it all onto one page (Markel, 2012).

Jane F. Doe
55 Pier Street
Law, New York 12345
(555) 555-5555
jfdoe@gmail.com

Summary of Qualifications

Collecting, coding, and analyzing crime data using Excel, SPSS, STATA, ArcGIS, Link Analysis. Presenting crime trends, patterns, and forecasting models to internal and external audiences using PowerPoint and Prezi. Communicating effectively in written, verbal, and graphical form and collaborating with others to develop and present intelligence reports and other data products.

Education

MS, Criminal Intelligence Analysis   2016–2018
Justice College
Bridge, New York
GPA: 3.92
Relevant courses: Advanced Crime Theory, Statistics II, Statistics III, Assessing Evidence, Data Visualization, Social Network Analysis, Crime Forecasting

BS, Criminal Justice   2012–2016
Rule College
Path, New York
GPA: 3.95
Relevant courses: Criminological Theory, Criminological Research Methods, Criminal Intelligence, Data Analysis in Criminal Justice, Criminal Justice Communications, Organized Crime

Employment

Junior Crime Analyst   2017–present
Bridge Police Department
Bridge, New York
Responsibilities: Researches and analyzes crime and law enforcement data regarding criminal activity and crime trends; compiles statistical and strategic analyses and reports, develops and maintains databases; attends regional and state law enforcement meetings; conducts briefings and presentations of analytical findings, conclusions, and recommendations; works with senior command, police personnel, and other city employees on crime research and analysis projects

Page 1 of 2

Research Assistant   2013–2016
Rule College
Path New York
Responsibilities: Conducting and drafting annotated bibliographies and literature reviews; assisting with survey design; entering and cleaning data in SPSS and STATA; performing preliminary data analyses and interpretations; preparing applications for the Human Subjects Committee

Organizational Memberships

Professional
International Association of Law Enforcement Intelligence Analysts, Member   2017–present
American Society of Criminology, Member   2016–present
Academic of Criminal Justice Sciences, Member   2016–present

Student
Student Senate, President, Rule College   2015–2016
Alpha Phi Sigma, Member, Rule   2014–2016

References

Available upon request.

Page 2 of 2

FIGURE 2.2   Sample Résumé

Figure 2.2 provides an example résumé for a criminal analyst position at a local police department. In this example, the hypothetical résumé author, Jane Doe, was a great student but did not have much professional experience. Here are some additional formatting tips:

- Use one font type (e.g., Times New Roman or Calibri) and size (e.g., 10–12) for all main text. You can use a larger font size for your name and section headings.
- Put your name (at the top) and section headings (throughout the document) in bold. You can use bold with italics for any subsection headings. Italicize rather than bolding other information.
- Consider inserting horizontal lines between major sections—especially if you are bolding any other information (e.g., names of academic institutions and places of employment).
- Single space, using left-aligned text for all material except your name and contact information at the top (which should be centered). Use 1-inch margins on all four sides.
- Put listed material in bulleted format. Then use parallel structure starting with strong, action verbs for each bullet's material.
- Be consistent, such as with verb tense and use of capitalization.
- Omit page numbers unless your résumé exceeds one page, in which case consider the "Page 1 of 2" page-numbering format.

Best Practices

It is a good idea to look at some examples of cover letters and résumés before you make yours. Looking at examples can give you an idea of appropriate language as well as a solid idea for how to format your job application materials. You can search online, such as with the search terms "effective cover letters and résumés." Remember, however, that different fields can have different expectations and standards (e.g., marketing and design résumés might have more "flare" than criminal justice résumés). So, you need to be circumspect in any search for a good model to adopt.

What follows is a list of best practices for cover letters and résumés:

1. **Research the job before you apply.** Learn what you can from the company's website, particularly about its goals and mission. A Google search also might show some news stories, such as particularly good aspects (e.g., humanitarian efforts, innovative approach) and particularly bad aspects (e.g., sexual harassment, bankruptcy).

2. **Personalize your cover letter and résumé for each job.** Resist the urge to use standard application materials for multiple jobs, though it can make sense to copy and paste specific information once you determine its relevance (e.g., courses taken, software used).

3. **Use key words from the job ad in your materials.** If the job ad says the organization is looking for someone with "data analysis skills, communication skills, and an ability to work in teams," then work those terms into your materials. Use those terms in your letter, and then list courses where you acquired and refined these skills as well as assignments where you have successfully demonstrated mastery of these skills.

4. **Be assertive in making your case that you are the best person for the job.** Without being too pushy or overconfident (e.g., "I have no doubt that I am the very best person for this job"), be confident and clear. Use your educational and employment experiences and accomplishments as evidence of your suitability, logically linking your credentials and expertise to the description of duties in the job ad.

5. **Do not act desperate.** Avoid giving the impression that you really need for a job and/or that money is the driving force behind your desire to work for the organization. Instead, focus on the apparent fit between (a) the organization and its mission and the advertised position and (b) your goals, aspirations, interests, skills, and knowledge. Certainly do not put in a letter that your first choices turned you down.

6. **Be honest.** Do not lie or exaggerate your qualifications and experience. Dishonesty in job application materials can be detected in a reference check, may become apparent over time in conversations or your performance, and even could result in termination.

7. **Maintain a clear, concise, and formal writing style.** In keeping with the nine principles presented in this text, be brief and use simple language. You might need to use more sophisticated terms in some places, such as presenting your experience with operating systems or statistical procedures. But avoid flowery, elaborate language as well as being too chatty and conversational.

8. **Use the active voice.** In your résumé, avoid "I" and instead use the active voice to list positions, functions, and responsibilities. For example, "Created code. . . ." and "Developed software. . . ." In this context, it is perfectly acceptable to write in incomplete sentences.

9. **Make sure all your information is correct and current.** On the one hand, all of *your* information needs to be accurate and up to date, particularly your educational and employment material and your contact information. On the other hand, all of the *organization's* information should be right. Spelling organizations' and people's names incorrectly is a fatal flaw. You also want to ensure that you accurately represent what the job ad says the position requires, and to avoid problems such as your cover letter to company A accidentally being addressed to the hiring manager of company B.

10. **Edit to catch and correct any typos.** Read your materials aloud to yourself to catch errors in writing mechanics, and then review it closely to catch punctuation errors and formatting inconsistencies and other flaws. If possible, ask someone else to review these materials for you before you submit them.

Performance Evaluation Reviews

Organizations often have employee **performance reviews**, which are typically annual written assessments by supervisors of employees' performance in meeting job expectations. There also may be semi-annual or quarterly meetings between supervisors and employees that serve as less formal check-ups on how well (or poorly) the employee is doing and what that person needs to do differently to meet expectations and thus have a positive annual performance review. These periodic check-ups focus on progress in meeting the goals as well as career development. An annual review covers all the employee's performance since the last annual review. It does not just cover the most recent events, negative events, or positive events (Heathfield, 2018a). Both because the review covers everything since the previous review and because of the periodic check-ups, employees cannot underperform for 11 months, deliver a stellar performance in the 12th month, and then get a positive evaluation review. Previously set goals are evaluated, and new goals are set. Thus, performance evaluation reviews facilitate constant professional monitoring, assessment, and development.

The review is not a secret; that is, the employee being evaluated will receive a copy. Because of this, there is transparency to the review process, which can be helpful to the employee in terms of meeting goals but also can be uncomfortable when the review is less than completely positive. An employee who receives a partly negative evaluation might feel self-conscious or even hostile, but it is important to maintain professionalism when confronted with critical feedback. After all, "Professionals aspire to be masters of their emotions, not enslaved by them" (Wiersma, 2010–2011, p. 213). But it is not just the employee who needs to maintain professionalism during the review process. For this process to be successful, the supervisor must construct an accurate, professional review document.

Contents and Organization

Organizations generally have a set format for their employees' performance evaluation reviews. What evaluation reviews have in common, however, is that they revolve around goals: What are the goals for the employee's performance, how are the goals measured, and how well did the employee do meeting those goals? Table 2.10 shows the basic structure and contents of performance evaluation reviews.

TABLE 2.10   Contents and Structure of a Performance Evaluation Review

Part	Specific Contents
Basic Information	• Employee name, position, and department • Reason for evaluation (standard/periodic or incident-based) • Job description
Performance Goals	• Employee's main work performance goals for the period: specific duty, goal, tools needed for the goal, and completion date • Additional tools or training needed • Discussion and measurement
Personal and Professional Development Goals	• Employee's main personal and professional developmental goals for the period: specific goal, how success in meeting the goal will be determined, tools needed for the goal, and completion date • Additional tools or training needed • Discussion and measurement • Employee comments • Employee suggestions for supervisor or department development • Date for next developmental meeting
Closing Information	• Employee signature and date • Supervisor signature and date

Source: Heathfield (2018b)

Employees and supervisors should be aware of the organization's performance evaluation process as soon as they are hired/promoted. Orientation should stress this process and its importance to the organization as well as to the employee's professional development. Having a solid understanding of this process and how it unfolds, employees can use the time between annual reviews working on their performance goals, while supervisors can spend that time observing and documenting the employee's performance. As a supervisor, keep a file on each employee, so you can collect relevant information all year (both positive and negative), which will give you valuable details on which to base your annual review.

Keep in mind that while the ultimate goal of the performance review process is to ensure high-quality organizational performance via high-quality individual performance, the review says as much about the person writing it as it does about the person being reviewed. A sloppy, inaccurate, unprofessional report reflects a sloppy, inaccurate, and unprofessional supervisor. Everyone is accountable to someone, and thus supervisors can expect their reviews ultimately to be used as evidence of their own effectiveness in meeting performance goals.

Best Practices
To maximize the usefulness of performance evaluation reviews, follow these best practices (Caramela, 2018; Heathfield, 2018a):

1. **Focus on specific, clearly defined goals.** The research you do to prepare the review and the review document itself should emphasize and be organized around performance goals. The goals and their measurement should be as specific and objective as possible.

2. **Be explicit.** "Do better," as an extreme example, is far too broad: Do better at what, exactly, and how? If the employee knew how to do better, assume that person

would have done better. Thus, if an employee needs to do better, the employee needs clear, actionable guidance on what "better" means and how to do better.

3. **Base goals on the employee's position and on the organization's needs.** Goals should be appropriate given the employee's job description as well as the organization's goals. Goals should also be realistic, reflecting the employee's qualifications and organizational resources. Intermediate goals might be a helpful approach.

4. **Ensure goal measures are realistic.** When you specify how a goal will be measured, make sure that measurement is possible and will not stretch your capabilities or organizational resources. As an extreme example, you would not want to measure a goal by "surveying every citizen" who came into contact with the employee.

5. **Get your facts correct.** Make sure your information is accurate. Both when setting and when evaluation goals, consider multiple sources. Try not to over-rely on one person or on subjective measurements. When you talk with other people about the employee being evaluated, take careful notes.

6. **Ground each conclusion in evidence.** Provided goal measurement has been clearly outlined, you do not have to get creative with your assessment of the employee's performance. The point here is to use evidence to reach conclusions and then to explain how the evidence led to each conclusion.

7. **Consider positives and negatives.** With positive aspects, discuss how the employee can continue. Try to lead with and spend more time on the positive aspects. With negative aspects, discuss what the employee needs to do differently. Be clear without being overly critical. Try to end on a positive note as well.

8. **Replace abstract, vague language with more concrete, measurement-oriented language.** Avoid vague words such as "good" and "bad"; instead, use words that specify what you mean by "good" or "bad." Thus, rather than "did a good job on report submission," for example, write, "submitted reports on time." Include specific examples wherever possible (e.g., if the employee submitted late reports, which reports and how late?).

9. **Be serious.** Resist the urge to tell an employee who gets upset over negative feedback that it "is no big deal." Do not trivialize the importance of the performance review process. The goal is for the employee to improve, and that goal will be impeded to the extent that the employee believes that the process is unimportant.

10. **Give the employee a copy of the review before you meet to discuss it.** Doing so helps ensure that you both are prepared for an efficient meeting and also can diffuse tension by giving the employee time to process any negative feedback.

EXERCISES
Matching
These exercises are designed to assess Chapter 2 Learning Objective 1 (see Box 2.1). Match each numbered statement to the lowercase letter corresponding to the key word it defines. Each key word will be used only once.

1. Moral standards governing decision-making and behavior
2. Multiple words joined together with an apostrophe and by abbreviating one of the words

3. Fabrications, misrepresentations, and omissions of material facts
4. Reusing your own work, either in part or in whole, such as submitting the same paper in two courses or using a part of a paper written in one course for a discussion post in another course, without the express permission of both instructors
5. The communication style that involves being forthright about your purpose without being antagonistic or evasive
6. Written assessments, often conducted annually, by supervisors of an employee's performance in meeting job expectations
7. A choice between options having moral implications
8. Pronouns, such as I, me, you, we, and ours
9. As it pertains to academic dishonesty, the giving or getting unauthorized assistance in the completion of graded work
10. A document listing a job applicant's education, skills, and employment history
11. Making only superficial alterations—substituting some words for others, reorganizing the order of words in a sentence, or putting sentences in a different order to source text—and then claiming both the idea and the words as your own by omitting a citation
12. Informal expressions, such as "have a good one" and "no problem"
13. Failing to acknowledge properly the source of information—whether intentional or unintentional
14. Attitude toward the subject and the communication task itself
15. Rules for ethical decision-making and action prescribed by organizations for members to follow
16. A letter written by an applicant to the organization to which one is applying, which expresses the applicant's interest in and suitability for a job
17. Words or phrases with a positive or negative connotation
18. The consistent exhibiting of certain personal characteristics in addition to technical competence that inspires trust
19. Word choice
20. The characteristic of people who hold moral principles that are reflected in their words and behavior
21. Making only superficial alterations—substituting some words for others, reorganizing the order of words in a sentence, or putting sentences in a different order to source text—and then giving the source credit for the idea by including a citation but claiming the words as your own by omitting quotation marks

a. assertive communication style
b. cheating
c. colloquialisms
d. contractions
e. cover letter
f. diction
g. ethical codes of conduct
h. ethical dilemma
i. ethics
j. inappropriate paraphrasing
k. integrity

l. loaded terms
m. lying
n. mosaic plagiarism
o. performance reviews
p. personal words
q. plagiarism
r. professionalism
s. résumé
t. self-plagiarism
u. tone

Multiple Choice

These exercises are designed to assess Chapter 2 Learning Objective 3 (see Box 2.1). Indicate the single most appropriate response to each item below.

1. Is the following answer professional or unprofessional? *Question*: "What does the research say about public defenders?" *Answer*: "The public defenders I've worked with are just as good as any other attorney."
   a. professional
   b. unprofessional

2. Is the following suspect description professional or unprofessional? "The suspect has black hair and is wearing black shoes, tan pants, and a black jacket. He was last seen crossing Main Street in a white pickup truck with no license plate."
   a. professional
   b. unprofessional

3. Is the following suspect description professional or unprofessional? "The suspect has black hair and is wearing black shoes, tan pants, and a black jacket. He is about 5 feet tall. He was last seen crossing Main Street in a rust-covered white pickup truck without a license plate."
   a. professional
   b. unprofessional

4. Is the following suspect description professional or unprofessional? "The suspect has black hair and is wearing black shoes, tan pants, and a black jacket. Suspect is a midget at about 5 feet tall. He was last seen crossing Main Street in a rust-covered white pickup truck without a license plate."
   a. professional
   b. unprofessional

5. Which of the following is an example of a *professional* communication?
   a. I know what needs to get done. Just do it.
   b. I'm not sure. I just can't make up my mind. What do you think we should do?
   c. Thank you for your suggestions, which I've seriously considered. Here is how we are going to proceed.
   d. I'm not interested in your thoughts on how we should proceed.

6. Which of the following is an example of a *professional* communication?
   a. There have been more residential burglaries this year than in the past 3 years combined.
   b. This year, we have witnessed an epidemic of residential burglaries.
   c. Residential burglaries are out of control this year.
   d. Our city has become infested with residential burglars.

7. Which of the following is an example of an *un*professional communication?
   a. Unlike criminal justice officials, legal scholars maintain that perp walks are unconstitutional.
   b. Based on the available evidence, I think perp walks are unconstitutional.
   c. Based on the available evidence, perp walks are unconstitutional.
   d. The evidence indicates that perp walks are unconstitutional.

8. Which of the following is an example of an *un*professional communication?
   a. Yes, sir, I can hear you.
   b. Indeed, I can hear you.
   c. I can hear you.
   d. Yeah, man, I can hear you.

9. Which of the following is an example of an *un*professional communication?
   a. They alert the media so that the media doesn't miss the arrest.
   b. They notify the media so that the media is there to witness the arrest.
   c. They alert the media so that the media does not miss the arrest.
   d. The media are notified so that they can witness the arrest.

10. Looking at Table 2.11, compare the original source material, which is presented verbatim from the source indicated, with how the source material is used in a report. Indicate which of the following best describes how the original passage was used:
    a. ethical use of source material
    b. mosaic plagiarism
    c. inappropriate paraphrasing
    d. plagiarism

TABLE 2.11   Passages for Multiple Choice Exercise #10

Original Source Material	Use of Source Material
Moreover, our finding that mental illness and preradicalization criminal behavior are consistent predictors of postradicalization violence suggests that there is potentially much to be gained from measuring dynamic indicators that may change over the individual's life course.	Also, the finding that postradicalization is consistently predicted by mental illness and criminal behavior indicates there could be a lot to be gained from studying factors that might change over the life course of people.

Source: LaFree, G., Jensen, M. A., James, P. A., & Safer-Lichtenstein, A. (2018). Correlates of violent political extremism in the United States. *Criminology, 56*(2), 233–268. (Quoted text is from page 256.)

11. Looking at Table 2.12, compare the original source material, which is presented verbatim from the source indicated, with how the source material is used in a report. Indicate which of the following best describes how the original passage was used.
    a. ethical use of source material
    b. mosaic plagiarism
    c. inappropriate paraphrasing
    d. plagiarism

TABLE 2.12   Passages for Multiple Choice Exercise #11

Original Source Material	Use of Source Material
Moreover, our finding that mental illness and preradicalization criminal behavior are consistent predictors of postradicalization violence suggests that there is potentially much to be gained from measuring dynamic indicators that may change over the individual's life course.	Two predictors of violent political extremism are mental illness and prior criminality, which "suggests that there is potentially much to be gained from measuring dynamic indicators that may change over the individual's life course" (LaFree, Jensen, James, & Safer-Lichtenstein, 2018, p. 256).

Source: LaFree, G., Jensen, M. A., James, P. A., & Safer-Lichtenstein, A. (2018). Correlates of violent political extremism in the United States. *Criminology, 56*(2), 233–268. (Quoted text is from page 256.)

12. Looking at Table 2.13, compare the original source material, which is presented verbatim from the source indicated, with how the source material is used in a report. Indicate which of the following best describes how the original passage was used.
    a. ethical use of source material
    b. mosaic plagiarism
    c. inappropriate paraphrasing
    d. plagiarism

TABLE 2.13   Passages for Multiple Choice Exercise #12

Original Source Material	Use of Source Material
Moreover, our finding that mental illness and preradicalization criminal behavior are consistent predictors of postradicalization violence suggests that there is potentially much to be gained from measuring dynamic indicators that may change over the individual's life course.	Mental illness and preradicalization criminal behavior are consistent predictors of postradicalization violence and suggests that there is potentially much to be gained from measuring dynamic indicators that may change over the individual's life course.

Source: LaFree, G., Jensen, M. A., James, P. A., & Safer-Lichtenstein, A. (2018). Correlates of violent political extremism in the United States. *Criminology, 56*(2), 233–268. (Quoted text is from page 256.)

13. Looking at Table 2.14, compare the original source material, which is presented verbatim from the source indicated, with how the source material is used in a report. Indicate which of the following best describes how the original passage was used.
    a. ethical use of source material
    b. mosaic plagiarism
    c. inappropriate paraphrasing
    d. plagiarism

TABLE 2.14   Passages for Multiple Choice Exercise #13

Original Source Material	Use of Source Material
Moreover, our finding that mental illness and preradicalization criminal behavior are consistent predictors of postradicalization violence suggests that there is potentially much to be gained from measuring dynamic indicators that may change over the individual's life course.	Two predictors of violent political extremism are mental illness and prior criminality.

Source: LaFree, G., Jensen, M. A., James, P. A., & Safer-Lichtenstein, A. (2018). Correlates of violent political extremism in the United States. *Criminology, 56*(2), 233–268. (Quoted text is from page 256.)

14. Looking at Table 2.15, compare the original source material, which is presented verbatim from the source indicated, with how the source material is used in a report. Indicate which of the following best describes how the original passage was used.
    a. ethical use of source material
    b. mosaic plagiarism
    c. inappropriate paraphrasing
    d. plagiarism

TABLE 2.15   Passages for Multiple Choice Exercise #14

Original Source Material	Use of Source Material
Moreover, our finding that mental illness and preradicalization criminal behavior are consistent predictors of postradicalization violence suggests that there is potentially much to be gained from measuring dynamic indicators that may change over the individual's life course.	Two predictors of violent political extremism are mental illness and prior criminality (LaFree, Jensen, James, & Safer-Lichtenstein, 2018).

Source: LaFree, G., Jensen, M. A., James, P. A., & Safer-Lichtenstein, A. (2018). Correlates of violent political extremism in the United States. *Criminology, 56*(2), 233–268. (Quoted text is from page 256.)

15. Looking at Table 2.16, compare the original source material, which is presented verbatim from the source indicated, with how the source material is used in a report. Indicate which of the following best describes how the original passage was used.
    a. ethical use of source material
    b. mosaic plagiarism
    c. inappropriate paraphrasing
    d. plagiarism

16. Choose the most professional term to complete this sentence: "The suspect is ____."
    a. fat
    b. pleasantly rotund
    c. grotesquely overweight
    d. approximately 300 pounds

TABLE 2.16   Passages for Multiple Choice Exercise #15

Original Source Material	Use of Source Material
Moreover, our finding that mental illness and preradicalization criminal behavior are consistent predictors of postradicalization violence suggests that there is potentially much to be gained from measuring dynamic indicators that may change over the individual's life course.	Also, the finding that postradicalization is consistently predicted by mental illness and criminal behavior indicates there could be a lot to be gained from studying factors that might change over the life course of people (LaFree, Jensen, James, & Safer-Lichtenstein, 2018).

Source: LaFree, G., Jensen, M. A., James, P. A., & Safer-Lichtenstein, A. (2018). Correlates of violent political extremism in the United States. *Criminology, 56*(2), 233–268. (Quoted text is from page 256.)

17. Choose the most professional term to complete this sentence: "The crime rate is ____."
    a. soaring
    b. through the roof
    c. increasing
    d. alarming

18. Choose the most professional term to complete this sentence: "Human trafficking is a ____ social problem."
    a. horrific
    b. tragic
    c. widely recognized
    d. big

19. Choose the most professional term to complete this sentence: "Victims of online auction fraud tend to exhibit ____ of warning signs."
    a. lack of awareness
    b. ignorance
    c. stupidity
    d. foolishness

20. Choose the most professional term to complete this sentence: "The man spanked his son in the ____."
    a. ass
    b. buttocks
    c. seat
    d. tush

Editing

These editing exercises are designed to assess Chapter 2 Learning Objective 5 (see Box 2.1). Identify the problem(s) in each of the following passages, and then rewrite them, editing as needed to achieve professionalism.

1. In this paper, I will talk about the major categories of terrorism, comparing and contrasting the different types of terrorism in terms of goals, tactics, targets, and consequences. By the end of the paper, you will have a better understanding of what terrorism is and of its many faces.
2. Terrorists believe that by freaking people out, they can achieve change.
3. Terrorism is a hot topic in the news as well as in the entertainment media.
4. There are many ways to guard against terrorism, but governments really just need to do one thing: Don't piss off the people with explosives.
5. Are you scared of terrorism? Do you dread the next terrorist attack? What can we do to prevent terrorism?
6. This paper covers the harrowing crime of terrorism.
7. Edit the unethical use of source material on the right side of Table 2.17.
8. Edit the unethical use of source material on the right side of Table 2.18.

TABLE 2.17 Passages for Editing Exercise #7

Original Source Material	Use of Source Material
First, our finding that stable employment seems to decrease the risk that individuals with extreme views will engage in violent behavior is relevant for several reasons.	The first finding that a stable job appears to decrease the chance the people with extreme views will become violent is relevant for many reasons (LaFree, Jensen, James, & Safer-Lichtenstein, 2018).

Source: LaFree, G., Jensen, M. A., James, P. A., & Safer-Lichtenstein, A. (2018). Correlates of violent political extremism in the United States. *Criminology, 56*(2), 233–268. (Quoted text is from page 257.)

TABLE 2.18 Passages for Editing Exercise #8

Original Source Material	Use of Source Material
We argued before that criminology has paid insufficient attention to violent extremists as an important subgroup of criminals.	Criminology needs to pay more attention to violent extremists.

Source: LaFree, G., Jensen, M. A., James, P. A., & Safer-Lichtenstein, A. (2018). Correlates of violent political extremism in the United States. *Criminology, 56*(2), 233–268. (Quoted text is from page 258.)

Writing

These writing exercises are designed to assess Chapter 2 Learning Objectives 2, 4, 6, and 7 (see Box 2.1).

1. Argue for the importance of professionalism in criminal justice communications.
2. Outline strategies for achieving professional communication as a criminal justice student and professional.
3. Find an advertisement for a criminal justice position. Craft a professional cover letter and résumé as though you really were applying for this job. If this exercise is a class assignment, then submit the position advertisement along with your cover letter and résumé so your instructor can assess the responsiveness of your job application materials to the advertised job.
4. Assume the role of your own boss and draft a professional performance review of yourself. You will need to play both roles: that of your boss doing the evaluation and that of yourself being evaluated. If you do not have a job, then you could review your performance as a student, athlete, parent, or spouse/significant other.

REFERENCES

Caramela, Sammi. (2018, January 26). 4 tips for writing an effective performance review. *Business News Daily*.

Gowen, Anne A. (2018, January 26). How the judge in Larry Nassar's case undermined justice. *Time*. Retrieved from http://time.com/5119433/larry-nassar-judge-rosemarie-aquilina-justice/

Harris, Robert A. (2017). *Using sources effectively: Strengthening your writing and avoiding plagiarism* (5th ed.). New York: Routledge.

Heathfield, Susan M. (2018a, April 8). 10 key tips for effective employee performance reviews. *The Balance Careers*. Retrieved from https://www.thebalancecareers.com/effective-performance-review-tips-1918842

Heathfield, Susan M. (2018b, June 1). Performance management: Sample performance development plan form. *The Balance Careers*. Retrieved from https://www.thebalancecareers.com/performance-development-plan-form-1918849

LaFree, Gary, Jensen, Michael A., James, Patrick A., & Safer-Lichtenstein, Aaron. (2018). Correlates of violent political extremism in the United States. *Criminology, 56*(2), 233–268.

Markel, Mike. (2012). *Technical communications* (10th ed.). Boston, MA: Bedford/St. Martin's.

Meeler, David. (n.d.). *Five basic approaches to ethical decision-making*. The Markkula Center for Applied Ethics. Retrieved from https://ethicallyphilosophical.wordpress.com/2018/05/03/five-basic-approaches-to-ethical-decision-making/

Roberson, Cliff, & Mire, Scott. (2010). *Ethics for criminal justice professionals*. Boca Raton, FL: CRC Press.

Roig, Miguel. (2015). *Avoiding plagiarism, self-plagiarism, and other questionable writing practices: A guide to ethical writing* [module]. Retrieved from https://ori.hhs.gov/avoiding-plagiarism-self-plagiarism-and-other-questionable-writing-practices-guide-ethical-writing

Sherman, Ruth. (n.d.). *Understanding your communication style*. Women's Business Center. Retrieved from http://www.au.af.mil/au/awc/awcgate/sba/comm_style.htm

Tyler, Tom R. (2003). Procedural justice, legitimacy, and the effective rule of law. *Crime and Justice, 30*, 283–357.

Tyler, Tom R., Goff, Phillip Atiba, & MacCoun, Robert J. (2015). The impact of psychological science on policing in the United States: Procedural justice, legitimacy, and effective law enforcement. *Psychological Science in the Public Interest, 16*(3), 75–109.

Wiersma, Bill. (2010–2011). *The power of professionalism: The seven mind-sets that drive performance and build trust*. Los Altos, CA: Ravel Media.

CHAPTER 3

Principle 2: Responsiveness

| BOX 3.1 | Learning Objectives |

After reading this chapter, you will be able to

1. Recognize terminology relevant to responsive communications.
2. Distinguish between purpose, coverage, and thesis statements.
3. Argue for the importance of responsive communications in criminal justice.
4. Differentiate between responsive and nonresponsive communications.
5. Revise ineffective thesis statements communications to make them effective.
6. Craft responsive answers to essay questions.
7. Develop responsive emails.

If your writing falls apart, it probably has no primary idea to hold it together.

—SHERIDAN BAKER

Imagine going to see a doctor about a pain in your stomach. Doctor appointments take time and cost money; plus, they are not particularly fun. At the end of your appointment, the doctor proudly tells you he found nothing wrong with your chest. The problem in this scenario boils down to a lack of responsiveness to the task at hand.

Responsiveness describes something that directly and thoroughly reflects, or reacts to, the situation at hand. While the doctor might have done a first-rate job of examining your chest, the end result is that you have the same stomach pain as before your appointment. Time and resources have been wasted, and you are no closer to your goal. In this chapter, we learn how to make sure a similar problem does not occur in our criminal justice communications. In short, unlike the doctor in the scenario above, we want to ensure that our communication products are directly and fully responsive in three important respects.

This chapter makes a case for the importance of responsive communications and presents three guidelines for ensuring that a communication is responsive. The chapter then addresses the significance of and ways to achieve responsiveness in two forms of criminal justice communications: answers to essay questions and emails. After having read this chapter, you should not only be convinced of the importance of responsiveness but also be able to construct responsive communications.

GUIDELINES

Responsive communications require that we recognize and satisfy the following three key aspects of the communication:

1. Address the objective.
2. Adhere to parameters.
3. Target the audience.

Address the Objective

Addressing the objective involves both the topic and the way the topic will be handled. To address our objective successfully, we need to do three things: (1) understand the objective, (2) state the objective, and (3) achieve the objective.

Understand the Objective

To begin, we need to identify the objective: What topic will we cover, and how will we cover that topic? Generally speaking, narrower topics are better than broader topics. Narrower topics not only facilitate a clearer and more focused communication, but they also tend to require proficiency with a smaller body of information and allow for a more manageable research process. Sometimes—especially for less experienced researchers and practitioners—research is needed to identify a specific topic. Figure 3.1 shows how an initially broad topic can be narrowed. At the base of the inverted triangle in Figure 3.1, we start with a broad topic. As we move up the triangle, the topic becomes more specific and easier to manage.

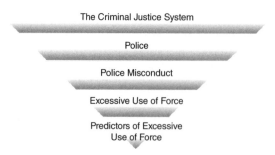

FIGURE 3.1 Narrowing a Topic

TABLE 3.1 Informative Versus Persuasive Communications

	Informative	Persuasive
Primary Purpose	To inform people	To influence people
Example Topics	Outlining the history of the death penalty Describing how executions are conducted Explaining why some people support capital punishment for convicted murderers	Arguing that the death penalty should be abolished Proposing that all executions use lethal injections Contending that convicted rapists be sentenced to death

Once we have established our topic, we need to determine what we will do with that topic. In other words, what is our primary objective in writing about that topic? Table 3.1 distinguishes between two broad objectives of technical communications: to inform and to persuade.

Informative communications impart information with the objective of rendering the audience (more) knowledgeable about the topic than before. An informative communication might seek to make the audience aware of the various forms of consumer fraud, the diverse ways in which consumer fraud is perpetrated, or the behavioral characteristics of consumer fraud victims. With informative communications, we seek to educate our audience.

Persuasive communications, in contrast, impart information with the objective of influencing the audience in terms of beliefs, attitudes, and/or actions. A persuasive communication might seek to convince government officials to devote more resources to the prevention and detention of consumer fraud, coax consumer fraud victims to report their victimization to law enforcement entities, or induce people to minimize certain purchasing behaviors that expose them to increased odds of consumer fraud victimization. While persuasive communications also provide information and thereby inform the audience, their primary objective is to influence the audience.

Table 3.2 shows some different types of communications that reflect these alternative communication objectives. A crime report is written by a police officer, for example, who objectively and thoroughly describes the crime and police response. Presentence investigation reports, on the other hand, end with a recommendation for how the defendant should be punished. Funded agencies often produce annual reports, which detail their operations and accomplishments each year.

To obtain additional funding, such agencies might apply for a grant to conduct research and/or provide service, and the purpose of a grant application is to convince the soliciting entity that the applying agency is best suited to accomplish the task and

TABLE 3.2 Examples of Communication Types with Different Purposes

Informative	Persuasive
Crime Report	Presentence Investigation Report
Annual Report	Grant Application
Policy Analysis	Policy Proposal
Jury Instructions	Closing Argument

therefore deserves the funding. A policy analysis identifies the goal of a policy and then describes the operations and outcomes associated with achieving the policy goal.

A policy proposal, in contrast, points to a problem and then recommends the implementation of a particular policy to solve the problem. In the jury instructions, a judge explains relevant law to the jurors to help them arrive at a verdict (e.g., defining "beyond a reasonable doubt," outlining the elements of the crime). And in their closing arguments, prosecutors review and interpret evidence in an attempt to convince jurors to find the defendant guilty.

State the Objective

Second, we need to clearly state our objective early on in a communication. As shown in Table 3.3, there are three basic ways we state our objective: (1) a purpose statement, (2) a coverage statement, and (3) a thesis statement.

PURPOSE STATEMENTS. A **purpose statement** identifies the specific objective(s) of the communication. In a single, succinct sentence, it tells the audience both the topic and the objective (i.e., to inform or to persuade) of the communication. A good purpose statement tells the audience what the communication is about and intends to do, but it does not convey the author's position on the topic or describe how the topic will be covered. As such, purpose statements are the simplest, most straightforward ways of conveying the point of your communication to your audience.

Purpose statements are best suited to informative communications. For example, a judge might preface his jury instructions with such a statement as, "The purpose of these instructions is to guide you to a just and lawful verdict." An example of a purpose statement in a research paper is, "The purpose of this paper is to determine whether white-collar criminals are sentenced more leniently than street criminals."

TABLE 3.3   Options for Stating a Communication's Objective

	Purpose Statement	Coverage Statement	Thesis Statement
Definition	Explicitly states the communication's topic and purpose(s)	Explicitly states the communication's topic and contents	Explicitly states the communication's topic and stance
Appropriate Uses	Informative communications, with essentially complete coverage of the topic	Informative communications, with intentionally limited coverage of the topic	Persuasive communications
Example 1	The purpose of this paper is to compare and contrast incarceration and probation in the United States.	Looking solely at the contemporary U.S. criminal justice system, this paper compares incarceration with probation in terms of public safety, cost, and deterrence.	This paper argues that probation has become more punitive than incarceration in the United States.
Example 2	This paper's purpose is to outline the history of drug control legislation in the United States.	This paper outlines the history of U.S. drug control efforts and examines laws designed to control drug use rather than their manufacture or distribution.	Examining the history of U.S. drug control efforts, this paper contends that marijuana use should be decriminalized.

COVERAGE STATEMENTS. A **coverage statement** identifies the topic and gives the audience a sense of the breadth or depth in which the topic will be covered. It is a way to articulate how—and perhaps why—you are narrowing down a broad topic. Compared with purpose statements, coverage statements tend to give the audience more detail regarding what the communication is about.

Most appropriate in informative communications, coverage statements can be an effective way to prepare readers for an intentionally focused treatment of an otherwise broad topic. An example of a coverage statement is, "Focusing on the United States and without delving into the moral issues related to gun ownership, this paper will examine statistics regarding gun ownership and gun control." Gun ownership and control is a broad topic, and this example shows both the author's (a) awareness that this topic involves moral considerations and applies beyond the United States, and (b) intention to limit this particular communication to non-moral considerations and the United States.

THESIS STATEMENTS. Where a coverage statement is best suited to informative communications and does not express a position, thesis statements are ideal for persuasive communications and do express a position. A **thesis statement** identifies the topic as well as the author's stance (e.g., for or against) on the topic.

Thesis statements prepare the reader for an argument that follows, where the argument can be judged in terms of whether or not the author has satisfactorily proven the thesis statement. If the thesis statement is that capital punishment should be abolished, for example, then the rest of the paper should contain reasons and evidence for why capital punishment should be abolished. If the communication does not intend to make an argument, then a thesis statement is not an appropriate method for introducing the communication's purpose.

Table 3.4 contrasts thesis statements with other expressions. A thesis statement can be one or more sentences. Consistent with the principle to be concise in the context of technical communication, however, single-sentence thesis statements are preferable to longer thesis statements. Thesis statements can be placed toward the beginning or end of the introduction section of a paper. To guide the decision of where to place the thesis statement, consider your audience and the popularity of your topic. If the audience is

TABLE 3.4   Distinguishing Characteristics of a Thesis Statement

Thesis Statement	Not a Thesis Statement
A complete sentence *Example*: The federal government should decriminalize marijuana use.	**A word, phrase, or incomplete sentence** *Example*: decriminalization of marijuana
A declarative sentence *Example*: Mentally ill adults should not be allowed to own guns.	**A question** *Example*: Should mentally ill people be allowed to own guns?
An expression of a position on a topic *Example*: Disenfranchisement of ex-offenders is unconstitutional and should be abolished.	**A statement of topic, purpose, or coverage** *Example*: The topic of this paper is disenfranchisement of ex-offenders.
Explicit, clear, concrete, and possible to argue against *Example*: Violent sex offenders and sex offenders who victimize children should be castrated.	**Vague, unclear, nebulous, or impossible to argue against** *Example*: It is possible that some sex offenders should be castrated.

generally unfamiliar with your topic, then it might be effective to place the thesis statement deeper in the introduction—after you have had some time to introduce your topic and establish its significance. If, on the other hand, you have a popular topic and/or an audience familiar with your topic, then you could state your thesis earlier in the introduction, and then move on to the "meat" of the communication.

Achieve the Objective

Third, we achieve our objective by presenting relevant material in an effective organizational structure. We need to ensure a logical and seamless flow of information from introduction to body to conclusion. Irrelevant information and poorly organized material can confuse our audience. One reason for outlining before we start drafting is to help us ensure that each part of the communication relates to and advances our objective. An outline can expose gaps as well as extraneous content.

As we research, write, and revise our communication, we constantly want to return to our objective and make sure we do everything in our power to achieve it. We must resist the urge to include information just because it is interesting, comes from a credible source, or helps us reach the page requirement. We need to put ourselves in the position of our audience, moreover, asking what additional information they might need. Informative transitions and section headings, repetition of key words, and graphics can be effective in helping an audience follow along. Chapter 4 will take a closer look at organizational structures and devices that reinforce our purpose and thereby maximize the effectiveness of communications. For now, the bottom line is that achieving our objective involves consideration of the information we have in a communication as well as information we need to add to the communication.

Adhere to Parameters

Beyond the topic and objective, we need to be aware of and adhere to additional requirements for our communications. Being aware of and conforming to the parameters not only will lead to a more effective communication, but also it can save time and energy in the long run when you do the job right the first time.

As students, common written communication parameters concern length, resources, and style. College/university paper instructions typically specify a page range (e.g., 3–5 pages, 20–25 pages), and these instructions often include requirements for resources (e.g., "at least 5 credible sources"; "at least 10 sources, 5 of which must be peer-reviewed empirical research") and identify a style guide to be followed (e.g., APA, Chicago, MLA). Common oral communication requirements for students include a time range (e.g., 3–5 minutes, 8–10 minutes), visual aide (e.g., poster board, PowerPoint, handouts), and dress/demeanor (e.g., "professional attire").

Advanced researchers (e.g., doctoral students, professors) need to pay special attention to publication requirements. When seeking publication in a peer-reviewed journal, for instance, authors must conform to the journal's requirements concerning length, title page content, omission of identifying information, abstract structure, in-text citations and References, table and figure format, and so on. Some journals decline to consider papers that deviate from their requirements. And when presenting at professional academic conferences, these researchers must share months or even years of research in the space of 15 or fewer minutes.

Such requirements are not unique to academia. Rather, professionals employed in the field of criminal justice often need to follow instructions for length/time, content, style, and format. Agencies responsible for producing annual reports, for example, need to ensure that the writing style and formatting are consistent from chapter to chapter even though different people (or teams of people) might be responsible for producing the various chapters. Meeting agendas, furthermore, might specify how long each person can speak. Importantly, practitioners often need to use standard forms and formats, such as chain-of-custody reports for law enforcement officers and evidence analysts. We are probably familiar with some parameters involved in trials from watching television; when trial lawyers deviate from prescribed parameters, the opposing side can object. Common objections include the following:

- No good-faith basis for question
- Argumentative
- Misquoting witness
- Assuming facts not in evidence
- Compound question
- Asked and answered
- Beyond the scope of direct
- Hearsay

Just like how each sport has rules by which the players must abide, each type of criminal justice communication has rules that need to be followed. As the creator of the communication, we need to make ourselves aware of the rules, and then we need to ensure that we follow those rules.

Target the Audience

A successful communication is written for—that is, targeted at—its audience. As such, an important set of steps in producing an effective communication is to (1) identify, (2) learn about, and then (3) customize the communication for the audience.

Identify the Audience

First, determine who your audience is. Keep in mind that a single communication can have more than one audience. Indeed, we can distinguish between primary, secondary, and tertiary audiences. This can be an unfamiliar concept for most students who are used to writing only for professors. For students, then, the primary audience generally is the professor of the course in which the communication is assigned. For criminal justice practitioners, the primary audience varies. When delivering an opening statement, for example, a trial lawyer's primary audience would be jurors, the secondary audience would be the presiding judge, and the tertiary audience could include other lawyers and the general public.

The **primary audience** is the key person or people for whom the communication is intended. These are the people who will use the communication to prescribe decision-making and/or action. There is always at least one primary audience.

The **secondary audience** will be a consumer of the communication but is more removed from the communication process than the primary audience. The secondary

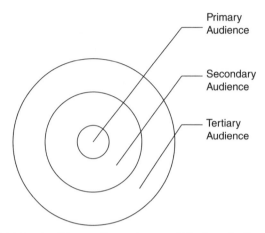

FIGURE 3.2   Primary, Secondary, and Tertiary Audiences

audience's decisions or actions might be influenced by the communication but will not be dictated directly by the communication.

The **tertiary audience** is even more remote than the primary audience. It consists of other people or groups who might for some reason or another be interested in the communication. Like the secondary audience, the tertiary audience might use the communication to guide—but not de facto dictate—decisions or action. However, the tertiary audience tends to be distant from the communication in terms of time and space.

As a general rule, as we move out from the center of Figure 3.2, the communication becomes less relevant while the size and diversity of the audience tends to increase. As we move outward from the center, moreover, the immediacy and impact of the communication lessen. In other words, the primary audience tends to use the information first and most, while the tertiary audience tends to use the information last and least.

Learn About the Audience

There are five important questions to ask about your audience:

1. Need: What do they need the communication for?
2. Expectation: What do they expect of the communication?
3. Knowledge: How much do they know about the material in the communication?
4. Experience: What relevant experiences do they have?
5. Use: How will they use the communication?

Remember that this chapter is about responsiveness. With regard to *need*, then, it is imperative that the communication be designed and delivered to meet the audience's needs. If your boss needs a brief comparison of two policies to use in reaching a decision of which policy to adopt, for instance, then a communication would be useless if it instead gave a detailed description of one policy.

Closely related to need is *expectations*. If someone communicates the need to you in assigning a communication, then they expect you to satisfy that need. Beyond that, expectations might be based on the quality, length, and timeliness of the communication. When their expectations go unmet, people can become disappointed or irritated. To the extent that we seek to make a positive impression, then, failure to meet expectations is counter-productive. Furthermore, there can be practical reasons for being responsive to your audience's expectations. If people expect a 3-minute briefing, then they might schedule you for 3 minutes. Going over 3 minutes then might mean your audience does not hear your entire briefing and/or has to reschedule later appointments. If a middle manager expects a report written well enough to be handed up to a higher level manager, then the middle manager might reasonably be irritated with you for writing an error-ridden report that requires major editing.

It has been long recognized that human beings tend to resist change (`Coch & French, 1948). Implementing a new policy, therefore, often involves winning over an audience of skeptics. If you know you are addressing an audience that is hostile, you probably would proceed differently than if you are addressing an audience that is supportive. Some strategies when you have a skeptical or hostile audience are to

- Learn about and directly address the audience's objections;
- Sell the audience on the benefits of compliance; and
- Present your recommendation only after you have addressed objections and presented benefits (Markel, 2012).

To illustrate, police agencies increasingly have been moving toward the adoption of body-worn cameras (BWCs; Ariel, Sutherland, Henstock, Young, & Sosinski, 2017). Many police officers understandably might resist what they perceive to be an overly intrusive method of ensuring accountability. They might also be offended at the notion that they are not trusted enough. Of course, police captains could simply require the use of BWCs, but a more desirable outcome is to convince the officers of the legitimacy of BWCs and thereby gain cooperation. Thus, police captains might begin the process by addressing the officers' concerns about trust and privacy and then transition to the benefits of BWCs for police officers (e.g., protection from false allegations of misconduct).

Just as need and expectations are closely intertwined, so too are *knowledge* and *experiences*: Both provide a common base of familiarity with the subject matter. The more your audience knows about or has experience with the topic, the less background, foundation, and context you generally need to provide. The more familiar your audience, the more leeway you have to use specialized terminology. One lawyer talking to another lawyer, for example, probably will be able to use technical language and to omit background information. But once the legal team enters the courtroom for a jury trial, a very different communication style is needed. Jurors will not understand technical language and may require some foundation to interpret the evidence. Indeed, scientific evidence is becoming increasingly common in jury trials; and juries seem to have a particularly difficult time understanding statistical, economic, and DNA evidence (Hans, 2007). At the same time, however, jurors can become overwhelmed with detail. Visual aids, analogies, examples, and simple terms can make complicated scientific evidence easier for jurors to digest.

Another word of caution is necessary regarding your audience's knowledge and experiences: Familiarity does not necessarily lead to similarity. While your audience might be equally familiar with the topic, the audience's familiarity could be rooted in different understanding of or experience with the topic than you. Compared with Caucasian Americans, for instance, African Americans tend to have more negative experiences with and hence perceptions of law enforcement (Weitzer, 2002; Weitzer & Tuch, 2005). If you need to enlist the aid of a largely African American community, it probably would be unwise to launch into your proposal without first addressing these negative experiences and perceptions. In this situation, it can be helpful to use the strategies listed above for skeptical/hostile audiences.

How the audience will *use* the communication presents some very practical concerns. An important consideration regarding use is the basic goal of the communication. If the goal is to ensure that people properly perform a crucial yet complicated process, then you need to produce the communication in a format that facilitates the necessary uniform performance. For example, realizing that many police officers give Miranda warnings in the streets—and that errors in giving Miranda warnings (e.g., reading them too late, leaving one or more rights out) can lead to lost cases—the clever decision was made to print out a script on pocket-sized paper. If the goal is to create a favorable impression, on the other hand, then sharing some anecdotes can be effective. Perhaps, for example, one's goal in a presentation is to gain funding for boot camps for juvenile delinquents. The audience does not need to use the information for anything other than reaching a decision. The details will be handled by others. Here, the communication needs to make a powerful impact, perhaps even to the point of overshadowing research evidence on the general ineffectiveness of boot camps (Gültekin & Gültekin, 2012). An effective approach to convincing potential funders would be to have some former boot-camp participants share their personal experiences: how they had been headed down a bad path, but then the boot camp changed their lives for the better.

Customize the Communication for the Audience

Once you have answered the five questions above (listed in the beginning of the "Learn About the Audience" section), use that information to tailor the communication to your audience. The ideal approach is to design a communication to appeal directly to all audiences. The more alike your audiences are, especially the members of the primary audience, the simpler this task is. But sometimes the audiences are so different, a single communication cannot be equally effective for each audience. Table 3.5 shows how to customize a communication in various situations.

As shown in Table 3.5, the simplest situation is when we have an audience (or audiences) that are similar in terms of need, expectations, knowledge, experiences, and use and that will consume the communication at the same time. In this case, a single version of the communication is adequate. When the audience is similar but will consume the communication at different times—such as an orientation packet for new employees—we have two options. First, we could use a single version of the communication. Second, we could make some changes to reflect current conditions or just to make the communication stronger. Perhaps

TABLE 3.5   Decision Matrix When Formatting for Multiple Audiences

		Audience Characteristics	
		Similar	*Diverse*
Communication Consumption	*At the Same Time*	Same version	Modular form
	At Different Times	Same version, with updates and improvements as appropriate	Different versions

our organization has moved office locations or adopted a new policy on sexual harassment, or suppose we found some typos or realized we left some important information out about medical leave. These are examples of situations that would justify revising the communication, even though the audience remains the same.

If our audience is diverse and will be consuming the communication at the same time, then Markel (2012) recommends using a **modular design** wherein the communication is broken down into separate components that are designed for the different audiences. Though we might not have realized it before, most of us are familiar with modular design: Instruction manuals often contain an English version on one side and a Spanish version on the reverse side. The last cell in Table 3.5 addresses situations when we have a diverse audience who will consume the communication at different times. Say, for example, we want to get people to invest in a new technology product in the United States and in France. We would pitch the product in English when presenting to potential investors in the United States, and then we would pitch the product in French when in France. These are simple examples of diverse audiences, but they serve to illustrate the point that a single communication needs to be tailored to each of the audiences. If a choice ever needs to be made, the primary audience should be preferred over the secondary audience, while the secondary audience should be preferred over the tertiary audience.

APPLICATIONS

Here, we consider the importance of and how to achieve responsiveness in two types of criminal justice communications: answers to essay questions and emails.

Answers to Essay Questions

Many exams contain essay questions. Knowledge of the subject matter is half of the challenge, and the other half of the challenge in answering essay questions effectively revolves around being directly responsive to the question asked. One part of the essay question is particularly important to our attempts to be responsive: the essay verb.

The Essay Verb

As shown in Figure 3.3, there are two basic parts to an essay question: the essay topic and the essay verb. The **essay verb** is the word or phrase that specifies your purpose in drafting the essay. The essay verb is different from the **essay topic**, which is the general subject matter involved in the essay question. An example of an essay topic might be the plain-view doctrine. The essay verb tells you what about the essay topic your response should cover. For instance, should you describe the plain-view doctrine, outline Supreme Court decisions that have shaped the plain-view doctrine, or justify the need for the plain-view doctrine? An essay response might provide a thorough, accurate *description* of the plain-view doctrine. But if the essay question specified that the response should *justify* the need for the plain-view doctrine, then that response would exhibit little knowledge about why the plain-view doctrine is needed, and as such, the student might earn no credit for that response.

Table 3.6 presents popular essay verbs. As shown in Table 3.6, this single word has enormous meaning in essay questions and answers: You need to write not just about the topic of the question but to provide information that is directly and clearly responsive to what about the topic the question is asking.

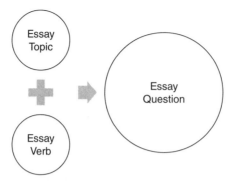

FIGURE 3.3   Basic Components of an Essay Question

TABLE 3.6   Popular Essay Verbs by Level of Detail Needed

	Meaning	Example
Brief		
Identify (or State)	Say what something is	Identify the amendment that protects U.S. citizens from unlawful searches and seizures.
List (or Enumerate)	Say what something involves or consists of, usually a group of things in a series	List the three conditions for legally seizing contraband under the plain-view doctrine.
Relatively Brief		
Define	Say what a term means	Define the term "plain view."
Summarize (or Outline)	Present the main points	Summarize the Supreme Court's ruling in *Terry v. Ohio* (1968).
Somewhat Detailed		
Describe	Say what, when, where, who, and how something is	Describe the landmark U.S. Supreme Court case *Terry v. Ohio.*
Illustrate	Provide one or more examples	Illustrate the need for exceptions to the requirement that police secure a search warrant.
Contrast (or Differentiate or Distinguish)	Present differences	Contrast lawful and unlawful searches and seizures.
Compare	Present similarities and differences	Compare the cases of *Terry v. Ohio* (1968) and *Minnesota v. Dickerson* (1993).
Detailed		
Discuss	Present multiple issues, sides, considerations, etc.	Discuss the role of probable cause in lawful search and seizure.
Explain	Tell why something is	Explain the relationship between police training and misconduct.
Analyze	Break something complex down into smaller parts	Analyze the decision to conduct a warrantless search.
Evaluate	Present an assessment of the value/ quality of something	Evaluate the effectiveness of citizen review boards in addressing allegations of police misconduct.
Justify	Present rationale for something	Justify Supreme Court involvement in American policing policy and procedure.
Argue	Present claims and evidence supporting a position on a controversial subject	Argue for the need for "good faith" exceptions with regard to improper searches and seizures.

Sample Essay Questions and Answers

Table 3.7 illustrates how to write answers on the same topic that are responsive to the different essay verbs. Notice how, in all three examples in Table 3.7, the key parts of the question are repeated in the answer, which immediately communicates to the audience that the communicator understands what the question is asking for and intends to answer it directly. As the questions call for increasingly detailed answers from the top to the bottom of the table, more signals are provided to help the audience easily follow along and locate each piece of the required information. The *listing* question used numbers in parentheses to indicate clearly the three items. The *distinguishing* question begins with numbers in parentheses, uses ordering transitions, and breaks each item into its own paragraph.

TABLE 3.7 Sample Essay Questions and Answers

Question	Answer
Identify the most stringent standard of proof in court proceedings.	The most stringent standard of proof in court proceedings is "beyond a reasonable doubt."
List the three common standards of proof in court proceedings.	The three common standards of proof in court proceedings are (1) "proof beyond a reasonable doubt," (2) "clear and convincing evidence," and (3) "preponderance of the evidence."
Distinguish between the three common standards of proof in court proceedings.	The three common standards of proof in court proceedings are (1) "proof beyond a reasonable doubt," (2) "clear and convincing evidence," and (3) "preponderance of the evidence."
	First, the standard of "proof beyond a reasonable doubt" is the strictest standard. For the prosecution to secure a guilty verdict in a criminal, felony case, the evidence presented at trial must establish the criminal charge to a degree of probability that crosses the 0.9 or 0.95 threshold. This means that not only must there be a plausible explanation for the evidence that includes all elements of the crime, but also there must be no plausible explanation that is inconsistent with evidence.
	Second, the standard of "clear and convincing evidence" lies somewhere between the other two standards. To meet this standard, the evidence supporting the claim must be substantially better than the evidence supporting the alternative claim, to a degree of probability that is somewhere between 0.5 and 0.9.
	Third, the standard of "preponderance of the evidence" is the least strict standard. For a plaintiff in a civil case to satisfy this standard, there must be—on the basis of all evidence presented at trial—more than a 0.5 probability of the plaintiff's claim being true. This means that there must be more evidence tending to show that the plaintiff's claim is true than there is evidence showing that the plaintiff's claim is not true.

BOX 3.3   Plagiarism Pointer

Copying text verbatim from the textbook or other course materials may be considered plagiarism. Check with your instructor before the exam to determine whether it is permissible to copy text verbatim, or whether you will need to write in your own words.

Best Practices

Following these seven best practices will help you craft an effective, responsive answer to essay questions:

1. **Determine exactly what the essay question is asking you to do.** Accomplish this by identifying the essay topic and then by locating the essay verb. Make sure your response directly and thoroughly addresses both the essay topic and the essay verb.

2. **Outline your response before you write.** Identify each part of the answer, and then arrange each part in order (where applicable). You need not use perfect standard outline formatting, yet mapping out the key parts of a complete and relevant response can guard against leaving out important material. As time dwindles, for instance, you might have a harder time thinking, which might cause you to forget important components of questions. You can add to your outline if additional information comes to mind.

3. **Preface your essay response with an introductory sentence that explicitly states what your essay is doing.** Use language directly from the essay question to signal to the professor that you intend to be directly responsive to the question asked. But avoid merely repeating the question in the same or different words. Each sentence should contain information that is directly responsive to the essay question. (You can skip this practice when the response is only a sentence or two, such as the first example in Table 3.6.)

4. **Clearly identify each part of your response.** If the question asks for two items of information, number them. When the question involves multiple parts and goes beyond simple listing, write a separate paragraph for each part of the answer. These paragraphs need not be lengthy, but paragraph breaks will help your professor locate the information and follow along with your response. Begin each paragraph with a brief yet informative transition, announcing the topic of the paragraph.

5. **Pace yourself.** Divide the total available time by the number of questions you need to answer plus one. The extra time is for outlining (see best practice #2). If, for instance, you have 60 minutes to complete four questions, then allot yourself 12 minutes to outline all responses and 12 minutes per question to write your responses.

6. **Begin with the answer you believe is your strongest, and then finish with the answer you believe is your weakest.** This strategy prevents running out of time to communicate your knowledge where you are strongest, and it buys you time to think more about the answer where you are weakest.

7. **Use any extra time to edit for clarity and comprehensiveness.** Make sure you transferred all material from your outlines to your essay answers. Ensure that your responses are coherent. If not, use lines and arrows to add clarification in the margins of handwritten exams, or insert text into typed exams.

Emails

Emails are one of the most common form of communication, both in school and the workplace. Emails can be formal or informal. Emailing a colleague who is a friend to see when she wants to talk about an upcoming deadline is usually an informal email, for instance, while emailing a client to arrange a meeting is a more formal email. Because they are so common and convenient, most of us use email on a daily basis for a variety of purposes. But precisely because they are so convenient, emails have plenty of potential to be used ineffectively. Here, we look at ways to craft effective formal emails.

When to Use Email

Email is not always the best communication method. Some types of information are better suited to other communication channels. More delicate or personal information, for example, is ideally communicated in a more personal way: face-to-face conversation, videoconferencing, or a phone call ("Communication channels," n.d.). More technical, official, or serious information, on the other hand, should probably be communicated using a more formal channel: written letters, memos, format documents, or spreadsheets ("Communication channels," n.d.). Email is quicker than "snail mail," but it is not as quick as a phone call or walking down the hall to talk to someone face to face—especially when you expect some going back and forth, such as questions that need answering. Serious discussions are not ideal for emails. Instead, you might use email to arrange a time to meet to have the serious discussion.

Contents and Structure

Figure 3.4 is an example of a standard workplace email. The numbers in Figure 3.4 indicate the typical components of a professional email:

1. Recipient's email address
2. Subject line
3. Greeting (salutation and recipient's name)
4. Body
5. Closing (closing and your name)
6. Your full contact information
7. Attachment (where applicable)

Greetings and closings can be especially tricky. You want to be professional without being either too formal or too informal, and striking the right balance involves considering a variety of factors such as the following:

- Whether you are emailing an individual or a group;
- Whether or not you know the name of the person you are emailing;
- Whether or not you know the sex of the person you are emailing;
- Whether or not you know the marital status of the person you are emailing;
- The closeness of your relationship with the recipient; and
- The gravity of the situation.

In other words, your choice of greetings and salutations should be responsive to the situation. There is no "silver bullet" for greetings and closings. For greetings, Cullen (2017a, 2017b) recommends the following when your recipient is an individual:

- For formal communications outside your organization on first contact, and as a default for professional/workplace emails
  - Dear [Title] [Last Name]:
  - Dear [First Name]:

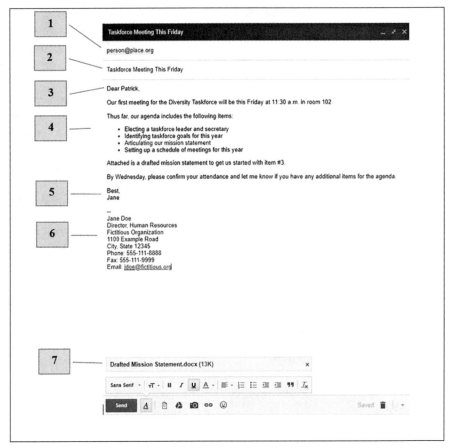

FIGURE 3.4 Example of a Workplace Email

- For more personal business (e.g., congratulations or appreciation)
  - Dear [Title] [Last Name],
  - Dear [First Name],

- For lighter subjects when you have a close relationship to recipients within your organization
  - Hello [First Name],
  - Hi [First Name],

Observe how the recipient's name is always part of the greeting in an email to an individual. Also note that colons are used with more formal greetings, while commas are used with less formal greetings. With titles, prefer earned titles (e.g., Lieutenant, Officer, Dr.) to sex-based titles (e.g., Mr. or Ms.).

When you are emailing a group, Cullen (2017a) recommends the following:

- For small groups
  - Dear [First Name], [First Name], and [First Name]:

- For a group that is a team
  - o Dear [Team Name]:

- For a group with members sharing the same position as you
  - o Dear Colleagues:
  - o Dear Coworkers:

- In general (more formal)
  - o Greetings:
  - o Greetings All:

- In general (less formal)
  - o Hello, everyone:
  - o Hi Team,

Some greetings that are *not* recommended are (Gillett, 2018)

- Dear Ma'am,
- Dear Sir or Madam,
- Hey there,
- To whom it may concern,

Fortunately, closings are a lot less complicated than greetings: Just go with "Best," followed by your name on the next line (Smith, 2016). While other closings can be appropriate in certain situations, they can be inappropriate in others. "Thanks," for example, is only appropriate when your email really is thanking someone for something they have already done; while "Respectfully," "Sincerely," Take care," and abbreviations (e.g., V/R) are not recommended for contemporary professional emails (Smith, 2016).

Best Practices

What follows is a list of best practices for workplace (and school) emails:

1. **Use organizational email addresses.** Use work email accounts for work emails. This applies both to you (the sender) and the recipients. If you do not have one (e.g., before you get hired), then use your school email (when possible), or ensure that your personal email address is professional (e.g., *not* partyanimal@— or hottie@—).
2. **Include a concise, informative subject line.** The goal of the subject line is to give the recipient an immediate idea of what the email is about. It is like the headline to a news article. Research indicates that 6–10 words is the ideal length for a subject line (Stillman, 2014). Use title case, capitalizing the first letter of all major words
3. **Start with a greeting and the recipient's name.** Use titles and last names where appropriate. When in doubt, err on the side of using titles and last names rather than just first names. Triple check to make sure you are spelling names correctly.
4. **Be clear and to the point.** Put the key information (i.e., a request, an answer to a question) in the first line of the text. Provide all pertinent information for the

recipient to understand the issue, either in the text of the email, as hyperlinks, or as attachments. But do *not* provide extraneous information that might distract from the main point of the email and/or slow down the response time.

5. **Maintain a professional writing style throughout the email.** Write emails the same way you would write any other professional communication. Avoid informal writing practices such as emoticons/emojis, text slang (e.g., LOL, OMG), lowercase "i," exclamation points, and incomplete sentences.

6. **Do *not* use all caps.** All caps in an email is the equivalent of yelling at someone. To emphasize something, use bold, italics, a different color font, or text highlighting.

7. **Use spaces between chunks of information.** Include a blank line space between the greeting and body, between paragraphs within the body, and between the body and closing.

8. **End with a closing and your name.** Type your name immediately below the closing.

9. **Include your full contact information.** Provide all the information that would appear on a business card in each email. You probably can make this an automated setting in your email.

10. **Be sure to include any attachments referred to in the email.** A helpful way to remember to do so is to attach the document either (a) before you start writing or (b) as soon as you refer to it in your email. If you wait until you are done typing the email, you might forget to attach the document before clicking send.

11. **Avoid sending emails when you are angry, frustrated, or otherwise not in a logical frame of mind.** We do not think as clearly when we are emotional as when we are calm and collected, and emails can do damage to our reputation as well as our relationships with others. Sleep on it, go on a walk, take deep breaths—but do not let your anger or frustration impugn your credibility and professionalism.

12. **Monitor your email regularly, and respond to emails promptly.** Be sure that in your responses you answer any questions. Respond within 24 hours during the workweek. Use an "out of office" automated message to warn senders if you will not be able to reply promptly. Consider providing the name and contact information of someone else senders can contact for help while you are out of the office.

13. **Give the recipient time to respond before following up.** Be prepared to wait at least 24 hours during the workweek before following up with another email or form of communication. If you need an answer sooner than that, consider going to the person's office (if they are in the same building) or calling the person.

14. **Adhere to all organizational email policies.** For example, do not use your work email for personal emails, such as sharing jokes or forwarding chain emails.

15. **Edit before you send.** Make sure that you are clear and to the point. Check to make sure any attachments are there and hyperlinks are working. Also, ensure that you have the correct email address for your recipient and that you have used proper grammar, spelling, and punctuation throughout.

EXERCISES

Matching

These exercises are designed to assess Chapter 3 Learning Objective 1 (see Box 3.1). Match each numbered statement to the lowercase letter corresponding to the key word it defines. Each key word will be used only once.

1. A type of communication that imparts information with the main goal of rendering the audience (more) knowledgeable about the topic
2. The person or people who will read/listen to a communication and whose decisions/actions may be influenced but will not be directly dictated by the communication
3. A way of stating a communication's objective that identifies the topic as well as the communicator's stance on that topic
4. A way of formatting a communication that breaks down the communication into separate parts tailored to different audiences
5. The word or phrase in an essay question that specifies the objective in drafting the response
6. A way of stating a communication's objective that identifies the topic and gives the audience a sense of the breadth or depth in which the topic will be covered
7. People or groups who might be interested in a communication and whose decisions/actions may be influenced by the communication although they are remote from the communication in terms of time and space
8. A characteristic of a communication that directly and thoroughly reflects, or reacts to, the situation at hand
9. The general subject matter to which an essay question pertains
10. A way of stating a communication's objective that, in a single, succinct sentence, tells the audience both the topic and purpose of the communication
11. A type of communication that imparts information with the main goal of influencing the audience's beliefs, attitudes, and/or actions
12. The key person or group for whom a communication is intended and will use the communication to guide decision and/or action

a. coverage statement
b. essay topic
c. essay verb
d. informative communications
e. modular design
f. persuasive communications
g. primary audience
h. purpose statement
i. responsiveness
j. secondary audience
k. tertiary audience
l. thesis statement

Multiple Choice

These exercises are designed to assess Chapter 3 Learning Objectives 2 and 4 (see Box 3.1). Indicate the single most appropriate response to each item.

1. Which of the following is a purpose statement?
   a. This paper will argue that home confinement with electronic monitoring is an effective alternative to incarceration.

    b. The purpose of this paper is to evaluate the effectiveness of home confinement with electronic monitoring.

    c. This paper will compare and contrast traditional probation and home confinement with electronic monitoring in terms of cost-effectiveness and recidivism likelihood.

    d. All of the above are purpose statements.

2. Which of the following is a coverage statement?

    a. This paper will argue that home confinement with electronic monitoring is an effective alternative to incarceration.

    b. The purpose of this paper is to evaluate the effectiveness of home confinement with electronic monitoring.

    c. This paper will compare and contrast traditional probation and home confinement with electronic monitoring in terms of cost-effectiveness and recidivism likelihood.

    d. All of the above are coverage statements.

3. Which of the following is a thesis statement?

    a. This paper will argue that home confinement with electronic monitoring is an effective alternative to incarceration.

    b. The purpose of this paper is to evaluate the effectiveness of home confinement with electronic monitoring.

    c. This paper will compare and contrast traditional probation and home confinement with electronic monitoring in terms of cost-effectiveness and recidivism likelihood.

    d. All of the above are thesis statements.

4. Which of the following is a purpose statement?

    a. The main objective of this research is to describe the type of offenders for whom home confinement with electronic monitoring is most effective.

    b. There are many types of offenders for whom home confinement with electronic monitoring can be effective.

    c. Examining adult felony offenders in the United States, this paper evaluates the effectiveness of home confinement with electronic monitoring.

    d. Is electronic monitoring more effective for some types of offenders than for others?

5. Which of the following is a coverage statement?

    a. The main objective of this research is to describe the type of offenders for whom home confinement with electronic monitoring is most effective.

    b. There are many types of offenders for whom home confinement with electronic monitoring can be effective.

    c. Examining adult felony offenders in the United States, this paper examines the effectiveness of home confinement with electronic monitoring.

    d. Is electronic monitoring more effective for some types of offenders than for others?

6. Which of the following is a thesis statement?

    a. The main objective of this research is to describe the type of offenders for whom home confinement with electronic monitoring is most effective.

    b. There are many types of offenders for whom home confinement with electronic monitoring is effective.

    c. Examining adult felony offenders in the United States, this paper examines the effectiveness of home confinement with electronic monitoring.

    d. Is electronic monitoring more effective for some types of offenders than for others?

7. Which of the following is an effective thesis statement?

    a. Shaming penalties are cost-effective in addition to effective in reducing recidivism.

    b. Do shaming penalties save costs as well as reduce recidivism?

    c. Shaming could be a form of cruel and unusual punishment.

    d. The purpose of this paper is to delineate between the different forms of shaming.

8. Which of the following is an effective thesis statement?

    a. It is possible for juveniles accused of murder to be tried in adult courts.

    b. Some juveniles accused of murder have been tried in adult courts.

    c. Juveniles accused of first-degree murder should be tried in adult courts.

    d. Can juveniles accused of first-degree murder be tried in adult courts?

9. Which of the following is an effective thesis statement?

    a. This paper will define and provide a history of disenfranchisement for ex-offenders.

    b. Does denying the vote to ex-offenders affect election outcomes?

    c. Denying the vote to ex-offenders is called disenfranchisement.

    d. Disenfranchising ex-offenders should not be legal because it serves as punishment after the offenders have completed their sentence in addition to influencing election outcomes.

10. Which of the following is an effective thesis statement?

    a. Incarceration is one way of sanctioning convicted criminals.

    b. Other than incarceration, what other ways exist for sanctioning convicted criminals?

    c. Compared with intensive supervision probation, incarceration is actually a less punitive way to sanction convicted criminals.

    d. It has been said that incarceration is an ineffective way to sanction convicted criminals.

11. Determine which of the following is most responsive to this essay question: Identify the two major approaches to shaming offenders.

    a. Throughout history, shaming has been one method for punishing criminals. The adulteress Hester Prynne was shamed when she was forced to wear the letter "A" on her gown. This is considered shaming because it used embarrassment to punish her for her crime.

    b. The two major approaches to shaming offenders are disintegrative shaming and reintegrative shaming.

12. Determine which of the following is most responsive to this essay question: Differentiate between disintegrative and reintegrative shaming.

    a. Disintegrative and reintegrative shaming are distinguishable in terms focus, approach, and effectiveness. First, while disintegrative shaming focuses on the deviant actor, reintegrative shaming emphasizes the deviant act. Second, disintegrative shaming expresses disapproval of the deviant actor, shunning and treating the offender as a social outcast. In contrast, reintegrative shaming expresses disapproval of the deviant act, condemning the deviant act while welcoming the actor back into the community. Third, disintegrative shaming is generally ineffective in reducing reoffending, whereas reintegrative shaming tends to be effective in reducing reoffending.

b. Shaming punishments have been used throughout history in many different countries. Contemporary criminal justice systems use shaming penalties mostly for juvenile offenders, and many societies have shifted from disintegrative to reintegrative shaming. Shaming can be effective in preventing future crime, and shaming is less costly than incarceration and other traditional forms of punishment (e.g., probation).

13. Determine which of the following is most responsive to this essay question: Evaluate the effectiveness of disintegrative shaming.

a. There are two criteria by which the effectiveness of disintegrative shaming can be evaluated. The first criterion is recidivism reduction. In this regard, most research has found that disintegrative shaming is not effective in reducing future offending. In condemning lawbreakers, shaming punishments turn lawbreakers into social outcasts. As social outcasts rejected by a law-abiding society, they embrace a deviant lifestyle that includes law-breaking. The second criterion is cost-effectiveness. In general, owing to the lack of recidivism reduction, disintegrative shaming in the long run is not cost-effective. Although the shaming sanction is itself less expensive than incarceration and therefore has some cost-saving benefit in the short term, the recycling of offenders through the system when they recidivate undermines any long-term fiscal benefit.

b. Effectiveness has to do with success in achieving a goal. The criminal justice system's primary goal is to reduce crime and victimization. Shaming can be evaluated as to whether or not it reduces crime and victimization. Crime is when someone breaks the criminal law, while victimization is when someone has a crime committed against them. Examples of crime are murder, assault, robbery, burglary, fraud, arson, drug dealing, and counterfeiting. Some crimes are more serious than others, and more serious crimes tend to result in more severe punishments. Effective punishments cause people to stop breaking the law. Crime and victimization have been decreasing since the 1990s, and so it can be argued that the criminal justice system and its use of punishment has been effective.

Editing
These exercises are designed to assess Chapter 3 Learning Objective 5 (see Box 3.1). Rewrite each of the following statements, editing them as needed to make them effective thesis statements.

1. Should shaming be used as a sanction for convicted white-collar criminals?
2. Home confinement with electronic monitoring
3. I am interested in studying problems associated with felon disenfranchisement.
4. The purpose of this paper is to examine the argument for marijuana decriminalization.
5. There are lots of ways to punish criminals.
6. Sex offender registration and community notification has become popular in the United States over the past few decades. There is a lot of research on this issue, and this is an important social issue. Not all sex offenders are the same;

there are many different kinds of sexual offenses that can result in someone having to register and notify the community. There are also differences across jurisdictions in how registration and notification work.

Writing

These discussion items are designed to assess Chapter 3 Learning Objectives 3, 6, and 7 (see Box 3.1).

1. Why is being responsive important in both academic and professional criminal justice communications?
2. Identify and distinguish between guidelines for achieving responsive criminal justice communications.
3. Differentiate between a purpose statement, a coverage statement, and a thesis statement. Using the same basic topic, provide an example of each.
4. Differentiate between primary, secondary, and tertiary audiences. Use the example of a specific type of criminal justice communication in your response, identifying its primary, secondary, and tertiary audience.
5. Suppose you are going through the application process for a job in the criminal justice system. Identify a particular position at a particular agency. Search the Internet, and use one that really exists. You may also need to research the agency a bit to complete this exercise properly. Write a series of emails, with each email being responsive to each of the following scenarios:

   - Draft an email to a current instructor asking for a letter of recommendation.
   - Draft an email to your classmates letting them know about this available position. Include an attachment or hyperlink to the job ad.
   - Draft an email to the contact person for the position, asking that person to clarify some specific requirement for the position and/or your job application.
   - Draft an email to the person or people who interviewed you for the position, thanking them for the interview.

Rather than actually sending these emails, take a screenshot of each one (for an example, see Figure 3.4). Compile the screenshots of your emails into a single Word document with your name at the top and the job ad between your name and screenshots.

REFERENCES

Ariel, Barak, Sutherland, Alex, Henstock, Daren, Young, Josh, & Sosinski, Gabriela. (2017). The deterrence spectrum: Explaining why police body-worn cameras "work" or "backfire" in aggressive police–public encounters. *Policing: A Journal of Policy and Practice, 12*(1), 6–26.

Coch, Lester, & French, John R. P. (1948). Overcoming resistance to change. *Human Relations, 1*(4), 512–532.

"Communication channels." (n.d.). Model 19: Communication in Organizations. *lumen: Principles of Management.* Retrieved from https://courses.lumenlearning.com/principlesmanagement/chapter/12-5-communication-channels/

Cullen, Mary. (2017a, January 19). Business email salutations to a group. *Instructional Solutions.* Retrieved from https://www.instructionalsolutions.com/blog/email-salutations-to-group

Cullen, Mary. (2017b, January 23). Business letter and business email salutations. *Instructional Solutions*. Retrieved from https://www.instructionalsolutions.com/blog/business-letter-and-business-email-salutations

Gillett, Rachel. (2018, July 20). The perfect way to start an email—and 29 greetings you should usually avoid. *Business Insider*. Retrieved from https://www.businessinsider.com/the-perfect-way-to-start-an-email-and-greetings-you-should-avoid-2016-5

Gültekin, Kübra, & Gültekin, Sebahhattin. (2012). Is juvenile boot camp policy effective? *International Journal of Human Sciences*, *9*(1), 725–740.

Hans, Valerie P. (2007). Judges, juries, and scientific evidence. *Journal of Law and Policy*, *16*(1), 19–46.

Markel, Mike. (2012). *Technical communication* (10th ed.). Boston, MA: Bedford/St. Martin's.

Smith, Jacquelyn. (2016, April 21). Here is the perfect way to end an email—and 27 sign-offs you should usually avoid. *Business Insider*. Retrieved from https://www.businessinsider.com/how-to-end-an-email-2016-4/#-1

Stillman, Jessica. (2014, June 20). The perfect length for an email subject line. *Inc.com*. Retrieved from https://www.inc.com/jessica-stillman/the-perfect-length-for-an-email-subject-line.html

Weitzer, Ronald. (2002). Incidents of police misconduct and public opinion. *Journal of Criminal Justice*, *30*(5), 397–408.

Weitzer, Ronald, & Tuch, Steven A. (2005). Racially biased policing: Determinants of citizen perceptions. *Social Forces*, *83*(3), 1009–1030.

CHAPTER 4

Principle 3: Organization

BOX 4.1	Learning Objectives

After reading this chapter, you will be able to

1. Recognize terminology relevant to the organization of communications.
2. Argue for the importance of organization in criminal justice communications.
3. Distinguish between various organizational structures and devices.
4. Construct effectively organized topic and sentence outlines.
5. Replace ineffective transitions with effective transitions.
6. Develop an effectively organized persuasive paper.
7. Create an effectively organized intelligence briefing.

Writing means organizing your thoughts. If your mind is scattered, your writing is scattered. If your mind is focused, your writing will be clear. Then your reader will say, "Yes, I get it."

—ROBERT PEATE

You might have excellent ideas and strong sources to support them, but your communication easily could be a disaster if it is not well organized. The same is true of just about any complicated endeavor. Take moving from one house to another, for example. Organization will save considerable time, money, and angst. We might be tempted to pack as quickly as possible, spending little time folding clothes and linens, wrapping dishes, putting like items in boxes together, and labeling boxes. But the less time we spend on these front-end (admittedly tedious) steps, the more time we will have to spend on the back end. We will not be able to wear the wrinkled clothes until we have ironed them, we will have to buy new dishes to replace the broken ones, and we will have to search through boxes until we find items we need. If boxes are not labeled, moreover, the movers will put some of them in the wrong rooms, perhaps in the basement instead of up on the second floor where they belong. Thus, we will even have to go back and re-move some boxes. But—had we organized the move in the first place—we could have made the move much less painful.

In communication, **organization** refers to the arrangement of information as well as to the process of planning and arranging information. In both cases, the key ingredient is that the arrangement of information is sensible and reflective of the communication's objective, parameters, and audience.

If our goal is to teach someone how to do something, for instance, then we would want to present steps sequentially rather than as we think of them. Further, if we have only 5 minutes, we want to make sure we fit all the important information into our time allotment without having to rush, skip, or gloss over key material. We might choose to use one organizational structure for a more knowledgeable audience and another organizational structure for a less informed audience, or for a hostile audience versus a friendly audience.

In technical writing generally and criminal justice communications specifically, organization is not always a concern. That is, we will not always have a choice in what to cover and how to organize what we say. Some criminal justice communications involve completing forms, writing brief emails, and recording meeting minutes. In such cases, organizational devices have no role. But even short communications can usually be made better when we structure the communication in a clear and logical way. To this effect, this chapter covers methods for organizing material in an effective manner. After presenting five guidelines for developing well-organized communications, this chapter discusses the organization of two types of communications common in the study and field of criminal justice: persuasive papers and intelligence briefings. Reading this chapter will equip you with a variety of strategies for producing effectively organized communications.

GUIDELINES

Follow these guidelines to develop a well-organized communication:

1. Have a beginning, a middle, and an end.
2. Outline before you write.
3. Adopt an appropriate organizational structure.
4. Employ organizational devices to highlight your structure.
5. Use structural variation to distinguish between major and minor material.

Have a Beginning, a Middle, and an End

Most communications begin with an introduction and end with a conclusion. The body or "meat" of the communication lies between the introduction and conclusion. The shorter and less formal the communication, the shorter each of these three elements

---

BOX 4.2	Credibility Connection

Boost your credibility by exploiting an effective organizational structure: You can look like an expert as you guide your audience through a well-structured communication.

tends to be. Still, however, these three elements should be present in just about any communication. Think of the introduction and conclusion as bookends and the body as the books: The books will fall over if either bookend is missing or inadequate.

The Beginning

The introduction should engage the audience, identify the topic, specify the communication's goal, and describe how the communication will proceed. It might be important in the introduction to establish the significance of the subject matter so as to answer the question, "Why would I bother to read (or listen to) this?" or "Who cares about this?" Establishing the significance of the subject matter is important when you are speaking to an audience that is generally unfamiliar with the subject matter and/or when the audience might be skeptical of the subject matter's importance.

The introduction should end with a "road map" that tells the audience what the rest of the communication contains and how it is organized. Table 4.1 contains examples of road maps. In shorter communications, the road map can be relatively short—perhaps just a sentence. But in longer communications, the road map should probably be longer—perhaps its own paragraph. After our introduction, our audience should have a clear idea of what is coming, in what order, and how it all will fit together.

The Middle

The body tends to be the longest, most detailed section. In a research paper, the body should be replete with evidence and citations. This is the part that should really deliver on the thesis statement (or coverage or purpose statement). If the purpose of the paper is to compare jails and prisons, for example, then the middle of the paper is where all of the comparisons should be presented and discussed. If the thesis statement is that the insanity defense should be abolished, then the middle of the presentation is where the reasons why the insanity defense should be abolished should be presented and substantiated with evidence.

The End

The conclusion should summarize key points and, as appropriate, suggest directions for moving forward based on the material presented. The conclusion should not merely repeat the introduction, nor should it introduce new material that will not be developed. We want the conclusion to give our audience a sense of closure and leave them with a

TABLE 4.1   Introduction "Road Maps"

In a Shorter Communication	In a Longer Communication
This paper proceeds as follows: Section II distinguishes between the various sentencing options, Section III shows how women tend to receive more lenient sentences than men, and Section IV presents conclusions and considers the implications of the identified sentencing disparities.	The next section, Section II, reviews the empirical literature comparing the sentencing of convicted women and men. Next, Section III discusses the current study's methodology: research design, sampling method, variable measures, and statistical procedures. Following that, Section IV presents the current study's findings, beginning with bivariate results and continuing with multivariate results. Finally, Section V reaches general conclusions and discusses the implications of the current findings.

positive impression of us. We also might want to leave them inspired, which could be accomplished by returning to the significance of the subject matter, outlining actionable steps suggested by the body of the communication, and/or ending with a memorable example. An effective conclusion ensures that any questions raised in the introduction or body have been answered as well as that the audience is assured the communication achieved its stated goal(s).

Outline Before You Write

An outline is to writing a paper as a blueprint is to building a house: Both are detailed plans of what you are going to make. An effective outline shows what information will be included in addition to distinguishing between major and minor elements. Some of the best outlines, moreover, include in-text citations and references and specify the estimated length of each section. A blueprint shows how many rooms, where each room goes, and how big each room is. Blueprints also include a list of materials that will be needed to construct the building. Thus, builders do not begin building until they know exactly where everything is going—how each part fits into the whole—and exactly what they will need to get from start to finish. In sum, know where you are going before you begin.

Outlining is beneficial to us in at least three ways. First, just like a blueprint, an outline can be used as an agreement. The writer is like the contractor, while the audience is like the client, and the outline is of course like the blueprint. Before we start construction, we can make sure that our plan for the final product is what it should be. Like a topic proposal, an outline helps us ensure that we are heading in the right direction.

Second, outlining forces us to organize our thoughts about the material in a logical and coherent way. In this sense, an outline can expose errors in thinking and gaps in information that we need to address. Similarly, an outline helps us remember what we need to include in the communication. Once we start writing, we might forget some ideas; but an outline reminds us what to say and when. Further, an outline can serve as a guard against repetition. If we have carefully planned out what we are going to say and where, and if we stick to that plan, then we are unlikely to make the mistake of saying the same thing twice.

Third, although less experienced writers often view outlining as a waste of time, outlining actually increases our efficiency. This is because it tackles the big picture first and details second. In the outline, we decide what information to include and in what order. Especially when we outline on a computer, it is easy to move information around, delete material, and make additions. Only after we have decided on content and arrangement will we worry about how best to word and punctuate passages and make one idea flow to the next. When we skip the outlining stage, we run the risk of spending a lot of time revising a sentence that we end up deleting later. Worse, we might retain an irrelevant sentence merely because we already spent lots of time making it "sound good."

Basic Outline Format

Start organizing your material by putting the material into basic outline format. Figure 4.1 is an example of basic outline format. There are four general rules to follow when outlining:

1. Put your thesis (or purpose or coverage) statement at the top of the outline.
2. Have a beginning, a middle, and an end.

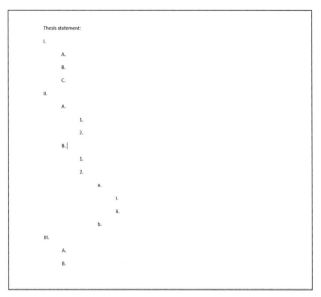

FIGURE 4.1 Outline Format

3. Distinguish between major and minor elements two ways:
   a. Use Roman numerals (e.g., I, II, III) to indicate level-1 (major) sections, capital letters (e.g., A, B, C) for level-2 (sub)sections, numbers for level-3 material, lowercase letters for level-4 material, and lowercase Roman numerals for level-5 information; and
   b. Indent appropriately: Roman numerals are not indented, capital letters are indented once (1/2 inch), numbers are indented twice, lowercase letters are indented three times, and lowercase Roman numerals are indented four times.
4. Identify at least two items on each level. For example, wherever you have a "1," you should at least have a "2"; wherever you have an "a," you at least should have a "b"; and so forth.

Types of Outlines

There are two types of outlines: (1) topic outlines and (2) sentence outlines. Whereas a **topic outline** consists of key words and phrases in a way that conveys what information will be presented and in what order without going into detail, a **sentence outline** combines key words and phrases (for section and subsection headings) with complete sentences to convey more specifically what information will be presented and in what order. Each sentence in a sentence outline should succinctly capture the main point you plan to make in that part of the paper. Someone reading a topic outline might understand that you intend, for instance, to cover various sanctioning options in the second major section of your paper. But someone reading a sentence outline would also have an idea of what you would be saying about those various sanctioning options.

Figure 4.2 contrasts topic and sentence outlines for the same paper. Sometimes it makes sense to use a topic rather than a sentence outline (or vice versa), and other times it makes sense to start with a topic outline and then flesh it out into a sentence outline.

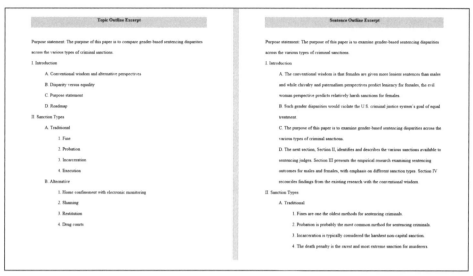

FIGURE 4.2   Excerpts of Topic Versus Sentence Outlines

From Outline to Draft

Convert the outline to a draft of your paper. Make sure you look at your outline repeatedly as you develop your draft, or you might leave out information. Here, we can liken the outline to a grocery list: If you make a grocery list but leave it in your pocket as you shop, then you might forget to buy an item or two.

The paper's major (level 1) sections will correspond directly to the Roman numerals, the paper's (level 2) subsections will correspond directly to the capital letters, and so on. Figure 4.3 shows how the outline from Figure 4.2 translates to a paper's section

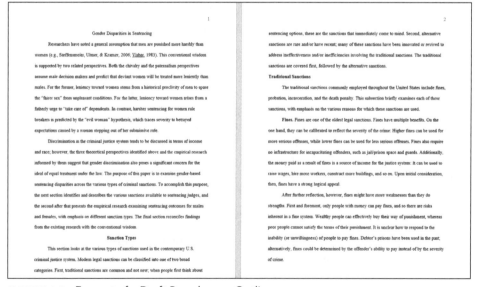

FIGURE 4.3   Excerpt of a Draft Based on an Outline

headings. The formatting of these headings should be consistent and should follow an appropriate style guide (e.g., APA, Chicago). For instance, according to APA style, the level-1 section headings should all be centered, bold, and in title case, with no extra line spaces above or below them; the level-2 section headings should all be left aligned, bold, and in title case, with no extra line spaces above or below them; and the level-3 headings should all be lead-in paragraph headings in sentence case that are bold and end with a period.

Generally speaking, you need to include at least a sentence between section/subsection headings so that you never have back-to-back section/subsection headings. For example, refer back to the "Topic Outline" in Figure 4.2. Between the level-1 section heading "Sanction Types" and the level-2 section heading "Traditional" sanctions directly below it, there must be some text. Notice how in Figure 4.3, the paragraph immediately following "Sanction Types" and the paragraph directly below "Traditional Sanctions" both provide a succinct overview of the section. This is generally an effective way to avoid back-to-back headings that is essentially a combination of a coverage statement and road map for the section.

Adopt an Appropriate Organizational Structure

Sometimes you will have no choice about how to structure a communication, such as if you are given specific requirements for content as well as for organization. In many cases, however, you will need to determine how to arrange the communication. An **organizational structure** is a method for arranging information. When you have the choice of how to organize a communication, the primary determinant of your organizational structure should be your objective: Pick the organizational structure that best fits the communication's objective. Fortunately, you do not need to reinvent the wheel here because there are several common structures available from which you can choose, as shown in Table 4.2.

It is possible to use more than one organizational pattern in the same communication. In this event, you would have a *primary* organizational structure to reflect your primary purpose and a *secondary* organizational structure to (a) reflect your secondary purpose and/or (b) impose additional order on the information. For example, your primary purpose might be to distinguish between probation and incarceration. As such, the most effective primary organizational structure would be compare-and-contrast. However, within each of these domains (i.e., compare and contrast), how will you organize the information? Most to least important (or least to most important) and advantages–disadvantages are logical secondary organizational structures.

Employ Organizational Devices to Highlight Your Structure

Suppose your audience consists of travelers visiting a place they never have been before. You are the guide, and it is your job to give them ample clues as to where they are and how to get to their destination. Some travelers will need more help than others, but you want all travelers to reach the destination. Thus, it is wise to err on the side of giving too much direction rather than too little direction. Along these lines, an **organizational device** is a signal to the audience about how some information fits into, or advances, the overall communication.

TABLE 4.2   Organizational Structures

Organizational Structure	Arranges Information . . .	Appropriate When . . .	Example
Chronological	From the earliest to the most recent	1. Describing how a policy, problem, or other condition came about 2. Chronicling the history of people, places, or other things	Tracing the evolution of shaming sanctions
Sequential	From the first to the last step	1. Describing how a process takes place 2. Instructing how to perform a procedure	Outlining the stages of criminal justice processing
Spatial	According to different physical locations	1. Showing where different items are 2. Linking items in terms of their location to each other	Describing the physical layout of a prison
Classification	Into separate categories	1. Using one or more criteria to categorize multiple items 2. Organizing multiple items into logical categories	Creating a typology of criminal behavior based on methods for perpetrating specific crimes
Partition	Into component parts	1. Breaking apart a single item into logical parts 2. Dividing a whole item into separate parts	Delineating the different components of the criminal justice system
General to specific	From the most general to the most specific	1. Giving the audience a framework for understanding details 2. Emphasizing the conclusion reached on the basis of evidence	Providing an introduction to a statistical software program
Specific to general	From the most specific to the most general	1. Building a case for a general conclusion 2. Emphasizing the evidence used to reach a logical conclusion	Investigating the circumstances resulting in a prison riot
Most to least important	From the most to the least important	1. Starting out with your strongest material to engage the audience 2. Convincing an audience early on	Interviewing for a job when the interview process has been going poorly
Least to most important	From the least to the most important	1. Ending on a strong note to leave a positive impression 2. Enhancing the salience of the strongest material	Interviewing for a job when the interview process has been going well
Compare-and-contrast	According to similarities and differences	1. Using a familiar (or simpler) topic to facilitate understanding of an unfamiliar (or more complicated) topic 2. Differentiating between phenomenon	Describing how intensive supervision probation differs from traditional probation
Advantages–disadvantages	According to pros and cons	1. Showing how something has both positive and negative effects 2. Performing a cost-benefit analysis	Documenting the rationale used to select one program rather than another for funding
Cause and effect	From independent variable to dependent variable(s)	1. Explaining how one phenomenon results in other phenomena 2. Demonstrating that a phenomenon has both intended and unintended consequences	Elucidate how poor performance in school can lead to juvenile delinquency

Organizational Structure	Arranges Information . . .	Appropriate When . . .	Example
Effect and cause	From dependent variable to independent variable(s)	1. Explaining how one phenomenon is the result of other phenomena 2. Demonstrating that a phenomenon is determined by other factors	Tracing desistance from crime to marriage and employment
Problem–cause–solution	From describing a problem, then explaining the problem, and then proposing a logical solution to the problem	1. Identifying a solution that is responsive to the nature and root of a problem 2. Developing a modified or supplementary solution to a problem	Proposing a strategy to reduce an emerging crime problem
Problem–process–solution	From describing a problem, then outlining steps already taken to solve the problem, and then proposing a logical solution to the problem	1. Identifying a solution that is responsive to the problem while improving on current approaches 2. Uncovering gaps or other flaws in current approaches to a problem	Proposing a multipronged approach to reduce a crime problem

Sources: Markel (2012); "Patterns of Organization" (n.d.); University of Maryland University College (2011)

Organizational Devices in Papers

Effective organizational devices for papers are shown in Table 4.3. Some of these organizational devices make sense in any type of communication: "road map" paragraphs, transitions, and bulleted and numbered lists. But other organizational devices can be unnecessary in short and simple communications with a single audience: table of contents, executive summaries and abstracts, and headings and subheadings.

In most cases, these organizational devices should be viewed as complementary rather than as alternative strategies. One exception is that we should use either an executive summary or an abstract—but not both—in a single communication. As a rule of thumb, scholarly publications use abstracts while more applied, practitioner-oriented publications use executive summaries. Two of these organizational devices will receive special attention here: lists and transitions.

TABLE 4.3   Organizational Devices

Organizational Device	Function
Table of contents	Lists the major parts of the paper in the order in which they appear along with page numbers
Executive summaries or abstracts	Summarizes the paper in several paragraphs (executive summary) or in one or two paragraphs (abstract)
"Road map" paragraphs	Outlines the paper's contents and the order in which they appear
Headings and subheadings	Labels new sections and subsections in such a way as to convey what they contain
Transitions	Specifies how present information relates to earlier information and/or the overall purpose of the communication
Lists	Lists components, items, stages, types, examples, and other parts or examples

TABLE 4.4   Formatting Options for Lists

	Unnumbered	Numbered
Horizontal	Traditional sentencing options include (a) fines, (b) probation, and (c) incarceration.	The three levels of registered sex offenders are (1) low risk, (2) moderate risk, and (3) high risk.
Vertical	Examples of organizational offenses for which federal fine provisions do not exist are • Environmental pollution, • Food, • Drugs, • Agricultural or consumer products, • Civil/individual rights, • Administration of justice, and • National defense (Office of General Counsel, 2015).	The seven stages involved in imposing a criminal fine on organizations in the federal justice system are 1. Determining the offense level, 2. Calculating the base fine, 3. Determining the culpability score, 4. Identifying the maximum and minimum multipliers for the culpability score, 5. Determining the guidelines fine range, 6. Determining the fine amount, and 7. Increasing the fine amount to reflect any gains made from the offense (Office of General Counsel, 2015).

LISTS. As shown in Table 4.4, there are different ways to format lists, and the list format should logically reflect the relationship of the items to each other as well as to the whole. Of course, information can be listed quite simply in a sentence with nothing more than punctuation separating the listed items. However, using labels (e.g., letters, numbers, bullets) can be a more effective way to list information in technical communications; hence, this section looks at approaches for labeling items in lists: unnumbered labels (esp. bullets) and numbered labels.

The first decision to make when listing is whether to use a horizontal or vertical list. To make this decision, consider length, importance, and complexity. First, the longer the list, the more sense a vertical list can make whenever you have the space available. It can be difficult to follow a lengthy list when it is in the text (i.e., horizontally formatted), especially when the listed items themselves are long. Second, vertical format draws attention to the list, which can be an effective strategy for emphasizing particularly important information. Third, vertical listing can make complex information easier to follow. Particularly if there are rather subtle differences between listed items, vertical listing can help the reader see those subtle differences.

The second decision when listing is whether to use a numbered or an unnumbered system. This decision should be governed by the nature of and relationship between listed items. If the number of items is important and/or there is an order to the items, then use a numbered list. If the number of items is unimportant and there is no order to the items, then use an unnumbered list. Some additional guidelines for using lists as an organizational device are presented in Table 4.5. Be sure to use terms and punctuation correctly and consistently in lists. The more familiar your audience is with writing mechanics, the more confused they might be when errors are made in a list's lead-in and punctuation. For example, improper or inconsistent comma use can make it difficult for the reader to determine when the list moves from one item to the next.

TRANSITIONS. The communication is unlikely to be effective if our audience is wondering, "What does this have to do with anything?" It is precisely this predicament that transitions prevent. Simply put, a **transition** connects ideas. It can be a single word, a phrase, a complete sentence, or a set of sentences. To be effective, transitions should be

TABLE 4.5   Listing Lead-In and Punctuation Guidelines

List lead-in	Use terms such as "consist of" when presenting a complete list: Primary colors consist of red, yellow, and blue.
	Use terms such as "include" when presenting a partial list: Colors include red, green, yellow, blue, and purple.
List punctuation	Use a comma between single and double items being listed: (1) a and b, (2) c and d, (3) e, (4) f, and (5) g and h.
	Use a semicolon between triple or more items being listed, with commas between the parts of the listed items: (1) a, b, and c; (2) d, e, and f; (3) g and h; (4) i; and (5) j, k, l, and m.

1. *Present*: Use them. Do not assume that readers will be able to follow along and see how parts connect to each other and to the whole.
2. *Consistent.* Avoid using transitions haphazardly. Instead, use them throughout the document. If you identify one major point as "First," for instance, then make sure you identify the next major point as "Second," and so on.
3. *Informative.* Some transitions are more informative than others. Be as clear and specific as possible about what the information is and how it relates to the rest of the information in the document. For instance, if you are listing steps, then use transitions that indicate the ordering of the steps (e.g., first, second) rather than less informative transitions (e.g., another, yet another).
4. *Logical.* The best transitions cohere with and accentuate the paper's organizational structure. Ensure that the transitions you use fit with your message and organizational structure. Unless you are using a cause and effect organizational pattern, for example, it will probably not make sense to use transitions such as "Because" and "As a result."

Table 4.6 presents some common transitions according to their role in a communication. Generally speaking, use some form of transition at the beginning of each section and at the beginning of each paragraph. Transition words and phrases need not be the first word(s) in a sentence; rather (just as done here with "rather"), they can be placed in the middle or even at the end of a sentence. That said, to serve the purpose of notifying your audience how present information relates to previous information, transitions are most effective at or near the beginning of a sentence. And yet to avoid monotony and provide some variety in sentence structure—which also is a good thing—some transitions can be placed later in sentences.

A particularly effective way to use transitions is to combine them. On the one hand, you can create a **compound transition** where you combine two or more transitional terms to create a single transitional phrase. Examples include "Generally, however" and "Therefore, as a consequence." On the other hand, your paper might benefit from **layered transitioning**, which is when you combine two or more transitional structures to distinguish between lines of thought or major versus minor elements. You might have a relatively simple, straightforward paper. In this case, you might need just one set of transitions (e.g., "First," "Second," and "Third"). Oftentimes, however, your paper will be more complex and thus would benefit from layered transitions. Suppose you are writing a paper comparing and contrasting capital punishment with life imprisonment. Figure 4.4 shows an example of layered transitioning that uses three transitional structures.

TABLE 4.6   **Transitional Words and Phrases**

Uses	Transitions
Indicates order Lists complementary points Builds a case	First, second, third . . . The first, the second, the third . . . Next, then, finally
Indicates temporal/chronological order Outlines how an event transpired	after, afterward, before, concurrently, currently, during, earlier, immediately, immediately thereafter, meanwhile, now, later, prior to, recently, simultaneously, soon, subsequently, then
Indicates spatial relationships Indicates geographic layout and proximity	above, adjacent, around, behind, below, beyond, close by, further away, here, in front, in back, nearby, next to, on the right/left, surrounding, to the right/left, to the east/west/north/south, under
Indicates frequency	as a general rule, frequently, generally, more often than not, often, rarely, sometimes, typically, usually
Continues a point Connects similar ideas Supplements a point	additionally, again, also, analogous to, another, as well, equally important, further, furthermore, in a like manner, in addition, in the same way, likewise, moreover, similarly
Distinguishes ideas Shows contrast Points out a different idea	alternatively, but, conversely, despite, however, in contrast, instead, nevertheless, notwithstanding, on the contrary, on the one hand/on the other hand, rather, whereas, while, yet
Illustrates a point Provides an example	as a case in point, for example, for instance, in particular, namely, specifically, to illustrate
Reinforces a point Simplifies an idea	briefly, in brief, indeed, in other words, plainly put, put simply, thus
Qualifies a point Leaves room for exceptions/serves as hedging	at any rate, frequently, generally, often, oftentimes, rarely, sometimes, that said, this is not to say, to some extent
Concedes a point Dismisses an idea	although, at least, despite, granted that, regardless, still, though, while it might be true that, while this might be true
Shows a causal relationship Relates a cause to an effect	accordingly, as a consequence, as a result, because of, consequently, hence, so, therefore, thus
Introduces material Provides background	as background, before getting to, to begin, to give a little context
Concludes a communication Summarizes a point	in brief, in conclusion, in short, in sum, in summary, overall, to conclude, to summarize

Sources: IOE Writing Centre (2018); Markel (2012); Taraba (n.d.); The Writing Center (n.d.)

Organizational Devices in Presentations

Many of the same devices used in papers can be adapted to presentations. Although Chapter 11 addresses this topic in detail, for now we should note two key differences regarding organizational devices in papers and in presentations. First, whereas these devices are written into the paper like the rest of the content, in presentations, organizational devices are typically part of the narrative. Rather than putting them on the slides, that is, these devices often will be oral.

The second important difference between organizational devices in papers and presentations is audience control: A paper's readers who become lost can flip back to the table of contents or road map or even reread the last couple of pages to orient themselves, but presentation audiences rarely can go back and forth. So, to guard against your audience becoming lost, consider using some other strategies to exploit your communication's organizational structure and overall coherence. Ultimately, then, although organizational

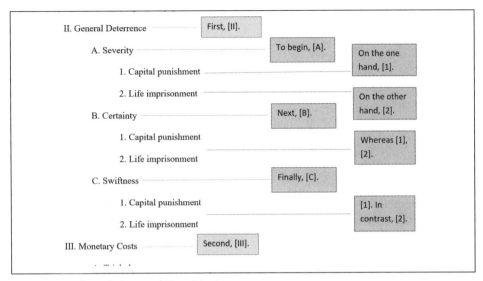

FIGURE 4.4   Sample Layered Transitioning

devices are woven into a presentation differently than into a paper, they are at least as important in presentations as they are in papers.

Use Structural Variation to Distinguish Between Major and Minor Material

Some elements of a communication are more important than others. The most important elements are the major elements, and it is to these major elements that we want to call the most attention. This guideline applies to the structure of paragraphs as well as the structure of sentences.

Paragraph Structure

Each paragraph should present and develop a single idea. In general, each paragraph should start with a transition and contain a topic sentence. We have covered transitions already in this chapter, so we can focus on topic sentences now. A **topic sentence** is a clear statement of what the paragraph is about. Because a paragraph deals with one idea, the key decision is how best to convey that idea to your audience. You certainly want a clear statement of that idea, but where should it go? Here, you have two options: in the beginning or in the end. Rarely is there a good reason to place the most important information in the middle of a paragraph. Table 4.7 distinguishes between these options. As shown in Table 4.7, you could begin with the main idea, and then devote the rest of the paragraph to elaborating on that idea using evidence, examples, clarifications, qualifications, and so on. Alternatively, you could begin with specifics, using the paragraph to build up to the main idea in the last sentence. In most cases, it is probably best to use variation, sometimes putting the key information at the beginning, and other times putting it at the end. But try not to bury the most important information in the middle.

Order of information within a paragraph is one decision; *length* of a paragraph is another decision. Some paragraphs will have more important information than others, and some ideas will need more development than others. As a general rule, more important and/or complex ideas warrant longer paragraphs than less important and/or simpler

TABLE 4.7   Placement of a Paragraph's Main Idea

	At the Beginning	At the End
How it works	Start with the main idea, and then develop it with details	Start with details, using them to build up to the main idea
When it is effective	Complicated material, for which the audience might need to know the "big picture" to make sense of specifics	Controversial material, for which the audience might need to be "prepped" for the general idea
	Time-sensitive material, with an audience who is likely only to skim the communication	Dramatic material, with an audience you want to leave with a strong, emotional impression

ideas. For example, some paragraphs exist only to link together two other, more substantive paragraphs. Such linking paragraphs can be relatively short—perhaps just a sentence or two. From this general rule it follows that most papers will have paragraphs of varying rather than uniform length.

Sentence Structure

Each sentence should express a single thought. As in the case with paragraph structure, the most important material usually should go at the beginning or end of a sentence. Less important information generally belongs in the middle, with a noteworthy exception: You can draw attention to an important part of a sentence by using the em dash ("—"). In the middle of a sentence, important material can be set off from the rest of the sentence by enclosing it between em dashes. For example, "The mother alleged that the father—who had been drinking heavily earlier in the day—was last seen with the child." If the important part is at the end of a sentence, however, then you just need one em dash to separate that important part from the rest of the sentence. For example, "The woman said she had looked everywhere for the child—though neighbors reported that the women hadn't left her house that day." Because the em dash is so noticeable, it should not be used to set off unimportant material, nor should it be overused. To set off less important material, prefer parentheses and commas. As a rule of thumb, restrict yourself to a maximum of one use of the em dash per paragraph.

In addition to Table 4.8's suggestions, when less important material is not part of a sentence containing important material, it can be put in a footnote (at the bottom of the page), an endnote (at the end of the paper), or an appendix. Footnotes and endnotes work well with material that is a short paragraph or less, while an appendix can be appropriate when the less important material is lengthy. Footnotes/endnotes and appendices make sense when keeping the material in the main text might disrupt the flow of the

TABLE 4.8   Arrangement of a Sentence's Major Versus Minor Elements

	Major Element	Minor Element
Placement	The beginning	The middle
	The end	
Punctuation	Set off with em dash	Set off with commas
		Enclosed in parentheses

communication, distract from the main point, or overwhelm the primary audience with less-than-essential details.

Another sentence structure consideration is the length of sentences. Avoid limiting yourself to only long sentences or only short sentences, either of which will give the paper a monotonous feel. Variety in sentence length is ideal. In general (and as with paragraphs), longer sentences are best for more complicated thoughts, while shorter sentences are best for simpler thoughts. Beyond that, variation in sentence length entails more creative concerns. To highlight a particularly important point, to distinguish a simple concept from more complicated concepts, or to reach a succinct bottom line—especially if you want to emphasize the simplicity of the bottom line—you might use a brief sentence.

APPLICATIONS

This section looks at two situations where organization is approached differently: persuasive papers in academia and intelligence briefings in the field. With the former, we need to make decisions about how to arrange the material to best convince an audience. With the latter, we use a particular organizational structure that emphasizes the bottom line in a manner that recognizes time constraints.

Persuasive Papers

A **persuasive paper** addresses a controversial topic and argues for a particular position on that topic. A controversial topic is an issue that has more than one side to it. There is disagreement about controversies. The job of a persuasive paper is to provide reasons supporting the stance taken on the controversial issue.

Topic and Stance

Unless you are assigned a topic or given a list of topics from which to choose, your first step in developing a persuasive paper is to identify an appropriate topic. To determine whether a topic is controversial, phrase it as a question, and then consider whether there are two opposing answers to the question (yes or no). Another test is to imagine a debate: Are there two opposing sides such that there could be a debate on the topic? Examples of controversial issues in criminal justice are provided in Table 4.9.

After you have selected a topic, your second task is to take a position on that topic. Basically, are you for it, or are you against it? Resist the urge to take a position based on how you *feel* about the topic. Instead, conduct research and take the side that is best supported by available evidence. Here, consider both the amount of evidence and the credibility of that evidence (topics to which we return in Chapter 6).

As you conduct your research, it can be helpful to record your information in the format shown in Figure 4.5. Remember to keep track of your sources as you do your research, collecting full bibliographic information so you do not have to go back later to build a complete References list.

Contents and Organization

Once you have done your research and taken a side, you are ready to organize and outline your paper. As usual, you need an introduction and a conclusion. The main part of the body should be the justification for your position on the controversy, but the body also

TABLE 4.9   Sample Controversial Issues in Criminal Justice

Intelligence and crime: Do those with less intelligence commit more crime?

Biology and crime: Is criminal behavior determined biologically?

Video games and crime: Do video games contribute to violent crime?

Pornography and rape: Is exposure to pornography related to increased rates of rape?

Legal status of euthanasia: Should euthanasia be a crime?

Domestic battery and arrest policy: Does arresting batterers do more harm than good?

Cameras in courtrooms: Should cameras be in the courtroom during criminal trials?

Prison and deterrence: Do prisons deter crime?

Private prisons: Should private, "for-profit" corporations be allowed to run U.S. prisons?

Juvenile murderers: Should juveniles who commit murder be sentenced to life in prison without the possibility of parole?

Megan's Law: Should neighbors be notified when a sex offender is released into their community?

Castration and sex offenders: Should serious sex offenders be castrated?

Effectiveness of three-strikes laws: Do three-strikes laws work?

Capital punishment: Does the death penalty reduce homicide?

Marijuana legalization: Should marijuana be legalized?

Partial identifications in police lineups: Should partial identifications be accepted in police lineups?

Exclusionary rule: Should the United States abolish the exclusionary rule of evidence in criminal cases?

Police and body cameras: Should the police be required to wear body cameras?

Source: Berlatsky (2010); Hickey (2017)

Topic: _____

	Yes	No
Reason 1		
Evidence supporting reason 1		
Reason 2		
Evidence supporting reason 2		
Reason 3		
Evidence supporting reason 3		
Reason 4		
Evidence supporting reason 4		

FIGURE 4.5   Recording and Organizing Information for a Persuasive Paper

needs to address the opposing position on the controversy. Addressing your opposition demonstrates that you are aware of both sides, including why some people take a different position than you. You want to give the impression that you have considered both

BOX 4.3	Plagiarism Pointer

Taking careful notes is a safeguard against plagiarism. As you collect information from a source, clearly indicate which information comes from which source, and record the source's full bibliographic information. Also, in your notes, use quotation marks to indicate when you are using this source's exact language—whether a phrase, sentence, or more.

sides rationally and objectively, and you have taken the side with the most support. If you are successful in creating this impression, then the subtle implication is that another person who weighs both sides will inevitably reach the same conclusion as you.

Drawing from social psychological research on sequencing effects (e.g., Crano, 1977; Nai & Seeberg, 2018), Figure 4.6 suggests a potentially effective organizational structure for the typical persuasive paper. As illustrated in Figure 4.5, both volume and sequencing of information are important. Unless you have a good reason to do otherwise, follow these rules when you organize a persuasive paper:

1. Use the introduction section to achieve a **primacy effect**, whereby the audience is strongly affected by material encountered first. This notion is consistent with the widely recognized value of "first impressions." Thus, explicitly indicate your position on the issue, and clearly identify the reasons that support your position.

FIGURE 4.6 Suggested Organizational Structure for Persuasive Papers

2. Vary length to achieve a **volume effect**, whereby the audience is strongly affected by material encountered the most. Here, devote the most space to your strongest reason, followed by your next strongest reason, and then your least strong reason. Do not oversimplify the opposing argument, but neither should you present it in such a way that it eclipses your position and supporting points.

3. Present your strongest point last to achieve a **recency effect**, whereby the audience is strongly affected by material encountered last, and then place your weaker points in the middle. Do not bury your strongest point in the middle of the paper, nor should you break apart your points by placing the opposing argument between them or dilute the conclusion with more than a passing reference to the opposing argument.

Keep your purpose in mind as you flesh out your outline and develop your draft: Your goal is to persuade your audience. Your goal is not merely to describe, compare and contrast, or otherwise inform your audience. The essence of the persuasive paper is to give *reasons* why your position is the preferred—that is, more logical and evidence-based—position on a controversial issue. We will use abolition of the death penalty as an example controversial issue, taking the side that, yes, the death penalty should be abolished. If you have three reasons, then you would be able to complete these three sentences:

1. The first reason why the death penalty should be abolished is because _____.
2. The second reason why the death penalty should be abolished is because _____.
3. The third reason why the death penalty should be abolished is because _____.

If it does not make sense to put the material into this form, then you probably do not have *reasons*. (See Chapter 5 for more on reasons and their role in an argument.)

So, what does this mean for the opposing argument? Keeping with the same example, the opposing argument would be, no, we should not abolish the death penalty. Reasons work the same way with the opposing argument as with your argument (e.g., "The first reason why the death penalty should not be abolished is because ____"). Ensure that you use transitions and topic sentences—and perhaps section headings—that make it unmistakably clear when you are presenting the opposing argument rather than developing your own argument.

Best Practices
To summarize this discussion, here are some best practices for preparing compelling persuasive papers:

1. **Select a controversial topic.** A persuasive paper should not merely inform. Nor should a persuasive paper be written where there is no argument.

2. **Take a logical, evidence-based stance on the selected topic.** Try to avoid picking a side merely because of how you feel or what you believe. Instead, do some preliminary research to help you pick the strongest side.

3. **Identify claims (reasons) supporting and opposing your stance.** Try to identify at least three reasons supporting your stance and as many reasons as possible supporting the opposing stance.

4. **Identify and critically evaluate the evidence for and against your stance.** The success of your argument might hinge on the quality of the evidence used to support it. Thus, weak evidence—such as flawed or irrelevant evidence—will lead to a weak argument.

5. **Make your stance clear as soon as possible.** Do not delay in clearly articulating your position. Your audience will have trouble processing information until it knows your stance.

6. **Present the opposing argument before your own argument.** Show your audience that you have seriously considered both sides. If you are debating, this is an excellent opportunity to steal your opponent's fire.

7. **Start with your weakest reason, and end with your strongest reason.** You want multiple reasons, but some will be stronger than others. The strongest reasons are the most logical and evidence-based reasons. End on a strong note.

8. **Spend the most time discussing your argument, especially your strongest reasons and evidence.** Make your stance and your strongest reason(s) the most salient part of your argument.

9. **Maintain a professional, educated tone and writing style.** Do not jeopardize your credibility by personally attacking your opponent, engaging in sensationalism, or making the issue personal. Also, errors in writing mechanics are like chinks in a knight's armor: They expose weakness. Errors in minor details can make your audience wonder if you make errors in major details. Once your competence is questioned, your credibility is lost.

Intelligence Briefings

Routinely used in the military, an **intelligence briefing** (hereinafter abbreviated as "intel" briefing or report) is "designed to accomplish a specific purpose: to impart information, to obtain a decision, to exchange information, or to review important details. The objective common to every briefing is that of facilitating a rapid, coordinated response" (GlobalSecurity.org, n.d.). Intel reports use data to suggest a specific course of action. As such, intel reports are evidence-based, action-oriented communications usually intended for an audience of agency leaders, such as military commanders and police chiefs.

Sometimes written and sometimes oral, intel reports are useful ways of answering such real-world questions as the following:

- What are the most effective ways to prevent guns from entering schools?
- How can we prevent Medicaid provider fraud committed by health professionals?
- What is the most pressing crime problem in our jurisdiction?
- Where and when in the agency's jurisdiction is the most crime occurring?
- Should the agency implement an anonymous reporting system for whistleblowers to report misconduct by their colleagues?
- Should the agency use one-officer or two-officer patrol units?
- What can we do to increase citizen confidence in the criminal justice system?

Common to all of these topics is the need for data to be collected, analyzed, and presented in a manner designed to facilitate informed and speedy decision-making.

Contents and Organization

The overriding organizational imperative for intel reports is to present the "bottom line up front" (**BLUF**; Jensen, McElreath, & Graves, 2013). There are two main reasons for BLUF formatting. First, the audience might not listen to the entire briefing. Thus, presenting the conclusion at the beginning ensures that the audience hears the most important part. Second, BLUF format can serve as an advance organizer: Knowing your conclusion helps the audience make sense of the data—which at times can be detailed and complicated—as you move quickly through the briefing. Table 4.10 shows the typical structure and contents of an intel report.

An intel briefing exemplifies a combination of the general-to-specific and most-to-least important organizational structures covered earlier in this chapter. The general-to-specific structure is most evident in the presentation of the bottom line (in the Key Judgments section) before the details supporting them (in the Substantiation section). Most-to-least important is perhaps best seen in the formatting and structure of each paragraph in the body of the briefing: The main point (or bottom line) of the paragraph is the first sentence, and it is in bold. This sentence summarizes the rest of the paragraph. The rest of the paragraph provides details necessary to understand and support that main point, with sentences ordered in terms of most to least important. This feature is one of BLUF format's most distinguishing features.

The BLUF intel report is designed to communicate key information efficiently. In doing so, some additional organizational and formatting practices can be employed. First, in addition to bolding the key points when they are the first sentence of a paragraph, use graphics and text boxes to reinforce those points. Second, detailed information can be presented in footnotes or endnotes. Details of how a cost estimate was calculated or how recidivism was measured, for example, could be placed in a footnote.

Figure 4.7 provides an example of the Key Judgments part of an intel briefing on drug courts and their potential as an alternative sanction to reduce recidivism among nonviolent drug offenders. Following along with the example in Figure 4.7, the Introduction would cover the problem of high recidivism rates among nonviolent drug offenders, while the Background section would describe how drug courts operate.

The bulk of the intel briefing would be the Substantiation section, which would devote at least a paragraph to each of the bullets in the Key Judgments (with the first sentence of each paragraph in bold). To help the reader follow along and easily locate

TABLE 4.10   BLUF Format

	Section	Purpose/Contents
1	Title	Captures the essence of the report succinctly and directly
2	Key Judgments	• Functions as an Executive Summary • Presents the bottom line clearly and concisely • Suffices as a stand-alone document
3	Introduction	• Serves as a less detailed Executive Summary • Presents the bottom line clearly and concisely
4	Background	Provides details that are necessary to understand the information that follows
5	Substantiation	• Provides the evidence basis for the claims presented in the Key Judgments and Introduction sections • Is usually the longest and most detailed section • Avoids opinions and commentary
6	Context	• Supplements the Background section • Provides additional information to help the reader make sense of the issue and your analysis of it
7	Outlook	• Summarizes the main points presented • Avoids introducing new ideas
8	Sources	Identifies the source of information

Source: "How to write an intelligence product in the bottom line up front (BLUF) format" (n.d.).

Assessment

Drug Courts and Recidivism

June 1, 2018

Key Judgments

Drug courts are a promising alternative for sentencing first-time nonviolent drug offenders. Although they are less suitable for violent and repeat drug offenders, research indicates that they reduce recidivism and associated costs among nonviolent, first-drug offenders.

- Drug offenders constitute a considerable portion of federal and state prison populations.
- Drug offenders are among the most likely to recidivate after completing sentences of probation or incarceration.
- Drug courts were designed specifically to increase rehabilitation and decrease recidivism among drug offenders.
- In addition to treatment for drug abuse/addiction, drug courts involve close monitoring by specially trained judges.
- Drug offenders who complete drug court treatment <u>are</u> significantly less likely to be arrested or convicted of new crimes.
- Drug courts can save money in the long run by breaking the cycle of drugs, crime, and recidivism.

FIGURE 4.7   Sample Key Judgments in an Intel Briefing

particular pieces of information, present material in the same order in the Substantiation section as in the Key Judgments section of the briefing, as seen in Figure 4.8. Observe how footnotes are used for details so as not to clutter the main text with methodological details in which the primary audience might have no interest.

The material presented in Figure 4.7 and Figure 4.8 could be accompanied by a diagram illustrating the main components of the drug court model, as shown in Figure 4.9. The Context section might outline how the figures reported in the Substantiation section were obtained, while the Outlook section could review the key points and conclude that drug courts should save money over time as recidivism and its associated

Drug courts have several distinguishing features that are tailored to the specific needs of drug offenders, including treatment and monitoring by specially trained judges. Although the drug court model varies to some extent across jurisdictions, its common features include: (1) offender screening and risk assessment, (2) training for judges, (3) close monitoring by judges, (4) drug testing, (5) treatment and rehabilitation services designed to promote successful community reintegration, and (6) incentives and graduated sanctions.

Evaluation studies have found that drug courts are effective in reducing recidivism, with some qualifications. First, recidivism reductions appear contingent upon program completion.[1] Second, recidivism reductions might diminish over time.[2] Third, drug courts might only work for nonviolent drug offenders.[3] And fourth, recidivism reductions appear greater among adult compared with juvenile drug offenders.[4] Moreover, these recidivism reductions might only be realized when drug courts are used as an alternative to traditional probation or incarceration.[5]

---

[1] Goldkamp et al. (2001) reported mixed results regarding the effect of drug court participation on reoffending, such that drug court reduced recidivism but only if the drug offender successfully completed the drug court program. Mitchell et al. (2001) reported less recidivism among program completers than noncompleters.

[2] Wilson et al. (2006) found evidence drug courts reduce recidivism, but this effect weakened in some cases with longer follow-up periods.

[3] Mitchell et al. (2001) found greater reductions in recidivism among adult drug court participants than among juvenile drug court participants.

[4] Mitchell et al. (2012) found greater reductions in recidivism drug court participants convicted of nonviolent crimes than among drug court participants convicted of violent crimes.

[5] Spohn et al. (2001) found that drug offenders participating in drug court have much lower recidivism rates than do traditionally sentenced drug offenders but not drug offenders who participated in a diversion program.

FIGURE 4.8   Excerpt of the Substantiation Section in an Intel Briefing

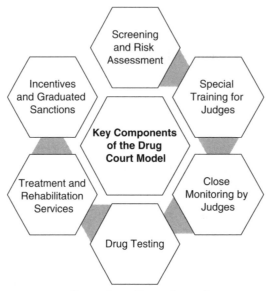

FIGURE 4.9   Illustration of Drug Court Components

costs are reduced. Finally, the Sources section would include bibliographic information for each of the sources used to write the report, providing sufficient detail so that a curious reader could locate each source to confirm information reported in your briefing or to learn more about the topic.

Best Practices

What follows is a list of best practices for intel briefings:

1. **Present the main conclusions first:** Following BLUF style, begin with the critical information—that is, the Key Judgments. Do not mix other material (e.g., background, context) in with the Key Judgments.
2. **Substantiate each Key Judgment:** Justify each conclusion, supporting each one with a balance of evidence and logic. Do not skimp on evidence. Instead, provide as strong a case as possible for each Key Judgment.
3. **Be clear and concise:** Avoid unnecessary material, including irrelevant, superfluous, and redundant material. Also omit flowery, fancy language; vague terms, euphemisms; clichés and colloquialisms; and equivocation.
4. **Be professional:** Maintain a focused, formal writing style. Refrain from personal opinions, experiences, and commentary. Stick to the issues and the evidence.

EXERCISES
Matching

These exercises are designed to assess Chapter 4 Learning Objective 1 (see Box 4.1). Match each numbered statement to the lowercase letter corresponding to the key word it defines. Each key word will be used only once.

1. A formal written communication that addresses a controversial topic and argues for a particular position on that topic by providing reasons that support the position taken on the issue
2. A word or collection of words that connects ideas within a communication
3. The format of a communication that is arranged with the "bottom line up front"
4. A signal to the audience about how some information fits into, or advances, the overall communication
5. The phenomenon whereby an audience is strongly affected by the material encountered the most
6. A clear statement of what a paragraph is about
7. The arrangement of information or the process of planning and arranging information in the manner reflective of the objective, parameters, and audience
8. The phenomenon whereby an audience is strongly affected by the material encountered last
9. A combination of two or more transitional (idea-linking) structures to distinguish between lines of thought or between major and minor elements
10. The blueprint for a communication that arranges key words and phrases in a way that conveys what information will be presented in what order without going into detail
11. A method for arranging information in a communication
12. A combination of two or more transitional (idea-linking) terms to create a single transitional phrase
13. A formal written or oral communication that suggests a specific course of action based on the analysis of data
14. The phenomenon whereby an audience is strongly affected by the material encountered first
15. The blueprint for a communication that arranges complete sentences along with key words and phrases (for section headings) in a way that conveys what information will be presented in what order

a. BLUF	**i.** primacy effect
b. compound transition	**j.** recency effect
c. intelligence briefing	**k.** sentence outline
d. layered transitioning	**l.** topic outline
e. organization	**m.** topic sentence
f. organizational device	**n.** transition
g. organizational structure	**o.** volume effect
h. persuasive paper	

Multiple Choice

These exercises are designed to assess Chapter 4 Learning Objective 3 (see Box 4.1). Indicate the single most appropriate response to each item below.

1. Which of the following transitions are most appropriate when your objective is to distinguish between ideas and/or show contrast?

    a. after, currently, subsequently
    b. first, second, third
    c. as a general rule, more often than not, typically
    d. alternatively, conversely, whereas

2. Which of the following transitions are most appropriate when your objective is to connect similar ideas?
    a. although, regardless, still
    b. additionally, further, moreover
    c. as a general rule, frequently, usually
    d. accordingly, hence, thus

3. Which of the following transitions are most appropriate for illustrating a point?
    a. this is not to say, that said, rarely
    b. to begin, to give a little context, as background
    c. often, generally, sometimes
    d. namely, as a case in point, for example

4. Which of the following transitions are most appropriate for qualifying a point and/or leaving room for exceptions?
    a. while it may be true that, regardless, despite
    b. next, then, finally
    c. that said, this is not to say, at any rate
    d. in short, to summarize, overall

5. Which of the following organizational structures is most appropriate for determining the impact of some new policy?
    a. partition
    b. advantages–disadvantages
    c. sequential
    d. spatial

6. Which of the following organizational structures is most appropriate for describing the crime scene in a mugging case?
    a. spatial
    b. chronological
    c. compare-and-contrast
    d. problem–cause–solution

7. Which of the following organizational structures is most appropriate for recounting the process that was followed to implement a new policing program?
    a. specific to general
    b. general to specific
    c. advantages–disadvantages
    d. chronological

8. Which of the following organizational structures is most appropriate for describing what a courtroom workgroup is?
    a. effect and cause
    b. cause and effect

    c. partition

    d. sequential

9. Which of the following organizational structures is most appropriate for determining which of two possible programs to implement?

    a. compare-and-contrast

    b. problem–process–solution

    c. classification

    d. partition

10. The effect-and-cause organizational structure is most appropriate when the objective is to . . .

    a. Assess the credibility of an eyewitness

    b. Generate a theory of why the defendant murdered the victim

    c. Find a legal precedent to support a motion

    d. Justify your decision to charge a person with first-degree rather than second-degree murder

11. The problem–cause–solution organizational structure is most appropriate when the objective is to . . .

    a. Distinguish between federal and state sentencing guidelines

    b. Describe how sentencing guidelines work for different types of crimes

    c. Outline the origins of and developments in federal sentencing guidelines

    d. Make a case for revising federal sentencing guidelines in a certain, specified way

12. The classification organizational structure is most appropriate when the objective is to . . .

    a. Show the proximity of different gang territories in a city

    b. Delineate between different types of gangs in a city

    c. Recount the rise and fall of a particular gang in a city

    d. Attribute a particular crime to a particular gang in a city

Editing

These editing exercises are designed to assess Chapter 4 Learning Objective 5 (see Box 4.1). Rewrite each of the following passages, editing them as needed to achieve effective use of transitions.

1. There are two good reasons to report crime. As a case in point, reporting crime increases the odds that the perpetrator will be apprehended and punished. To illustrate, reporting crime also increases the validity of crime statistics.

2. There are advantages and disadvantages to reporting crime. To begin, reporting crime increases the odds that the perpetrator will be apprehended and punished. Next, reporting crime can expose the person to danger, such as if the perpetrator wants revenge for being reported. Then, reporting crime increases the validity of crime statistics. Finally, reporting crime may lead to the person having to testify in court, which takes time and can be stressful.

3. Whether or not a crime is reported depends on a series of conditions. There needs to be a crime. There needs to be some knowledge of the crime. There needs to be

some desire, or motivation, to report the crime. There needs to be an ability for the crime to be reported.

4. Some crimes suffer more from under-reporting than other crimes. More robberies than rapes are reported.

5. Crime reports can emerge in different ways. Victims can report. Nearby, eyewitnesses can report. Simultaneously, people who overhear or find some evidence, like a diary, can report. Police officers can discover a crime and report, too.

6. People who are victimized by fraudsters sometimes don't report. They feel embarrassed that they fell for a scheme.

7. Many victims choose do not report their victimization. Some victims are not aware that they were victimized by a crime. Some victims are embarrassed that they were victimized. Some victims don't want to deal with the police. Some victims might think that reporting the crime will be a waste of time. Many victims do report their victimization. They trust the police to do their best to apprehend the perpetrator. They think they will get a sense of satisfaction if the perpetrator is punished. They think reporting is their duty as a U.S. citizen.

8. It is understandable that Andrew Smith did not report it when he saw someone steal cigarettes from a convenience store. Andrew had been victimized several times in the past and, each time, felt as though the police didn't take his victimizations seriously.

9. Blame and shame go a long way toward explaining under-reporting of crimes such as rape and fraud. People are unlikely to report if they will be blamed or shamed for being victimized.

10. There is a substantial "dark figure" of crime because of under-reporting. Crime statistics are not entirely useless. We can use crime statistics to identify trends over time and space.

Writing

These writing exercises are designed to assess Chapter 4 Learning Objectives 2, 4, 6, and 7 (see Box 4.1).

1. Why is organization important in both academic and professional criminal justice communications?

2. Identify and distinguish between guidelines for achieving effective organization in criminal justice communications.

3. Pick a controversial issue in criminal justice, take a position on the issue, conduct some research, and then develop, in this order, (1) a topic outline, (2) a sentence outline, (3) a draft, and (4) a final paper. Ensure that you address the opposing argument and then present at least three reasons—each with supporting evidence—for your position on the issue.

4. Prepare an intel briefing on a significant controversial issue in contemporary criminal justice. The question is, What are best practices for a police officer using a Taser with a crime suspect?

REFERENCES

Berlatsky, Noah (Ed.). (2010). *America's prisons: Opposing viewpoints*. Detroit, MI: Greenhaven Press.

Crano, William D. (1977). Primacy versus recency in retention of information and opinion change. *Journal of Social Psychology, 101*(1), 87–96.

GlobalSecurity.org. (n.d.). *FM 34–80: Brigade and battalion intelligence and electronic warfare operations. Appendix B: Briefing techniques*. Retrieved from http://www.globalsecurity.org/intell/library/policy/army/fm/34-80/appb.htm

Goldkamp, John S., White, Michael D., & Robinson, Jennifer B. (2001). Do drug courts work? Getting inside the drug court black box. *Journal of Drug Issues, 31*(1), 27–72.

Hickey, Thomas (Ed.). (2017). *Taking sides: Clashing views in crime and criminology* (2th ed.). McGraw Hill Education.

"How to write an intelligence product in the bottom line up front (BLUF) format." (n.d.). Retrieved from https://www.utep.edu/liberalarts/nssi/student-resources/BLUF-Writing-Format.pdf

IOE Writing Centre. (2018). *Cautious language and hedging*. University College London. Retrieved from http://www.ucl.ac.uk/ioe-writing-centre/develop-academic-voice/caution-hedging

Jensen, Carl J. III., McElreath, David H., & Graves, Melissa. (2013). *Introduction to intelligence studies*. Boca Raton, FL: CRC Press.

Markel, Mark. (2012). *Technical communication* (10th ed.). Boston, MA: Bedford/St. Martin's.

Mitchell, Ojmarrh, Wilson, David B., Eggers, Amy, & MacKenzie, Doris L. (2012). Assessing the effectiveness of drug courts on recidivism: A meta-analytic review of traditional and non-traditional drug courts. *Journal of Criminal Justice, 40*(1), 60–71.

Nai, Alessandro, & Seeberg, Henrik Bech. (2018). A series of persuasive events: Sequencing effects of negative and positive messages on party evaluations and perceptions of negativity. *Journal of Marketing Communications, 24*(4), 412–432.

Office of General Counsel, U.S. Sentencing Commission. (2015, June). *Primer: Fines under the organizational guidelines*. Retrieved from https://www.ussc.gov/sites/default/files/pdf/training/primers/2015_Primer_Organizational_Fines.pdf

"Patterns of organization." (n.d.). Retrieved from http://faculty.washington.edu/ezent/impo.htm

Steffensmeier, Darrell, Ulmer, Jeffrey, & Kramer, John. (2006). The interaction of race, gender, and age in criminal sentencing: The punishment cost of being young, black, and male. *Criminology, 36*(4), 763–798.

Spohn, Cassia, Piper, R. K., Martin, Tom, & Frenzel, Erika Davis. (2001). Drug courts and recidivism: The results of an evaluation using two comparison groups and multiple indicators of recidivism. *Journal of Drug Issues, 31*(1), 149–176.

Taraba, Joanna. (n.d.). *Transitional words and phrases*. University of Richmond Writer's Web. Retrieved from http://writing2.richmond.edu/writing/wweb/trans1.html

The Writing Center. (n.d.). *Transitions* [handout]. College of Arts and Sciences, University of North Carolina–Chapel Hill. Retrieved from https://writingcenter.unc.edu/tips-and-tools/transitions/

University of Maryland University College. (2011). Patterns for presenting information. *Online Guide to Writing and Research*. Retrieved from http://www.umuc.edu/current-students/learning-resources/writing-center/online-guide-to-writing/tutorial/chapter3/ch3-11.html

Visher, Christy A. (1983). Gender, police arrest decisions, and notions of chivalry. *Criminology, 21*(1), 5–28.

Wilson, David B., Mitchell, Ojmarrh, & MacKenzie, Doris L. (2006). A systematic review of drug court effects on recidivism. *Journal of Experimental Criminology, 2*(4), 459–487.

Principle 4: Logic

BOX 5.1 **Learning Objectives**

After reading this chapter, you will be able to
1. Recognize terminology relevant to logical communications.
2. Argue for the importance of logic in criminal justice communications.
3. Diagram arguments.
4. Detect logical fallacies.
5. Distinguish between conclusions based on adequate and inadequate reasoning.
6. Construct logical policy analyses and policy proposals.
7. Develop logical presentence investigation reports.

Fear is a disease that eats away at logic and makes man inhuman.

—MARIAN ANDERSON

In the morning of January 21, 1998, 12-year-old Stephanie Crowe's murdered body was found on the floor of her bedroom in Escondido, California. The night before, police had received several calls from the Crowe's neighbors reporting that an unknown man had been wandering through the neighborhood and looking in windows. The man, Richard Tuite, was a diagnosed schizophrenic with a criminal record. He was questioned for 20 minutes before being released on January 21—despite having cuts and scrapes on his body, blood on his clothing, and some items from the Crowe's home on his person (Phillips, 2013). All of these circumstances point to Tuite as the most logical primary suspect.

But the police did not arrest Tuite. They did not even seriously consider Tuite. Instead, they found no signs of forced entry at the Crowe residence; Stephanie's 14-year-old brother Michael was perceived to be acting "distant and preoccupied" after his sister's body was found, and Michael had a reputation for being fascinated with death (Phillips, 2013; Sauer, 2012). Police also know the statistic that most children are killed by people close to them. And so, without further ado, the police zeroed in on Michael and two of his friends.

After a coerced quasi-confession, Michael was charged with his sister's murder and then was detained for 6 months awaiting trial. As the trial drew near, the blood on Tuite's previously confiscated clothing finally was tested and proved to be a match with Stephanie (Phillips, 2013). Charges against Michael and his friends were dismissed soon thereafter, but it took 4 years before Tuite was brought to trial (only to have his conviction overturned years later) and another 14 years before the San Diego Superior Court declared Michael and his friends to be factually innocent of Stephanie's murder (Phillips, 2013; Sauer, 2014).

Michael's wrongful arrest and pretrial detection were at least partly the product of flawed logic. As examined here in the context of producing successful criminal justice communications, **logic** is the reasoning process used to justify claims and reach conclusions. A conclusion is logical when it is supported by adequate reasoning.

It was a bad decision to focus so exclusively on Michael so early in the case. It was another bad decision to eliminate Tuite as a suspect so quickly, given the neighbors' reports and bloody clothes. And—like a snowball rolling down a hill, gaining speed and size—early bad decisions lead to even more bad decisions later on, until ultimately three innocent teenagers were behind bars while the killer remained at large.

Logic, then, can serve as a coat of armor, shielding us from making poor decisions and taking ill-advised action. To be just and fair, effective and efficient, those involved in criminal justice system policy and practice—and the scholarly study of it—must make a firm commitment to logical and evidence-based decisions and actions. We need to ensure that our criminal justice communications are consistently governed by logic and evidence—not by our feelings and habits. And we need to recognize that the people with whom we are communicating often are being influenced by emotions and instincts—not by logic and evidence.

This chapter is about how to be a logical criminal justice communicator. It presents five guidelines for consistently producing logical communications and two types of writings that illustrate the role and importance of logic in academic and professional criminal justice communications. After reading this chapter, you should have a solid understanding of how logic does—and often does not—work in criminal justice communications.

GUIDELINES

To be a logical criminal justice communicator, follow these guidelines:

1. Be a habitual critical thinker.
2. Be informed.
3. Avoid logical fallacies.
4. Diagram arguments.
5. Advance defensible claims.

Be a Habitual Critical Thinker

This first guideline is about making critical thinking a part of our daily lives. **Critical thinking** involves conscious reflection, wherein we base beliefs on a fair and logical assessment of available information. Think of critical thinking as a muscle: The more we use it, the stronger it becomes. However, the less we use it, the weaker and harder it is to use it—the less effective it will be when we need it.

To be a habitual critical thinker, we need to be self-aware, open-minded and objective, and actively skeptical. And we need to do these things constantly—not just when we are writing a paper, but whenever we are thinking, talking, listening, or reading about crime, criminals, and the criminal justice system. Figure 5.1 illustrates the centrality of logic in all aspects of communication.

Self-Awareness

Self-awareness refers to conscious reflection on what we think, feel, want, and do. When we are self-aware, we are more in tune to our own decision-making process. We recognize more situations as choices rather than as givens. And when we recognize a choice situation, we tend to pay more attention and devote more resources to making a good—that is, logical—decision. We might play the role of devil's advocate with ourselves, for instance, questioning why we reached the conclusion we reached or if there is a better explanation for what we have seen. Self-awareness thus helps us detect and correct flaws in our own thinking and actions.

Self-awareness also means that we are more likely to recognize a conflict of interest, or to notice when our personal biases are beginning to interfere with the exercise of our professional duties. Paying close attention to ourselves might expose favoritism, such as when we treat similar cases differently or critique an opposing viewpoint more harshly than our own viewpoint. It might also reveal that we do not actually have a reason to believe what we believe, or that we can identify as many reasons against as for the stance we hold on a controversial issue.

When we are self-aware, we can separate what we feel or want from what we should do. This is a matter not just of being logical but often also of being an ethical professional. Here are some strategies for prioritizing logic and evidence over more personal influences:

- Constantly stop and reflect on whether you have any personal feelings, experiences, expectations, or interests that are relevant to the task at hand.
- Distinguish between personal concerns and professional concerns, and make a conscious effort to prevent the former from intruding on your professional performance.
- Try not to act when you are emotional or otherwise not in full control of your senses. Whenever possible, hold off on speaking or taking action until you have calmed down and can focus properly on logic and evidence.
- Be open, honest, and explicit about your decision-making process, such as by mapping (or diagramming) out your argument to identify all parts of the reasoning and how they lead to your conclusion.

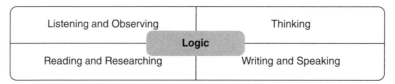

FIGURE 5.1   Centrality of Logic

Open-Mindedness and Objectivity

Open-mindedness and objectivity can help us guard against tunnel vision, such as we saw in the case at the beginning of this chapter with the false arrest of Michael Crowe. This is because one aspect of being open-minded and objective is to consider alternative perspectives and options. For most topics and situations, there are multiple interpretations, values and goals, and ways of doing things. Considering alternatives can help us determine the best conclusion as well as yield a more well-rounded communication. Whether we are advancing our own argument or listening to someone else's argument, we are more likely to make good decisions when we identify and rule out alternatives.

Another aspect of being open-minded and objective is to be balanced and fair when considering alternatives. For both sides of a controversial issue, we need to consider the pros and the cons. We should be equally critical of all options and positions. If we accept that our goal is to reach the best possible decisions, then we want to make sure we have considered all of our options and that we have used a fair and rigorous process to weigh our options.

Skepticism

Not all information deserves to be trusted. People sometimes make mistakes, and so information could be mistaken (unintentionally untrue). Other times, people want to deceive, and so information might be fabricated or misrepresented (intentionally untrue). Intentional or not, as rational actors, untrue information is bad information, and we want to avoid bad information. We do not want to believe, repeat, or be swayed by that which is false. Accordingly, it becomes necessary for us to be on the active lookout for bad information. That is, we need to assume the role of active skeptic.

Being an active skeptic means that we pay close attention, doubt information, and question claims. To be **skeptical** is thus to doubt rather than to believe automatically. Our default response to new information should be to question rather than accept it.

Being skeptical acts as a check on bad information: It filters out bad information that is trying to come into our heads, and it filters out bad information that is trying to leave our heads in our written or spoken words. Just like a filter, however, some information— the good information—needs to get through. Thus, we cannot infinitely question each piece of information, never reaching conclusions or taking action. Asking questions such as the following can help us maintain a healthy amount of skepticism:

- How could someone know that? What information would someone need to reach that conclusion?
- Why do I think this? What is the basis for this belief?
- Why is this person taking that position? What might be influencing this person's thinking on this topic?
- How might that information be flawed? What are the common, or typical, limitations of this type of data or data on this topic?
- Is this claim consistent with other related claims? Do other things I know corroborate or contradict this claim?

Be Informed

As discussed here, being informed is a matter of **competence**. Professionals are competent. They have the substantive knowledge and the technical skills necessary to do well that which needs to be done. Competence relates to logical criminal justice communication in two ways. First, there is the matter of substantive knowledge. Compelling criminal justice communicators know what they are talking about. Second, there is the matter of procedural knowledge. They know how to reason properly to reach and justify decisions; they know how logic and argumentation work.

Subject Matter

If you are not already knowledgeable on the subject matter about which you will be communicating, then make yourself an expert on it. If we have an upcoming presentation on a new contraband problem in our jail, then we need to keep ourselves aware of all news and developments relating to that contraband problem. Knowing and staying current with the topic can involve researching and investigating, attending meetings, taking notes, and asking questions.

Familiarity with a topic means we know what the alternative perspectives are, what claims are commonly made, what evidence is typically offered, what obstacles are frequently encountered, and where the most disagreement occurs. If we know the topic well, furthermore, then we can distinguish between "facts" that need no proof and claims that require substantiation. We can better anticipate what questions and criticisms others might have and can be proactive in addressing such concerns.

Argumentation

As logical communicators, we have a reasonable basis for what we believe, say, and do. We gather evidence and give reasons to support a conclusion, thereby creating an argument. An **argument** is a fusion of claims, evidence, and inference used to reach a conclusion.

ARGUMENT COMPONENTS. Figure 5.2 shows the basic parts of any argument. As used in Figure 5.2, *basis* is a broad term for all those parts of the argument that are offered as direct or indirect support for the conclusion. These parts of the basis can take on two forms: premise and evidence. First, a **premise** (P) is a claim that is offered to support some other claim, where a **claim** is a contention—an arguable assertion of fact (i.e., this is the case), value (i.e., this is better than that), or policy (i.e., this is what we should do). Second, **evidence** (E) is proof. Evidence is used to justify claims. Table 5.1 distinguishes further between these two forms of basis.

A **conclusion** (C) is a claim for which support is offered. Thus, claims can be distinguished in terms of the role they assume in a given argument: as premise or as conclusion. A claim can be a premise in one argument but the conclusion of another argument, and so we have to understand the context to determine which role a claim is assuming. In Table 5.1, the premise examples distinguish between conclusions and premises.

FIGURE 5.2   What Makes an Argument

TABLE 5.1   Premises and Evidence

	Premise	Evidence
Definition	A claim offered in support of some other claim	Something offered as proof of some claim
Examples	1. To support a motion to suppress evidence (C):	1. To support the claim that a search was illegal (C):
	P_1: Illegally obtained evidence is inadmissible at trial.	E_1: A search warrant with the wrong address or time
	P_2: The search in question was illegal.	E_2: Eyewitness testimony that the search went beyond the scope of the warrant
	2. To support an argument against capital punishment (C):	2. To support the claim that capital punishment does not deter crime (C):
	P_1: It is too expensive.	E: Statistical evidence that states with the death penalty have as many homicides as states without the death penalty
	P_2: It does not deter crime.	

Looking back to Figure 5.1, there is one more piece we have not covered: the inference. An **inference** (I) is the logical connection between the different pieces of an argument. It is the reasoning we do to get from one piece of the argument to the next piece. Inferring one thing from another happens in our head, though we need to be able to articulate it so that people can follow along with our argument. Together with the basis, the inference constitutes the rationale (or justification) for the conclusion. These inferences are our primary concern in this chapter, as they embody the logical component of argumentation.

REASONING STYLES. Table 5.2 presents two reasoning styles. **Deductive logic** involves reasoning from general principles (premises) to a more specific conclusion, while **inductive logic** involves reasoning from specific observations (evidence) to a more general conclusion. In other words, the basis in a deductive argument is one or more claim, while the basis in an inductive argument is one or more piece of evidence.

Deductive Logic. The deductive argument in Table 5.2 works like this: We know P_1 and we know P_2, and so we also know C. C is the logical product of P_1 and P_2. C could only have been true or false; there is no middle ground. On the basis of P_1 and P_2, C is true. Valid deductive logic leads to a conclusion that is true given the premise(s).

Thus, to ensure we are using deductive logic properly, we (1) suppose our premise(s) are true and (2) ask if the conclusion is guaranteed by the premise(s). If no, then our logic is bad and does not support the conclusion. If yes, then our logic is good and renders our conclusion a certainty. Table 5.3 distinguishes between valid and invalid deductive conclusions.

To help determine if your deductive reasoning is valid, you can use these questions as tests:

1. **Is the conclusion compatible with the premises?** How is C related to the premise? Is it reasonable to believe C in light of the premises? Or are the conclusion and premise mutually exclusive, logically incompatible ideas or conditions?

TABLE 5.2   Deductive Versus Inductive Logic

Deductive Logic	Inductive Logic
P_1: It is illegal to drive under the influence of alcohol.	E_1: Tina was in the driver's seat when the police pulled her over.
P_2: A blood alcohol level (BAL) above .08 indicates intoxication.	E_2: Tina's car had been swerving all over the road at 2:30 a.m.
C: Thus, it is illegal to drive with a BAL above .08.	C: Thus, Tina was probably drinking and driving.

TABLE 5.3   Valid and Invalid Deductive Reasoning

Argument 1	Argument 2
P_1: Criminals are people who have been convicted of a crime.	P_1: Criminals are people who have been convicted of a crime.
P_2: Larry is a criminal.	P_2: Larry is a criminal.
C: Larry has been convicted of a crime.	C: Larry committed a crime.

2. **Is the conclusion fully accountable by the premises?** Do the premises fully explain, or account for, the conclusion? Or does some other information or condition need to be established to render C?

3. **Are there zero exceptions to the conclusion?** Or can we think of even one possible instance where the premises could be true but the conclusion be false?

4. **Are we completely convinced of the conclusion, given the basis?** Or do we have even a shred of doubt about the truth of C, given the truth of the premises?

5. **Does accepting the premise(s) as true force us—for the sake of logical consistency—to accept the conclusion as true?** Would it be irrational for us to believe the premises but not to believe the conclusion?

Affirmative answers to these questions indicate that the deductive logic is valid. Our argument is unsound if it is not deductively valid, and our argument is sound if it is deductively valid and if the premises are accepted as true. An unsound deductive argument is "worthless" (Phelan & Reynolds, 1996) and therefore should play no role in effective criminal justice communication.

Inductive Logic. In Table 5.2, the inductive argument works differently than the deductive argument: We start by knowing nothing—not E_1, E_2, or C. But we need to make a decision about C. And so we collect evidence (E_1 and E_2), and then use that evidence to arrive at the most convincing conclusion possible (C). We are not aiming to be 100 percent convinced of C because evidence does not carry with it the same degree of certainty as the principles that serve as our basis in deductive logic. So, instead of being certain, we need to be sufficiently convinced of inductive conclusions.

To make sure we are using proper inductive logic, we (1) set aside any questions about the credibility of the evidence itself for the time being, and then (2) ask if the evidence renders the conclusion probable. If no, then our logic is bad, and our rationale is inadequate to support the conclusion. If yes, then our logic is good, and our conclusion is adequately justified.

Strong inductive logic leads to conclusions that are sufficiently convincing based on the evidence. Where a deductive inference is either valid or invalid, inductive inferences are of varying degrees of strength. The stronger the connection between the proof and the claim, the stronger the inference.

To explore this point further, Table 5.4 distinguishes between more and less convincing inductive conclusions. Argument 1 is the weakest because E is irrelevant to C. Argument 3 is the strongest, because E has a very tight logical connection with C. Argument 2 is between Argument 1 and 3. In it, E has a logical connection with C, but that logical connection is a bit loose. The looser the connection, the less weight the evidence has in establishing the claim.

TABLE 5.4   Varying Strength of Inductive Inferences

Argument 1	Argument 2	Argument 3
E: Lisa's neighbor's birth certificate says his middle name is Elmo. C: Therefore, it was Lisa's neighbor who stole her car.	E: Lisa's brother said her neighbor told him he was going to steal her car. C: Therefore, it was Lisa's neighbor who stole her car.	E: Lisa's brother saw her neighbor take her car. C: Therefore, it was Lisa's neighbor who stole her car.

The following questions can help you check the strength of your inductive logic:

1. **Is the conclusion compatible with the evidence?** How is C related to the evidence? Is it at all reasonable to believe C in light of the evidence? Or are the conclusion and evidence mutually exclusive, logically incompatible ideas or conditions?
2. **Does the evidence render the conclusion more likely than the conclusion would be without the evidence?** Does the evidence sway us one way or the other? Does the evidence reduce our uncertainty, to some extent, about C? Or are we equally confident (or unconfident) about the claim, with and without the evidence?
3. **Is this conclusion more plausible than alternative conclusions based on the same evidence?** Have you considered alternative explanations? Which explanation is the best fit for the evidence?
4. **Are we sufficiently convinced of the conclusion, given the evidence?** In light of the evidence, are we reasonably confident of C? Or do we have nontrivial doubts about C?

Answering these questions affirmatively tells us that our inductive logic is valid.

Naturally, whether or not evidence is trustworthy also affects the probability of the conclusion being true, but this is a question not of logic but of proof, to which we turn in Chapter 6. Chapter 6 will also take up the question of how much proof is needed to make us sufficiently convinced. For now, please take from this discussion the importance of knowing which reasoning style we are using and then of using that reasoning style properly.

ARGUMENT STRUCTURE. Arguments differ in terms of how many parts are in the rationale and how those parts fit together. Figure 5.3 shows how arguments can vary in simplicity/complexity in terms of number of parts.

Notice how what began as its own argument in Panel A has become an argument within an argument in Panel C: Panel A's conclusion has become one of Panel C's premises (i.e., P_1). To distinguish them from the one main argument, we can call such arguments *interior arguments*. The one main argument then can be called the *ultimate argument*, while its conclusion is called the **resolution**. An ultimate argument can contain any number of interior arguments, but it can have only one resolution. The resolution is the heart of the argument; it is the claim that must be resolved to end the argument.

Avoid Logical Fallacies

A **logical fallacy** is an error in reasoning. This term refers to any number of situations wherein an argument's conclusion is not really justified by the premise(s) and/or evidence. Logical fallacies can be hard to spot because they often seem logical when we first

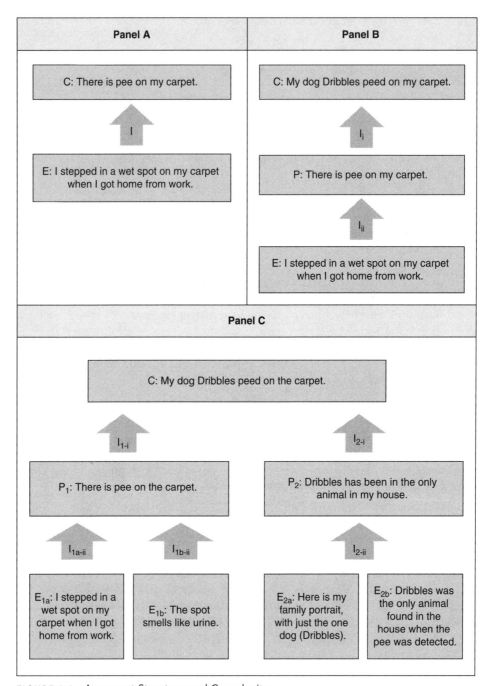

FIGURE 5.3   Argument Structure and Complexity

BOX 5.2	Credibility Connection

Attacking our opponents and exploiting fear and emotions are unethical and can be dangerous. Criminal justice communicators need to consciously avoid intentionally or unintentionally engaging in logical fallacies.

hear them. But numerous logical fallacies can be found in popular, academic, and even professional discourse on crime, criminals, and the criminal justice system.

Fallacies of Inconsistency

Fallacies of inconsistency occur when we hold and/or express beliefs that contradict each other. These fallacies are a form of **logical paradox** because it is impossible for two beliefs that are logically incompatible to both be true. For example, it makes no sense and therefore is irrational to believe both that the person is Tom and the person is not Tom. It also makes no sense to insist that everyone should obey the law but that it is okay for us not to. Table 5.5 shows two forms that a logical paradox can take.

Fallacies of Irrelevance

Fallacies of irrelevance occur when we justify a conclusion in terms of unrelated reasoning. For example, suppose I say that I know my son came home late last night (C) because there was a rerun of *Golden Girls* on this morning (E). In this example, there is no logical connection between E and C; hence, E does not really support C. A rerun of *Golden Girls* is not proof that my son was out late. In contrast, it is logical to believe my son came home late last night because his car still was not in the driveway when I checked at midnight. His car not being there earlier is proof that my son was out late. Table 5.6 presents various forms in which such fallacies of irrelevance can take shape.

Fallacies of Vacuity

Setting fallacies of vacuity apart from the other logical fallacies is their common feature of a lack of information. These are reasoning errors that revolve around some information gap or deficiency on the topic, which results in a conclusion devoid of any real justification. Sometimes, people mistakenly believe that lack of evidence can tell us something. Others exploit evidence holes, treating it as evidence itself. Regardless, with fallacies of vacuity, the conclusion is improperly based on an absence rather than a presence of information. Table 5.7 distinguishes between several ways that fallacies of vacuity can occur.

TABLE 5.5   Fallacies of Inconsistency

Name of Fallacy	Description of Fallacy
Contradictory assumption	Making an assumption that contradicts a previous claim or assumption
Contradictory premise	Making a claim that contradicts a previous claim or assumption

Sources: LaBossiere (2010); Wheeler (2018); Zarefsky (2005)

TABLE 5.6   Fallacies of Irrelevance

Name of Fallacy	Description of Fallacy
Appeal to emotion	Exploiting emotions such as fear and outrage to convince an audience to accept a conclusion
Appeal to force	Coercing the audience to accept a conclusion by threatening force or some other unpleasant consequence
Appeal to improper authority	Arguing that, because the authority says so, it is true—even though the authority has no expertise on the subject
Appeal to tradition	Claiming that, because it is what we have always done, it must be the right thing to do
Argument from adverse consequences	Basing acceptance of a conclusion on whether doing so is beneficial to us rather than on whether it is supported by adequate reasoning
Bandwagon approach	Claiming that, because everybody else is doing it, it must be a good thing to do
Ignoring the question	Shifting the argument from its conclusion and justification by introducing unrelated ideas
Irrelevant conclusion	Providing justification for one conclusion but then advancing a different conclusion
Personal attack	Criticizing the advocate of an argument instead of the argument itself

Sources: LaBossiere (2010); Wheeler (2018); Zarefsky (2005)

TABLE 5.7   Fallacies of Vacuity

Name of Fallacy	Description of Fallacy
Appeal to a lack of evidence	Treating a lack of available evidence to support some claim as proof that the claim is false; arguing that something must be false because there is no evidence to support its truth
Argument from personal incredulity	Arguing that because you cannot understand something, it cannot be true
Argument from the negative	Contending that because an alternative position on an issue is not adequately justified, our position is adequately justified
Begging the question	Making a claim where that claim requires the establishment of other conditions—and those other conditions are not addressed
Circular reasoning	Offering justification that is merely a restatement of the conclusion
Complex question	Asking a question that presupposes some other, as-yet-unestablished, condition; also called a loaded question
Self-sealing argument	Advancing an argument that is so broad and ill-defined that it cannot be refuted

Sources: LaBossiere (2010); Wheeler (2018); Zarefsky (2005)

Fallacies of Distortion

Distortion means misrepresentation and, in keeping with other logical fallacies, can occur either intentionally or unintentionally. When we intentionally distort aspects of our argument, we are trying to rig the argument—making the argument look like it has a stronger justification than it does. Table 5.8 distinguishes between common fallacies involving distortion.

Fallacies of Mistaken Relationship

The last category of logical fallacies covered here center on a mistaken belief in how two or more conditions are related to each other. Two of these fallacies, for instance, involve false causes: *non causa pro causa* and *post hoc ergo propter hoc*. Like when a suspect is falsely

TABLE 5.8   Fallacies of Distortion

Name of Fallacy	Description of Fallacy
Cherry picking	Basing a conclusion only on evidence that supports your conclusion, while ignoring contradictory evidence; also called stacking the deck
Faulty analogy	Making a point about one thing on the basis of that thing's similarity with another thing, even though the items being compared are dissimilar in relevant regards
False dilemma	Treating an issue as though there are only two possible outcomes; also called the either/or fallacy
Hasty generalization	Reaching a conclusion on the basis of too few cases
Straw man	Exaggerating or oversimplifying the opposing argument to make it easier to attack; also called a red herring or smoke screen

Sources: LaBossiere (2010); Wheeler (2018); Zarefsky (2005)

TABLE 5.9   Fallacies of Mistaken Relationship

Name of Fallacy	Description of Fallacy
Composition	Assuming that what is true of the parts also must be true for the whole
Division	Assuming that what is true of the whole must also be true for the parts
Hypothesis contrary to fact	Asserting that if one hypothetical condition were to exist, then some consequence would or would not follow
Non causa pro causa	Identifying a false cause for some condition; erroneously saying that one thing caused some other thing to happen
Post hoc ergo propter hoc	Assuming that because one condition happened earlier, it must be the cause of another condition that happened later
Slippery slope	Arguing that taking one step in a direction will necessarily lead to taking more steps in that same direction

Sources: LaBossiere (2010); Wheeler (2018); Zarefsky (2005)

accused of causing a victim's murder, these false cause fallacies involve implicating something as a cause that really is not a cause. Table 5.9 presents several fallacies involving a mistaken relationship.

Diagram Arguments

Graphically delineating the parts of an argument and how they relate to each other helps us understand arguments as well as expose logical fallacies and other weaknesses, such as evidence deficiencies.

Creating the Diagram

Imagine there is a law against eating in public: Public eating is a felony. You are the prosecutor, and it is your job to secure the conviction of Defendant X for breaking this law. To persuade the jury to convict Defendant X, you as the prosecutor need to establish three conditions:

1. P_1: The act in question is eating.
2. P_2: The act in question was observed in a public place.
3. P_3: The act in question was committed by Defendant X.

These conditions are the premises. Having identified our conclusion and the premises, we are ready to start diagramming. Figure 5.4 shows how the beginning of our diagram would look like with just the claims.

Now, we need to consider how the premises lead to the conclusion. Are they all necessary to produce the conclusion, or are only some necessary? If the premises are satisfied, is the conclusion guaranteed? First, the conclusion depends on all three of them, which we denote with a plus sign between the premises. Second, were P_1 and P_2 to be established, C would be certain. C would not just be possible or even probable. We can show this in our diagram by adding a single, solid arrow leading from the premises to the conclusion. Figure 5.5 illustrates these logical connections.

Now that we know what we need to prove, we are ready to gather our evidence and then infuse it into our diagram. Ultimately, we will need sufficient evidence to establish each of the three premises. Figure 5.6 shows how this argument might look with evidence.

The last step is to add in the inferences leading from evidence to premise. For each piece of evidence, add an arrow pointing to the premise for which the proof is being offered. This is true even when there are multiple pieces of evidence supporting the same premise: Each one requires its own inference. Figure 5.7 shows the diagram with these inferences added.

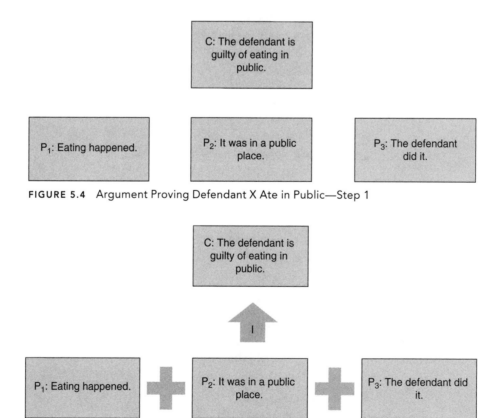

FIGURE 5.4   Argument Proving Defendant X Ate in Public—Step 1

FIGURE 5.5   Argument Proving Defendant X Ate in Public—Step 2

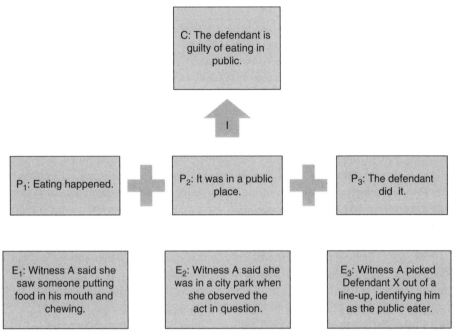

FIGURE 5.6 Argument Proving Defendant X Ate in Public—Step 3

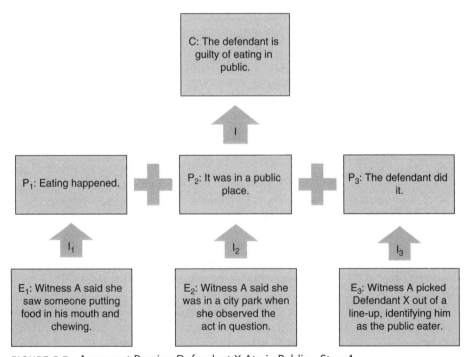

FIGURE 5.7 Argument Proving Defendant X Ate in Public—Step 4

In Figure 5.7, notice how the inference connecting E_1 to P_1 is labeled I_1, while the inference connecting E_2 to P_2 is I_2, and the inference connecting E_3 to P_3 is labeled I_3. These numbers indicate separate lines of reasoning. E_1 supports P_1 but not P_2 or P_3. Invalidating E_1 therefore is an attack on P_1 but not on P_2 or P_3; the same goes for E_2 and E_3. Distinguishing between lines of reasoning can be useful when it comes to evaluating and attacking arguments.

We can use the same basic technique to diagram just about any other argument. Next, consider an argument where the conclusion does not necessitate accepting all the premises. Suppose, for instance, our assignment is to debate a classmate about whether or not outlawing assault weapons will reduce school shootings. We are assigned the position that the United States needs to outlaw assault weapons to reduce school shootings (C). After some reading and critical thinking, we are able to identify three reasons: Assault weapons are more lethal than other guns (P_1), outlawing assault weapons reduces school shootings (P_2), and an assault weapon ban would mean that would-be shooters would not be able to get an assault weapon (P_3).

Now, we consider how the premises are connected to each other and to the conclusion. First, we do *not* need to establish all three of them to make an adequate case for C. The more premises we can establish, all else equal, the stronger the argument will be. But establishing all three premises is not essential for accepting C. Thus, we do not need to add a plus sign between premises. Second, accepting P_1, P_2, and P_3 does *not* force us to accept C. Accepting the premises makes C likely but does not guarantee the truth of C. To reflect that we are talking about probability rather than certainty, we will use hollow rather than solid arrows. And to reflect that each premise has its own, independent logical connection to C, we place a hollow arrow between each premise and the conclusion.

Next, we would look for evidence to support the premises. Regarding P_1, Chivers, Buchanan, Lu, and Yourish (2018) reported that assault weapons allow shooters to fire more rounds per second than civilian weapons (E_1). For P_2, Guis's (2017) research documented how school shootings increased when the federal assault weapons ban expired (E_2). Having added our evidence, our last step is to insert inference arrows for each piece of evidence, connecting it to the claim for which it is offered as proof. Figure 5.8 shows how this argument can be diagrammed.

Correcting the Diagram

To resolve an argument, it is not enough to map out those pieces that have been explicitly stated as part of the rationale. Instead, we need to go two steps further:

1. Is anything relevant and absent? If so, then we need to add it.
2. Is anything irrelevant and present? If so, then we need to cross it out.

RELEVANT BUT ABSENT ELEMENTS. Looking at an argument map can make it clear when our rationale is insufficient. In Figure 5.7, for example, our diagram reveals that we have no evidence to support P_3. Therefore, we either need to locate evidence or drop P_3 from our argument.

Looking at our diagram, we should also ask if anything else would need to be true (or probably true) for us to accept the conclusion. Here, a major concern is with unstated **assumptions**, which are beliefs taken to be true that can influence the argument. Therefore, the problem is that they are not only unstated but also relevant. Consider Figure 5.8 once more. The persuasiveness of C hinges on another, as-yet-specified condition: that

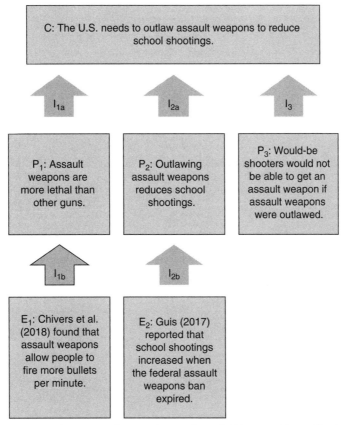

FIGURE 5.8 Argument Supporting an Assault Weapons Ban—Version 1

assault weapons are used in a lot of school shootings (P_A). After all, if assault weapons are not used in school shootings, then outlawing them would make no more sense than outlawing extension cords if our goal is to reduce school shootings. Taking P_A into account, Figure 5.9 shows a more fully specified, or fleshed-out, version of the argument shown in Figure 5.8.

IRRELEVANT BUT PRESENT ELEMENTS. Having added relevant but absent elements, we can use our diagram to purge the argument of any superfluous parts (i.e., irrelevant but present elements). One way to do this is to look for logical fallacies. When we find a logical fallacy, we place a big "X" over it and everything below and connected to it, thus ending that fallacious line of reasoning. When a line of reasoning is ended, it cannot legitimately serve as part of the rationale for C.

Figures 5.10 and 5.11 show an argument with an either/or fallacy as the fourth premise (P_4): Either people are for outlawing assault weapons, or they want children to die. Figure 5.11 shows how we can add a big "X" to indicate that the line of reasoning beginning with I_4 and continuing to P_4 is fallacious.

Advance Defensible Claims

To be compelling is to be convincing. To convince others, we need to make sure that the claims we make are adequately justified as well as resistant to attack. Let us begin this

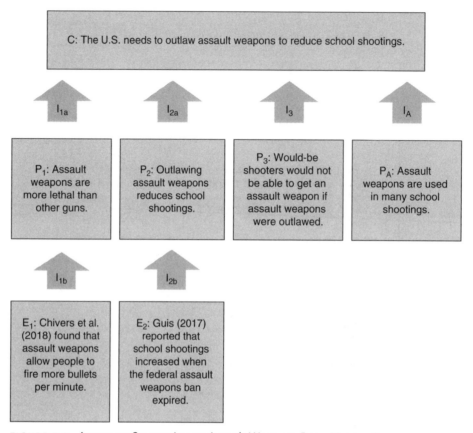

FIGURE 5.9   Argument Supporting an Assault Weapons Ban—Version 2

discussion with a quick glimpse at how arguments are attacked and then move into some specific strategies for making our arguments as impervious to attack as possible.

Fortifying Arguments

Argument attack and defense does not necessarily happen in the same room, in a formal debate setting. We might make a statement, and days later that statement might be applauded or criticized. Argument attack and defense also need not be competitive or aggressive. Instead, it can involve questions from colleagues that—while polite— undermine our argument. Any time we advance a claim, we need to be prepared for it to be challenged in some way. If we can anticipate how our argument might be challenged, then we might be able to take steps to fortify our argument, thereby advancing a stronger, more defensible, and ultimately more productive conclusion.

The key is to stay focused on the argument itself, systematically assessing its parts and their interconnections. As you do so, keep the following argumentation rules in mind:

1. Attacks are launched against the rationale—not the conclusion itself. Just like we build an argument by fusing inferences, premises, and evidence, we dismantle an argument by chipping away at the inferences, premises, and evidence.

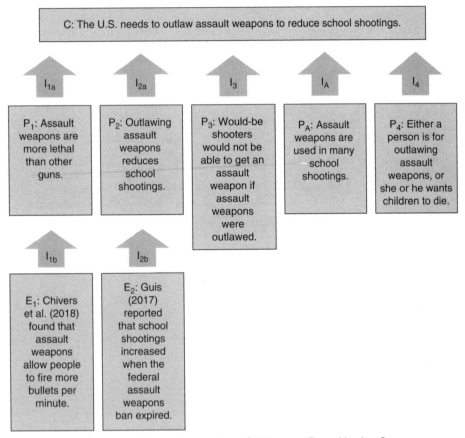

FIGURE 5.10   Argument Supporting an Assault Weapons Ban—Version 3

2. Inferences can be challenged, which means we question or do not automatically accept the reasoning. We can contest the connection between premise and conclusion or between evidence and claim.

3. Premises can be challenged, which means we doubt or do not automatically accept them as true or as agreed-upon facts. We can contest whether a rule, law, or other "fact" has been properly established as such and interpreted in the present case.

4. Evidence can be challenged, which means we question its credibility or do not accept it as trustworthy. We can contest the authenticity, honesty, integrity, and so on of a piece of evidence.

5. Concessions should be made when an inference, premise, or piece of evidence is challenged and cannot be justified. We should not be contentious except insofar as needed to resolve the argument in favor of the most logical and evidence-based conclusion.

6. Once challenged, inferences, premises, and evidence require concession or justification. Agreement on the conclusion usually cannot be reached while disagreement remains over challenged parts of the rationale.

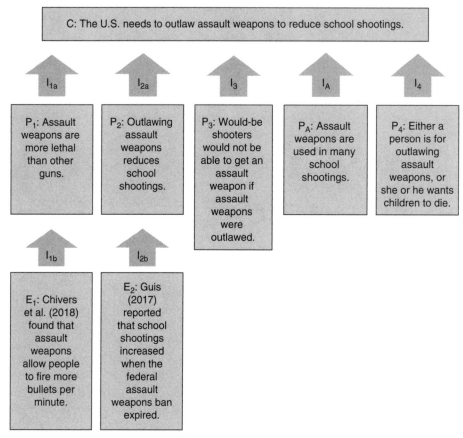

FIGURE 5.11   Argument Supporting an Assault Weapons Ban—Version 4

Given these rules, a fortified argument becomes one where each part and each connection can be convincingly established. A conclusion needs a basis, and premises that are not things that "everybody knows" need evidence. And all of these components need to logically relate to one another.

Stating Conclusions

So, we first need to have a reason for what we believe and do. Second, that reasoning should be solid. Third, having arrived at a justified conclusion, it becomes necessary to state that conclusion in a manner that preserves its logic. Poor word choice can alter meaning, thereby making an otherwise strong argument look illogical. Of primary concern here is for our conclusion to be phrased and to be proportionate to our rationale. That is, we should neither overstate a probable conclusion nor understate a certain conclusion.

UNDERSTATING CERTAIN CONCLUSIONS. Understatements occur when the conclusion is weaker than is warranted given the rationale. Sometimes, we deliberately understate to be delicate, or to avoid committing to a definite belief or position. Other times, we might not mean to understate our conclusions, and yet we do so anyway because we are rushing and not paying close enough attention to our word choice. Intentional or not, however, understated conclusions can weaken an otherwise strong argument, and they can distort and deceive. To avoid such understatements, try not to use phrases that imply uncertainty (e.g., "seems," "might be the case," "possibly," "could be") unless you really are uncertain.

OVERSTATING PROBABLE CONCLUSIONS. Whereas understatements dilute strong conclusions, overstatements oversell weak conclusions. We might want to push a certain conclusion, but yet lack a sufficiently convincing rationale for it. It can be tempting in this case to word the conclusion in a way that implies a stronger rationale than we have, but of course this is a temptation to which no criminal justice student or professional should succumb. There are a variety of strategies we can use to ensure that our conclusion does not overstate our rationale.

First, avoid phrases that imply certainty unless we are certain via valid deductive logic (e.g., "proves true," "shows XXX is a fact," "disproves the theory"). Similarly, take care with extreme language, such as "all," always, "every," "never," and "none." Words like these permit no wiggle room—no margin of error. A single exception—exceptional or no—can falsify an extreme conclusion. Unless you are 100 percent confident of your deductive logic, play it safe and avoid such terms. Along these lines, inductive conclusions are often couched in such cautionary language as "generally," "indicates," "suggests," "supports," and "contradicts."

Second, consider ways to improve the alignment between rationale and conclusion. Perhaps the conclusion goes too far beyond the evidence—so far that it is not quite convincing. If we interview five victims and then present our results as though they are facts about crime victims as a whole, then we have gone too far. In this case, we could rephrase the conclusion, toning it down until it appropriately reflects the evidence. For example, we could say that a small number of interviews suggest or are indicative of what might be a broader pattern experienced by other crime victims. Or we could collect additional evidence (e.g., interviews with more victims), until we reach the point where the evidence sufficiently substantiates our conclusion.

And third, acknowledge limitations in our arguments. Our ego cannot lead us to hide flaws in our arguments. Instead, be explicit about what you do know and what you do not know, as well as how that affects the level of confidence that should be placed in your conclusion. After all, withholding relevant information impedes the open and honest flow of accurate information that we as logical criminal justice communicators strive to accomplish.

APPLICATIONS

The rest of this chapter considers two criminal justice communications that involve the integration of logic and evidence to guide high-stakes decisions: (1) policy analyses and policy proposals and (2) presentence investigation reports.

Policy Analyses and Policy Proposals

A **policy analysis** is an applied research product that examines the effectiveness of some policy in achieving its stated goal(s), while a **policy proposal** is an applied research product that assesses some phenomenon and proposes a policy for addressing it. Thanks

---

BOX 5.3	Plagiarism Pointer

Properly attributing information to its source not only helps us avoid plagiarism but also can prevent an argument from getting too personal and allowing emotions to cloud judgment. Clearly and consistently noting that our claims are based on evidence collected and reported by others creates a buffer between us and our position on a controversial issue.

---

to the increasing emphasis on an evidence-based approach to criminal justice policy, these are common forms of writing and presentation assignments in upper-level college/university courses as well as in scholarly publications and funded research.

Policy Analyses

Because the purpose of a policy analysis is to determine whether a particular policy is effective in achieving its goal(s), the conclusion is a statement of whether or not the policy has been successful. The premises in a police analysis are therefore a series of reasons supporting the conclusion of effectiveness (or ineffectiveness).

Consider using the 5WH questions in two steps as a framework for understanding and describing the crime problem and policy, giving detailed responses to each question, as shown in Table 5.10. Step 1 is to answer these questions about the policy's goals and intentions from the outset, and Step 2 is to answer these questions about the policy's effects and outcomes after it has been implemented. As a rule of thumb, the greater the correspondence in your answers from Step 1 to Step 2, the more successful the policy is.

After using the two-step 5WH process outlined above, you are ready to assemble your report. Table 5.11 suggests a structure for organizing the main contents in a policy analysis.

Policy Proposals

Policy proposals have a lot in common with policy analyses, particularly the necessary logical nexus between a crime problem and crime policy. But the main purpose is different: to propose, or recommend, a policy to address a crime problem. Accordingly, the conclusion differs from that in a policy analysis. With a policy proposal, the conclusion

TABLE 5.10 Using the 5WH Questions in Policy Analysis

	Step 1 Intention/Goals	Step 2 Reality/Outcomes
What?	What problem(s) should the policy affect?	What problem(s) did the policy affect?
Who?	Who should the policy affect?	Who did the policy affect?
Where?	Where should the policy affect the problem?	Where did the policy affect (or not) the problem?
When?	When should the policy affect the problem?	When did the policy affect (or not) the problem?
Why?	Why should the policy affect the problem?	Why did the policy affect (or not) the problem?
How?	How should the policy be implemented and operated?	How was the policy implemented and operated?
	How should the policy affect the problem?	How did the policy affect the problem?
	How much should the policy affect the problem?	How much did the policy affect the problem?

TABLE 5.11   Outline of a Policy Analysis

Main Section	Contents
I. Introduction	*Required* • Introduce the topic • State the purpose of the policy analysis • Establish the significance of the policy • Provide a "road map" of the rest of the policy analysis
II. Policy Context	*Required* • Link the policy to the relevant crime problem • Define the crime problem • Describe the nature and extent of the crime problem *Optional* • Outline historical/comparative approaches to the crime problem • Discuss relevant social, economic, and political factors
III. Policy Description	*Required* • Answer the 5WH questions regarding policy intentions/goals (Step 1 from Table 5.10), drawing as appropriate from criminological theory and existing research *Optional* • Discuss factors relevant to the conceptualization and implementation of the policy
IV. Policy Evaluation	*Required* • Outline the methodology used to determine effectiveness, including data sources and focusing on how success was measured • Answer the 5WH questions regarding policy reality/outcomes (Step 2 from Table 5.10) • Specify whether and to what extent the policy was effective in terms of each of its intended goals
V. Discussion	*Required* • Summarize the policy context, description, and evaluation • Reinforce the main findings regarding the policy's effectiveness • Recommend how the findings should be used to in decisions about the policy *Optional* • Present any limitations to the evaluation of effectiveness • Identify any unintended effects of the policy • Discuss any broader implications of the policy analysis findings

is the claim that the policy being proposed is the best approach for reducing the crime problem. Hence, there is a stronger comparative element to a policy proposal than to a policy analysis because "best approach" implies a comparison between at least two policies that could potentially reduce the crime problem.

Presenting options and then recommending the most promising one is similar to the process and logic of ruling out alternatives in hypothesis testing and ruling out other suspects in a crime investigation. The path we eventually take will make more sense to our audience to the extent that we convince them that we seriously considered other possible paths but have chosen the single path that has the most logical and evidentiary support in terms of leading to our goal.

Table 5.12 presents a suggested outline for a policy proposal. Notice how, like the policy analysis, a major element in a policy proposal is the answering of the 5WH questions.

TABLE 5.12   Outline of a Policy Proposal

Main Section	Contents
I. Introduction	• Introduce the topic • State the purpose of the policy proposal • Establish the significance of the crime problem • Provide a "road map" of the rest of the policy proposal
II. Description of the Crime Problem	• What is the crime problem? • Who is involved in the crime problem (esp. offenders, victims)? • Where is the crime problem? • When is the crime problem? • How does the crime happen?
III. Explanation of the Crime Problem	• Why does the crime happen?
IV. Comparison of Policy Options	• What is/are the goals of a policy for reducing the crime problem? • What are the criteria for comparing policy options? • How do the possible policy options compare with regard to the criteria?
V. Policy Recommendation	• Which policy is the most promising based on the comparison? • How should the policy be implemented to maximize the potential for success? • How should the policy's effectiveness be evaluated?
VI. Discussion	• Summarize the key conclusions in the policy proposal, emphasizing the basis for the policy recommendation • Identify and qualifications/limitations to the recommended policy

To start this process, we need to identify different approaches to reducing the crime problem. Then, we need to identify relevant criteria by which to compare the identified possibilities. Drawing loosely from Rummens (2016), here is a list of items that could be used to compare and contrast crime-control policies:

1. **Goals:** What is/are the intended goal(s) of the policy?
2. **Crime mechanism:** By what process(es) is the policy supposed to reduce crime?
3. **Empirical research support:** Has the policy's effectiveness been evaluated; if so, does the evaluation research indicate that the policy is effective?
4. **Theoretical support:** Is the policy derived from or consistent with criminological theory; if so, which one(s)?
5. **Effect size:** How much of a crime decrease does the policy generate?
6. **Effect duration:** How long does the policy effect persist?
7. **Affected population:** For whom is the policy effective?
8. **Cost:** How much does the policy cost? What other resources are involved in the policy (e.g., training, personnel, equipment, technology)?
9. **Replicability:** Is adequate information provided in sufficient detail for the policy to be implemented?
10. **Evaluability:** Is the policy capable of being evaluated?
11. **Implementation/operation impediments:** What challenges/problems have others experienced when implementing the policy?
12. **Unintended consequences:** Has the policy had effects other than on the stated goals?

Best Practices

Despite multiple differences between policy analyses and policy proposals, the following list of best practices can be used to capture the most important considerations in preparing both types of policy papers:

1. **Expect modest crime reductions.** It is unreasonable to expect or promise complete crime eradication or problem elimination.
2. **Specify the program's goals clearly.** Try to determine goals in consultation with program stakeholders and by reviewing and citing programmatic literature. Do not assume you know the goal(s).
3. **Articulate the nexus between the crime problem and crime policy.** Specify how the policy is supposed to affect the goal. By what process should the program, for example, decrease crime?
4. **Identify objective criteria to guide the analysis ...**
    a. For determining success (in policy analyses and proposals); and/or
    b. For comparing policies (in proposals).
5. **Use the 5WH question framework to describe ...**
    a. The intended and actual crime policy (in analyses); or
    b. The crime problem (in proposals).
6. **Consider unintended consequences and implementation/operation deviations.** Keep in mind that policies can have multiple effects. Success in achieving its intended goal could be outweighed by (unintended) negative outcomes.
7. **Base conclusions on logic and evidence.** Ground the ultimate conclusion on evidence and logic rather than on intuition and ideology.

Presentence Investigation Reports

Ordered by a judge and completed by a probation officer, a **presentence investigation report** (PSI) is a written report of an investigation into a defendant's life that will assist the judge in making an informed sentencing decision. PSI requirements differ across states and the federal system. Here, we will focus on PSIs used in federal criminal proceedings, where PSIs have five functions:

1. To aid the court in determining the appropriate sentence;
2. To aid the probation officer in supervision efforts during probation and parole;
3. To assist the Federal Bureau of Prisons in classification, institutional programs, and release planning;
4. To furnish the U.S. Parole Commission with information pertinent to consideration of parole; and
5. To serve as a source of information for research (Administrative Office of the United States Courts Probation Division, 1984, p. 1).

Used to guide the appropriate sentencing of convicted defendants, the PSI has no role in police investigations or prosecutorial efforts to convict.

Contents and Organization

The Administrative Office of the United States Courts Probation Division (1984) sets forth instructions for the contents and organization of PSIs, as shown in Table 5.13.

TABLE 5.13   Outline of a Federal Presentence Investigation Report

Fact Sheet (Identifying Information)

(1)	Name
(2)	Date
(3)	Address
(4)	Legal Residence
(5)	Docket Number
(6)	Race
(7)	Citizenship
(8)	Age
(9)	Date of Birth
(10)	Place of Birth
(11)	Sex
(12)	Education
(13)	Marital Status
(14)	Dependents
(15)	Social Security Number
(16)	FBI Number
(17)	U.S. Marshal Number
(18)	Other Identifying Numbers
(19)	Offense(s)
(20)	Penalty
(21)	Custodial Status
(22)	Date of Arrest
(23)	Plea
(24)	Verdict
(25)	Detainers or Charges Pending
(26)	Other Defendants
(27)	Assistant U.S. Attorney
(28)	Defense Counsel
(29)	Disposition
(30)	Disposition Date
(31)	Sentencing Judge

Body of the Report (Core Information Categories)

(1)	Offense
	Prosecution's Version
	Victim Impact Statement
	Defendant's Version
	Codefendant Information
	Statement of Witnesses and Complainants
(2)	Prior Record
	Juvenile Adjudication

	Adult Record	
(3)	Personal and Family Data	
	Defendant	
	Parents and Siblings	
	Marital	
	Education	
	Employment	
	Health	
	Physical	
	Mental and Emotional	
	Military Service	
	Financial Condition	
	Assets	
	Liabilities	
(4)	Evaluation	
	Probation Officer's Assessment	
	Parole Guidelines Data	
	Sentencing Data	
	Special Sentencing Provisions	
(5)	Recommendation	
	Recommendation and Rationale	
	Voluntary Surrender	

Source: Administrative Office of the United States Courts Probation Division (1984, p. 6)

(For detailed information—including distinctions between required and non-required material—interested readers are encouraged to download and read pages 7–17 of the Administrative Office of the United States Courts Probation Division's [1984] *The Presentence Investigation Report*.)

Looking at Table 5.13, in the body of the PSI ("Body of the Report"), Sections 1, 2, and 3 present evidence; Section 4 provides the probation officer's assessment of the evidence; and Section 5 contains the sentencing recommendation and rationale for the sentencing recommendation. The conclusion in the PSI is the sentencing recommendation. Premises (i.e., reasons supporting the conclusion) are provided in the probation officer's assessment, while evidence is presented in the first half of the PSI. A strong PSI is both logical and evidence based. That is, the recommendation is logically based on the evidence and the probation officer's assessment of the evidence. A weak PSI, by way of contrast, recommends a sentence that is not logically connected to the evidence and/or to the probation officer's assessment of that evidence.

The probation officer's assessment should critically examine the evidence related to: (1) the offense, (2) the community, and (3) the defendant. Table 5.14 lists the relevant questions to be answered for each of these three areas. The answers to the questions in Table 5.14 should serve as the basis for the recommended sentence.

TABLE 5.14   Questions to Answer in the Probation Officer's Assessment

Offense	Community	Defendant
Is it situational in nature or indicative of persistent problems?	Does the defendant pose a direct threat to the safety and welfare of others?	What developmental factors were significant in contributing to the defendant's current behavior pattern?
Was violence threatened or used?	Would a disposition other than incarceration tend to depreciate the seriousness of the crime?	What is the history of antisocial behavior and when did it begin?
Was the defendant armed?	Is probation a sufficient deterrent?	Does the defendant acknowledge responsibility for the offense?
Was the offense against person or property?	Would the most benefit derive from working with the defendant in the community?	Is the defendant motivated to change his behavior?
What is the relative culpability of the defendant and codefendants?	What community resources are available?	What are his strengths or weaknesses?
What was the motive for the offense?		Is the defendant employable?
What was the amount of financial loss to an individual or the government?		Does he have a supportive family?
		What are the positive features that can affect supervision?
		Does he demonstrate remorse?

Source: Administrative Office of the United States Courts Probation Division (1984, p. 6)
Note: These questions are quoted directly from the source.

Best Practices

Drawing from the Administrative Office of the United States Courts Probation Division (1984), best practices for the construction of a PSI include the following:

1. **Differentiate clearly between information that "is factual, inferred or alleged"** (p. 3).
2. **Verify evidence whenever possible, and then distinguish between verified and unverified information.** Identify your sources (unless confidential).
3. **Interpret evidence; do not merely list evidence.** Your goal is to present pieces of evidence "in a manner which reveals their relevance to the problems of the defendant and the protection of the community" (p. 4).
4. **Ensure coherence between core categories.** The recommendation must logically derive from the assessment, while the assessment should be grounded in the evidence.
5. **Meet with the defendant at least twice during the investigation,** with at least one of these meetings occurring at the defendant's residence. In the residence, try to learn from your surroundings.
6. **Address discrepancies in information,** preferably by re-interviewing the source to reconcile the discrepancy. Note any discrepancy that cannot be reconciled.

7. **Focus on the present;** report information from the past "only to the extent they assist in understanding what motivates the defendant's behavior or aid in predicting what kinds of behavior may be anticipated in the future" (p. 4).
8. **Be concise:** "A simple, direct, lucid style is effective. The report need not be elaborate nor seek a dramatic effect" (p. 5). Summarize rather than merely repeating the indictment; avoid irrelevant and repetitive material; and use clear, concrete terms rather than abstract, vague terms. Omit specialized terms and jargon.
9. **Build rapport.** Use the investigation process as an opportunity to establish a positive relationship between supervisor and parolee.

EXERCISES
Matching
These exercises are designed to assess Chapter 5 Learning Objective 1 (see Box 5.1). Match each numbered statement to the lowercase letter corresponding to the key word it defines. Each key word will be used only once.

1. An error in reasoning
2. The characteristic of a person who doubts rather than automatically believes
3. Beliefs taken to be true that can influence the argument but often remain unstated
4. Reasoning from specific observations (evidence) to a more general conclusion
5. Substantive knowledge and technical skills necessary for doing well what needs to be done
6. Proof; that which is used to justify a claim
7. Conscious reflection that leads us to base beliefs on a fair and logical assessment of available information
8. An applied research product that assesses some phenomenon and proposes a policy for addressing it
9. Reasoning from general principles (premises) to a more specific conclusion
10. A claim offered to support some other claim
11. The fusion of claims, evidence, and inference used to reach a conclusion
12. An irrational situation involving contradictory, or logically incompatible, beliefs
13. An applied research product that examines the effectiveness of some policy in achieving its stated goal(s)
14. A claim for which support is offered
15. The reasoning process used to justify claims and reach conclusions; a conclusion is logical when it is supported by adequate reasoning
16. The one main conclusion that must be resolved to end the argument; the heart of the argument
17. A contention; an arguable assertion of fact (this is), value (this is better), or policy (this is what we should do)
18. The logical connection between the different pieces of an argument; the reasoning we do to get from one piece of the argument to the next piece

19. A written report of an investigation into a defendant's life that will assist the judge in making an informed sentencing decision

a. argument
b. assumptions
c. claim
d. competence
e. conclusion
f. critical thinking
g. deductive logic
h. evidence
i. inductive logic
j. inference

k. logic
l. logical fallacy
m. logical paradox
n. policy analysis
o. policy proposal
p. premise
q. presentence investigation report (PSI)
r. resolution
s. skeptical

Multiple Choice

These exercises are designed to assess Chapter 5 Learning Objectives 4 and 5 (see Box 5.1). Indicate the single most appropriate response to each item below.

1. "The guy down the street just got busted for distributing child pornography on the Internet. It wouldn't surprise me to learn that he's also dealing drugs." Which logical fallacy best describes this faulty reasoning?
   a. false dilemma
   b. bandwagon approach
   c. stacking the deck
   d. non sequitur

2. "So, they're saying that the death penalty discriminates against minorities, and so we should get rid of it. But there's no way abolishing the death penalty is going to eliminate racial discrimination, so I'm going to continue supporting the death penalty." Which logical fallacy best describes this faulty reasoning?
   a. complex question
   b. argument from adverse consequences
   c. contradictory premises
   d. straw man

3. "If you don't support bail reform, then you must be a racist." Which logical fallacy best describes this faulty reasoning?
   a. false dilemma
   b. contradictory assumption
   c. bandwagon approach
   d. *non causa pro causa*

4. "So the new police captain wants us to go from one-man patrols to two-man patrols. What's next? Fifty-men patrol teams?" Which logical fallacy best describes this faulty reasoning?
   a. false cause
   b. slippery slope
   c. stacking the deck
   d. begging the question

5. "The death penalty is wrong. I know this, because it is immoral for us humans to decide to kill someone." Which logical fallacy best describes this faulty reasoning?
   a. false dilemma
   b. contradictory premises
   c. argument from the negative
   d. circular reasoning

6. "Did you hear about that group of teenagers who toilet papered the house down the street? It just goes to show that teenagers have no respect for the law or personal property." Which logical fallacy best describes this faulty reasoning?
   a. hasty generalization
   b. faulty analogy
   c. false dilemma
   d. slippery slope

7. Which of the following lines of reasoning reflects the logical fallacy of *appeal to tradition*?
   a. I know it's okay to walk around with an open container of alcohol in New Orleans because people always do that there.
   b. I know it's okay to walk around with an open container of alcohol in New Orleans because the bartender told me so.
   c. I know it's okay to walk around with an open container of alcohol in New Orleans because a textbook on open container laws in the United States says so.
   d. I know it's okay to walk around with an open container of alcohol in New Orleans because my roommate told me so.

8. Which of the following lines of reasoning reflects the logical fallacy of *appeal to a lack of evidence*?
   a. My parents vacationed in Hawaii and had their wallets stolen, so I know that tourists are at an increased risk of theft victimization.
   b. I read a study showing that tourists are the least likely to be assault victims, so it stands to reason that they also have a low likelihood of being the victim of theft.
   c. There are no data showing that tourists are at an increased risk of being theft victims, so it's simply not true.
   d. The data showing that tourists are at an increased risk of theft victimization are flawed, so they should be accepted cautiously.

9. Which of the following lines of reasoning reflects a logical fallacy of *appeal to emotion*?
   a. Why isn't there a traffic light at that intersection near the park? All other intersections in that area have traffic lights.
   b. Why isn't there a traffic light at that intersection near the park? Most parks have some form of traffic control.
   c. Why isn't there a traffic light at that intersection near the part? In last year's Town Hall meeting, there was a unanimous vote to install one.
   d. Why isn't there a traffic light in that intersection near the park? Do they want our children to be slaughtered?

10. Is the following argument deductively valid or invalid? People charged with a crime either have the charges dropped, plea bargain, or go to trial. Jim was charged with a crime and did not have the charges dropped or plea bargain. Therefore, Jim must be going to trial.
    a. deductively valid
    b. deductively invalid

11. Is the following argument deductively valid or invalid? Trials are either bench trials or jury trials. No bench trial is a jury trial. Jim's trial was a bench trial. Therefore, Jim's trial was not a jury trial.
    a. deductively valid
    b. deductively invalid

12. Is the following argument deductively valid or invalid? If a police officer uses excessive force, then that officer is suspended. Officer Jones did not use excessive force. Therefore, Officer Jones could not have been suspended.
    a. deductively valid
    b. deductively invalid

13. Is the following argument deductively valid or invalid? All judges are lawyers. All lawyers have law degrees. Therefore, all lawyers are judges.
    a. deductively valid
    b. deductively invalid

14. Is the following argument deductively valid or invalid? In some trials, no one on probation can serve as a juror. In those trials, some smart people are on probation. Therefore, in some trials, some smart people cannot serve as a juror.
    a. deductively valid
    b. deductively invalid

15. Is the following argument deductively valid or invalid? All prisoners wear orange. Pumpkins are orange. Therefore, pumpkins are prisoners.
    a. deductively valid
    b. deductively invalid

16. Based on the following arguments, which inductive conclusion is the strongest? I always speed on my way to work, and I have never gotten pulled over and been given a ticket. Therefore, I conclude …
    a. There is no way I will be pulled over and ticketed for speeding on my way to work tomorrow.
    b. No one will be pulled over and ticketed for speeding on their way to work tomorrow.
    c. I am unlikely to be pulled over and ticketed for speeding on my way to work tomorrow.
    d. I am likely to be pulled over and ticketed for speeding on my way to work tomorrow.
    e. I will definitely be pulled over and ticketed for speeding on my way to work tomorrow.

17. Based on the following arguments, which inductive conclusion is the strongest? I always speed on my way to work, and I have never gotten pulled over and been given a ticket. But this evening, there was a news report about a speed trap that will be on my route to work tomorrow. Therefore, I conclude …
    a. I will never be pulled over and ticketed for speeding on my way to work tomorrow.
    b. No one gets pulled over and ticketed for speeding on their way to work tomorrow.
    c. I am unlikely to be pulled over and ticketed for speeding on my way to work tomorrow.
    d. I am likely to be pulled over and ticketed for speeding on my way to work tomorrow.
    e. I will definitely be pulled over and ticketed for speeding on my way to work tomorrow.

18. Based on the following arguments, which inductive conclusion is the strongest? I am on the varsity soccer team, and none of my teammates drink alcohol. Therefore, I conclude …
    a. Soccer players probably do not drink alcohol.
    b. Athletes probably do not drink alcohol.
    c. I probably do not drink alcohol.
    d. My teammates probably do not drink alcohol.
    e. My teammates probably do drink alcohol.

19. Based on the following arguments, which inductive conclusion is the strongest? I am on the varsity soccer team, and all of my teammates say they do not drink alcohol. But I was at a party last weekend where I saw some of my teammates drinking alcohol. Therefore, I conclude …
    a. Some of my teammates probably drink alcohol.
    b. All of my teammates probably drink alcohol.
    c. None of my teammates probably drink alcohol.
    d. All of my teammates probably are liars.
    e. I probably drink alcohol.

20. Based on the following arguments, which inductive conclusion is the strongest? I read a blog about how there is less crime in neighborhoods with more vegetarians than in neighborhoods with less vegetarians. Therefore, I conclude …
    a. Vegetarians are less likely than non-vegetarians to commit crime.
    b. Most carnivores are criminals.
    c. Convincing my neighbors to become vegetarians will probably reduce crime in our neighborhood.
    d. If I continue to eat meat, I will probably become a criminal.
    e. There is probably some other factor related to both vegetarianism and crime.

Editing

The next set of exercises is designed to assess Chapter 5 Learning Objective 3 (see Box 5.1).

1. Diagram the following argument.

   There are many ways to sanction convicted criminals, such as fines, community service, probation, incarceration, and execution. It is expensive to incarcerate people for life. Incarcerated inmates with no hope of parole have little incentive to behave, and so three-strikes laws may increase the level of prison misconduct. Also, three-strikes laws do not decrease crime. Stolzenberg and D'Alessio (1997) analyzed crime rates before and after California imposed three-strikes, and they found similar levels of serious crime or petty theft in the two time periods. Stolzenberg and D'Alessio's (1997) study indicates that crime does not go down when three-strikes laws are implemented. Mauer, King, and Young (2004) reported that "lifers" require more security, for example, while elderly prisoners require more medical care. Because more security and medical care is needed for lifers than non-lifers, lifetime prison sentences are costlier than less permanent prison sentences. In sum, you would have to be ignorant or cruel to want to lock someone up forever. Thus, three-strikes laws should be abolished.

2. Assess the argument diagrammed in #1 in terms of its adequacy.
3. Building off #1 and #2, craft an improved argument.

Writing

These writing exercises are designed to assess Chapter 5 Learning Objectives 2, 6, and 7 (see Box 5.1).

1. Argue for the importance of logic in criminal justice communications.
2. Outline strategies for producing logical criminal justice communications.
3. Select a single, specific criminal justice system policy that has been around long enough to have generated some research (e.g., drug courts, problem-oriented policing, sex offender registration, police body-worn cameras, gun buy-back programs, supermax prisons). Do some research on the policy, and then develop a logical policy analysis. Use Tables 5.10 and 5.11 to structure your policy analysis.
4. Select a single, specific crime problem that has been around long enough to have generated some research (e.g., youth gangs, investor fraud, motor vehicle theft, underage drinking, intimate partner violence, cyberbullying, income tax evasion). Do some research on the crime problem, and then develop a logical policy proposal that recommends one single, specific policy for addressing the crime problem. Use Table 5.12 to structure your policy proposal.
5. Pick a famous criminal, choosing one for which there are abundant details about both the crime and the criminal and his/her crime(s). You could choose a high-profile case, such as O.J. Simpson or Casey Anthony. Learn as much as you can about the criminal and crime(s). Suppose the criminal is going to be sentenced for his/her crime(s) and develop a logical presentence investigation report (PSI) to aid the judge in determining an appropriate sentence. Use Tables 5.13 and 5.14 to structure your PSI.

REFERENCES

Administrative Office of the United States Courts Probation Division. (1984). *The presentence investigation report*. Publication 105. National Institute of Justice, U.S. Department of Justice. Retrieved from https://www.ncjrs.gov/pdffiles1/digitization/101715ncjrs.pdf

Chivers, C. J., Buchanan, Larry, Lu, Denise, & Yourish, Karen. (2018, February 28). With AR-15s, mass shooters attack with the rifle firepower typically used by infantry troops. *New York Times*. Retrieved from https://www.nytimes.com/interactive/2018/02/28/us/ar-15-rifle-mass-shootings.html

Guis, Mark. (2017). The effects of state and federal gun control laws on school shootings. *Applied Economics Letters, 25* (317–320). doi:10.1080/13504851.2017.1319555

LaBossiere, Michael C. (2010). *42 fallacies*. Retrieved from http://www.triviumeducation.com/texts/42Fallacies.pdf

Mauer, Marc, King, Ryan S., & Young, Malcolm C. (2004, May). *The meaning of "life": Long prison sentences in context*. Washington, DC: The Sentencing Project. Retrieved from https://www.sentencingproject.org/wp-content/uploads/2016/01/The-Meaning-of-Life-Long-Prison-Sentences-in-Context.pdf

Phelan, Peter, & Reynolds, Peter. (1996). *Argument and evidence: Critical analysis for the social sciences*. London: Routledge.

Phillips, Sandra. (2013, November 14). Stephanie Crowe's brother cries as he recalls her murder. Fox 5, San Diego. Retrieved from https://fox5sandiego.com/2013/11/14/stephanie-crowes-brother-cries-as-he-recalls-her-murder/

Sauer, Mark. (2012, May 22). Michael Crowe found "factually innocent" in sister's murder. KPBS, San Diego State University. Retrieved from https://www.kpbs.org/news/2012/may/22/michael-crowe-found-factually-innocent-sisters-mur/

Stolzenberg, Lisa, & D'Alessio, Stewart J. (1997). "Three strikes and you're out": The impact of California's new mandatory sentencing law on serious crime rates. *Crime & Delinquency, 43*(4), 457–469.

Wheeler, L. Kip. (2018). Logical fallacies handlist. Retrieved from https://web.cn.edu/kwheeler/fallacies_list.html

Principle 5: Evidence

After reading this chapter, you will be able to

1. Recognize terminology relevant to evidence-based communication.
2. Argue for the importance of evidence in criminal justice communications.
3. Distinguish between different forms of evidence.
4. Identify and describe criteria for evaluating evidence.
5. Revise statements that use evidence ineffectively so that they use evidence effectively.
6. Construct an evidence-based research paper.
7. Develop an evidence-based affidavit for a search warrant.

I say, sir, that you can never make an intelligence judgment without evidence.

—MALCOM X

Whether our concern is the academic study or the professional practice of criminal justice, evidence plays a central role. Moreover, the division between academic and professional criminal justice evidence has become blurred for at least two reasons. First, scientific evidence has entered the courtrooms more and more. In its third edition, the Federal Judicial Center and National Research Council's *Reference Manual on Scientific Evidence* (2011) includes chapters on such forms of evidence as DNA, statistics, survey research, estimation of economic damages, epidemiology, toxicology, neuroscience, and engineering. Second, recognition of the widespread existence of programs and policies without any reliable evidence of their effectiveness, and despite accumulating evidence that they are harmful, has fueled a "movement for evidence-based crime policy" (Walker, 2011, p. 10). Officially embraced in 2000, this evidence-based policy movement demands rigorous and replicated empirical evidence of effectiveness (Walker, 2011). In sum, scholarly, scientific evidence has assumed a prominent role throughout the criminal justice system.

Criminal justice scholars and practitioners of the 21st century are not satisfied with assumptions, traditions, speculation, or opinion. We are motivated and trained to question rather than assume effectiveness and to pursue credible evidence of what works. "Prove it" is our mantra. Therefore, we are constantly looking for evidence to substantiate beliefs, and we are constantly considering the quality of that evidence. Moreover, we generally expect the same of our audience: that the people who read our work or listen to our presentations will demand strong evidence to believe us. This demand for evidence—for proof, that is— underlies the pivotal role of evidence in criminal justice communications.

It is beyond the scope of this or probably any other single textbook to cover all aspects of evidence in both the study and practice of criminal justice. Readers are referred to textbooks on criminal evidence and police investigations to learn about the various forms of evidence of criminal activity (e.g., DNA, toxicology, handwriting, email trails), and how to collect and process these forms of evidence. Likewise, readers are directed to textbooks on social science and criminological research methods to learn how to conduct their own empirical research (e.g., experiments, surveys, content analysis, crime mapping). In this chapter, these topics are covered only briefly in relation to their role in written and oral communications.

Thus, this chapter focuses on how evidence is used in the development and delivery of compelling criminal justice communications. It begins with four guidelines for developing evidence-based communications and then shows how these guidelines can be applied to research papers and search warrant affidavits. By the end of this chapter, readers will know where and how to use evidence.

GUIDELINES

Follow these guidelines to develop a solid, evidence-based communication:

1. Identify where evidence is needed.
2. Determine what evidence is needed.
3. Evaluate evidence.
4. Explain evidence.

Identify Where Evidence Is Needed

Recall from Chapter 5 that **evidence** is proof. It is the grounds for believing something, or that which justifies a claim. As such, the general rule is that we need evidence any time we make a claim. In Chapter 5, we learned that a claim is an assertion of fact, value, or policy. If it would be reasonable for someone to question a claim, then we should provide evidence to substantiate that claim.

From this it follows that we need not provide evidence for a claim if it would be unreasonable for someone to question that claim. For example, we should not need to prove such common knowledge as that the Declaration of Independence was signed in 1776;

BOX 6.2	Credibility Connection

The evidence we present reflects on us: We look good when we use strong sources, but we look bad when we use weak sources.

Florida is south of New York; 1 + 1 = 2; and fish swim in the water. It also seems silly to expect evidence of our own sensations and perceptions (e.g., apples taste good to me, you hurt my feelings). And, given that evidence relates to the real, empirical world, we also cannot have logical, evidence-based arguments about supernatural claims (e.g., the devil causes criminal behavior, guardian angels watch over us).

Determine What Evidence Is Needed

The first step—identifying where evidence is needed—is considerably more straightforward than the second step of determining what evidence is needed. This second step involves three considerations: (1) what type of claim is being made, (2) what requirements must be met to prove the claim, and (3) which form(s) of evidence is/are appropriate. Following these steps is critical to effective use of evidence because different types of claims require different types of evidence.

Claim Type

There are three general types of claims (e.g., Duckart, n.d., McGaan, 2016). First, a **claim of fact** asserts that a condition has (or has not) existed, exists (or does not exist), or will (or will not) exist. These claims include definitions and categorizations of things, relationships between things, and predictions of things. Second, a **claim of value** argues that one condition is better than another (or other) conditions. Claims of value address issues of philosophy, ethics, and morality. And third, a **claim of policy** asserts that some condition should (or should not) exist.

An example of a claim of fact is that solitary confinement causes psychological problems; an example claim of value is that solitary confinement is immoral; and an example claim of policy is that solitary confinement should be illegal. So that we have a concrete idea of what types of statements require evidence, Table 6.1 distinguishes further between various subtypes of claims.

TABLE 6.1   Subtypes of Fact Claims

	Assertion	Example
Definition	To assert the meaning of a term	Solitary confinement is when a prisoner is isolated in a separate cell from other prisoners for at least 22 hours per day (Yoo, 2015).
Classification	To assert that one thing is an instance/example of something broader	Pelican Bay is an example of a prison designed to house prisoners in solitary confinement (Sullivan, 2006).
Generalization	To assert that one smaller group of things is a subtype of a bigger group of things	Disciplinary segregation and administrative segregation reflect the majority of solitary confinement use (Weir, 2012).
Past Condition	To assert that something happened in the past	The United States began using solitary confinement in 1829 at the Eastern State Penitentiary in Philadelphia (Sullivan, 2006).
Present Condition	To assert that something is happening now	The majority of U.S. citizens in solitary confinement are African American males housed in federal prisons (Nolan & Amico, 2017).
Future Condition	To assert (predict) that something will happen in the future	Nevada prisons are projected to hold 12,431 male prisoners by 2020 (Ware, Austin, & Thomson, 2010).
Correlation	To assert a (noncausal) relationship between two things	Recidivism is more common among solitary confinement inmates than among general population inmates (*Recidivism in Connecticut*, 2001).
Causation	To assert that one (or more) thing causes or influences another thing(s)	Solitary confinement can cause delirium, which is a severe psychological illness (Grassian, 2006).

Proof Requirements

Looking at Figure 6.1, we see that moving from the center of the circle out, more steps are needed to resolve a claim. Thus, claims of fact are both the simplest to resolve and at the core of all other claims. Table 6.2 outlines suggested steps for using evidence to resolve the three claim types. Remember, however, that the first step is to determine what type of claim is being asserted.

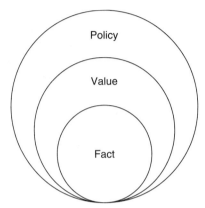

FIGURE 6.1 Claims of Fact, Value, and Policy

TABLE 6.2 Proof Requirements by Claim Type

Claim of Fact	Claim of Value	Claim of Policy
1. Identify appropriate evidence for the fact claim	1. Identify objective criteria on which to base judgement	1. Identify an existing problem (Steps 1–6 under Claim of Value)
2. Make a judgment on the fact claim based on the evidence	2. Specify how the criteria judgments will be combined to reach a decision	2. Propose a specific solution for the problem
	3. Reach agreement on criteria and how they will be used to reach a decision	3. Identify alternative solutions to the problem
	4. Articulate a fact claim for each criterion	4. Identify objective criteria by which to compare and contrast alternative solutions
	5. Evaluate each fact claim (Steps 1–2 under Claim of Fact)	5. Specify how the criteria judgments will be combined to reach a decision
	6. Make a judgment on the value claim based on the judgment of fact claims	6. Reach agreement on criteria and how they will be used to reach a decision
		7. Articulate a fact claim for each criterion
		8. Identify evidence for each fact claim
		9. Make a judgement on the policy claim based on the judgment of fact claims

PROVING FACT CLAIMS. To argue a claim of fact (e.g., solitary confinement causes psychological problems [a claim of causation]), we need to locate evidence of the asserted condition. We might need to define "psychological problems" or specify what conditions constitute "psychological problems" (e.g., hallucinations, depression, hysteria, anxiety, suicidal ideation), but defining and classifying still are claims of fact.

PROVING VALUE CLAIMS. To argue a claim of value, we have to start by identifying criteria. For the value claim that solitary confinement is immoral, then, we would need to start by identifying objective standards for judging immorality. Such standards might include need (What is the goal of solitary confinement?), costs (What are the negative consequences of solitary confinement?), benefits (What are the positive outcomes of solitary confinement?), and alternatives (What alternatives are there to solitary confinement?). We want to reach agreement on what these criteria should be and how the overall determination should be made (e.g., How many standards of morality must be met to conclude that solitary confinement is immoral?).

Next, we would need to express each criterion in the form of a fact claim. Having done so, we are in a position to locate evidence related to each fact claim. We can then determine whether or not the evidence establishes the fact claims and, ultimately, determines whether the established fact claims support the value claim.

PROVING POLICY CLAIMS. To argue a claim of policy (e.g., solitary confinement should be outlawed), we have to go even further. We need to follow the steps necessary to establish the fact and value claims within the policy claim, but we also will need to identify alternatives and establish the superiority of the advocated policy.

Having demonstrated that solitary confinement does cause psychological problems and that solitary confinement is immoral, what should we do instead with especially dangerous prisoners? The policy claim needs to identify a suitable alternative and provide evidence of the alternative's potential effectiveness in filling the void created by the prohibition of solitary confinement. In other words, what other prison management strategy can control dangerous prisoners without causing such severe psychological problems (or posing other significant concerns)? The policy being advocated might be a totally different policy (e.g., treatment, incentives), or it could be a modified form of the critiqued policy (e.g., time limits for isolated prisoners).

Having identified alternatives to the recommended policy, we next generate a list of objective criteria for weighing the options. (Later in this chapter, we look at policy analyses and proposals, including a list of criteria for assessing policy options.) Expressed as fact claims, we can gather and assess evidence to determine which options best meet the criteria. By breaking down value and policy claims into fact claims that can be argued and assessed using evidence, we are keeping our communications as logical and evidence-based as possible.

Evidence Forms

As shown in Table 6.2, the proof requirements outlined for the three claim types all boil down to the need to locate evidentiary support for claims of fact. So, what options do we have when it comes time to prove fact claims? Here, it is helpful to separate out scholarly communications from field communications.

SOURCE EVIDENCE IN SCHOLARLY COMMUNICATIONS. In their research and communications, students and professors tend to use source evidence. A **source** is the origin of some information. The term **source evidence** refers to proof that originates outside of the communication, offering it as substantiation of some claim. The most common sources in academic writing are written communications such as books, journals, newspapers, magazines, and websites. Other (nonwritten) sources include videos, movies, TV shows, audio recordings, podcasts, interviews, speeches, and photographs. This chapter covers three major classifications of written source evidence: (1) primary and secondary sources, (2) empirical and nonempirical research, and (3) level of scholarliness.

Primary and Secondary Sources. The first important distinction in academic sources is between primary and secondary sources. Table 6.3 shows what these terms mean and how they are different. The key difference is that, where a **primary source** is the original source of some piece of information, a **secondary source** is not the original source of some piece of information.

Thus, secondary sources are more vulnerable to error than are primary sources, as the author of the secondary source could intentionally or mistakenly misrepresent the original source (e.g., present a finding out of context, misinterpret how a variable was measured, omit an important qualification). Think of this like the classic game "telephone," where people line up and someone whispers a message into the ear of the first person in line. As the message is relayed from person to person and eventually reaches the end of the line, it has morphed: Some words have changed, others are in a different order, and sometimes the meaning has changed. All else equal, then, primary sources are superior to secondary sources.

Because primary sources are to be preferred over secondary sources, secondary sources should be used with care. First, we should have a legitimate reason for using a secondary source. Second, we must state explicitly that we are using a secondary source and avoid stating or implying that a secondary source is a primary source. A sentence such as, "Researchers found that X happened after Y occurred (SOURCE)," indicates a research result; accordingly, the reader would assume that the source cited is where that research result was reported. If, instead, you are citing a secondary source, you at minimum need to clarify the citation, such as "(SOURCE citing SOURCE)," where the first source listed is the source you consulted and the second source listed is the primary source of the information being presented.

Empirical and Nonempirical Research. The second important distinction in academic sources is between empirical and nonempirical research, where **research** is a purposeful,

TABLE 6.3   Primary and Secondary Sources

Primary Sources	Secondary Sources
An original source of information	Not an original source of information
A first-hand account; the foundational source that all the secondary sources make use of	A relayed account that makes use of primary sources; a discussion of one or more primary sources
Includes empirical research reports, historical documents, literary works, court testimony transcripts, and interviews	Includes most student research papers, literature reviews, encyclopedia entries, criticisms of literary works, and book reviews
EX: Your interview with a prison warden about conditions preceding prison riots, which you include in a research paper	EX: A newspaper article reporting on some other article writer's interview with a prison warden about conditions preceding prison riots

TABLE 6.4   Empirical and Nonempirical Research

Empirical Research	Nonempirical Research
Based on original observations of the real world	Based on existing information about the real world
Involves the collection, analysis, and reporting of original data and unique findings	Involves location, synthesis, and presentation of findings previously reported
Includes reports of experiments, surveys, field research (e.g., observation, intensive interviewing), focus groups, content analysis, crime mapping, analysis of government data (e.g., Census, Uniform Crime Report [UCR]), and meta-analysis	Includes most student research papers, literature reviews, policy essays, response/reaction essays, and editorial introductions
EX: A research article presenting findings that peoples' trust in police increases the likelihood that they will report crime based on a survey of New York City residents	EX: A book summarizing research on trust in the police and proposing a new theory to explain why trusting police increases citizen cooperation with agents of the criminal justice system

systematic investigation designed to increase knowledge. Research is conducted to explore, describe, explain, or evaluate some phenomenon. Research is not casual, everyday human inquiry; nor is it a reflection of personal tastes, beliefs, or attitudes.

Table 6.4 delineates between two categories of research. Both empirical and nonempirical research are research (i.e., systematic investigations). Beyond that, however, **empirical research** is based on unique observations of the real world, whereas **nonempirical research** is based on information that already exists. With the exception of authors who publish the same results more than once, all empirical research is primary research. Nonempirical research can be primary or secondary research.

All else equal, empirical research is superior to nonempirical research. If we want to substantiate a claim that crime rates have been declining for the past two decades, for example, our argument will be stronger if our evidence includes data on crime trends for the last 20 years than if it is based on a paper without crime trend data. As with primary and secondary research, then, we should (a) only use nonempirical research when we have a legitimate reason to use it, and (b) distinguish between empirical and nonempirical research sources.

Unlike primary and secondary research, however, situations are more common when using nonempirical research is justified. A claim such as "Researchers generally agree that X causes Y" need not be based on empirical research, and such claims often are made in academic writings. But a claim such as "Researchers generally have found that X causes Y" should be based on empirical research. The difference here is that the second sentence, but not the first sentence, makes a claim about (empirical) findings.

Level of Scholarliness. The third important distinction in academic sources is based on their level of scholarliness. Table 6.5 distinguishes between four levels of scholarliness across different types of sources. As we move from the left side to the right side of Table 6.5, the level of scholarliness declines. All else equal, professional sources are superior to other sources, substantive sources are superior to popular and sensational sources, and popular sources are superior to sensational sources. And, as with the other types of academic sources, we should (a) prefer more scholarly sources to less scholarly sources and (b) distinguish carefully and clearly between more and less scholarly sources.

TABLE 6.5   Level of Scholarliness in Source Evidence

Professional	Substantive	Popular	Sensational
Written by academics, scientists, or experts	Written by staff writers or experts	Written by staff writers or freelance journalists	Written by staff writers or freelance writers
Audience is other academics or those trained in the field	Audience is the well-educated public	Audience is the general reader	Audience is less well-educated
Purpose is to share findings or present theories; to inform	Purpose is to inform and entertain	Purpose is to entertain and inform	Purpose is to entertain
Discussion is often highly specific and sophisticated	Discussion is more general, easier to understand	Discussion is general and simplified	Discussion is sensational and simplistic
References are always included	Some sources are cited	Sources are often not cited	Sources are not cited
Article has been peer-reviewed by other scholars in the field	Article has been approved by an editorial board	Article has been approved by an editorial board or editor	Article has been approved by an editor

Source: Harris (2017)

The last row in Table 6.5 is particularly important. It shows a major reason for the superiority of professional publications: peer review. **Peer review** is the process whereby subject matter and/or methodological experts in the field review the paper for strengths and weaknesses, screening out flawed studies so that only the strongest studies are published. In academia, the peer-review process is either single blind or double blind. In single-blind peer review, the reviewers know who wrote the paper, but the paper author does not know who the reviewers are. In double-blind peer review, neither the reviewers nor the author knows each other's identity. The purpose of blind peer reviews is to facilitate open and honest reviews while guarding against personal biases.

CRIMINAL EVIDENCE IN FIELD COMMUNICATIONS. Within the criminal justice system, police, lawyers, and judges work with evidence on a daily basis. Police, and lawyers collect and analyze evidence, while judges (and juries) assess criminal evidence. **Criminal evidence** is proof of or relating to law-breaking behavior. This chapter covers three major classifications of criminal evidence: (1) real, demonstrative, testimonial, and documentary evidence; (2) direct versus circumstantial evidence; and (3) presumptions and judicial notice.

Real, Demonstrative, Testimonial, and Documentary Evidence. The first important distinction in criminal evidence is real versus demonstrative and testimonial evidence, as shown in Table 6.6. **Real evidence** is tangible. It can be observed in the courtroom using the five senses. **Demonstrative evidence** is a substitute for real evidence. It is some representation of real evidence. **Testimonial evidence** is what people say, while **documentary evidence** is what people have written (with the word *written* being broadly construed to include any form of "data compilation" [Federal Rules of Evidence, 1001, https://www.law.cornell.edu/rules/fre/rule_1001]).

Real evidence is considered primary evidence, whereas demonstrative, testimonial, and documentary evidence are considered secondary evidence. As with the previous

TABLE 6.6   Real, Demonstrative, Testimonial, and Documentary Evidence

Real Evidence	Demonstrative Evidence	Testimonial Evidence	Documentary Evidence
Tangible proof	A representation of, or substitute for, real proof	Someone's spoken words offered as proof	Documents or writings offered as proof
EX: weapons, drugs, bloodstains, clothing, masks, fake IDs, condoms, documents, fire accelerant	EX: simulations and reenactments, scale models, x-rays, artists' renditions, plaster casts, scientific tests, photographs	EX: witness recollections of the events leading up to the crime, victim account of the crime, expert explanation of the evidence	EX: letters, emails, contracts, diaries, tweets, blogs, test messages, wills, trusts, employment records

discussion of scholarly evidence, primary evidence is considered less vulnerable to error than secondary forms of evidence.

Despite being considered the gold standard of criminal evidence, real evidence can present some challenges. First, it might not be discernible to the human eye. The judge and jury will not be able to look at a bloodstained sock, for example, and be able to determine the blood type. In this case, a DNA expert's testimonial evidence would be a necessary supplement to the real evidence of a bloodstained sock. Second, real evidence might not make sense to a judge or jury. An expert might be able to determine that a substance found at the scene of a fire is a commonly used accelerant, but the typical judge and juror would not know that. Here, real evidence has a role in the courtroom, but it would need some help—such as the testimony of an arson investigator—to explain how it can be used to burn down a building. Third, real evidence can be inappropriate, such as the mutilated body of a murder victim. In this situation, demonstrative evidence—such as autopsy photographs—would be an acceptable substitute for the real evidence of the victim's corpse. Fourth, it is impractical or impossible to bring into a courtroom some real evidence, such as a crime scene for a hit-and-run or a barroom brawl. Instead, crime-scene photographs, scale models, and/or computer simulations can serve as a substitute for the real evidence of the crime scene.

Advances in technology are likely increasing both the role and effectiveness of demonstrative evidence in the criminal justice system, but most evidence tends to be testimonial. Testimonial evidence can be provided orally or in writing by oath or affirmation before or during a trial (Nemeth, 2011). Testimonial evidence therefore can include confessions, depositions, and sworn testimony during a court proceeding. **Lay witnesses** have some personal knowledge relevant to the case—they might have seen a domestic battery defendant beat his wife before, for example; or have been threatened by the defendant before; or have been lied to by the defendant in the past. **Expert witnesses**, on the other hand, have some "scientific, technical, or specialized knowledge [that] will assist the trier of fact to understand the evidence or to determine a fact in issue" (Federal Rules of Evidence 702). Thus, an expert witness might be educated in toxicology, DNA evidence, or psychology in a case where toxicology, DNA, or psychology is relevant to some disputed fact.

In earlier times, documentary evidence played a lesser role because most people could not read. These days, most U.S. citizens can read and write, and therefore we have a formalized system for determining the integrity of documentary evidence in the criminal justice system. Echoing the preference for primary over secondary sources in academic writings, Federal Rules of Evidence 1002 calls for primary documents to be used unless there are legitimate reasons for using secondary or duplicate documents. A primary, or original, form of documentation is "the writing or recording itself or any counterpart intended to have the same effect by a person executing or issuing it" (Federal Rules of Evidence 1001). An example of a legitimate reason for not using a primary document is when the primary document has been lost or destroyed.

Direct and Circumstantial Evidence. The second major distinction in criminal evidence is between direct and circumstantial evidence. Table 6.7 differentiates between these two categories of criminal evidence. **Direct evidence** substantiates some fact by itself with near certainty. **Circumstantial evidence**, on the other hand, substantiates some fact indirectly. While direct evidence is considered superior to circumstantial evidence, most criminal evidence is circumstantial (Nemeth, 2011; Worrall, Hemmens, & Nored, 2018).

There is one main reason for the superiority of direct evidence over circumstantial evidence: Direct evidence does not require much inference. (Recall that an inference is the reasoning used to link the evidence to the claim.) The reasoning process creates room for doubt. The longer and more circuitous that process is, the more room for doubt there is. And the more room for the doubt that exists, the less certain we are.

Based on the direct evidence of a video-recorded confession, for instance, we might be fairly certain (e.g., 95 percent sure) that the defendant committed the assault. We can trust that the confession is credible because the video showed no coercion, and the exclusionary rule should have prohibited it from being introduced in the trial had it been illegally obtained. Based on the circumstantial evidence of a DNA match, however, we might be less certain (e.g., 60 percent sure) because there are other explanations for the DNA match, such as someone other than the defendant having the same blood type and having committed the assault, or someone having planted the evidence.

There are two reasons for the greater use of circumstantial evidence. First, direct evidence is harder to come by. That is, there tends to be less of it to begin with. Second, because circumstantial evidence is less convincing than direct evidence, more pieces of circumstantial evidence are needed to prove a claim, such as that the defendant has a history of behaving aggressively. If we think in terms of the prosecution's burden to prove the defendant guilty *beyond a reasonable doubt* (i.e., 90–95 percent sure), then the distinction between direct and circumstantial evidence becomes even clearer—and we can understand why some trials take so long. Indeed, the longest portion of a criminal jury trial is the presentation of the plaintiff's case (Sipes, Oram, Thornton, Valluzzi, & Van Duizend, 1988).

Presumptions and Judicial Notice. The third major distinction in criminal evidence relates to presumptions and judicially noticed evidence. Presenting evidence in a trial can

TABLE 6.7   Direct and Circumstantial Evidence

Direct Evidence	Circumstantial Evidence
Straightforward proof of something	Roundabout, or indirect, proof of something
Requires very little conjecture to believe in the truth of that which is being asserted	Requires moderate to major conjecture to believe in the truth of that which is being asserted
EX: A defendant's confession that he punched the victim is direct evidence of assault	EX: DNA evidence that the blood on the defendant's knuckles matches the victim's blood type is circumstantial evidence of assault

TABLE 6.8   Presumptions and Judicial Notice

	Presumption	Judicial Notice
Definition	A conclusion reached on the basis of established or accepted facts	A conclusion reached on a basis other than formal evidentiary procedures
Function	A *substitute* for evidence (no evidence is needed to establish the conclusion)	A *shortcut* for evidence (waived-in evidence is used to establish the conclusion)
Forms	Of law (e.g., innocence, sanity, knowledge of what is illegal)	Of law (e.g., court decisions, statutory law, constitutional provisions, administrative regulations, municipal ordinances)
	Of fact (e.g., a blood-alcohol level of 0.08% or higher indicates intoxication; an email sent to the person's correct email address reached that person)	Of fact (e.g., common knowledge; laws of science and natural events; definitions of terms, symbols, and abbreviations)

Sources: Boulder County Bar Association (2014); Nemeth (2011); Worrall, Hemmens, and Nored (2018)

be a time-consuming process, and presumptions and judicial notice are essentially ways to bypass this process. Table 6.8 differentiates between these two concepts.

A **presumption** is a conclusion reached on the basis of established or accepted facts. As a substitute for evidence, a presumption requires no evidence to establish the conclusion. Indeed, a presumption *forces* a conclusion. This is essentially a matter of logical deduction. If we accept the initial claim (called a premise), then we must accept the claim derived from it. Most of us are familiar with the presumption of innocence. The premise—the presumption of innocence—demands the conclusion that a given defendant is innocent … unless proven guilty.

Where a presumption *replaces* proof, judicial notice is a kind of evidence that *expedites* the proof process. **Judicial notice** is a conclusion reached on some basis other than the formal evidentiary process. Judicial notice is to law what common knowledge is to academia (Worrall et al., 2018). A judicially noticed fact is not contested by the other side, and the person offering the evidence does not have to prove relevance or meet other admissibility standards (Nemeth, 2011); instead, it is taken as a given. That guns can kill, it is dark at night, apples grow on trees—these are types of common knowledge that cannot be reasonably argued. Were they to be argued, it would be quick and simple for an average citizen to look them up in an authoritative source, such as an encyclopedia, and realize the truth of these assertions. Examples of a legal matters subject to judicial notice are the elements of the crime or the statutory penalty for the crime. These matters can easily be resolved by looking to the relevant penal code, and so there is no need for such conclusions to be debated to the same extent as, say, whether or not the defendant had a motive to commit the crime.

Evaluate Evidence

Whether or not an argument is strong is heavily determined by the evidence used to support the claims. This is a matter not only of the evidence itself but of the connection between evidence and claim. In this way, we can think of each piece of evidence as a brick. Just as we put bricks together to build a wall, we put pieces of evidence together to build a case (B. Hyman, personal communication, January 26, 2018). Keeping with this analogy of a brick wall, cement is to the wall as inference—or reasoning—is to the case: It holds it together.

Strong evidence is relevant and credible. This is true whether we are talking about source evidence in scholarly communications or criminal evidence in field communications. When it comes to evaluating evidence, perhaps the biggest difference between school and the field is the formality of the process. Unlike scholarly communications, there are official and explicit standards and rules in the field for getting evidence admitted into court and determining whether sufficient evidence exists to find a defendant guilty. But these standards and rules reflect concerns that should implicitly govern the scholarly evidence-evaluating process as well. Given this similarity, we do not need separate sections here on evidence evaluation. Instead, we can borrow the criminal justice system process to guide our evaluation of scholarly evidence. As we do so, we will look at two dimensions of evidence evaluation: (1) evaluating a single piece of evidence and (2) evaluating the total evidence.

Single Pieces of Evidence

When we think of boxing, we usually envision the actual match between the two contestants: throwing jabs, ducking punches, and so on, in the ring. But before the boxers can enter the ring and compete, they must first pass a series of qualifying exams, including drug tests and a weigh-in. Once the boxer gets in the ring, the fight begins to determine the winner. In a similar vein, when most people think about criminal evidence, they think about the presentation of evidence in court by the prosecution and defense. Yet before evidence gets admitted to trial, evidence—like boxers—must pass a number of tests before it can be presented in a trial and used to determine the verdict.

Table 6.9 outlines eight tests to use when deciding whether or not a single piece of evidence should (in academia) or can (in the field) be used. We need an affirmative answer to each question relevant to the type of evidence in consideration.

TABLE 6.9   Determining Whether a Single Piece of Evidence Can and Should Be Used

Test	Question to Ask
1. Ethical Acquisition	Has the evidence been legally/ethically obtained?
2. Relevance	Is the evidence logically connected to the claim it seeks to prove?
3. Materiality	Is the claim to which the evidence relates logically connected to the ultimate issue to be decided?
4. Value Versus Risk	Does the probative value of evidence outweigh the risks of using the evidence?
5. Competence	Does the person providing the evidence have the ability to narrate events and understand the duty to tell the truth?
6. Credibility	Should the person providing the evidence be believed?
7. Authenticity	Is the evidence what it is claimed to be?
8. Best Evidence	Is the evidence the original source/version?

Source: Worrall et al. (2018)

The point of the first test is that we should not include illegally or unethically obtained evidence. In the criminal justice system, the exclusionary rule guards against the use of evidence that has been illegally obtained. Academic honor codes and professional codes of ethics serve a similar purpose in ensuring the integrity of the scholarly communication process. In both cases, wrongfully acquired evidence is "fruit of the poisonous tree" and should not be used in the communication.

Tests two and three revolve around the connection between the piece of evidence and the claim we are trying to prove and the ultimate issue in the case. These tests make the point that we should not offer evidence just because we have the evidence, there is a requirement for evidence, or we do not have better evidence. On the contrary, there must be a logical connection between the evidence and claim. The timing should be consistent between the evidence and the claim, for instance. Evidence of some condition in 2000 (e.g., a person was not using drugs) often cannot substantiate a claim of that condition existing in 2010 (e.g., a person does not use drugs). Also, the claim must have an important role in our argument. That is, the claim must be logically connected to the ultimate issue. If we are arguing that a person is a drug addict, however, it is unlikely that the person's middle name is an important (or material) fact. Consequently, evidence of the person's middle name should not enter into the argument. Alternatively, if we are arguing that a person is a liar and the person provided a false middle name, then evidence of the person's real middle name is relevant and material.

The fourth test refers to probative value. **Probative value** means usefulness in proving the truth or falsity of the proposition to which it is logically connected. Even though a piece of evidence might be relevant and material, its probative value could be outweighed by practical concerns, such as potential for causing prejudice or confusion, for misleading the audience, or for taking too much time. An example might be if there are 100 witnesses to the exact same event. In this situation, a judge might rule that not all 100 witnesses are admissible because somewhere along the line between the first witness and the hundredth witness, the probative value would diminish and become overshadowed by how long it took and how little additional information was added.

The fifth, sixth, seventh, and eighth tests are equally important as the first four tests. While these four tests do not apply to all forms of criminal evidence, they do apply in most forms of academic communications. Tests 5 and 6 concern testimonial evidence. In law, competence relates to testimonial evidence, and witnesses are presumed competent unless otherwise proven. Minors and people with significantly diminished capacity might not be able to relate events accurately or understand the need to be truthful or the consequences of being untruthful, while spouses have been considered incompetent witnesses for multiple reasons (e.g., self-interest and marital harmony, husbands and wives being one person and the right against self-incrimination). A witness's credibility can be called into question on such grounds as bias or prejudice, inconsistent/contradictory statements, and reputation.

Test seven requires that nontestimonial evidence be authenticated before being presented at trial, while test eight holds that the documentary evidence in question be the best possible evidence. Criminal evidence can be authenticated—that is, shown to be genuine—in a variety of ways, such as witnesses testifying that s/he recognize the handwriting in a letter or voice in a recording, saw the letter being written, or wrote the letter her/himself. Consistent with the preference for primary over secondary sources as discussed previously in the section "Criminal Evidence in Field Communications," the best evidence rule values original/primary sources over secondary/duplicate sources. While the best evidence rule is not an ironclad prohibition of secondary documents, it does mandate that whenever possible, the primary version should be used instead of other versions.

Evidence that passes the tests above qualifies for use to prove a claim. As stated, these tests can and should be used in scholarly communications in addition to field communications so the rigor of scholarly dialogues is not compromised flawed evidence. Just as we want to make sure only qualified boxers enter the ring on fight night, we want only relevant and credible evidence to drive thinking and action about crime and its control.

Total Evidence

Because the goal of using evidence is to prove a claim, we are concerned with quantity of evidence as well as quality. On the one hand, the weaknesses of one piece of evidence can be overcome by strengths of another piece of evidence. And on the other hand, if we have several pieces of less-than-ideal evidence, the fact that they all point to the same conclusion increases our confidence that that conclusion is correct. But how do we know when we have enough good evidence to make our case? Here again, formal standards exist in the criminal justice system that can be adapted to scholarly communications. Three concepts help us determine the sufficiency of a body of evidence: total evidence, burden of proof, and standard of proof.

The term **total evidence** refers to all available relevant evidence. The expectation is that our audience will make a decision based on the total evidence—not on a single piece or some subset of total evidence. Returning to the brick wall metaphor used earlier, the decision to accept or reject the ultimate issue should be based not on the quality of any single brick or portion of the brick wall, but rather on the entire brick wall. In a criminal case, the person making the claim is usually the prosecution. In the case of scholarly communications, the person making the claim is usually the person writing the paper or giving the presentation.

Unless the total evidence supports the claim being made, our audience should not accept our claim. This is because the person making the case usually has the burden of proof, where **burden of proof** means the obligation to provide evidence to prove what is being asserted. In criminal law, where there is a presumption of innocence, the burden of proof is on the state (or prosecution) to prove that the defendant is guilty of the crime(s) with which that defendant is charged. Thus, the defense does not have any obligation to provide evidence of innocence. If no evidence were presented, then, the court would rule in favor of the defendant because the state would have failed to meet its burden.

In a like manner, the burden of proof in scholarly communications is on the party who is advancing the argument. In a research paper asserting that solitary confinement should be abolished, for instance, the burden of proving this claim would be on the paper's author. The burden is not on the audience to disprove the claim that solitary confinement should be abolished.

So, the party with the burden of proof must provide sufficient evidence to prove the claim. Well, how much evidence does it take to conclude that the evidence is sufficiently

TABLE 6.10   Standards of Proof

Case type	Degree of Certainty	
	100%	Absolutely certain
Criminal cases	90%	Beyond a reasonable doubt
	80%	
Some civil and criminal cases	70%	Clear and convincing
	60%	
Civil cases	> 50%	Preponderance
	40%	
Arrests and search warrants	30%	Probable cause
Stops and searches	20%	Reasonable suspicion
	10%	
	0%	Absolute lack of evidence

Note: These percentages are approximations meant for illustrative purposes.

strong for the audience to accept the claim? Academia provides no guidelines for this quandary, but the criminal justice system does in the form of legal standards of proof. The **standard of proof** is the level of probability necessary to conclude that enough evidence has been presented to prove a claim. Table 6.10 distinguishes between standards of proof used throughout different points in the criminal justice system, while Figure 6.2 delineates the different meanings of these standards of proof. Notice how higher standards are used in weightier decisions, such as in felony cases where life or liberty are at stake.

Overall, then, the party with the burden of proof must offer sufficient evidence to satisfy the relevant burden. The prosecution in criminal trials generally must convince the judge or jury of the defendant's guilt beyond a reasonable doubt, which means approximately 90 percent certain. In contrast, the plaintiff in a civil case must meet the lesser burden of preponderance of the evidence—at least 51 percent certainty.

Although academia does not have official standards of proof like the legal system does, there is no reason the legal standards of proof cannot be adapted to academic communications. At the very least, it makes sense to demand that higher-stakes academic communications (e.g., program evaluations) be held to a higher standard of proof than lower-stakes academic communications (e.g., term papers).

Explain Evidence

Remember that evidence does not lead directly to a claim. Instead, it is connected to the claim via an inductive inference, which is the reasoning process used to get from a piece of evidence to the claim for which it is offered as proof. Effective use of evidence therefore requires us to articulate exactly how the evidence we present supports a given claim that we are making. The more complicated the evidence and/or the less informed our audience, the more important it is to specify how the evidence supports the claim.

Here, we will focus on source evidence in scholarly communications, where evidence should be like the supporting cast and claims should be the star of the show

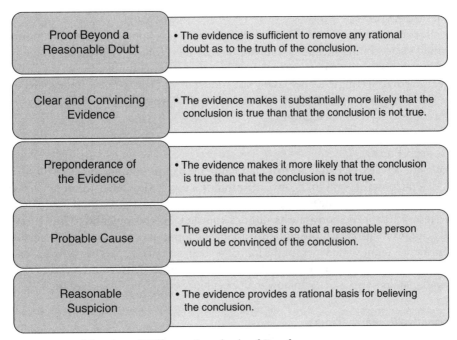

FIGURE 6.2 Meaning of Different Standards of Proof

(Harris, 2017). Among other things, this means that we should not merely string together pieces of evidence, with little or no commentary to link them to our claims and overall argument. Imagine ordering an assembly-required shed and getting no instructions. Unless you happen to be a shed expert, you are probably going to have a tough time figuring out how all the parts fit together to make a shed. You might even return the shed rather than invest your time and energy in figuring out how to put it together. Well, as a criminal justice communicator, the last thing you want is for your audience to give up because your evidence is too hard to follow to a conclusion. Nor do you want them to reach the wrong conclusion or fail to see the strength of your evidence in supporting your claims.

Overall, then, using effective use of evidence requires that we explicitly integrate our evidence into the argument we are making. Strategies for explaining evidence include

1. Introduce each piece of evidence.
2. Explicitly state how each piece of evidence proves the claim.
3. Acknowledge limitations of each piece of evidence and the total evidence.
4. Address the contradictory evidence and claims based on contradictory evidence.
5. Summarize the total evidence and how it satisfactory proves each claim as well as the main conclusion (i.e., the resolution).

The guideline that we explain our evidence reflects the fact that evidence does not speak for itself, and we should not assume that our audience understands the evidence or how it proves a claim.

APPLICATIONS

Not all criminal justice communications involve evidence. But two particularly common criminal justice communications revolve around evidence: research papers and affidavits for a search warrant. Note, however, that this discussion will not address the issue of generating or collecting evidence, as in the conduct of scholarly empirical research or the investigation of a crime. Rather, the focus here is on how to use evidence to make for a more compelling communication.

Research Papers

Simply put, a **research paper** is a formal document that communicates the results of the author's purposeful, systematic investigation of a topic. Thus, the author locates and synthesizes evidence on the topic, presenting it in an organized and ethical way. Not only can a research paper demonstrate its author's knowledge of the topic and communication skills, but it can also teach the audience about the topic, and/or it can seek to persuade the audience about some aspect of the topic. As such, research papers can be informative or persuasive (see Chapter 4). This section will distinguish between these two forms of research papers, with a focus on how to use evidence effectively in each of them.

Informative Research Papers

An informative research paper typically begins with a coverage and/or purpose statement and then is devoted to presenting relevant evidence in a reasonably comprehensive manner so as to deliver on its coverage/purpose statement. Papers chronicling the history of white-collar crime, comparing and contrasting white-collar and street offenders, presenting a typology of white-collar crimes, outlining various theoretical perspectives on the causes of white-collar crime, and describing different methods for controlling white-collar crime are all examples of informative research papers.

While an informative research paper is not an argument, it will contain claims of fact. The very definition of white-collar crime, for example, is a claim of fact about which considerable controversy exists. Thus, from the outset, any of the sample topics listed above would require evidence to substantiate that it is indeed a credible definition of white-collar crime. Appropriate evidence for such a claim would be academic or governmental publications that contain a definition of white-collar crime, the logic being that the definition is valid because it has been defined that way by an authoritative source.

Persuasive Research Papers

A persuasive research paper begins with a thesis statement and then proceeds to outline claims and supporting evidence to prove that thesis. Thus, the persuasive research paper is a form of complex argument where the thesis serves as the ultimate issue, and

BOX 6.3	Plagiarism Pointer

It is a common misunderstanding that too many citations weaken a paper. But, by definition, a research paper should be replete with evidence. Always identify the source of your evidence. Not only does doing so strengthen the evidentiary support for your claims, but doing so also protects you from plagiarism.

the body of the paper consists of claims that speak to the ultimate issue and evidence that supports those claims. Examples of persuasive research paper topics are that white-collar crime should be defined according to the offender rather than offense, white-collar crime is more serious than street crime, white-collar criminals are more rational than street criminals, white-collar criminals are not punished harshly enough, and compliance-oriented policies are more effective than coercive policies in reducing white-collar crime. Each of these example topics takes a position on a controversial issue.

Many persuasive papers involve claims of value and/or policy as well as claims of fact. Much of the advice presented previously for informative research papers applies to persuasive research papers too, but a key difference central to our discussion of evidence is controversy: That persuasive communications address a controversial issue suggests a higher standard of proof is warranted than in informative communications. The more controversial the issue, the more and the stronger evidence you may need to succeed in convincing your audience.

Best Practices

This section provides some suggestions for developing strong research papers that hold true for both informative and persuasive research papers.

First, using standard dictionaries to look up a definition when you are reading is reasonable, such as when you encounter a word you are unfamiliar with and need to know what it means. But it is poor practice to cite—or even worse, quote—a standard dictionary in a research paper. This is because dictionary definitions tend to be unhelpful (e.g., vague, condensed), and they tell us how a word *is* used, not necessarily how a word *should be* used (Harris, 2017). This caution does not mean, however, that there is never a good reason to cite a standard dictionary. On the contrary, if you need evidence of a claim about how a word is used in contemporary society (e.g., "Today, when lay people say 'white-collar crime,' they mean …"), then a standard dictionary is a logical source.

Second, as with any use of evidence, remember to rely on strong sources to support your claims. If you cannot find evidence that supports a claim, do something about it. Do not just ignore a lack of fit between evidence and claim and hope that your audience will not notice it. One way to handle this situation is to reconsider the claim. Ask yourself if you really need to make that claim to prove the ultimate issue. If no, then delete it. If yes, then reexamine how it is phrased. The claim might just need to be toned down. Consider the difference between these two claims:

1. Rich people are punished less severely than poor people.
2. Empirical research has found that rich people are less likely to be incarcerated than poor people.

As written, the first claim asserts an empirical correlation, whereas the second claim presents a conclusion from existing research without actually making an assertation about punishment disparities between the wealthy and poor themselves. The second claim is therefore far easier to substantiate and harder to critique. In sum, make sure your claim is not too strong given the evidence available to you for supporting it.

Third, in addition to the preceding information, here are some general best practices for developing a strong research paper:

1. **Conduct preliminary research to select a suitable topic.** The topic should be appropriately specific and suitable given the parameters and audience.
2. **Conduct thorough research to learn about your topic and collect sources.** Screen sources for credibility before you use them. Note any weaknesses of sources, such as if they are outdated or rely on a biased sample.
3. **Select an organizational structure for the paper that best reflects the information you have** (see Chapter 4). Remember to build your paper around your ideas and main points instead of around your evidence.
4. **Outline your paper.** Include your evidence and sources, and then conduct additional research as needed to flesh out and complete your outline. Ensure that you have evidence to support each claim.
5. **Draft your paper.** Use your outline to create a draft of your complete paper. Your first draft is done when you believe you not only have met the content, length, and resource requirements for the assignment, but also have provided evidence to support each claim and have articulated exactly how the evidence supports claims.
6. **Check closely to confirm that each fact claim is supported by evidence, and then revise as needed until you have no unsupported claims.** You might want to ask a classmate, friend, family member, or tutor to review your paper specifically for such gaps. Having written the paper, you might think it is clear how evidence supports a claim, but other people might need a bit more explanation. Thus, a second pair of eyes might be able to detect where additional explanation would be helpful to your audience.
7. **Edit before you submit.** A second pair of eyes is also ideal at this stage, checking not just format and style but also writing mechanics and adherence to parameters.

Search Warrant Affidavits

Before the police can search a home, they usually must prepare an affidavit requesting a search warrant and present the affidavit to a neutral judge. An **affidavit** is a written statement of facts made under oath. One form of affidavit is a **search warrant affidavit**, which is an affidavit submitted from a police officer to a judge to request a search warrant. The purpose of the search warrant affidavit is to convince the judge that there is probable cause to believe that a particular item is in a particular location.

While different states have somewhat different requirements, there are four key components to a proper search warrant affidavit:

1. It specifies the location to be searched;
2. It describes in detail the item to be seized;
3. It provides sufficient evidence to establish probable cause; and
4. It includes the police officer's signature, which means the officer swears to the contents.

If a judge believes there is probable cause on the basis of the information provided in the search warrant affidavit, then the judge will sign a search warrant. The search warrant affidavit or the search warrant itself can be the subject to pretrial motions by the defense to exclude evidence. The importance of a properly prepared search warrant affidavit is therefore twofold. First, it must convince the judge to issue the requested search. Second, it must be capable of withstanding later scrutiny by others.

Convincing the Judge to Issue a Search Warrant

Recall from Table 6.10 how probable cause means approximately 30 percent certainty. Probable cause exists when there is a legitimate and reasonable basis for believing that evidence of a crime is in the place to be searched (e.g., Legal Information Institute, n.d.; Tsay, 2014). Simply put, probable cause exists when there is a rational belief that is supported by some credible evidence.

Providing evidence to establish probable cause is the key to a successful search warrant affidavit. Police officers' observations and information from third parties (e.g., victims, witnesses, informants) are examples of acceptable forms of evidence for demonstrating probable cause. When the evidence is based on something other than the police officer's own knowledge (such as from an informant), the affidavit needs to provide information so that the judge can assess the credibility of the source (Wallace & Roberson, 2013). Thus, the search warrant affidavit needs to articulate facts (based on evidence) that support the officer's belief that evidence of a crime probably would be discovered if the place identified were searched.

In addition to probable cause that there is evidence of criminal activity, the search warrant affidavit must be particular as opposed to vague. Search warrants are governed by the Fourth Amendment, which states that "no Warrants shall issue, but upon probable cause, supported by Oath or affirmation, and *particularly describing* the place to be searched, and the persons or things to be seized" (emphasis added). Search warrant affidavits therefore should neither identify general locations nor general items.

Withstanding Later Scrutiny

Police officers often are called into court to account for the information provided in the search warrant affidavit, so defects (typos/mistakes, lack of specificity) and dishonesty (fabrications, embellishments) can have consequences later on in the criminal justice process. One cause of defects, for example, is copying and pasting from a previous affidavit into a new affidavit (Rutledge, 2010). While this might be done with the intention of saving time and/or using tried and true language, it can invalidate the search if details from the previous case are not edited to reflect the current case. If the search warrant affidavit is later determined to have failed to establish probable cause, then evidence seized during the search can be ruled inadmissible, convictions could be overturned, and/or the officer(s) might face civil liability charges. Two examples follow to demonstrate the importance of a properly prepared search warrant affidavit.

The first example of a defective search warrant affidavit is *Mills v. City of Barbourville* (2004) wherein the affidavit failed to articulate a connection between criminal activity and the location to be searched. In 1999, three high school students were said to have purchased a marijuana cigarette from Lisa Mills. Two students had waited while the third, Leo Cox, went to buy the marijuana cigarette. It is the testimony of Leo Cox given to Officer Robert Brown and Police Chief Johnny Smith on which probable cause was said to be based. After preparing affidavits to search and arrest, police searched Lisa Mills's home and found rolling papers and plastic baggies but no drugs. She was arrested and taken to Knox County Jail. About 2 weeks later, one of the defendants recanted when he was re-interviewed, and no criminal charges were filed against Lisa Mills. In 2001, Lisa Mills claimed a violation of her Fourth Amendment rights in terms of

> Both the underlying validity, as well as the sufficiency, of the allegations in the affidavit underlying the search warrant. She contends that the affidavit was not supported by probable cause and, further, that a reasonable officer in Officer Broughton's or Chief Smith's position would have known there was not probable cause for issuance of the warrant, rendering the application for and execution of the warrant a violation of a clearly established right. Specifically, plaintiff asserts that there was no probable cause for the warrant because (1) the affidavit supporting the warrant was either deliberately false or made with "reckless disregard" for the truth and (2) the affidavit was insufficient because it failed to connect the place to be searched with any criminal activity and police failed to corroborate allegations made by Leo Cox in his statement, which served as the basis for the affidavit and warrant, or to ensure his reliability as a witness. (*Mills v. City of Barbourville*, 2004)

The district court ruled against the plaintiff, but the appeals court reversed and remanded, explaining that there was no probable cause, and a reasonable officer should have known there was no probable cause. The search warrant affidavit said nothing about why Lisa Mills's home was being searched. There was no connection made between that location and criminal activity or between Lisa Mills and that location.

The second example is *State of Tennessee v. Gregory Lamont Hall* (2014), in which the affidavit was based on "stale" evidence and lacked specificity. On hearing that drugs were being sold in a certain house, Detective Ronald Kumrow sent a confidential informant (CI) to that house to buy drugs. The CI did buy drugs, and then Det. Kumrow applied to search every person at that house 72 hours later, beginning the search warrant affidavit with the following:

> This affidavit is made by Detective Ronald L. Kumrow who has been a sworn police officer since 2002, now testifies herein which is based upon your affiant's personal knowledge, upon information received from other law enforcement officers, or upon information obtained from other sources as noted, which your Affiant believes to be true, is as follows. (*State of Tennessee v. Gregory Lamont Hall*, 2014)

The trial court overruled the defense's motion to suppress the evidence from the search, and then Hall pled guilty to one count of possession with intent to sell within 1,000 feet of a school and received a 10-year prison sentence.

The appeals court prefaced its ruling by explaining, "In reviewing a probable cause determination, we look solely to the affidavit itself and not 'to other evidence provided to or known by the issuing magistrate or possessed by the affiant'" (*State of Tennessee v. Gregory Lamont Hall*, 2014). The appeals court ruled in Hall's favor, vacating his guilty conviction and dismissing all charges against him, explaining thus:

> A panel of this court concluded that while "'the affidavit … contained information establishing a nexus between the [d]efendant's apartment and criminal activity, it

contained no information tending to establish how long the nexus would persist." ... Because the affidavit did not "contain any facts supporting an inference that the person who sold drugs to the CI was more than a one-time visitor to the apartment" or "that the CI observed any drugs other than the drugs he bought," the court concluded that "the information in the affidavit became stale as soon as enough time had passed for such a one-time seller to leave the apartment."

The State points to the boilerplate language at the beginning of the affidavit. ... However, a finding of probable cause requires the affidavit to contain "more than mere conclusory allegations by the affiant."

Because there was nothing in the affidavit to support Det. Kumrow's statement that he had received information that illegal narcotics were being sold at the target residence, it was a mere conclusory allegation and could not reliably establish ongoing criminal activity at the target residence (*State of Tennessee v. Gregory Lamont Hall*, 2014).

Thus, there was insufficient evidence to provide probable cause. The information that was provided was both stale and vague, with part of the vagueness resulting from the use of standard, boilerplate language at the beginning of the affidavit.

These are not the only cases involving defective search warrant affidavits, but they are illustrative of the importance of evidence and its proper use in the professional practice of criminal justice.

Best Practices

This discussion can be crystallized into the following list of best practices for preparing a search warrant affidavit:

1. **Specify the item(s) to be seized:** What item(s) will be found? Identify each item explicitly, and then describe each item in detail.
2. **Link the item(s) to be seized to *criminal activity*:** To what crime(s) is/are the item(s) connected? How do you know the item(s) is/are connected to criminal activity? Provide evidence supporting this belief.
3. **Link the item(s) to be seized to the *location*:** Where will you search? How did you determine the location to search? Identify the location explicitly, and then describe it in detail. Provide evidence supporting this belief.
4. **Link the item(s) to be seized to the *time*:** How do you know that the item(s) will be found in this specific location when the location is searched? Provide evidence supporting this belief.
5. **Establish the credibility of sources:** Present information so that the judge can determine that the evidence used to support your beliefs is trustworthy.
6. **Be open and honest:** Do not mislead, fabricate, exaggerate, or otherwise misrepresent the item, location, connection to criminal activity, evidence, or reasoning used. Admit limitations, such as gaps in knowledge or reservations about credibility.
7. **Take your time being specific, accurate, and clear:** Resist the urge to rush and cut corners, such as using boilerplate language or copying and pasting from previous affidavits. Proofread for current and correct information.

EXERCISES
Matching

These exercises are designed to assess Chapter 6 Learning Objective 1 (see Box 6.1). Match each numbered statement to the lowercase letter corresponding to the key word it defines. Each key word will be used only once.

1. Research that is based on unique observations of the real world
2. All available relevant evidence
3. Proof that originates outside of the communication, offering it as substantiation of some claim
4. An assertion that a condition has (or has not) existed, exists (or does not exist), or will exist (or will not exist)
5. Usefulness is proving the truth or falsity of the proposition to which it is legally connected
6. A written statement of facts made under oath
7. Research that is *not* based on unique observations of the real world; it is based on information that already exists
8. Proof of or relating to law-breaking behavior
9. Tangible evidence (proof) that can be observed in a courtroom using the five senses
10. A purposeful, systematic investigation designed to increase knowledge
11. Proof; that which is used to justify a claim
12. A source other than the primary source of some information
13. People who have some personal knowledge relevant to a case
14. An affidavit submitted by a police officer to a judge to request a search warrant
15. An assertion that some condition should (or should not) exist
16. The level of probability necessary to conclude that enough evidence has been presented to prove (substantiate) a claim
17. A formal document that communicates the results of the author's purposeful, systematic investigation of a topic
18. The process whereby subject matter and/or methodological experts in the field review a paper for strengths and weaknesses, screening out flawed studies so that only the strongest studies are published
19. People who have some professional, specialized knowledge relevant to the disposition of a case
20. The origin of some information
21. An assertion that one condition is better than another (or other) conditions
22. Evidence that serves as a substitute for real evidence; it is some representation of real evidence
23. Evidence that substantiates some fact indirectly
24. The original source of some piece of information
25. A conclusion reached on some basis other than the formal legal evidentiary process
26. The obligation to provide evidence to prove what is being asserted

27. A conclusion reached on the basis of established or accepted facts, which does not require evidence
28. Evidence that people say
29. Evidence that, on its own, substantiates some fact directly and with a great deal of confidence
30. Evidence written, typed, or otherwise compiled by people

a. affidavit
b. burden of proof
c. circumstantial evidence
d. claim of fact
e. claim of policy
f. claim of value
g. criminal evidence
h. demonstrative evidence
i. direct evidence
j. documentary evidence
k. empirical research
l. evidence
m. expert witnesses
n. judicial notice
o. lay witnesses

p. nonempirical research
q. peer review
r. presumption
s. primary source
t. probative value
u. real evidence
v. research
w. research paper
x. search warrant affidavit
y. secondary source
z. source
aa. source evidence
bb. standard of proof
cc. testimonial evidence
dd. total evidence

Multiple Choice

These exercises are designed to assess Chapter 6 Learning Objective 3 (see Box 6.1). Indicate the single most appropriate response to each item below.

1. Which of the options best identifies the following type of evidence: a newspaper article about a new study on the relationship between gun laws and suicide rates.
   a. primary source
   b. secondary source

2. Which of the options best identifies the following type of evidence: a newspaper article reporting interviews with psychologists about treatment patterns for suicidal patients.
   a. secondary source
   b. primary source

3. Which of the options best identifies the following type of evidence: a blog on suicide prevention written by a person who attempted suicide.
   a. primary source
   b. secondary source

4. Which of the options best identifies the following type of evidence: a research article reviewing existing research on suicide.
   a. secondary source
   b. primary source

5. Which of the options best identifies the following type of evidence: a journal article reporting the results of an analysis of mortality statistics on trends in the suicide rate.
   a. empirical research
   b. nonempirical research

6. Which of the options best identifies the following type of evidence: a research article summarizing the key findings in a cutting-edge book on suicide prevention.
   a. secondary source
   b. primary source

7. Which of the options best identifies the following type of evidence: a research article critiquing several theories of suicide.
   a. empirical research
   b. nonempirical research

8. Which of the options best identifies the following type of evidence: an encyclopedia entry about a famous suicide theory.
   a. primary source
   b. secondary source

9. Which of the options best identifies the following type of evidence: an opinion piece on what committing suicide is like.
   a. nonempirical research
   b. empirical research

10. Which of the options best identifies the following type of evidence: a doctoral dissertation reporting the results of an analysis of how newspaper articles depicted suicide events.
    a. nonempirical research
    b. empirical research

11. Which of the options best identifies the following type of evidence: a footprint left at the scene of a burglary.
    a. direct evidence
    b. circumstantial evidence

12. Which of the options best identifies the following type of evidence: a suspect's confession that she committed the burglary in question.
    a. direct evidence
    b. circumstantial evidence

13. Which of the options best identifies the following type of evidence: the defendant's fingerprints on the window at the scene of the burglary.
    a. direct evidence
    b. circumstantial evidence

14. Which of the options best identifies the following type of evidence: a neighbor's testimony that the defendant was fleeing the scene soon after the glass was heard shattering.
    a. expert witness
    b. lay witness

15. Which of the options best identifies the following type of evidence: a forensic scientist testifying that the fibers from the defendant's shirt match fibers found at the crime scene.
    a. expert witness
    b. lay witness

16. Which of the options best identifies the following type of evidence: an eyewitness seeing the defendant near the crime scene around the time of the crime used to prove the defendant's guilt.
    a. direct evidence
    b. circumstantial evidence

17. Which of the options best identifies the following type of evidence: an eyewitness seeing the defendant near the crime scene around the time of the crime used to prove the defendant was near the crime scene around the time of the crime.
    a. direct evidence
    b. circumstantial evidence

18. Which of the options best identifies the following type of evidence: an email written by the defendant to her sister talking about a burglary she committed.
    a. documentary evidence
    b. testimonial evidence

19. Which of the options best identifies the following type of evidence: the defendant's sister saying she got an email from her sister in which her sister talked about committing a burglary.
    a. documentary evidence
    b. testimonial evidence

20. Which of the options best identifies the following type of evidence: a computer simulation of how the defendant entered the home.
    a. demonstrative evidence
    b. real evidence

21. Which of the options best identifies the following type of evidence: a crowbar offered as evidence of how the defendant entered the home.
    a. demonstrative evidence
    b. real evidence

22. Which of the options best identifies the following type of evidence: a psychologist testifying about how she saw the defendant buy the crowbar.
    a. expert witness
    b. lay witness

23. Which of the options best identifies the following type of evidence: a psychologist testifying about how the defendant isn't competent to stand trial.
    a. expert witness
    b. lay witness

24. Which of the options best identifies the following type of evidence: the jewelry, cash, and paintings stolen from the crime scene and retrieved from the defendant's home.
    a. demonstrative evidence
    b. real evidence

25. Which of the options best identifies the following type of evidence: photographs of the electronics stolen from the crime scene and recovered from the defendant's home.
    a. demonstrative evidence
    b. real evidence

Editing

These editing exercises are designed to assess Chapter 6 Learning Objective 5 (see Box 6.1). Identify the flaw in each of the following passages, and then describe how it should be revised to achieve effective evidence-based writing. You do *not* need to look up the studies cited here.

1. The rate of cybercrime has been increasing steadily for years.
2. The leading cause of cybercrime victimization is low self-control (Hackers R Us, 2014).
3. People do not take cybercrime seriously enough. This is evidenced by peer-reviewed empirical research showing that cybercrime has increased over the years (Smith & Thomas, 2018).
4. People who fall victim to cybercrime have a lower IQ than others (Wikipedia, 2014).
5. At present, 1 in 4 people will fall victim to cybercrime at least once in their lifetime, according to a peer-reviewed empirical research article (Anderson & Davidson, 2004).
6. We talked to two eyewitnesses who said the same thing. Now we know that after hitting the boy, the girl stole his lunch.
7. The girl in the video footage was Amy. We can be certain of this because the girl in the video was wearing a red jacket and black pants, and Amy was wearing a red jacket and blank pants that day.
8. The witness's friend said that the witness didn't actually see Amy hit the boy.
9. The assailant was left-handed, and Amy was left-handed. Thus, Amy is the assailant.
10. Amy couldn't possibly be the person who hit and stole from the boy because Amy's computer was being used at the time of the attack 5 miles away.

Writing

These discussion items are designed to assess Chapter 6 Learning Objectives 2, 4, 6, and 7 (see Box 6.1). Write at least one full paragraph in response to each item below. Use proper spelling, punctuation, and grammar.

1. Argue for the importance of evidence in criminal justice communications.
2. Identify and describe criteria for evaluating evidence.
3. Write an evidence-based research paper on some crime-related topic of your choosing. Compare some crime-related topic across two countries, identifying similarities and differences in the chosen topic. For example, you might want to compare violent crime trends, incarceration use, drug control, gun control, handling of juvenile offenders, policing models, sentencing of sex offenders, trial process, or capital punishment. Identify credible evidence to substantiate each claim. Write 3–5 pages, using APA format.
4. Pretend it is illegal for people to brush their teeth. Pick a person you know well, and then develop an affidavit for a search warrant to search the person's home for evidence that s/he brushes her/his teeth. Get creative as needed to demonstrate your knowledge of how to construct an effective evidence-based search warrant.

REFERENCES

Boulder County Bar Association. (2014). 13.2. Judicial notice and presumptions. *Bar media manual*. Retrieved from https://www.red-point-design.com/boulder-bar.org/bar_media_manual/evidence/13.2.html

Duckart, Tracy. (n.d.). *Thesis statements: Characteristics of an effective thesis*. Retrieved from http://users.humboldt.edu/tduckart/Thesis-Statements.htm

Grassian, Stuart. (2006). Psychiatric effects of solitary confinement. *Washington University Journal of Law and Policy, 22*(1), 325–383.

Federal Judicial Center and National Research Council. (2011). *Reference manual on scientific evidence* (3rd ed.). Washington, DC: The National Academies Press. Retrieved from https://www.fjc.gov/sites/default/files/2015/SciMan3D01.pdf

Harris, Robert A. (2017). *Using sources effectively: Strengthening your writing and avoiding plagiarism* (5th ed.). New York: Routledge.

Legal Information Institute. (n.d.). *Probable cause*. Retrieved from https://www.law.cornell.edu/wex/probable_cause

Mills v. City of Barbourville. (2004). #02-6404, 389 F.3d 568 (6th Cir.).

Nemeth, Charles P. (2011). *Law and evidence: A primer for criminal justice, criminology, law, and legal studies* (2nd ed.). Sudbury, MA: Jones and Bartlett Publishers.

Nolan, Dan, & Amico, Chris. (2017, April 18). Solitary by the numbers. *Frontline*. Retrieved from http://apps.frontline.org/solitary-by-the-numbers/

Recidivism in Connecticut. (2001). Retrieved from http://www.ct.gov/opm/lib/opm/cjppd/cjresearch/recidivismstudy/2001recidivisminconnecticut.pdf

Rutledge, Devallis. (2010, November 11). Patrol: Avoid defective search warrants. *Police*. Retrieved from http://www.policemag.com/channel/patrol/articles/2010/11/avoid-defective-search-warrants.aspx

Sipes, Dale Anne, Oram, Mary Elsner, Thornton, Marlene A., Valluzzi, Daniel J., & Van Duizend, Richard. (1988). *On trial: The length of civil and criminal trials*. Williamsburg, VA: National Center for State Courts.

State of Tennessee v. Gregory Lamont Hall (2014). M2013-02841-CCA-R3-CD (Tenn. R. App. P. 3).

Sullivan, Laura. (2006, July 26). Timeline: Solitary confinement in U.S. prisons. *NPR Special Series: Life in Solitary Confinement.* Retrieved from https://www.npr.org/templates/story/story.php?storyId=5579901

Tsay, Jenny. (2014, February 11). What evidence is needed for a search warrant? *FindLaw Crime & Criminals* [Blog post]. Retrieved from https://blogs.findlaw.com/blotter/2014/02/what-evidence-is-needed-for-a-search-warrant.html

Walker, Samuel. (2011). *Sense and nonsense about crime, drugs, and communities* (7th ed.). Belmont, CA: Wadsworth.

Wallace, Harvey, & Roberson, Cliff. (2013). *Written and interpersonal communication: Methods for law enforcement* (5th ed.). Upper Saddle River, NJ: Pearson Education Inc.

Ware, Wendy, Austin, James, & Thomson, Gillian. (2010). *Nevada Department of Corrections ten-year prison population projections, 2010–2020.* Washington, DC: JFA Associates.

Retrieved from http://doc.nv.gov/uploaded-Files/docnvgov/content/About/Statistics/Forecast_and_Planning/Prison_Population_Forecast_Report_2010_2020.PDF

Weir, Kirsten. (2012, May). Alone, in "the hole": Psychologists probe the mental health effects of solitary confinement. *Monitor on Psychology, 43*(5), 54. Retrieved from http://www.apa.org/monitor/2012/05/solitary.aspx

Worrall, John L., Hemmens, Craig, & Nored, Lisa S. (2018). *Criminal evidence: An introduction* (3rd ed.). New York: Oxford University Press.

Yoo, Sahng-Ah. (2015, November 19). *A look into solitary confinement: Present and future* [Blog post]. University of Oxford, Faculty of Law, Centre for Criminology. Retrieved from https://www.law.ox.ac.uk/centres-institutes/centre-criminology/blog/2015/11/look-solitary-confinement-present-and-future

Principle 6: Completeness

After reading this chapter, you will be able to

1. Recognize terminology relevant to complete communications.
2. Argue for the importance of complete communications in criminal justice.
3. Outline methods for producing complete communications.
4. Distinguish between complete and incomplete communications.
5. Revise topics in terms of breadth and depth.
6. Construct a complete lab report.
7. Produce a complete crime scene report.

If a writer omits something because he does not know it then there is a hole in the story.

—ERNEST HEMINGWAY

A **complete** communication is thorough, containing all pertinent parts and information, where **pertinent** means relevant and important. For students, completeness goes beyond reaching the minimum page requirement for a paper to making sure all pertinent information is in the paper and is presented with an appropriate level of detail. People who do not recognize this distinction tend to produce inferior communications. Being less concerned with producing a strong paper, they are content merely to be "done" with the communication. They do not review drafts for logic and flow, which would allow them to catch a possible gap in the information provided. They do not ask others to review their work, moreover, which is a step that can detect a missing stage in instructions.

For a variety of reasons, however, an incomplete communication creates problems. First, it can imply that the person who created it does not care—that person did not put enough thought and effort into the product's development to identify and include everything important. Second, an incomplete communication can imply that the person who created it is ignorant—that person did not know the subject. Third, an incomplete communication might have to be redone until it is complete. Having to repeat tasks is an inefficient consumption of valuable resources (e.g., time, manpower). Fourth, an incomplete communication can be difficult if not impossible to follow. The audience might not be able to understand or implement the message if vital material is left out. And fifth, an incomplete communication can result in poor, ineffective, unsafe, and/or illegal actions. If the audience is unaware of missing steps and/or has no choice but to use the communication to guide action, then the missing information can cause significant problems.

Consider the potential consequences of incomplete information in the following scenarios:

- An arrest report that neglects to mention an argument between the arrestee and arresting officer;
- Instructions for new employees on how to book a suspect that omit a step such as checking for contraband;
- A prosecutor's discovery disclosure to the defense that omits the name of a key witness;
- Incident reports in correctional institutions that name some but not all inmates involved in a riot;
- An essay exam in which a student leaves out one of three components of the criminal justice system;
- A student paper that fails to include an in-text citation to document the source of information or fails to include quotation marks to indicate the source's exact words;
- Job applications that fail to disclose a prior conviction; and
- Resumes that leave out contact information for references.

Echoing the oath sworn by trial witnesses, a compelling criminal justice communication must consist of "the truth, *the whole truth* and nothing but the truth" (emphasis added).

This chapter addresses the importance of completeness and presents some strategies for ensuring that the communications you produce are complete. We then look at the importance of completeness in the context of lab reports and crime scene reports. After reading this chapter, you will have a concrete understanding of what completeness entails and how to achieve completeness.

GUIDELINES

Follow these guidelines to develop a complete communication:

1. Include all pertinent information.
2. Address any coverage constraints.

A word of caution is warranted before we proceed: Do not confuse complete with long. A *complete* communication covers everything it needs to cover, while a *long* communication has lots of words but might not be complete. Keeping in mind the goal of concise writing (see Chapter 10), an effective criminal justice communication uses as few words as possible to present all the pertinent information.

BOX 7.2	Credibility Connection

Credible people are thorough. The completeness of your communications thus reflects on you and the quality and quantity of attention you are willing and able to devote to your work. Gaps in information make you look ignorant and/or careless.

Include All Pertinent Information

A complete communication contains all pertinent information, and what is pertinent is dictated by your communication's objective. The following list contains tips for ensuring that you have included all pertinent information:

1. **Understand your objective, parameters, and audience** (see Chapter 3). Completeness involves a thorough treatment of your objective in a manner that adheres to any parameters (e.g., length, number of resources, specific information to be included) and is tailored to your audience (e.g., what they know about the topic, what they need to get out of the communication).

2. **Do your research.** Read and talk to people to learn about your topic. Consider alternative perspectives, historical context, culture, pros and cons, and multiple angles. Criminal justice spans sociological, psychological, biological, economic, and more academic fields of study, which means (among other things) there are often multiple ways of looking at a single issue. Criminal justice practices vary across time and space, moreover, which means there are diverse ways of approaching crime and its control.

3. **Present both sides of issues.** "Pertinent" is not the same thing as "supportive" or "consistent." As such, information relevant to your topic might include contradictory positions and evidence. Merely presenting one side or including supportive evidence gives an incomplete understanding of the issue.

4. **Outline before you write.** You can save a lot of time by outlining before you develop the communication. An outline can serve as a visual representation of your information, which can guard against leaving out important information. (For more on outlining, see Chapter 4.)

5. **Deliver on promises.** Do what you explicitly or implicitly tell your audience that you are going to do. If you say, for instance, that "there are similarities and differences," then you need to identify both similarities and differences. If you say "there are five reasons," then you need to present five reasons.

6. **Present balanced coverage.** Treat similar items with a similar level of reflection and detail. If, for example, you present two viewpoints on an issue, avoid such practices as critiquing one but not the other, providing an example of one but not the other, listing pros for one but cons for the other, and providing substantially more details for one than the other.

7. **Remember to cite the source of all ideas, information, and words.** Do not assume that your reader will understand that a citation at the beginning of a paragraph means that citation applies to all information in the rest of a paragraph. Also, be sure to provide complete bibliographic information for each cited source.

8. **Be your own critic.** When you think you are done, review your communication critically looking for gaps in information. While reading aloud is particularly useful for catching writing mechanics errors (e.g., missing word, subject–verb disagreement), mapping out your communication can be especially helpful for detecting informational gaps. If you cannot see how one paragraph connects to the next, figure out why: Is it because some information is missing that would connect them, because one of the paragraphs is not actually relevant, or perhaps just because a transition is needed to clarify the connection between paragraphs?

9. **Get feedback.** Ask one or more other people to review your communication with attention to missing information. Sometimes a second set of eyes can see things you do not. Whenever possible, try to get someone from your target audience to review your communication and provide feedback.

10. **Give yourself time.** Start as soon as possible so that you have time to take the steps listed here to ensure that your communication is complete.

Address Any Coverage Constraints

There might be arguably pertinent information that is beyond the scope of a given communication, and you do not want to look ignorant or lazy for leaving out information your audience might expect you to cover. Two sources of this problem are (1) when there is too much information and (2) when there is too little information.

Too Much Information

Sometimes you need to cover a broad topic in a short amount of time or space. In this case, the challenge is to decide on a manageable yet legitimate way to cover the topic without sacrificing completeness.

The key consideration when you believe there is too much information on your topic is the trade-off between depth and breadth. **Breadth** refers to the range or extent of a topic. There are broader topics (e.g., white-collar crime), and there are narrower topics (e.g., insider trading, Ponzi schemes, embezzlement). **Depth** refers to the level of detail and specificity. Some topics are covered in minute detail (e.g., steps involved in alternative processes for detecting white-collar crime), and other topics are covered in little detail (e.g., overview of alternative models for detecting white-collar crime). Generally speaking, the broader your treatment of a topic, the less depth you can achieve.

Figure 7.1 illustrates this trade-off between breadth and depth. Moving from left to right, we go from more to less breadth. Moving from the bottom to the top, we go from less to more detail. Suppose your job is to write a pamphlet about ways to guard

BOX 7.3	Plagiarism Pointer

Think about how movie credits list everyone who contributed to the movie along with the type of contribution they made—which character they played or their job on the set. We would consider the movie credits to be incomplete if they left out any of the actors or other workers. Likewise, a communication is incomplete if it fails to give credit for each contribution, whether that contribution is an idea, picture, words, or some other form of information.

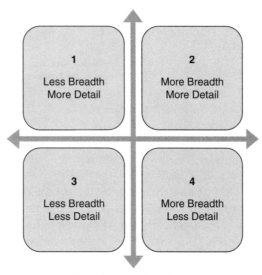

FIGURE 7.1   Breadth and Depth

against robbery victimization. In square 1, you are going to define your topic narrowly and, once you have done so, you would go into specific details. You might narrow your focus to residential robbery, for example, and then provide very detailed steps for each preventative measure identified. In square 3, you are going to keep a narrowed topic—in this case, residential robbery—and then list preventative measures without going into detail about how to implement each preventative measure. In squares 2 and 4, you would have a broader focus, such as residential and commercial burglary. While in square 2, you would list preventative measures as well as provide details on how to implement each preventative measure, in square 4 you would simply list the preventative measures.

Beyond that, Table 7.1 presents some suggestions for how to handle this problem at different points in a communication. To illustrate how Table 7.1 works, suppose your task is to present different models of policing in a brief presentation. There are multiple typologies of policing models, so the first step would be to choose one that best fits in the time allotted to you. Compare the two typologies presented in Table 7.2. Selecting the

TABLE 7.1   Strategies for Being Comprehensive When There Is *Too Much* Information

Where in the Communication You Are		
In the Beginning	*In the Middle*	*In the End*
Choose an approach that best fits the communication's objective, parameters, and audience	Focus on the most important material	Remind your audience of how you handled the topic and why
Specify (a) how you are handling the topic, and (b) why you are handling it that way (see coverage statements in Chapter 3)	Note when a topic or details are beyond the scope of the present communication	Direct the audience to additional resources on topics about which you cannot go into depth

TABLE 7.2   Different Ways to Classify Policing Models

5-Category Typology	3-Category Typology
1. Traditional policing	1. Reactive policing
2. Zero-tolerance policing	2. Predictive policing
3. Community-oriented policing	3. Community-oriented policing
4. Problem-oriented policing	
5. Intelligence-led policing	

5-category typology would give less time to cover each of the five policing models, while selecting the 3-category typology would give more time to cover each of the three policing models. If the communication's main purpose is to expose people with little knowledge on the topic to the idea that police agencies operate in different styles, then the 3-category typology is probably sufficient. If, however, the communication's main purpose is to make the point that there are many different policing models, then the five-category typology will probably be more appropriate.

After selecting one of the typologies, you might begin the presentation by noting that there are multiple typologies, and you selected the one best suited to your purpose in giving the presentation. You could invite audience members to speak with you after the presentation if they are interested in alternative typologies. Supposing the choice was the 3-category typology: you could identify and briefly describe different subtypes of predictive policing (e.g., problem-oriented policing; intelligence-led policing; scanning, analysis, response, action policing). Because you would not be able to go into detail on the subtypes, you might choose to focus your comparison around the major similarities and differences across subtypes. In this situation, you might inform your audience of your focus and that there is much more to these different policing models than can be covered in this particular presentation. At the end of your presentation, you could remind the audience of how you handled the topic and why as well as where to go for more information.

Too Little Information

Sometimes, there might seem to be no information on a topic; other times, the information might be flawed; and yet other times the information might be close to but not a perfect fit with your topic. Rarely is there absolutely no information. When you can choose your topic, you usually want to choose a topic about which there is readily available information. This is especially true for students writing papers or preparing presentations for class. Far more common are the other two situations: flawed information and loosely related information, both of which could be encountered with a single topic. Most research has one or more flaws. But flaws do not necessarily render information useless. Rather, we just need to be aware of them and address them, noting their existence and how they might affect our conclusion. The same is true of loosely related information.

Table 7.3 provides some specific strategies for handling these situations throughout the communication process. Across all strategies listed in Table 7.3, the key is to be open and honest. Do not try to ignore the lack of relevant, credible information. It can be tempting to gloss over or sidestep gaps and flaws in information. But—as professionals—we need to deal with information deficits directly and transparently. If asked to develop

TABLE 7.3   Strategies for Being Comprehensive When There Is *Too Little* Information

No Information	Flawed Information	Loosely Related Information
Acknowledge the lack of information on the topic	Acknowledge the limitations of existing information on the topic	Acknowledge the loose connection between topic and available information
Try to draw on information that is loosely related (when appropriate)	Try to reach conclusions based on the flawed information, but then clearly articulate how those conclusions are tentative due to the flawed information on which they are based	Try to reach conclusions based on the loosely related information, but then clearly articulate how those conclusions are tentative due to their loose connection with the information on which they are based
Try to conduct research/investigation to produce pertinent information	Try to conduct research/investigation to produce stronger information	Try to conduct research/investigation to produce more relevant information

a communication on a newly emerging crime problem or policy, we should expect and be prepared for a lack of information.

To illustrate how Table 7.3 works, imagine that your job is to draft an ethics code for the potentially new "space force"—President Trump's proposed organization for policing space travel (Bachman, 2018; Insinna, 2018). Well, clearly you could not find and draw from existing information on ethics codes for space policing. But you could locate less perfectly connected information sources. It was not that long ago, after all, that there was a new need for Internet policing, but it has been long enough that a wealth of information exists on ethical concerns and guidelines for policing cyberspace. Just as space policing is the new frontier for law enforcement in the 21st century, Internet policing was a novel expansion of law enforcement in the 20th century. While cyberspace policing thus might contain some ideas for ethical issues relevant to a newly emerging form of law enforcement, the air force might provide some added guidance pertaining to ethical issues involved in flight; and NASA and other space traveling entities likely could be consulted on how they approach and regulate ethics in space travel. When perfectly relevant information does not yet exist, then, one approach is to identify the next-best source(s) of information.

Another approach—listed in Table 7.3 for all information-gap situations—is to conduct research to produce credible information. Here, consider conducting surveys and/or interviews with relevant people. Use email, phone calls, or Skype sessions to get input from several people with as much as possible subject-matter expertise. What do they think key ethical issues will be, and do they have any suggestions for ethical guidelines for a space force? The presentation could summarize your survey/interview results, such as by presenting a ranking of the most commonly mentioned potential ethical problems and a listing of recommended components of ethical guidelines. Consider prefacing the results with some background data establishing the credibility of your sources, such as listing job titles and relevant educational and professional expertise.

Before leaving this topic, it might be helpful to look at another example of troubleshooting an information deficit. Say your assignment is to identify a list of evidence-based best practices for educating delinquent youths in juvenile justice institutions. While there is some research on this exact topic, there is not a great deal of strong research identifying effective strategies for incarcerated delinquents. The ideal source would report the results of an empirical evaluation of the effectiveness of one or more educational practices using an appropriate research design with a sample of incarcerated youth.

You would start by finding all those ideal sources, which might yield a short list of best practices. To lengthen your list, might be able to do some more digging to find additional ideal sources, but ultimately you would need to lower your standards to include flawed and loosely related information. Further, if you have the time, you could do some additional research of your own. You might not have the means to conduct a rigorous empirical evaluation of best practices with incarcerated youth, but you might be able to do some interviews with researchers who have done such studies and/or with teachers whose job is to educate incarcerated youth.

In terms of flawed research, you might include studies with less than ideal research designs. And in terms of loosely related evidence, you might include studies whose sample was not incarcerated, such as students with conduct problems in regular public schools, or whose sample was adults rather than juveniles. If your focus was on academic education, other loosely related evidence might stem from studies of best practices in vocational education. In both cases, explain why you are adding these less-than-ideal studies and how their shortcomings provide less confidence than the ideal studies. Your reason for adding these less-than-ideal studies was to identify as many best practices as possible, which you would state at the outset of your communication.

Describe your process and criteria for deciding which studies to include in your research. Then, distinguish the best practices based on ideal studies from those best practices based on flawed and loosely related studies. You might do this by separating the two sets of best practices into two lists—one called "best practices" and the other called "promising practices"—and then clearly explaining the distinction in the two lists: that we should have more confidence in the effectiveness of the best practices in the first than the second list because the best practices in the first list are based stronger research (empirical evaluation research using appropriate research designs) that directly addresses your topic (best academic educational practices) with your target population (incarcerated youth).

APPLICATIONS

Sometimes, you will have flexibility in deciding how to approach a communication assignment, such as when your task is to learn about some topic (e.g., sentencing) in the breadth and depth of your choice (e.g., identification and brief description of as many types of sentences as possible vs. detailed comparison of home confinement and incarceration).

But many criminal justice communications have very specific requirements, wherein completeness is a less subjective matter. Here, you lack control over defining what complete will mean and typically do not have the choice to limit your focus to some aspects while excluding others. Two such communications are lab reports and crime scene reports. Your job in such communications is to include all required information, listing every step you take and each thing you see.

Lab Reports

Many college/university assignments are "hands-on,"—such as in science and psychology experiments, financial crime analyses, and computer forensics exercises—wherein students perform some procedure and record what happens. A **lab report** is a formal account of an experiment or some other procedure used to obtain results. The lab report details exactly what was done to produce the reported results. Just like how a good recipe lists ingredients and procedures so others can make the exact same dish, a good lab report lists the materials and methods used to generate findings. Both the recipe and lab report are complete when they list all the ingredients/materials and steps/methods, and they lack comprehensiveness if one or more ingredients/materials and/or steps/methods is missing. An effective lab report facilitates **replication**, which is when documented steps can be followed to achieve the same result.

To permit replication, not only must the lab report be complete but also it must be correct and precise. Returning to the recipe scenario, suppose I am writing a recipe for a cake. I greased the cake pans before adding the batter, but I forgot to record that step when I wrote my recipe. The person using my recipe will end up with cake stuck to the pans. S/he will not end up with a cake that is exactly like my cake, and this would be because my recipe lacked *completeness*. In terms of *correctness*, were I to incorrectly record the amount of sugar (e.g., 2 cups when it was actually 1 cup), then the cake baked by someone using my recipe will be sweeter than the cake I baked. In terms of *precision*, suppose I were vague with the amount of ingredients (e.g., ¼ to ½ cup of butter). One person using my recipe might use ¼ cup of butter, while another person using my recipe might use ½ cup of butter—these two people would not end up with the same cake.

Contents and Organization

Variation in the contents of lab reports exists across disciplines (e.g., biology, psychology, computer science, criminal justice), which makes it impossible to develop a uniform guide to the contents and structure of lab reports that will apply in every course you take. Noting that such variation exists, Table 7.4 presents the sections of a lab report required in a digital forensics course that teaches students how to prepare a real-world digital forensics lab report. A digital forensics investigation and lab report might be used to link evidence to a particular suspect, confirm or contradict alibis or other statements, determine intent, pinpoint location, create timelines, reconstruct crimes, and authenticate documents. For example, digital forensics was involved in the 2005 investigation of Josie Phyllis Brown's murder. Both cell phone and Internet evidence was used to track her locations prior to her death, show the suspect's pattern of using MySpace to meet women, and uncover a voice recording of a fight (Casey, 2010).

In Table 7.4, the Evidence Analyzed section is to the lab report what the list of ingredients is to a recipe. Likewise, the Steps Taken section is equivalent to the steps in a recipe. While some of the components listed are optional (denoted by an asterisk in Table 7.4), the more the assignment is intended to simulate real-world investigations of actual criminal conduct, the more likely a professor is to require all the components listed in Table 7.4.

TABLE 7.4   Content and Structure of a Lab Report

Section	Contents
Title Page	Give the project a title and/or other identifying information.Provide the name and contact information for the investigator of the lab report.
Table of Contents*	Identify the major sections of the report.Include a Table of Contents only if your report is long and/or a Table of Contents is required.
Executive Summary	Summarize the most important information in a short amount of space.Include an Executive Summary (≈ 1 page) if your report is long; otherwise, include a briefer Abstract (≈ 200 words).
Objectives	Specify the purpose(s) of the investigation.
Evidence Analyzed	Itemize all forms/pieces of digital evidence analyzed, such as serial numbers, hash values, and images.
Steps Taken	Identify each step you take to analyze the evidence in detail.Specify all software and hardware used.
Relevant Findings	Provide findings for each objective.Consider using subsections if your lab report is long (e.g., Documents of Interest, Internet Activity, Software of Note).
Timeline*	Present important events in chronological order.Consider using a graphic to communicate this information.
Conclusion	Summarize the key points succinctly using bullet-list format.
Signature	Provide a place for the lab report investigator's signed signature.
Exhibits*	Include any additional relevant material (e.g., investigator's resume, chain of custody report).

Source: Kelley (2012)

*These are optional (less common) components.

Best Practices

Lab reports exemplify technical writing, particularly the need for complete and correct information to be presented clearly and concisely. As with any student communication, the overarching principle is to follow your professor's instructions. Beyond that, here are some general best practices for compiling high-quality lab reports:

- **Use established procedures:** Rely on reputable, validated methods and mechanisms for analyzing digital data.
- **Be comprehensive:** List every step of every procedure used with every piece of digital evidence. Demonstrate how knowledgeable you are with regard to digital forensics, how thorough your investigation has been, and how responsive you have been to the objectives.
- **Interpret your results:** Explain what your analysis means. Do not just include a series of screenshots, assuming your reader will see and surmise the same things as you. Explicitly link your results to your objectives.
- **Be concise:** Be direct and brief. Focus on your (assigned) objectives, avoiding tangential or irrelevant issues. Use bulleted and numbered lists where appropriate.
- **Incorporate graphics:** Select appropriate graphics to convey your methods and results. Consider combining options for data presentation, such as a screenshot with a red circle around the critical information.
- **Remain objective and professional:** Maintain professionalism, including objectivity and neutrality. Do not allow others to pressure you into misrepresenting

your procedures or results. Be open and honest about what you have done and found.

- **Review and edit:** Double-check your work. Look for and correct any inaccuracies, missing steps, vague language, and typos. Try to get someone else to review your work in case a second pair of eyes can catch what you miss, such as information gaps and lack of clarity. Do not let a careless error or two cast doubt on your knowledge or credibility.

Note that this list of best practices is for the writing of the lab report. It does not cover the digital evidence investigation itself because this textbook focuses on communication, not investigation.

Crime Scene Reports

Most crimes involve a physical crime scene, such as the house where a burglary took place, the street corner where a person was assaulted, or the garage where a car was stolen. The **crime scene report** (CSR) is a document describing a crime scene in detail. The importance of a properly prepared crime scene report cannot be overstated. This report will be a critical piece both of the investigation of the crime and the prosecution of the perpetrator. An effective CSR can help others establish the timeline and chain of events and recreate the crime scene. More specifically, CSRs can be useful in such issues as identifying and ruling out suspects, confirming (or disconfirming) witness accounts, determining modus operandi and cause of death, uncovering signs of a struggle or accomplices (or lack thereof), and protecting against (or suggesting the need to pursue) charges of police tampering with evidence. To get a clearer idea of how the CSR can accomplish these things, watch some of the documentaries or read some websites about the O.J. Simpson murder trial.

Contents and Organization

Police departments have their own requirements for CSRs, but there are some commonalties. CSRs have three basic components: the written part, photographs, and diagrams/sketches. The written component often includes five categories of information, as outlined in Table 7.5. While Table 7.5 is somewhat general and in a narrative format, Table 7.6 provides a more specific list of information to document in a CSR using a checklist

TABLE 7.5   Content and Structure of a Crime Scene Report—Narrative Format

Component	Description
Summary	Describe briefly how the case was initiated, including how it is that you came to be at the crime scene.
Scene	Describe in detail what you see as you approach the crime scene.Include anything unusual or out of place. Identify evidence, including its location and condition. Provide identification markers for the evidence.
Processing	Describe anything you or other investigators did, identifying all investigators who have a role in the crime scene investigation.
Evidence Collected	Identify the evidence recovered from the scene, the location where it was recovered, and where the evidence goes for analysis.
Pending	Identify any tasks that need to be completed.

Source: Byrd (n.d.)

TABLE 7.6   Content and Structure of a Crime Scene Report—Checklist Format

Identifying Information	Department Name:
	Date:
	Offense:
	Case Number:
	Location:
	Time Notified:
	Notified By:
	Authorized By:
	Time Arrived:
	Victim's Name:
	Victim's Address:
	Victim's Phone Number:
Information About the Scene	First Officer at Scene:
	Scene Security:
	Method Secured (select all that apply):
	Officer
	Barrier tape
	Other
	Scene Security Log Started: Yes or No
	Scene Entry Log Started: Yes or No
	Search Warrant: Yes or No
Weapons Present	For Each Weapon Present:
	Type:
	Location:
	Information Found on Weapon:
Scene Processing	Evidence Recovered: Yes or No
	Evidence Custody Sheet: Yes or No
	Location of All Evidence:
	List of All Evidence Collected at Crime Scene: Yes or No
	Date and Time Recovered:
Items Processed at Scene	Fingerprinting: Yes or No
	Location Where Processed:
	Date and Time Began:
	Date and Time Ended:
	DNA: Yes or No
	Location Where Processed:
	Date and Time Began:
	Date and Time Ended:
	(Repeat to record information for each item processed.)
Trace Evidence	Blood: Yes or No
	Description:
	Location:
	(Repeat to record information for each item [e.g., hair, fibers, stains, glass fragments, soil/dirt, toolmarks, liquid].)

Shoe and Tire Tracks	Shoe Tracks: Yes or No
	Description:
	Location:
	Photographed: Yes or No
	Microstatic Lifting: Yes or No
	Tire Tracks: Yes or No
	Description:
	Location:
	Photographed: Yes or No
	Casted: Yes or No
Photo Log	Yes or No
Leaving the Crime Scene	Date:
	Time:
	Secured: Yes or No and/or Turned Over to the Victim

Source: Warrington (2012)

format. While the format and exact information should comply with your agency's policy for CSRs, these tables give an idea of the types of information to be recorded and the level of specificity needed in a CSR.

Best Practices

What follows are considered best practices for documenting a crime scene in the narrative section and sketches (Byrd, n.d.; Warrington, 2012; Wisconsin Department of Justice Crime Laboratory Bureau, 2017):

1. **Take careful, copious notes.** Use these notes to write your final report of the crime scene. Ensure that your notes are sufficiently detailed to allow you to construct a precise account of the crime scene.
2. **Draw sketches in addition to taking photographs.** Sketches can be used to simplify and highlight aspects of the crime scene. They also can capture angles and views that a photograph cannot, such as the layout of a crime scene spanning multiple rooms. Specify the location being sketched and the date and time of the sketch, label doors and windows, and indicate which direction is north.
3. **Use symbols to draw objects.** Use squares, circles, and so on, to represent objects. Do not worry about making a gun, for example, look like a gun. Then use the evidence labels (e.g., #3) for each piece of evidence. Ensure that the evidence labels in your sketches match the evidence labels in the photographs.
4. **Distinguish between sketches that are drawn to scale and those that are not.** When you can, take measurements, using triangulation from at least two points, so that sketches are drawn to scale. Record the measurements, preferably on the sketch.
5. **Use a systematic process to guard against leaving out any information.** Consider creating and using a checklist, such as that provided in Table 7.6.

6. **Present only the facts.** Be descriptive and objective, omitting any opinions, analyses, or conclusions. Your observations, not your thoughts, should be include in the CSR.

7. **Edit for clarity, precision, and completeness.** You do not want to be misinterpreted. Nor do you want an investigator or prosecutor asking questions about the crime scene that should have been but cannot be answered by consulting your CSR—either because you left something out or were too vague.

Note that these best practices address the compilation of the CSR, not the actual investigation of a crime scene, such as collection of evidence and chain-of-custody reports. These topics are well beyond the scope of this textbook.

EXERCISES

Matching
These exercises are designed to assess Chapter 7 Learning Objective 1 (see Box 7.1). Match each numbered statement to the lowercase letter corresponding to the key word it defines. Each key word will be used only once.

1. A document describing a crime scene in detail
2. In communication, level of detail and specificity
3. Relevant and important
4. In communication, range or extent of a topic
5. Occurs when documented steps can be followed to achieve the same results
6. A formal account of an experiment or some other procedure used to obtain results
7. Thorough, containing all pertinent parts and information

    a. breadth
    b. crime scene report
    c. complete
    d. depth
    e. lab report
    f. pertinent
    g. replication

Multiple Choice
These exercises are designed to assess Chapter 7 Learning Objective 4 (see Box 7.1). Indicate the single most appropriate response to each item below. Feel free to do some research if that will help you decide.

1. Read the following passage, and then determine whether it is complete or incomplete. "There are three main components to the U.S. criminal justice system. The first component is policing. The second component is the courts. And the third component is corrections."
    a. complete
    b. incomplete

2. Read the following passage, and then determine whether it is complete or incomplete. "UCR Part I crimes include murder/homicide, aggravated assault, rape, robbery, burglary, motor vehicle theft, and larceny-theft."
   a. complete
   b. incomplete

3. Read the following passage, and then determine whether it is complete or incomplete. "The courtroom work group is comprised of prosecutors and defense attorneys."
   a. complete
   b. incomplete

4. Read the following passage, and then determine whether it is complete or incomplete. "There are six major stages in the process of developing formal criminal justice communications: collect information, draft, synthesize, improve and finalize, and deliver."
   a. complete
   b. incomplete

5. Read the following passage, and then determine whether it is complete or incomplete. "The principles of effective criminal justice communication consist of professionalism, responsiveness, organization, conciseness, clarity, correctness, completeness, evidence, and logic."
   a. complete
   b. incomplete

6. Read the following objective and road map, and then determine whether it would be a complete or incomplete paper. "The purpose of this paper is to explore differences in how England and Germany determine guilt or innocence. This paper begins with an overview of English and German society. Next, the English legal system and sentencing practices are described, and then German sentencing practices are presented. The conclusion stresses the importance of presumption of innocence and burden of proof."
   a. complete
   b. incomplete

7. Read the following objective and road map, and then determine whether it would be a complete or incomplete paper. "This paper will argue that the presumption of innocence creates an inefficient and ineffective criminal justice system. The first section will discuss what it means to presume innocence and how the presumption of innocence affects the criminal justice system process. The second section compares and contrasts two countries, one that does and one that does not have the presumption of innocence. The third section is the paper's conclusion, which suggests how a government could move from away from the presumption of innocence."
   a. complete
   b. incomplete

8. Read the following objective and road map, and then determine whether it would be a complete or incomplete paper. "This paper will examine the presumption of innocence, presenting a series of case studies that illustrate problems caused by assuming suspects and defendants are innocent. The following three cases will be analyzed: O.J. Simpson, Casey Anthony, and George Zimmerman. The conclusion speculates how shifting to a presumption of guilt could reduce these problems."
   a. complete
   b. incomplete

9. Read the title and overview slides in Table 7.7, and then determine whether it would be a complete or incomplete presentation.
   a. complete
   b. incomplete

10. Read the following title and overview in Table 7.8, and then determine whether it would be a complete or incomplete presentation.
    a. complete
    b. incomplete

Editing

These editing exercises are designed to assess Chapter 7 Learning Objective 5 (see Box 7.1). Rewrite each of the following passages, editing them as needed to achieve completeness.

1. Edit the following topic to be less broad: "outlining the history of policing."
2. Edit the following topic to be broader: "identifying English words for police."

TABLE 7.7   Slides for Multiple Choice Exercise #9

TABLE 7.8   Slides for Multiple Choice Exercise #10

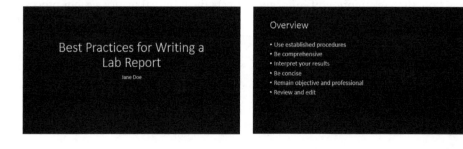

3. Edit the following topic to be less broad: "crime control."

4. Edit the following topic to be broader: "wrongful convictions in Oklahoma."

5. Edit the following topic to be more detailed: "enumerating the different reasons for wrongful convictions."

6. Edit the following topic to be less detailed: "a day-by-day chronology of Watergate."

7. Edit the following topic to be less broad and less detailed: "chronicling wrongful convictions throughout U.S. history, examining the details of the crime, people involved, and justice system process."

8. Edit the following topic to be broader and less detailed: "exploring reasons why larceny-theft crime victims lie to police and proposing methods for reducing lying for each reason."

9. Edit the following topic to be less broad and more detailed: "exploring reasons why larceny-theft crime victims lie to police, and identifying methods for reducing lying for each reason."

Writing

These writing exercises are designed to assess Chapter 7 Learning Objectives 2, 3, 6, and 7 (see Box 7.1). Write at least one full paragraph in response to each item below. Use proper spelling, punctuation, and grammar.

1. Argue for the importance of complete communications in criminal justice.

2. Outline methods for producing complete communications, including how to address coverage constraints.

3. Construct a complete lab report. Pick a controversial topic to research (e.g., racial profiling, sentencing inequality for rich and poor defendants, effectiveness of gun control, link between drugs and crime), and then identify three peer-reviewed scholarly journal articles that are directly relevant to your topic. The three studies you choose should—to the best of your knowledge— be the best available evidence. Record every decision you make and step you take (e.g., search engines, key words, why you might have passed over some studies in the search results) in sufficient detail that someone could repeat your procedures and obtain the same results. Create an APA-style References page that lists your studies and provides complete bibliographic information for them.

4. Produce a complete crime scene report. Pick a location to pretend is a crime scene (e.g., your dining room, garage, or back patio). The location should be free of any disturbance for a few hours to allow you to complete this exercise. Put two items in your crime scene that will be your evidence. Label the pieces of evidence with numbered cards. Write up a crime scene report with at least two sketches and a photograph. The first sketch should give a clear idea of the layout of the property and where on the property the crime scene is. The second sketch should focus on the evidence in the crime scene. Take a picture of the crime scene so that your narrative and second sketch can be compared with the actual crime scene. Submit your narrative along with your sketches and photograph.

REFERENCES

Bachman, Justin & Travis J. Tritten. (2018, August 10). Why Trump wants a space force for the final frontier. *Bloomberg*. Retrieved from https://www.bloomberg.com/news/articles/2018-08-06/what-s-a-space-force-and-can-trump-really-start-one-quicktake

Byrd, Mike. (n.d.). *Written documentation at a crime scene* (pp. 1–16). Retrieved from http://www.crime-scene-investigator.net/document.html

Casey, Eoghan. (2010). Introduction. In Eoghan Casey (Ed.), *Handbook of digital forensics and investigation*. Burlington, MA: Elsevier Academic Press.

Insinna, Valerie. (2018, September 5). Top US Air Force official is now on board with Trump's Space Force plan. *Defense News Conference*. Retrieved from https://www.defensenews.com/smr/defense-news-conference/2018/09/05/the-top-air-force-official-is-now-onboard-with-trumps-space-force-plan/

Kelley, Melia. (2012, May 30). Report writing guidelines. *Forensic Magazine*. Retrieved from https://www.forensicmag.com/article/2012/05/report-writing-guidelines

Warrington, Dick. (2012, October 18). Crime scene checklists: Value in the report. *Forensic Magazine*. Retrieved from https://www.forensicmag.com/article/2012/10/crime-scene-checklists-value-report

Wisconsin Department of Justice Crime Laboratory Bureau. (2017). Chapter 4: Crime scene sketch. *Physical evidence handbook* (9th ed.). Retrieved from WILEnet website: https://wilenet.org/html/crime-lab/physev-book/chapter4-crime-scene-sketch-2017.pdf

CHAPTER 8

Principle 7: Correctness

BOX 8.1　　**Learning Objectives**

After reading this chapter, you will be able to
1. Recognize terminology relevant to correct communications.
2. Argue for the importance of correct criminal justice communications.
3. Outline methods for producing correct communications.
4. Distinguish between proper and improper writing mechanics.
5. Edit statements to make them correct.
6. Develop a correct book or article critique.
7. Construct a correct arrest report.

If you're not accurate, you'll cause untold trouble.

—DAVID O. SELZNICK

In its broadest sense, **correct** means free from error. As such, correct pertains not just to the truth and accuracy of information itself but also to the proper presentation of the information. Correctness is perhaps the writing principle that many would believe is the most important—in criminal justice and elsewhere. But, if there is such widespread recognition of the importance of being correct, why is being incorrect so common? Incorrectness could stem from ignorance, caprice, or mistake. In any event, in our field, incorrectness can be confusing, expensive, counterproductive, offensive, and even lethal.

You think not? Since 1932, researchers have been investigating cases of wrongful conviction, including when innocent people have been executed. Where Borchard (1932) identified 65 cases of wrongful convictions "mainly from the 20th century" (p. v), Radelet, Bedau, and Putnam (1992) uncovered more than 416 cases of Americans wrongfully convicted in homicide cases in the 1900s. More recently, the Death Penalty Information Center (2018) lists 162 cases of death-row inmates later determined to be innocent since 1973—after having served an average of 11.3 years on death row. Some of these innocents were exonerated after the person they had been accused of killing showed up alive. In other cases, new evidence surfaced, eyewitness testimony was determined to be mistaken, "snitches" and prosecution witnesses were discovered to have given false testimony, the "real killer" was convicted, or DNA evidence was analyzed using new technology.

Wrongful conviction—and even more tragically, wrongful executions—exemplify the most obvious form of incorrectness: being wrong about the truth. We can also be wrong in how we represent the truth (i.e., how we present information). An early example is literally of biblical portion: The Ten Commandments. One version of the Holy Bible left out a key word: "not," the result being "Thou shalt commit adultery." We do not know how much swinging resulted in 17th-century England thanks to the *Wicked Bible*, as this version became known, but we do know that King Charles I ordered every copy burnt and took away the license of the printer who had published it (Smallwood, 2014). Here are just a few more examples to demonstrate the persistence of the problem as it applies specifically to contemporary criminal justice:

- A judge reduced a lawyer's fees because his documents were riddled with typos; the judge described the lawyer's writing as "vague, ambiguous, unintelligible, verbose and repetitive," explaining "Mr. Puricelli's complete lack of care in his written product shows disrespect for the court. . . . Mr. Puricelli's lack of care caused the court and, I am sure, defense counsel, to spend an inordinate amount of time deciphering the arguments" (Liptak, 2004).
- Christina FourHorn was wrongfully arrested and spent 5 days in jail before her husband could bail her out; the police had meant to arrest "Christina Fourhorn" (Chen, 2010).
- A drug dealer who had served 29 years in prison was released when an appeals court found a "fatal flaw": The judge had written 10:35 p.m. instead of 10:35 a.m. on the search warrant (WSMV News 4, 2011).
- Botched wording in federal legislation mandated that gun-carrying Amtrak passengers be locked in boxes. But the law meant to require that the guns be locked away for the journey instead of the people carrying them (Pergram, 2009).
- Mistaken use of a comma instead of a hyphen cost the U.S. government and hence taxpayers more than $2 million in 1872 when it exempted fruit—not just fruit plants, as intended—from tariffs: "fruit, plants" instead of "fruit-plants" (Crockett, 2014).
- Princeton University Press recalled more than 4,000 copies of Peter Moskos's book, *Cop in the Hood: My Year Policing Baltimore's Eastern District*, after finding more than 90 spelling and grammatical errors in the book's 245 pages (Howard, 2008).
- After the judge accidentally left off a single digit, a man charged with aggravated child abuse was freed on $25,000 bond instead of $250,000. And the man had been bailed out before the mistake was realized (Humphrey, 2016).
- A search warrant wrote the wrong year, 2003, when the officer meant 2004. But because 2003 was a year prior to the search, the probable cause was considered stale, and the evidence was suppressed (*State v. Greenstreet*, 2004).

This chapter looks at correctness in criminal justice communications and how to ensure that our communications are correct in terms not only of the truth and accuracy of the information we communicate but also of whether or not we present this information in consistently proper form. Although correctness is equally crucial in all criminal justice communications, this chapter looks at correctness in the context of critiques and arrest reports. Having read this chapter, readers should be convinced of the need to produce communications that are correct in both minor and major details.

GUIDELINES

Follow these guidelines to develop a correct communication:

1. Present only information that is true.
2. Present information in proper form.

Bear in mind that for a communication to be correct, both of these guidelines must be followed in all respects.

Present Only Information That Is True

Correct information is true information. **Truth** refers to an accurate reflection of reality. Three rules are presented here that, when combined, yield a truthful communication:

1. Know the truth.
2. Tell the truth.
3. Avoid untruths and half-truths.

Know the Truth

To tell the truth, we must *know* the truth. **Knowledge** is a justified true belief (Ichikawa & Steup, 2017). We know something when we believe it to be true based on evidence. If we do not believe it to be true, then we do not know it as truth. Likewise, if we are unable to justify it by pointing to supporting evidence, then what we have is a belief rather than knowledge of the truth. There are some exceptions to this rule, such as common knowledge (e.g., the sun rises in the morning and sets in the evening, an island is surrounded by water, plants need light and water to grow, there are three primary colors) and deductive logic (e.g., 5 + 5 = 10; 4 hours after noon, it will be 4:00 p.m.; today is Wednesday, because yesterday was Tuesday). Other than common knowledge, however, we need to be cautious about assuming we know the truth.

Chapter 6 covered evidence—its forms and its role in uncovering the truth. Here, the point is that we should refrain from assuming we know the truth until we have evidence supporting it. In other words, we need to have some basis for treating something as the truth. That basis could be common knowledge or evidence, but it should not be preference, intuition, opinion, assumption, or speculation.

BOX 8.2	Credibility Connection

Incorrect facts and information might give the impression that we are unethical (at worst) or ignorant (at best). Incorrect grammar, spelling, and punctuation just make us look sloppy and careless. None of this is consistent with fostering trust and projecting credibility.

Tell the Truth

Once we know the truth—or at least have a valid justification for believing something to be true—we should stick to the truth. Being truthful is more than being ethical (not that ethics is a small concern!). It is also a matter of being correct. To be correct, we must be truthful. Although as a criminal justice practitioner, our ability to tell the truth might be constrained by law and/or ethics (e.g., a defense attorney must not tell the jury his client is guilty, even if he knows that to be true), the general rule of thumb is to stick to the truth.

The truth involves communicating facts, and we need to get our facts straight and then stick to those facts. If we have less than a fact—such as a suspicion—then we need to be careful to avoid presenting it as a fact. It might be a fact, for instance, that Witness A told you that he saw Suspect B hit Victim C. But it is not a fact that Suspect B hit Victim C. We have some reason to believe Suspect B hit Victim C, but we do not know that Suspect B hit Victim C. Thus, it would be truthful to say, "Witness A said that Suspect B hit Victim C." But to say that "Suspect B hit Victim C" denies any possibility that Witness A lied or was mistaken. Thus, part of truth telling is using language in such a way as to distinguish between fact/truth and possibility/conjecture.

Truth telling is important not just in the practice of criminal justice but also in its study. College and university codes of academic integrity demand that students be truthful. Students and professors are expected not to pass assumptions off as facts, and sources of ideas and words should be accurately identified. When evidence supports a belief but leaves room for doubt, we are wise to use phrases such as "According to Study A . . .," "Study B indicates that . . .," and "Research has found. . . ." These phrases make a crucial difference as to the meaning of the sentence and the fact being asserted: In these examples, the fact asserted is that a study reported something—not that the something being reported is true. When using such language, as long as you interpreted and credited the source properly, you are telling the truth—regardless of whether or not the something being reported is actually true.

Avoid Untruths and Half-Truths

If a prerequisite for correctness is truth, then it follows that an untruthful communication is an incorrect communication. An **untruth** is a statement you know or believe to be false (i.e., a falsehood), while a **half-truth** is a statement that you know or believe to be only partially true—a combination of truth and falsehood. Only in very exceptional real-world situations (e.g., interrogations, hostage negotiations), are untruths and half-truths ever acceptable. There is no acceptable use of untruths and half-truths in academic communications.

Half-truths are probably more common than deliberate untruths in academic writing. Suppose you are researching reasons for parole revocations and how common they are,

---

BOX 8.3   Plagiarism Pointer

Clearly identifying the source of information not only prevents plagiarism but also can protect you from being wrong. Perhaps your source is mistaken about some fact. If you credit that fact to your source rather than claiming that you discovered it (e.g., "According to Smith (2016) . . ."), then you are not technically wrong. This is the idea behind statements in crime news reports such as "According to an eyewitness. . . ."

focusing on whether new crimes or technical violations are the more common reason people's parole gets revoked. Imagine you found one source reporting that new crimes are the main reason and another source reporting that technical violations are the main reason. If in your paper you report, "Research indicates that technical violations are the most common reason for parole revocation," and cite that one source—which might be tempting if it supports your beliefs or thesis—you would be telling only half of the truth. To be completely open and honest—and correct—you would instead need to say something along the lines of, "Although research is inconsistent on the issue, Study X found that technical violations are the most common reason for parole revocation"; or even, "While Study X found that technical violations are the most common reason for parole revocation, Study Y found just the opposite: that new offenses are the most common reason for parole revocation."

Present Information in Proper Form

Correct information is expressed in proper form. **Proper** means conforming to accepted standards. Here, the concern is with writing mechanics, particularly grammar, spelling, and punctuation. There is no way this chapter can present an exhaustive lesson on writing mechanics, but it will cover the fundamental rules as well as address some of rules particularly relevant to criminal justice. These five general strategies will help you present information properly:

1. Learn the rules.
2. Use proper grammar.
3. Use proper spelling.
4. Use proper punctuation.
5. Be consistent.

Learn the Rules

Just like knowing the truth is the first step to telling the truth, knowing the rules for writing mechanics is the first step to using proper writing mechanics. Accepted standards for writing are not universal. For example, even though the United States and the United Kingdom share the English language, the proper spelling of words sometimes differs (e.g., "offense" in the United States versus "offence" in the United Kingdom). Likewise, different organizations and academic disciplines have different rules for writing. This situation is akin to "house rules" when playing a game of cards. Aces might be high in one house but low in another house, twos might be wild in one house but not the next, and so forth. What is correct therefore differs from house to house. Unless otherwise indicated, this book uses Standard U.S. English and follows American Psychological Association (APA) rules governing writing mechanics. (Refer to Appendix B for APA rules governing format and style, including in-text citations, headings, references, etc.)

Use Proper Grammar

Grammar deals with fitting words together to express thoughts. As such, correct grammar involves the following:

(a) complete sentences, (b) subject-verb agreement, (c) noun-pronoun agreement, (d) verb tense, (e) placement of modifiers, (f) parallel construction, (g) capitalization, (h) italics, and (i) numbers.

TABLE 8.1   Complete Sentences, Sentence Fragments, and Run-On Sentences

	Example	Problem	Solution
Complete Sentences	A man broke into a house and stole electronics and jewelry.	—	—
	The homeowner reported a burglary.	—	—
	The police officer arrested the burglary suspect.	—	—
Sentence Fragments	Did not resist arrest.	There is no subject.	Add a subject: The suspect did not resist arrest.
	The police officer, responding to the call after being dispatched.	There is no verb.	Add a verb: The police officer, responding to the call after being dispatched, arrested the suspect.
	Because the homeowner reported a burglary.	This is not a complete thought.	Complete the thought: Because the homeowner reported a burglary, the police officer was dispatched to the scene.
Run-On Sentences	The homeowner reported a burglary the police officer was dispatched to the scene.	Two complete sentences are combined.	Divide them into two separate sentences: The homeowner reported a burglary. The police officer was dispatched to the scene.
	The police officer arrested the burglary suspect, the burglary suspect exhibited no signs of arrest.	Two complete sentences are combined by a comma (comma splice).	Add a coordinating conjunction: The police officer arrested the burglary suspect, and the burglary suspect exhibited no signs of arrest.
	The arraignment judge set bail, therefore the suspect's wife went to see a bail bondsman.	A transition is used improperly in the middle of a sentence (comma splice).	Replace the comma with a semicolon, and then add a comma after the transition: The arraignment judge set bail; therefore, the suspect's wife went to see a bail bondsman.

COMPLETE SENTENCES. A **complete sentence** has a subject and a verb, and it expresses one complete thought. In contrast, a **sentence fragment** lacks a subject and/or verb. As such, it does not express a complete thought. And a **run-on sentence** expresses more than one complete thought. Thus, it has two (or more) sets of subjects and verbs. Some examples are provided in Table 8.1. While some writing styles and situations (e.g., poetry, novels, entertainment) allow for fragments, technical writing does not.

SUBJECT–VERB AGREEMENT. The subject and verb must agree in number. For example: "A person writes" versus "People write." Though this is a fundamental grammar rule, it can be complicated to apply in some situations. Use this process to ensure subject–verb agreement:

1. **Find the verb.** A verb expresses action. If there are multiple verbs, perform this process for each verb.
2. **Find the subject that governs the verb.** The subject performs the action expressed by the verb. There might be multiple nouns in a sentence, and the subject might not be the noun nearest to the verb. Prepositional phrases (e.g., "of people," "in the prison," "around the corner") end with a noun (i.e., the object of the preposition), but that noun does not govern the verb.

3. **Ignore other words.** Just focus on the subject and verb. Consider striking through other words or writing the subject and verb right next to each other to help you focus.

4. **Determine whether the subject is singular or plural.** Usually, this will be simple, but sometimes is can be tricky. Words like "data" and "phenomena" are plural; thus, "data are" and "phenomena occur."

5. **Look to the noun closest to the verb when the subject consists of singular and plural nouns.** For example, "Neither the killers nor the gun was found," or "Neither the gun nor the killers were found."

6. **Reword the sentence as necessary to achieve subject–verb agreement.** Without changing the meaning or accuracy of the sentence, edit the subject and/or verb to make them agree.

NOUN–PRONOUN AGREEMENT. The pronoun and the noun it replaces must agree in number and in gender.

1. **Find the pronoun.** Pronouns are substitutes for nouns.

2. **Determine if the pronoun is feminine, masculine, or neuter.** Most pronouns are neuter. Table 8.2. distinguishes between pronouns in terms of gender.

3. **Determine if the pronoun is singular or plural.** Table 8.2 also distinguishes between pronouns in terms of number. Notice how all plural pronouns are neuter.

4. **Find the noun being replaced.** Usually, the noun appears earlier in the sentence or in a previous sentence. Sometimes, however, you might need to read the previous sentence or go back even further to determine what the noun is. (When this is the case, it is probably better to repeat the noun than to use a pronoun because we do not want to make our readers have to do a lot of work to figure out what a pronoun stands for.)

5. **Determine if the noun is feminine, masculine, or neuter.** Nouns such as Anne, Sarah, Jessica, girls, and ladies are feminine. Nouns like Tom, Dick, Harry, boys, and men are masculine. Nouns such as gun, DNA, gangs, policy, criminal justice system, and prisons are neuter.

6. **Determine if the noun is singular or plural.** Nouns such as Anne, Tom, gun, DNA, policy, and criminal justice system are singular. Nouns such as girls, boys, gangs, and prisons are plural.

7. **Reword the sentence as necessary to achieve noun–pronoun agreement.** Without changing the meaning or accuracy of the sentence, try to edit the noun and/ or pronoun. Sometimes this can produce awkward phrasing, and so you might need to rearrange some words or figure out a different way to express the idea.

TABLE 8.2 Pronouns

| | Singular | | Plural | |
	Feminine	*Masculine*	*Neuter*	*Neuter*
First Person	—	—	I, me, my, mine	we, us, our, ours
Second Person	—	—	you, your, yours	you, your, yours
Third Person	she, her, hers	he, him, his	it, its	they, them, their, theirs

A common mistake with noun and pronoun agreement involves *collective nouns* (e.g., gang, group, police). When a collective noun refers to a unified group (e.g., gang behavior, group process, police practice), then it should be treated as singular and be used with a singular pronoun and with a singular verb. For example: The gang deals drugs, and *it* also engages in robbery.

Another common mistake is a *vague pronoun reference*. Sometimes, there is more than one noun to which a pronoun could refer. In this case, it can be unclear to which of the nouns the pronoun refers. For example, Tom and Joe witnessed a crime, and *he* called the police to report it. In this example, who "he" is cannot be discerned. In such situations, the best corrective is to keep using the noun: Tom and Joe witnessed a crime, and *Joe* called the police to report it.

VERB TENSE. Verbs express action or a state of being. Although we generally think only of the simple tense forms—past, present, and future tense—there are also perfect and progressive forms for each of these three simple tenses. To express a thought, we need to pick the appropriate tense, and then we need to stick with it. Table 8.3 summarizes the different verb tenses and when they are appropriate.

A common problem with verbs is an unjustified shift in verb tense: "The probation officer *asked* for a urine sample. He then *explains* to the offender that urine samples are used to test for drugs." Assuming both the asking and the explaining occurred in the past, it is correct to say, "The probation officer *asked* for a urine sample. He then *explained* to the offender that urine samples are used to test for drugs." Remember that verb tense conveys meaning. Improper tense (e.g., using present tense to describe past events) and

TABLE 8.3   Verb Tenses

Tense	Description	Example
Simple Form		
Past	Describing conditions that occurred at a discrete time in the past	The victim <u>reported</u> the crime. The police officers <u>responded</u> to the call.
Present	Describing conditions that are occurring right now or that occur regularly	The victim <u>experiences</u> shame. Police officers <u>assist</u> crime victims.
Future	Describing conditions that will occur in the future.	The victim <u>will testify</u> in court. Police officers <u>will escort</u> the victim to the courthouse.
Perfect Form		
Past Perfect	Describing conditions that occurred and ended at an indefinite time in the past or conditions that occurred prior to other past conditions	The perpetrator <u>had planned</u> the attack. The police officers <u>had participated</u> in victim advocacy training before they were assigned to sexual assault cases.
Present Perfect	Describing conditions that occurred over an indefinite time period in the past or that began in the past and have continued into the present	The victim <u>has experienced</u> nightmares since the attack. The police officers <u>have collected</u> evidence of the crime.

(Continued)

Tense	Description	Example
Future Perfect	Describing conditions that will be completed in the future prior to some other future condition	The victim <u>will have testified</u> before the jury deliberates. The police officers <u>will have explained</u> the evidence before the victim testifies.
Progressive Form		
Past Progressive	Describing conditions that occurred over a period of time in the past	The victim <u>was living</u> with her parents. The police <u>were patrolling</u> the neighborhood when the assault was reported.
Present Progressive	Describing conditions that are occurring now and might continue to occur	The victim <u>is experiencing</u> psychological pain. The police <u>are waiting</u> for their turn to testify.
Future Progressive	Describing conditions that will occur over a period of time in the future	The victim <u>will be</u> anxious during her testimony tomorrow. The police <u>will be transporting</u> the victim to the courthouse.
Perfect Progressive Form		
Past Perfect Progressive	Describing conditions that began in the past and ended at a definite point in the past	She <u>had been walking</u> home from work when she was assaulted. The police <u>had been completing</u> paperwork when they got the call.
Present Perfect Progressive	Describing conditions that began in the past and ended in the present	She <u>has been depressed</u> since her parents died. The police officers <u>have been consoling</u> victims since they took a victim advocacy class.
Future Perfect Progressive	Describing conditions that began in the past, present, or future and will continue up to a definite point in the future	By 5:00 p.m. today, the victim <u>will have been waiting</u> to testify for 6 hours. When the police officers finish testifying, they <u>will have been working</u> on this case for 4 months.

Sources: APA (2009); Grammarly (2018c)

switching tenses (e.g., moving from present to past tense when describing present events) can be unclear and confusing as well as technically incorrect.

MODIFIER PLACEMENT. Both adjectives and adverbs are modifiers, and they should be placed as close as possible to the word they modify. Adjectives describe nouns (e.g., "a *credible* witness," "a judge who is *stern*," "*corrupt* evidence," "a *maximum-security* prison," "punishment is *swift*"), while adverbs describe verbs, adjectives, or other adverbs (e.g., "spoke *quickly*," "*sternly* chastised," "*unethically* cunning interrogation tactics," "testified *amazingly accurately*"). Adverbs also can be used as transitional or introductory words (e.g., "*Similarly*, there was . . ."; "*Consequently*, the man . . ."; "*Conversely*, the victim . . ."). Problems and solutions involving misplaced and dangling modifiers are presented in Table 8.4.

TABLE 8.4 Modifier Placement

	Misplaced Modifier	Dangling Modifier
Definition	Modifier placement makes the sentence confusing or incorrect	Modifier has no discernible referent; the sentence does not contain the word being modified
Incorrect	The <u>lengthy</u> victim's testimony caused jurors to cry.	The witnesses were interviewed <u>using a new procedure</u>.
Problem	Incorrect: The victim wasn't lengthy (though she might have been tall); it would have been the testimony that was lengthy.	Unclear: Was the new procedure (a) used to interview witnesses or (b) used by the witnesses who were interviewed? And who did the interviewing?
Solution(s)	Move the modifier as close as possible to the word/phrase it modifies	Switch from passive to active voice and/or move the modifier as close as possible to the word/phrase it modifies
Correct	The victim's <u>lengthy</u> testimony caused the jurors to cry.	<u>Using a new procedure</u>, <u>the officers</u> interviewed the witnesses.

The word "only" is a commonly misplaced modifier. Consider the sentence: "Tina only told a small lie." What does this sentence mean? Literally, it means that Tina said just one thing, and that one thing was a lie. If this is what the writer meant, then the sentence is unclear because the reader might wonder what "only" refers to. In contrast, perhaps the writer meant that what Tina did was not too bad because the lie was just a small one. But if this is the case, then the sentence is incorrect and should instead be written as "She told only a small lie" (or: "The lie she told was only a small one").

PARALLEL CONSTRUCTION. Similar ideas should be presented in similar form. Table 8.5 shows errors and corrections involving parallel construction for three situations. Notice how, in the third column, the incorrect version involves not only lacking parallel construction of verbs (indicated by single underlining) but also mismatched coordinating conjunctions (indicated by double underlining).

TABLE 8.5 Parallel Construction

	Lists	Single Coordinating Conjunctions	Paired Coordinating Conjunctions
Definition	Presenting items in a series	Joining items using "and," "or," "but," or "nor"	Joining items using "between . . . and," "both . . . and," "neither . . . nor," "either . . . or," or "not only . . . but also"
Incorrect	Bailiffs' duties include <u>providing</u> security, <u>maintain</u> order, and <u>to announce</u> the judge's entry and departure.	The bailiff <u>called</u> the witness and then <u>walks</u> her to the stand.	The bailiff <u>not only</u> <u>called</u> the witness <u>and</u> <u>walks</u> her to the stand.
Correct	Bailiffs' duties include <u>providing</u> security, <u>maintaining</u> order, and <u>announcing</u> the judge's entry and departure.	The bailiff <u>called</u> the witness and then <u>walked</u> her to the stand.	The bailiff <u>not only</u> <u>called</u> the witness <u>but also</u> <u>walked</u> her to the stand.

Parallel construction plays a critical role in PowerPoint presentations. Within a content slide, the material presented in a bulleted or numbered list should be expressed in parallel form (compare Figure 8.1a [not parallel form] and 8.1b [parallel form]). This includes not only phrasing but also use of capitalization and punctuation. If one item has a punctuation mark at the end, for instance, all items should have a punctuation mark at the end. Chapter 11 will go into more detail about parallel and consistent formatting within and across slides in PowerPoint presentations.

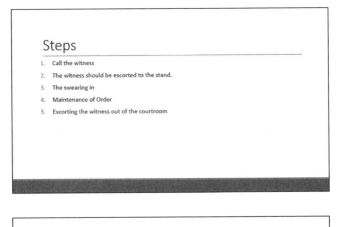

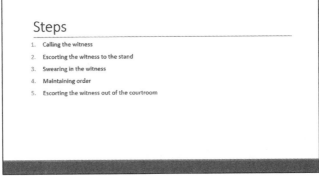

FIGURE 8.1A AND 8.1B   Achieving Parallel Construction in
PowerPoint Presentations

CAPITALIZATION. There are several fairly standard rules governing when words should be capitalized:

- **Words at the start of a complete sentence**
  - ○ The victim testified.
  - ○ Now is the time for her to testify.
- **Words beginning a title/heading and major words in titles/headings**
  - ○ The first word of titles and subtitles when using "Sentence case"
    - ■ The role of the bailiff
    - ■ The role of the bailiff: Every judge needs a henchman

- Major words in titles and headings when using "Title Case"
  - The Role of the Bailiff
  - The Role of the Bailiff: Every Judge Needs a Henchman
  - The Bailiff Versus the Judge: Who Really Is in Charge?
  - Table 1. The Bailiff's Duties
  - Figure 1. Where the Bailiff Stands in a Courtroom
- **Proper nouns**
  - Names of people, places, institutions/organizations, trade and brand names, and particular tests
    - John Doe
    - Washington
    - Sears Tower
    - Federal Bureau of Investigation
    - Xerox
    - Level of Service Inventory

Just as there are rules for when to capitalize, there are rules for when *not* to capitalize. Some common rules for when *not* to capitalize are

- **As ALL CAPS** (unless otherwise specified [e.g., by the required style guide])
  - Wrong: We should NOT capitalize for emphasis.
  - Right: We should not capitalize for emphasis. (Note: APA says not to italicize for emphasis either.)
- **For names of scientific theories, hypotheses, models, effects, and laws**
  - Wrong: Deterrence Theory
  - Right: deterrence theory
  - Wrong: Lead–Crime Hypothesis
  - Right: lead–crime hypothesis
  - Wrong: Prisoner's Dilemma Model
  - Right: prisoner's dilemma model
  - Wrong: Black-Sheep Effect
  - Right: black-sheep effect
  - Wrong: Law of Diminishing Returns
  - Right: law of diminishing returns

Use Proper Spelling

Spelling pertains to putting letters together to present terms that convey meaning. As such, correct spelling involves (a) word choice, (b) spelling, (c) hyphens and en dashes, (d) plurals and possessives, and (e) abbreviations.

WORD CHOICE. Start proper spelling by choosing the right word. Complicating this task is that some words are commonly misused or confused with other words. While these words might sound or look similar, they have different correct uses. Table 8.6 provides some examples of words that are commonly but incorrectly misused or confused with each other. Spell check might not catch these errors, and your own editing is unlikely to detect them (because you probably would not have made the error to begin with if you knew the difference). Being sensitized to the problem is thus your best protection against this problem. When you find yourself in doubt, look up the word(s) in a dictionary or do an Internet search with the two terms as keywords to see if/how they differ.

TABLE 8.6   Commonly Confused and Misused Terms

Terms	Distinction
ability, capacity	*Abilities* can be acquired; *capacities* cannot
adapt, adopt	*Adapting* means taking and modifying something for a new use; *adopting* means taking something for a new use
advisedly, intentionally	An action is taken *advisedly* when it has been carefully thought out beforehand; an action performed *intentionally* was merely done on purpose
affect, effect	*Affect* is a verb meaning to influence or have an effect on something else; *effect* is a noun referring to an effect or outcome (though effect also can be used as a verb meaning to bring something about—to effectuate)
arbitrator, mediator	*Arbitrators* weigh evidence and make judgments; *mediators* try to resolve disputes but lack the decision-making authority of arbitrators
beside, besides	*Beside* means next to; *besides* means in additional to or other than
between, among	*Between* is used with two items; *among* is used with more than two items
bias, prejudice, discrimination	*Bias* is a mental state predisposing someone toward unfair treatment; *prejudice* is either a preformed judgment or an opinion without a logical basis that could lead to unfair treatment; *discrimination* is unfair treatment
can, may	*Can* refers to ability to do something; *may* refers to permission to do something
compare to, compare with	To show similarity, use *compare to*; to show differences, use *compare with*
discover, invent	We *discover* something that already existed; we *invent* something to bring it into existence
doubtful, in doubt	*Doubtful* means we think otherwise; *in doubt* means we are unsure
fewer, less	Use *fewer* when you can count the difference and the increments matter; otherwise, use *less*
gender, sex	*Gender* is a grammatical and sociological term; *sex* is a biological term
historic, historical	That which is *historic* is a major, memorable past event; that which is *historical* merely happened in the past
impact, effect	*Impact* conveys the force with which an effect was brought about; *effect* can refer to any result
imply, infer	To imply is to *suggest*; to infer is to *surmise*
irregardless, regardless	*Irregardless* is not a meaningful word; *regardless* is a word, and it means "without regard to"
libel, slander	Both refer to defamation, but while *slander* is oral, *libel* is in written or visual form
literally, figuratively	*Literally* refers to the exact meaning of the words; *figuratively* means not according to the exact meaning of the words
may, might	*May* refers to a possibility; *might* refers to a particularly uncertain possibility
nauseous, nauseated	Something that makes us physically sick is *nauseous*; when that happens, we feel *nauseated*
practicable, practical	Something is *practicable* it if can be done; something is *practical* if it can be done and makes sense to do it
presumptive, presumptuous	Something is *presumptive* if it provides a reason to suppose; someone is *presumptuous* if they presume too much
principal, principle	A leader is a *principal*; a rule or guideline is a *principle*
recur, reoccur	*Recur* means something happens over and over; *reoccur* means something has happened once again

(Continued)

TABLE 8.6 *(Continued)*

Terms	Distinction
take place, occur	*Take place* refers to a planned event; *occur* refers to a spontaneous event
that, which	*That* should introduce a defining clause; *which* should introduce a nondefining clause
tortuous, torturous	*Tortuous* refers to something that is convoluted or indirect; *torturous* refers to something that produces pain
varied, various	*Varied* means to be made different; *various* means to be different
who, whom	*Who* refers to the subject of a sentence; *whom* refers to the object

Source: Bernstein (1965/1998)

Perhaps the most common mistake shown in Table 8.6 concerns "that" versus "which," and so this issue deserves some special attention. "That" and "which" are called relative pronouns; as such, they connect phrases to nouns or other pronouns. The rule is to use "that" in defining clauses and "which" in nondefining clauses when referring to non-humans (while "who" or "whom" are used to refer to humans). A **defining clause** is an essential part of the sentence. Removing it would alter the meaning of the sentence. A **nondefining clause** adds information but is not essential to the sentence. Removing it would not alter the meaning of the sentence. We do not set off defining clauses with a comma, but we do set off nondefining clauses by placing a comma directly before it. Here are some examples:

- Defining clause
  - o Nonhuman: The car that was vandalized last night had been parked on the street.
  - o Human: The man who was mugged last night carried a lot of cash.
- Nondefining clause
  - o Nonhuman: The car parked on the street, which had its rims stolen last year, was vandalized last night.
  - o Human: The man, who was walking alone at night, was carrying a lot of cash and was mugged.

SPELLING. Once we are sure we know what word we want to use, we can verify its correct spelling by consulting *Merriam-Webster's Collegiate Dictionary* or (as needed) *Webster's Third International Dictionary*. A dictionary is not always going to solve the problem, however, as some words sound the same but have different spellings (and meanings). These words are called **homophones**. Table 8.7 shows some examples of words with different spellings but that sound the same or very similar. Homophones can be especially tricky because they look and sound right upon a cursory review of a draft and also because spell checkers will not always flag them.

Before moving from spelling, be advised that spelling tests can be part of qualification exams for criminal justice professors. Police officers, for instance, are in some cases asked to look at a sentence and choose which of four words best completes that sentence. When taking such an exam, prospective police officers are not permitted to look up the spelling of words using their phones, computers, or other sources. Instead, they need to know these things. Some examples pulled from an actual Law Enforcement Spelling/Grammar Test (Ctoney, 2013) are provided in Figure 8.2.

TABLE 8.7   Same- or Similar-Sounding Words

aloud, allowed	alter, altar	accessary, accessory
be, bee	bear, bear	billed, build
bite, byte	boarder, border	but, butt
buy, by, bye	cite, sight, site	complement, compliment
daze, days	descent, dissent	desert, dessert
deer, dear	die, dye	dual, duel
fair, fare	find, fined	forth, fourth
foul, fowl	here, hear	genes, jeans
gorilla, guerilla	groan, grown	hall, haul
heroin, heroine	hi, high	holey, holy, wholly
hour, our	idle, idol	it's, its
I, eye	knead, need	knew, new
knot, not	know, no	knows, nose
lade, laid	laps, lapse	lead, led
lean, lien	lessen, lesson	licker, liquor
loot, lute	made, maid	male, mail
main, mane	mall, maul	marshal, martial
meat, meet, mete	medal, mettle	miner, minor
missed, mist	morning, mourning	muscle, mussel
naval, navel	oh, owe	one, won
packed, pact	pail, pale	pain, pane
pair, pare, pear	pause, paws	pores, pours
pea, pee	peak, peek	pedal, peddle, petal
piece, peace	plane, plain	praise, prays, preys
principal, principle	profit, prophet	rain, reign, rein
real, reel	red, read	residence, residents
reek, wreak	rest, wrest	retch, wretch
right, rite, write	road, rode	role, roll
rose, rows	rote, wrote	rough, ruff
rung, wrung	sea, see	sale, sail
scene, seen		seam, seem
seas, sees, seize	sew, so	side, sighed
soar, sore	sole, soul	some, sum
son, sun	stationary, stationery	sweet, suite
tail, tale	tea, tee	team, teem
their, there, they're	threw, through	throne, thrown
tide, tied	to, too, two	vain, vane, vein
vial, vile	wail, wale, whale	waist, waste
wait, weight	waive, wave	ware, wear, where
weak, week	we'd, weed	weal, we'll, wheel
weather, whether	wet, whet	while, wile
whine, wine	whirled, world	witch, which
who's, whose	wood, would	yore, your, you're
yoke, yolk	you'll, yule	zany, xani

I responded to the caller's _____ to make contact.
- A. Residence
- B. Residents
- C. Resident

I talked to three suspects and _____ going to come in for an interview.
- A. Their
- B. They're
- C. There

I arrested them for possession of drug _____.
- A. Parafanalia
- B. Paraphernalia
- C. Paraphanalia

The defense attorney issued a _____ for me to testify in court.
- A. Suhpena
- B. Subpoena
- C. Subpena

The Florida _____ for DWLSR is 322.34.
- A. Statute
- B. Statue
- C. Statyou

The crime _____ is described as....
- A. Scene
- B. Seen
- C. Sceine

The _____ reported a dog was barking all night.
- A. Complaintant
- B. Complainant
- C. Complanent

FIGURE 8.2 Sample Spelling Test Questions for Police Officers

HYPHENS AND EN DASHES. Hyphens (-) and en dashes (–) are used to connect words so as to make a new word (e.g., self-concept, police–community relations). There are considerably more situations that use hyphens than en dashes. When in doubt about hyphenation, first try looking the word up in *Merriam-Webster's Intercollegiate Dictionary* or (as needed) *Webster's Third International Dictionary*. If you cannot find the word there, then use the guidelines presented in Table 8.8.

It is not easy to apply these rules in all cases. And these are not even all the rules. These are just some of the more common situations when hyphenation is an issue. If you are unsure, then the best thing to do is make a decision—to hyphenate or not to hyphenate—and then be consistent. The same is true for en dashes. An en dash is a medium-length hyphen. We use an en dash instead of a hyphen when the two items being joined are of equal weight; for example, police–community relations, victim–offender relationship, attorney–client privilege, and male–female dynamics. (The en dash is also used with number ranges, but this will be covered later in terms of punctuation.)

TABLE 8.8   Hyphenation

	Use a Hyphen	Do *Not* Use a Hyphen
Compound Adjectives	With compound adjectives that could be misread without a hyphen (e.g., co-offender)	Unless it serves a purpose (e.g., cohabitant)
	With compound adjectives preceding the noun they modify (e.g., white-collar crime, low-crime area)	With compound adjectives following the noun they modify (e.g., crime that is white collar, area that is low crime)
	With compound adjectives where all words together in the compound modify the noun (e.g., long-term problem, high-impact practices)	With compound adjectives where the first word ends in "ly" (e.g., commonly known problem, highly regarded practice)
	With compound adjectives where the first part is a number (e.g., two-part question, 20-question quiz)	With compound adjectives where the first word is in comparative or superlative form (e.g., best performing trainee, higher scoring trainee)
Prefixes	With the prefix "self" (e.g., self-report, self-concept; except self psychology)	With certain prefixes unless needed for clarity or to follow other hyphenation rules: after, anti, bi, co, counter, equi, extra, infra, inter, macro, mega, meta, micro, mid, mini, multi, non, over, post, pre, pro, pseudo, re, semi, socio, sub, super, supra, ultra, un, under (e.g., antisocial, macrotheory, posttest, rearrest, unbiased)
	When the base word is capitalized, a number, an abbreviation, or more than one word (e.g., pre-Trump, pseudo-CIA, post-9/11, non-high-risk offenders)	
	When the prefix ends and the base word begins with the same vowel (e.g., meta-analysis, co-occurring)	

PLURALS AND POSSESSIVES. Nouns can be singular, plural, singular possessive, or plural possessive. Singular means one, plural means more than one, and possessive indicates ownership:

- Singular (s): Tom is an *offender*. This *offender* broke the law.
- Plural (p): Tom and Jane are *offenders*. These *offenders* broke the law.
- Singular possessive (sp): Tom is an offender. This *offender's* lawbreaking will lead to punishment.
- Plural possessive (pp): Tom and Jane are offenders. These *offenders'* lawbreaking will lead to punishment.

Make sure you know which form you need to use to convey meaning accurately and clearly, and then make sure you know how to express that form. Observe in the examples above how the apostrophe (') is used for possessive form but *not* for plural form. Table 8.9 shows the rules for using plural form, and Table 8.10 shows rules for using possessive form.

There are some exceptions to the rules for showing possession. For example, no apostrophe or "s" is added to possessive pronouns: my and mine, your and yours, her and hers, his, its, our and ours, and their and theirs. This is because these words are already in possessive form. "Its" versus "it's" is confusing to many, but it need not be. "Its" is possessive; for example, "The dog wants its bone." "It's" is a contraction, which is an abbreviation for "it is"; for example, "It's the dog's bone" or "It is the dog's bone." If ever you are unsure which one to use, replace "its"/"it's" with "it is." If the resulting construction makes sense, then use "it's." If the resulting construction does not make sense, then you are probably correct to use "its."

TABLE 8.9   Plural Form

Rules	Examples
Add "s" to the end of most nouns	prison → prisons
Add "es" to the end of most nouns ending in "s," "ss," "sh," "ch," "x," or "z"	tax → taxes
Add another "s" or "z" before adding "es" to some nouns ending in "s" or "z"	pass → passes
Change the "f" to "v" to "v" or "ve" in some nouns ending in "f" or "fe"	knife → knives loaf → loaves
Change the "y" to "ies" in nouns ending in a consonant followed by "y"	city → cities
Add "es" to some nouns ending in "o"	potato → potatoes
Change "us" to "i" in nouns ending in "us"	focus → foci
Change the "is" to "es" in nouns ending in "is"	analysis → analyses
Change the "on" to "a" in nouns ending in "on"	criterion → criteria
Don't make any changes to some nouns	series → series
Make special changes to irregular nouns	child → children foot → feet goose → geese man → men mouse → mice tooth → teeth woman → women

Source: Grammarly (2018a)

ABBREVIATIONS. Abbreviations can be effective, efficient ways to communicate. An abbreviation is a shortened form of a word. The four types of abbreviations are shown in Table 8.11. In technical writing, we should not use contractions because they are too informal. But we do use the other three types of abbreviations, and so we should follow these rules for their proper use:

- Introduce an abbreviation when you first mention the term: "The criminal justice system (CJS) consists of police, courts, and corrections." (Note: This rule does not apply to standard abbreviations for units of measurement [e.g., hrs, lb, a.m.].)
- Once an abbreviation is introduced, use it consistently thereafter. Do not go back and forth between the full and abbreviated versions.
- Do not introduce an abbreviation unless you will use it at least three times in the communication.
- Confine use of Latin abbreviations to within parentheses (e.g., etc., i.e., vs.).

TABLE 8.10   Possessive Form

Rules	Examples
Add an apostrophe followed by "s" to singular or plural nouns that don't already end in an "s"	judge → judge's men → men's
Add an apostrophe or an apostrophe followed by "s" to singular nouns that already end in an "s"	Jess → Jess' or Jess's
Add an apostrophe to plural nouns that already end in "s"	cities → cities'

TABLE 8.11 Abbreviations

Type	Description	Examples
Initialism	Taking the first letter of each major word and then pronouncing the abbreviation by saying each letter (e.g., "F-B-I")	FBI, CIA, CJS, USA
Acronym	Taking the first letter of each major word and then pronouncing the abbreviation as a word (e.g., "ice")	ICE, PIN, RAM, ZIP
Shortening	Using a shortened version of a full word(s) and then pronouncing the abbreviation as the real word (e.g., "doctor")	Dr., etc., in., St.
Contraction	Combining words in a shortened form and then pronouncing the abbreviation in its abbreviated form (e.g., "can't")	can't, I've, shouldn't, would've

- Capitalize letters in the abbreviation when the word being abbreviated is capitalized.
- Use periods when the abbreviation is initials of people's names, Latin abbreviations, and abbreviating "United States" as "U.S."

Use Proper Punctuation

Punctuation deals with use of devices for separating words and sentences and clarifying meaning. As such, correct punctuation involves (a) terminal points, (b) pausing points, (c) quotation points, (d) other points, and (e) spacing.

TERMINAL POINTS. **Terminal points**—period, question mark, and exclamation point—are punctuation marks at the end of a sentence. In technical writing, we use the exclamation point the least and the period the most. Table 8.12 provides some basic guidance on how to use these three terminal points.

PAUSING POINTS. **Pausing points**—comma, semicolon, colon, and em dash—are punctuation marks that go in the middle of a sentence to signal a halt and achieve clarity. The comma is the most common while the em dash is the least common, but all pausing points have their purposes. None should be over- or underused. Table 8.13 outlines appropriate situations for using each pausing point.

QUOTATION POINTS. Table 8.12 has already shown how terminal punctuation points are used with quotations. Four other forms of punctuation are commonly used when we directly quote a source: double quotation marks, single quotation marks, ellipses, and brackets. Table 8.14 summarizes when and how to use these other punctuation points.

OTHER POINTS. There are a couple of other punctuation marks we have yet to cover (i.e., parentheses and slashes) and one we already covered but only in the context of quotations (i.e., brackets). Table 8.15 shows when and how to use these punctuation points. Slashes only rarely should be used. Before using a slash, consider whether words would better communicate your meaning. If not, consider whether an en dash is more appropriate.

SPACING. The spacing issue revolves around the question, one space or two spaces following punctuation? With nonterminal points, it is one space after (although there is no space between points when points are used back-to-back). With terminal points, APA style specifies two spaces (and Chicago style specifies one space). Whether you should put one space or two spaces between sentences, therefore, is a function of which style guide you need to use. If you do not have to use a style guide, then you are free to choose

TABLE 8.12   Terminal Points

	Period	Question Mark	Exclamation Point
With no other punctuation mark	The judge instructed the jury prior to deliberation.	Did the judge instruct the jury prior to deliberation?	That judge was crazy when he forgot to instruct the jury!
With a parenthetical	The judge sequestered the jury (because he was being cautious).	Did the judge sequestered the jury (because he was being cautious)?	There is no way the judge will sequester the jury (even if he is being cautious)!
With an abbreviation ending in a period	The jury began deliberating at 2:00 p.m.	Did the jury begin deliberating at 2:00 p.m.?	The jury deliberated all the way until 10:00 p.m.!
With a direct quote ending in a period	The judge said, "You're dismissed."	When did the judge say, "You're dismissed"?	I can't believe the judge told her, "You're dismissed"!
With a direct quote ending in a question mark	The judge asked, "Has the jury reached a verdict?"	Did the judge ask, "Has the jury reached a verdict?"	That crazy judge forgot to ask, "Has the jury reached a verdict?"!
With a direct quote ending in an exclamation point	The bailiff yelled, "Gun!"	Did the bailiff yell, "Gun!"?	The bailiff yelled, "Gun!"

Source: Penn (2011–2019)

TABLE 8.13   Pausing Points

Uses	Examples
Comma	
Between all items in a simple series of three or more	The defendant, victim, and witnesses were female.
To set off a nonessential clause	The jury, which had been selected months ago, was brought into the courtroom.
After an introductory clause	Before the trial began, the judge conferred with the attorneys.
To separate two independent clauses joined by a conjunction	The jury was brought into the courtroom, and the witnesses waited outside the courtroom.
To set off the year when accompanied by the month and date	According to the records, February 2, 2018, was the first day of the trial.
To separate author names and publication year in in-text citations in APA style	Research indicates that . . . (Smith, 1999).
Between sets of three digits in numbers greater than or equal to 1,000	48,552
Semicolon	
To separate two independent clauses that are not joined by a conjunction	The jury was brought into the courtroom; the witnesses waited outside the courtroom.
To separate sets of items in a series when commas already are being used	Evidence includes weapons such as guns, knives, and poison; documents such as letters, diaries, notes, and contracts; and lay and expert witnesses. Research indicates that . . . (Smith, 1999; Thomas, 2002).

Uses	Examples
Colon	
Between a complete introductory clause and an incomplete clause that elaborates on the introductory clause	The trial judge considered two sets of factors: mitigating and aggravating.
Between a complete introductory clause and another complete clause that elaborates on the introductory clause	The trial judge explained his reasoning: The defendant poses a flight risk.
In ratios and proportions	The proportion of jurors voting guilty versus not guilty was 5:7.
Between the publisher's location and name in the References	New York: Oxford University Press. Washington, DC: American Psychological Association.
Em Dash	
To set off abruptly a phrase in the middle or end of a sentence	The jury felt—as anyone who witnessed the trial would feel—that the judge was unfair. The jury felt that the judge was unfair—as would anyone who had witnessed the trial.

Source: APA (2009)

Note: The sources cited in the examples in this table are fictitious.

TABLE 8.14   Quotation Points

Uses	Examples
Double Quotation Marks	
To indicate exact language	The judge said, "Order in the court."Smith (2017) reported "no evidence to support the hypothesis" (p. 264).
To introduce an ironic, coined, or otherwise distinctively stated term or phrase	The defendant acted with "deliberate indifference."
Single Quotation Marks	
To indicate a quote within a quote	To confirm what the witness said, the prosecutor asked, "Did you really say 'I shot him in the face,' or did I hear wrong"?
Ellipsis	
To indicate text omitted from a quote	The victim's mother explained, "She was terrified, anxious, . . . and sad."
	Smith (2010) explained, "The hypothesis started logically enough . . ." (p. 53).
Brackets*	
To indicate text added to a quote	The defendant had said, "If ever there was a time [for violence], it was then."
To indicate text edited in the quote	"Many thoughts were going through [my] head," explained the defendant.

Source: APA (2009)

Note: The sources cited in the examples in this table are fictitious.

*Additional uses for brackets are provided under "Other Points."

TABLE 8.15 Other Points

Uses	Examples
Parentheses	
To set off structurally independent elements	The victim did not testify (because she was deceased by the time of the trial).
To set off in-text citation material	Victim testimony has a powerful influence on juries (Thomas, 2010).
	Thomas (2010) explained how "juries are moved by victim testimony" (p. 12).
To introduce an abbreviation	The Centers for Disease Control and Prevention (CDC)
To set off numbers or letters identifying items in a series presented in a sentence	The lawyers followed the standard process of (1) direct examination, (2) cross-examination, (3) re-direct, and (3) re-cross.
	The jurors lunch options were (a) sandwiches, (b) burgers, or (c) salad.
To enclose statistical and mathematical information	The relationship was significant ($p <.01$).
	$(a + b)/(c—d)$
Brackets*	
To enclose material that is already in parentheses	The victim did not testify (because she was deceased by the time of the trial [after having been on life support for 2 weeks]).
Slashes	
To clarify a relationship when already using a hyphenated compound	public/private-prison debate
In to indicate "per" when presenting more than one unit of measurement	0.02 deg/s
	But: 70 mph, 0.08% BAC, 60 RPM
To cite a reproduced work	Smith (1972/2005)
Between numerators and denominators	R/S

Source: APA (2009); Penn (2011–2019)
Note: The sources cited in the examples in this table are fictitious.
*Additional uses for brackets are provided under "Punctuation Points."

between one or two spaces. Because one space is more conducive to reading comprehension than two spaces (R. L. Johnson, Bui, & Schmitt, 2018), the wise decision appears to be one space. But perhaps more important than which decision you make is to apply your decision consistently. That is, avoid haphazard spacing—with one space between some sentences and two spaces between other sentences.

Be Consistent

Consistency is a necessary but not sufficient condition for correctness. If your writing mechanics are consistent, they are correct to the extent that you are following appropriate writing rules. If your writing mechanics are inconsistent, the communication cannot possibly be correct.

Beyond its connection to correctness, consistency in writing mechanics is important for two reasons. First, inconsistent writing mechanics can confuse and frustrate readers, especially readers who are knowledgeable about writing mechanics. A reader might think you mean something different if you spell a word one way early on and another way later on, misunderstand your meaning if you put a comma in the wrong place, or have to re-read a passage to figure it out when you use a period instead of a question mark. Second, inconsistent writing mechanics can be more obvious than isolated errors, thus drawing the audience's attention. Like a shark smelling blood in the water, the reader becomes sensitized and skeptical, wondering if the writer is ignorant or just plain sloppy. This skepticism could translate into doubt regarding the substance of your communication. If a writer cannot be trusted to use commas correctly, for instance, how could that writer be trusted to report facts accurately or interpret evidence correctly? In short, inconsistent writing mechanics can chip away at one's credibility, thereby jeopardizing the effectiveness of the communication (not to mention the writer's reputation as a professional).

If you cannot locate a rule for a particular situation (e.g., whether or not to use a hyphen to join two words, to capitalize a word, to italicize a phrase, or to write out a number), you should create a logical rule for yourself to follow—drawing from the most appropriate existing rule (e.g., APA for grammar and punctuation, *Merriam-Webster's Collegiate Dictionary* for spelling)—and then be consistent in your application of that rule each time you encounter the situation.

APPLICATIONS

This section looks at critiques and police reports as forms of criminal justice communications that exemplify the need to be correct. As with all other principles presented in this book, however, the need for correctness is not limited to the two communication forms presented in this chapter.

Critiques

Students may be asked to read and critique a book, an article, or some other existing communication. A **critique** is a critical analysis and assessment of a communication. The goal of a critique is to make a determination about the strength or value of the thing being evaluated. A critique is not just a description, nor is it merely a laundry list of flaws. A critique also need not be entirely negative. On the contrary, it can conclude that the thing being evaluated is quite strong. One of the worst mistakes we can make is inaccurately portraying that which we are critiquing. Beyond that, we need a reasonable process to structure our evaluation.

Contents and Organization

Like any good formal communication, a critique should have a beginning, middle, and end. The focus of the beginning and end is your evaluation, while the focus of the middle is the communication being analyzed. That is, the paper needs to start with the purpose of and process for your critique, and then it needs to end with the conclusion you reached during your evaluation. Table 8.16 outlines the contents and structure of a critique.

TABLE 8.16   Contents and Structure of a Critique

Section	Description
Introduction	• Introduce the work being critiqued • State your purpose • Describe your method and criteria for evaluation • Provide a road map of the rest of your critique
Summary	• Present a concise summary of the work • Focus on the work's purpose, major parts, and main conclusions
Evaluation	• Present your assessment of the work • Organize your assessment around your evaluation criteria • Draw from the work to illustrate your points
Conclusion	• State your overall assessment of the work • Describe the rationale for your overall assessment

Knowing the purpose of a critique and how the critique should be organized leads us to the reasonable process for evaluating the communication. Identify and use criteria to guide your evaluation, such as the following:

1. Was the purpose of the communication stated in the introduction? Is the purpose clearly stated? Is the purpose appropriate given the author's intended audience?

2. Did the author achieve the stated purpose? Do the communication's organization, contents, and conclusions reflect the purpose? Did the communication meet your expectations, given the introduction and stated purpose?

3. Is the author's evidence relevant and credible? Are sources logically related to the point being made? Are source authors authorities on the subject matter? Are sources contemporary (or outdated)? Are sources nonbiased? Does the author establish the credibility of sources or distinguish between more and less credible sources?

4. Are the author's conclusions grounded in evidence? Is the conclusion at the end rationally derived from the evidence presented throughout the paper? Does the author explicitly state the connection between evidence and conclusion?

5. Does the author present multiple perspectives? If not, can you think of alternative perspectives? If so, is there balanced coverage of each perspective?

6. Is it complete? Can you think of anything relevant to the author's purpose that is missing? If so, do you think inclusion of the missing information/perspective might have altered the author's conclusion?

7. Does the author exhibit logical thinking? Does the author stick to evidence and logic, or does the author resort to emotional appeals, unfair attacks on alternative perspectives and people espousing them, or other fallacies, or other exaggerations or distortions?

Best Practices

What follows are some best practices for developing an effective critique:

1. **Keep it professional.** Do not let your personal opinions or preferences shape your critique. Put yourself in the role of an impartial judge who must reach the most reasonable, evidence-based decision.

2. **State your purpose and process clearly at the outset.** Clearly identify the work being critiqued, providing some context if possible. Present your plan for assessing the work in your introduction, and then stick to your plan. Explicitly identify your evaluation criteria.

3. **Provide a structured, well-balanced assessment.** Look at positives and negatives. Refrain from glossing over either strengths or weaknesses to help you arrive at a more definitive overall conclusion.

4. **Accurately present the communication being critiqued.** Get your facts straight when you summarize and cite the communication. Do not distort the material being critiqued so it is easier to attack. Make sure you are interpreting the material properly. Avoid "vicious abstraction," which means quoting out of context (Harris, 2017).

5. **Use concrete examples to substantiate your statements.** Explicitly present the rationale and evidence for each claim you make. If you claim, for example, that the author relied on outdated evidence, then give examples of outdated information and then examples of more current information that could have been used.

6. **Do not spend too much time summarizing the communication.** Remember that your goal is to assess the communication—not to regurgitate it. Spend no more than a fraction (perhaps one-fifth) of your time summarizing the information. Keep in mind that you will be incorporating material from the communication throughout your critique as examples, and you do not want to be repetitive.

7. **Arrive at a conclusion that logically reflects the entire work,** including all strengths and weaknesses and all evaluation criteria. State your overall impression of the work, and then explain your overall conclusion.

Police Reports

An **arrest report** is an official documentation of an arrest that is written by a police officer. Reports are a prominent part of working as a police officer. These reports are not just institutional records. They also are used in courtrooms, governmental and academic research, the news media, insurance companies, and other governmental agencies and officials. The general concept is the same as with crime scene reports (see Chapter 7): to create a detailed record of an event that can be consulted later. And like search warrant affidavits, errors in them can lead to dropped charges, suppressed evidence, overturned convictions, and civil lawsuits.

Contents and Organization

Although police departments differ with regard to whether they use a template and how the template looks, the basic components of an arrest report are essentially the same and are outlined in Table 8.17. While the first two sections are in fill-in-the-blank form, the narrative is detailed and lengthy.

TABLE 8.17 Contents and Structure of an Arrest Report

Section	Description
Front Sheet	• Provides procedural and identifying information, such as date/time, location, and case number • Provides names and contact information for the people involved in the crime, such as the victim(s), witness(es), suspect(s), informant(s), and other officer(s)
Narrative	• Describes what happened in detail, using chronological structure and past tense • Answer the 5WH questions: who, what, when, where, how, and why • Demonstrates probable cause
Conclusions and Recommendations	• Recommends what should be done next • Cites the crime code, charge, and/or statute number
Optional	• May include witness statements, property involved, and evidence collected

Sources: Grubb and Hemby (2019); Wallace and Roberson (2013)

The narrative should present evidence and factual information. To answer the 5WH questions, W. A. Johnson, Retting, Scott, and Garrison (2015, pp. 164–166 [citing Ross & Plant, 1977]) suggest dozens of more specific questions:

- **Who . . .**
  - Discovered the crime?
  - Reported the crime?
  - Saw or heard anything of importance?
  - Had a motive for committing the crime?
  - Helped the one committing the crime?
  - Committed the crime?
  - Associated with the suspect?
  - Is associated with or is known to the witness?
  - Is the suspect?
    - height
    - weight
    - nationality
    - complexion
    - eyes, eye color
    - glasses
    - visible scars, marks, tattoos
    - age
    - hat
    - hair (color and cut)
    - facial hair
    - shirt
    - necktie or scarf
    - jacket or coat
    - trousers or dress

- shoes
- weapons
- What . . .
  - Happened?
  - Crime was committed?
  - Are the elements of the crime?
  - Were the actions of the suspects?
  - Do the witnesses know about the case?
  - Evidence was obtained?
  - Was done with the evidence?
  - Tools were used?
  - Weapons were used?
  - Knowledge, skill, or strength was necessary to commit the crime?
  - Means of transportation was used in the commission of the crime?
  - Was the motive?
  - Was the method of operation?
- Where . . .
  - Was the crime discovered?
  - Was the crime committed?
  - Were the suspects seen?
  - Were the witnesses during the crime?
  - Was the victim found?
  - Were the tools and weapons obtained?
  - Did the suspect live?
  - Did the victim live?
  - Did the suspect spend their leisure time?
  - Is the suspect now?
  - Is the suspect likely to go?
  - Was the suspect apprehended?
- When . . .
  - Was the crime committed?
  - Was the crime discovered?
  - Was notification received?
  - Did the police arrive at the scene?
  - Was the victim last seen?
  - Was the suspect apprehended?
- How . . .
  - Was the crime committed?
  - Did the suspect get to the scene?
  - Did the suspect get away?
  - Did the suspect escape?
    - direction
    - license
    - vehicle description
    - additional remarks

- o Did the suspect get the information necessary to enable the suspect to commit the crime?
- o Was the crime planned?
- o Did the suspect secure the tools and weapons?
- o Were the tools and weapons used?
- o Much damage was done?
- o Much property was stolen?
- o Much knowledge, skill, or strength was necessary to commit the crime?
- **Why . . .**
  - o Was the crime committed?
  - o Was a particular type of tool used?
  - o Was the particular method employed?
  - o Was a witness reluctant to talk to you?
  - o Was the crime reported?

Best Practices

Adhere to this list of best practices to produce effective arrest reports:

1. **Use chronological structure.** Relate events in the order in which they occurred. Start with the point of your involvement, and end when you turn over the arrested suspect. Include any use of force or handcuffs.

2. **Use past tense.** Because you will be writing the report after the arrest has been completed, everything about which you write will have occurred in the past. Thus, consistently use past tense.

3. **Put the subject first.** Start each sentence with its subject. For example, edit "From the back of the room, the shopkeeper observed the suspect" to "The shopkeeper observed the suspect from the back of the room."

4. **Use active voice.** Like putting the subject first, using active voice keeps the sentence focused on the subject (i.e., who did what). With passive voice, we know something was done, but we might not know who did it. Thus, for example, edit "The door was slammed" to "The suspect slammed the door."

5. **Be specific and descriptive.** Avoid abstract terms. Instead, use clear, specific descriptions. For example, edit "The suspect behaved aggressively" to "The suspect yelled 'fuck you' and threw beer bottles at the wall." The word "aggressive" is broad, and different people reading your report of this could interpret it differently (e.g., one person thinking it means merely "standoffish" with another person thinking the suspect might have hit the arresting officer). Be too specific to leave room for alternative interpretations.

6. **Present facts.** Provide an objective, professional account of what happened. Omit personal commentary, such as "I was sure he was going to attack me"; "The smell made me feel sick"; and "The witness was acting weird." Instead, stick to facts such as "The suspect said he was going to attack me if I came any closer"; "There was a pile of rotting garbage in the corner of the room"; and "The witness kept humming while we spoke."

7. **Identify the source of information.** To be correct as well as clear, distinguish between what you know to be a fact and what might be a fact. If a witness told

you the suspect arrived at the house at 3:00 a.m., then say "The witness, [INSERT NAME], said that the suspect arrived at the house at 3:00 a.m." rather than "The suspect arrived at the house at 3:00 a.m." (which might not be true), or "It appears the suspect arrived at then house at 3:00 a.m." (which fails to indicate why it appears that way).

8. **Double-check everything.** Leave no room for confusion. Think ahead, and then imagine needing to use your report to jog your memory when you testify at trial or having to justify some aspect of your report to avoid a civil suit. Check all details—large and small—before you file your report. Look for accuracy as well as completeness and clarity.

EXERCISES
Matching
These exercises are designed to assess Chapter 8 Learning Objective 1 (see Box 8.1). Match each numbered statement to the lowercase letter corresponding to the key word it defines. Each key word will be used only once.

1. Free from error in terms of both the truth/accuracy of the information itself and the proper presentation of the information
2. Punctuation marks that go in the middle of a sentence to signal a halt and achieve clarity: comma, semicolon, colon, and em dash
3. Words that sound the same but have different spellings and meanings
4. A police officer's official documentation of an arrest
5. A statement that is known or believed to be false
6. A critical analysis and assessment of a communication
7. Punctuation marks at the end of a sentence: period, question mark, exclamation point
8. Information that is not essential to a sentence such that removing it would not alter the meaning of the sentence
9. A statement known or believed to be only partially true or to be a combination of truth and falsehood
10. A statement that expresses more than one complete thought and having two or more sets of subjects and verbs
11. A statement that expresses one complete thought and has a subject and verb
12. A justified true belief
13. An essential part of a sentence such that removing it would alter the meaning of the sentence
14. An accurate reflection of reality
15. Conforming to accepted standards
16. A statement that lacks a subject and/or verb and does not express a complete thought

a. arrest report	f. half-truth
b. complete sentence	g. homophones
c. correct	h. knowledge
d. critique	i. nondefining clause
e. defining clause	j. pausing points

k. proper

l. run-on sentence

m. sentence fragment

n. terminal points

o. truth

p. untruth

Multiple Choice

These exercises are designed to assess Chapter 8 Learning Objective 4 (see Box 8.1). Indicate the single most appropriate response to each item below.

1. Is the following passage in proper or improper form? "The store was robbed during shift change, which is why the store owner is implementing a new procedure for shift changes."

   a. proper

   b. improper

2. Is the italicized passage in proper or improper form? *"Police are not called to many crimes in progress.* Which is why reducing response time would not noticeably reduce crime (Walker, 2011)."

   a. proper

   b. improper

3. Is the italicized passage in proper or improper form? "Police are not called to many crimes in progress. *Which is why reducing response time would not noticeably reduce crime* (Walker, 2011)."

   a. proper

   b. improper

4. Is the following passage in proper or improper form? "Some suspects resist being arrested by police officers. In these situations, they often use force."

   a. proper

   b. improper

5. Is the following passage in proper or improper form? "The women, Mary and Alice, each took a picture of the robber fleeing the scene. Unfortunately, the picture she took did not reveal the robber's face."

   a. proper

   b. improper

6. Is the following passage in proper or improper form? "The suspects were questioned after reading their rights."

   a. proper

   b. improper

7. Is the following passage in proper or improper form? "The robber stole cash, cigarettes, and beer."

   a. proper

   b. improper

8. Is the following passage in proper or improper form? "Officer Collins collected the evidence, interviewed the witnesses, and arrested the suspect."
   a. proper
   b. improper

9. Is the following passage in proper or improper form? "The low-light conditions hindered the investigation. Specifically, low-light conditions can make it difficult for officers to see important evidence."
   a. proper
   b. improper

10. Is the following passage in proper or improper form? "The robber was no longer on parole. The parole board had determined that he was not high risk. High-risk cases often involve criminal histories."
    a. proper
    b. improper

11. Is the following passage in proper or improper form? "The victim heard a noise out in the alley. When the victim opened the door, he saw that a man dressed in black was trying to pry open a window."
    a. proper
    b. improper

12. Is the following passage in proper or improper form? "The employee only told some of what he had seen."
    a. proper
    b. improper

13. Is the following passage in proper or improper form? "The neighborhood's residents asked the police to tell them what had happened."
    a. proper
    b. improper

14. Is the following passage in proper or improper form? "According to the witness, the robber asked if anyone else was in the store?"
    a. proper
    b. improper

15. Is the following passage in proper or improper form? "The neighborhood residents fear was obvious."
    a. proper
    b. improper

16. Is the following passage in proper or improper form? "At the beginning of the interview the police officer asked the witness to state her full name."
    a. proper
    b. improper

17. Is the following passage in proper or improper form? "The police interviewed three groups of people: Mary, Alice, and Claire; Tom, Frank, and Bill; and Dan and Edith."
    a. proper
    b. improper

Editing

These editing exercises are designed to assess Chapter 8 Learning Objective 5 (see Box 8.1). Rewrite each of the following passages, editing them as needed to achieve correctness.

1. Listening to the first witness's story might have had an affect on the second witness's story.
2. The male witness stood besides the female witness.
3. From the victim's account, the officer implied that the victim felt responsible.
4. They suspect said he was innocent. Irregardless, he was arrested.
5. The new evidence might altar the timeline of events leading up to the crime.
6. The investigating officer thought the DNA evidence would compliment the video footage.
7. The interview served a duel purpose.
8. Because the child was a miner, the officer wanted the child's parent present for questioning.
9. The crime happened at work rather than at the victim's residents.
10. The principle investigator watched the video footage multiple times.
11. According to the witness, "The robber asked if I 'wanted to die today,' but I was too scared to say anything."
12. The store would not be open the next day, because it's windows were broken.
13. Under common law, "every final decision by a court creates a precedent (Worrall, Hemmens, & Nored, 2018, p. 35)."

Writing

These writing exercises are designed to assess Chapter 8 Learning Objectives 2, 4, 6, and 7 (see Box 8.1). Write at least one full paragraph in response to each item below. Use proper spelling, punctuation, and grammar.

1. Argue for the importance of correctness in criminal justice communications.
2. Outline methods for producing correct communications.
3. Pick a scholarly journal article. It does not need to be empirical, but it should be a primary source. (Do *not* pick a book review or a critique of some other publication.) Develop a correct book or article critique.
4. Watch an episode of *Law and Order, CSI, NCIS,* or some similar crime drama in which there is an investigation that leads to an arrest. Alternatively, watch a documentary of a (true) crime, ensuring that the documentary you select provides sufficient information for you to complete this exercise. Pretend you are the arresting officer, and construct a correct arrest report. Be sure to identify the crime/arrest that you are reporting.

REFERENCES

American Psychological Association (APA). (2009). *Publication manual of the American Psychological Association* (6th ed.). Washington, DC: Author.

Bernstein, Theodore M. (1998). *The careful writer: A modern guide to English usage.* New York: The Free Press. (Original work published 1965)

Borchard, Edwin M. (1932). *Convicting the innocent: Sixty-five actual errors of criminal justice.* Garden City, NY: Garden City Publishing Company, Inc.

Chen, Stephanie. (2010, February 15). Officer, you've got the wrong person. *CNN.* Retrieved from http://www.cnn.com/2010/CRIME/02/15/colorado.mistaken.identity.arrest/index.html

Crockett, Zachary. (2014, October 9). The most expensive typo in legislative history. *Priceonomics.* Retrieved from https://priceonomics.com/the-most-expensive-typo-in-legislative-history/

Ctoney. (2013, January 28). Law enforcement spelling/grammar test. *ProProfs.* Retrieved from https://www.proprofs.com/quiz-school/story.php?title=law-enforcement-spelling-grammar-test

Death Penalty Information Center. (2018). *The innocence list.* Retrieved from https://deathpenaltyinfo.org/innocence-list-those-freed-death-row

Grammarly. (2018a). Plural nouns: Rules and examples. *Grammarly* [Blog post]. Retrieved https://www.grammarly.com/blog/plural-nouns/

Grammarly. (2018b). Possessive case of nouns: Rules and examples. *Grammarly* [Blog post]. Retrieved https://www.grammarly.com/blog/possessive-case/

Grammarly. (2018c). Verb tenses. *Grammarly* [Blog post]. Retrieved from https://www.grammarly.com/blog/verb-tenses/

Grubb, Robert E., & Hemby, K. Virginia. (2019). *Effective communication in criminal justice.* Thousand Oaks, CA: Sage.

Harris, Robert A. (2017). *Using sources effectively: Strengthening your writing and avoiding plagiarism* (5th ed.). New York: Routledge.

Howard, Jennifer. (2008, May 2). Princeton U. Press recalls typo-filled book and says it will reprint. *Chronicle of Higher Education.* Retrieved from https://www.chronicle.com/article/Princeton-U-Press-Recalls/40917

Humphrey, Jeff. (2016, December 19). Typo allows alleged child abuser to be released on unusually low bond. *KXLY.com.* Retrieved from https://www.kxly.com/news/local-news/courthouse-typo-leads-to-alleged-child-abusers-release/222790329

Ichikawa, Jonathan Jenkins, & Steup, Matthias. (2017). Knowledge analysis. *Stanford Encyclopedia of Philosophy.* Retrieved from https://plato.stanford.edu/entries/knowledge-analysis/

Johnson, Rebecca L., Bui, Becky, & Schmitt, Lindsay L. (2018). Are two spaces better than one? The effect of spacing following periods and commas during reading. *Attention, Perception, and Psychophysics.* doi:10.3758/s13414-018-1527-6

Johnson, William A. Jr., Retting, Richard P., Scott, Gregory M., & Garrison, Stephen M. (2015). *The criminal justice student writer's manual* (6th ed.). Upper Saddle River, NJ: Pearson.

Liptak, Adam. (2004, March 4). Judge finds a typo-prone lawyer guilty of bad writing. *New York Times.* Retrieved from https://www.nytimes.com/2004/03/04/us/judge-finds-a-typo-prone-lawyer-guilty-of-bad-writing.html

Penn, Jordan. (2011–2019). *The punctuation guide.* Retrieved from https://www.thepunctuationguide.com/about-this-guide.html

Pergram, Chad. (2009, December 17). Typo in law establishes mandate to lock gun-toting train passengers in boxes. *Fox News.* Retrieved from http://www.foxnews.com/politics/2009/12/16/typo-law-establishes-mandate-lock-gun-toting-train-passengers-boxes.html

Radelet, Michael L., Bedau, Hugo Adam, & Putnam, Constance E. (1992). *In spite of innocence: Erroneous convictions in capital cases.* Boston, MA: Northeastern University Press.

Smallwood, Karl. (2014, May 4). Top 10 typos that almost changed the world. *TopTenz.* Retrieved from https://www.toptenz.net/top-10-typos.php

State v. Greenstreet. (2004). No. 2105, September Term, 2004. Retrieved from https://www.mdcourts.gov/data/opinions/cosa/2005/2105s04.pdf

WSMV News 4. (2011, March 2). Search warrant typo frees Tenn. drug dealer. *Officer.com*. Retrieved from https://www.officer.com/home/news/10246792/search-warrant-typo-frees-tenn-drug-dealer

Walker, Samuel. (2011). *Sense and nonsense about crime, drugs, and communities* (7th ed.). Belmont, CA: Wadsworth.

Wallace, Harvey, & Roberson, Cliff. (2013). *Written and interpersonal communication: Methods for law enforcement* (5th ed.). Upper Saddle River, NJ: Pearson.

Worrall, John L., Hemmens, Craig, & Nored, Lisa S. (2018). *Criminal evidence: An introduction* (3rd ed.). New York: Oxford University Press.

CHAPTER 9

Principle 8: Clarity

BOX 9.1	Learning Objectives

After reading this chapter, you will be able to
1. Recognize terminology relevant to clear communication.
2. Argue for the importance of clarity in criminal justice communications.
3. Outline methods for producing clear communications.
4. Distinguish between writing that is clear and writing that is unclear.
5. Rewrite unclear sentences to be clear.
6. Develop clear discussion posts.
7. Construct a clear expert witness testimony.

As George Orwell observed, fuzzy writing *always* reveals fuzzy thinking.

—PAULA LAROCQUE

Recall from Chapter 1 that communication is the process of transmitting information from sender to receiver. The process is judged a success to the extent that the receiver accurately decodes the message (i.e., understands the message in the way intended by the sender). This is like a shortstop throwing the ball to the first baseman: The goal of throwing the ball is for the first baseman to catch it. But if the ball is not thrown directly at the first baseman, then the odds of the first baseman catching it go down. If, for some reason, the shortstop throws a curveball, then the first basemen likewise will have a harder time catching it. It might be easier for the shortstop to get the ball out of his hands simply by chucking it in the general direction of the first baseman, yet doing so would not help the first baseman catch the ball. If we keep in mind that the shortstop and the first baseman share the goal of the first baseman catching the ball before the batter hits first base, then we can see that the shortstop should make every effort to facilitate that goal—even if doing so makes his job a little harder. A shortstop who cannot get the ball to the first baseman is replaced.

Just like throwing a ball we want someone to catch, the best way to communicate is to send a clear message—a message that will be as easy as possible for the receiver to understand. A communication has **clarity** when it is straightforward, unambiguous, and therefore able to be decoded accurately with as little effort as possible. When a communication lacks clarity, different people might infer different meaning, for example, or the audience might not be able to make any sense of it at all.

Clarity is a critical feature of effective criminal justice communications. As criminal justice communicators, we will not be judged merely by whether or not we can put words on paper—any more than a shortstop is judged just for throwing the ball. We must communicate effectively, which means our audience needs to be able to understand exactly what we write or say. We need to communicate in a way that prevents misunderstandings. For students, when a paper, presentation, or essay response lacks clarity, that communication cannot demonstrate either the student's substantive knowledge or communication skills. This is true even when the teacher is able to discern that some relevant terminology and sources are used. For practitioners, when a report or briefing lacks clarity, the people who read it might not be able to make sense of it, such as who did what to whom and when. Unclarity works against the critical functions of police to provide evidence that will help them solve crimes and prosecutors to secure guilty convictions. When pieces of evidence cannot be used because they are too vague, confusing, or unintelligible, the police and prosecution have a harder time doing their job and ensuring that justice is served.

This chapter shows us how we can ensure that the communications we produce have clarity and thereby assist the justice system to operate effectively and efficiently. It begins with five guidelines for achieving clarity and then discusses two communications in which clarity is essential. Throughout, a case is made for the importance of clarity in criminal justice communications. By the end of this chapter, readers should have a solid understanding of what clarity means for a communication and how to achieve it.

GUIDELINES

The goal of clear communication is to say exactly what you mean as directly as possible. To achieve this goal, follow these guidelines:

1. Be explicit.
2. Use plain language.
3. Be literal.
4. Prefer positive to negative constructions.
5. Avoid double-barreled questions.

Be Explicit

Being explicit means being straightforward and leaving no room for doubt as to what you mean. To be explicit, we need to (a) be direct, (b) be precise, and (c) avoid equivocating.

BOX 9.2	Credibility Connection

However well-meaning, speakers can look uncaring and dishonest, and may be perceived as trivializing a situation, when they engage in evasive maneuvering and linguistic trickery to make a point.

Be Direct

The shortest distance between two points is a straight line. The straight line is the direct path, while, conversely, taking a more circuitous route would take longer. To be **direct** is thus to be to the point. In communication, this means to know what your goal is and to target it unswervingly. Indirect language often stems from being uncomfortable with the more direct approach, and thus wanting to avoid having to come right out and say something. Indirect language also occurs when the communicator is unsure of the goals and therefore takes a roundabout approach ("beating around the bush") to the communication. Table 9.1 shows some examples of indirect statements accompanies by their more direct versions.

Like being concise, being direct means being an efficient communicator. Not only does being direct save time, but also being direct can prevent miscommunication. When we are subtle (intentionally or unintentionally) instead of direct, our audience might not understand us. To ensure that we are being direct, we should start by knowing the goal of the communication. Then we can make sure that there is a clear statement that is directly responsive to that goal. If the goal in writing a paper is to examine the effectiveness of a right-to-carry (RTC) laws on rates of gun violence, for example, there must be a statement explicitly indicating that, yes, RTC laws reduce gun violence or, no, RTC laws do not reduce violence. Such a paper should not merely describe evaluation studies one after another, present their findings, and then leave it up to the reader to deduce whether or not RTC laws reduce gun violence.

Before moving on, note that we do not want to be so direct that we are perceived as being unconcerned or rude. That is, being direct does not preclude or outweigh being respectful and tactful. **Tact** refers to showing consideration for others and their situations. Thus, we need to strike the proper balance between directness and tact. In general, the more sensitive the situation, the more tact we need to use. A victim's family member, for example, who asks, "Is there any hope?" deserves more than "No." Likewise, if someone who fell for a scam artist asks what they can do differently in the future to prevent falling for another scam, we should not say, "Use your brain." Curt, monosyllabic responses and blunt delivery of delicate or bad news can make us look callous and unapproachable. This point relates back to the importance of professionalism (see Chapter 2), which builds trust, confidence, and cooperation. The bottom line is that—while we certainly want to ensure that we are direct in answering questions, issuing commands, and relaying information—we also must endeavor to deliver news in a diplomatic manner.

TABLE 9.1   Indirect Versus Direct Language

Indirect	Direct
It sure would be nice if my friends voted for me.	Will you vote for me, please?
Hi, friend. Don't you think it's nice when friends support each other? Oh, by the way, did you hear I'm running for office?	
I'm thirsty.	Please get me a drink.
I usually have a drink after I go on a walk. I just finished my walk. Are you thirsty?	

Be Precise

Being direct is the first step to being explicit, and being precise is the second step. To be **precise** is to be exact. When we are vague, we open ourselves to misinterpretation and various interpretations. My daughter was eating pizza the other night, and she was making a mess. I noticed that her plate was too far away from her to catch the food that was falling out of her mouth, so I told her to "Move your plate closer to you." I meant for her to slide the plate until it reached the edge of the table, but my precocious 4-year-old instead picked up the plate to move up in the air, closer to her mouth. She then dropped the pizza and the plate, and we had an even bigger mess on our hands. The point of this story is that I was too vague. There was more than one meaning to my statement, and my daughter unfortunately inferred something other than what I intended. The fault was mine, as the burden of communicating is on the one sending the message.

We can prevent misunderstandings by being precise, which means being exact and using concrete, descriptive, and specific terms rather than abstract, vague, and general terms. Abstract terms are fuzzy. Different people can take them to mean different things. For example, "She appeared upset." An "upset" appearance can mean many different things, such as slumped shoulders, frown, slow gait, red eyes, puffy eyes, watery eyes, softly crying, sobbing. Instead of using the vague term "upset," then we should describe her appearance using specific adjectives: "She had red eyes, slumped shoulders, and a slow gait." Incidentally, when we use descriptive instead of evaluative language, we might realize that the description fits more than one condition, such as "upset" and "inebriated." As such, using specific, descriptive language can help guard against reaching premature conclusions.

Some words are themselves too vague to carry much meaning. Table 9.2 presents some of these weak words. Train yourself to avoid using these words. When you catch yourself using one, think about what you are trying to say, and then use a more specific term instead. Rather than writing "better," for example, say how one thing is better than the other thing (e.g., more effective in reducing crime, less costly).

While Table 9.2 lists words that are inherently weak, Table 9.3 lists words that were once powerful but have been so overused that they have become weak. As normally used today, the words listed in Table 9.3 no longer carry the same meaning. They are often used to exaggerate or understate without regard to their actual meaning. Should you catch yourself using one of these words, ask yourself if it is appropriate given what you are trying to say. Usually, these words are not appropriate, and so they should be replaced with a more appropriate term that more accurately conveys your meaning.

Pronouns can be another source of vagueness. Chapter 8 discussed vague personal pronoun references in terms of noun–pronoun agreement in gender and number, but pronouns can introduce unclarity in other ways, too. Consider this passage: "The autopsy

TABLE 9.2 Weak Terms

a lot, lots	about	and so on	and the like
and things like that	bad	better	big
etc.	good	great	issue, issues
many	really	roughly	stuff
that	the public	they	things

TABLE 9.3   Diluted Terms

absolutely, actually, honestly, literally, really, seriously, totally, truly
amazing, awesome, brilliant, genius, fantastic, incredible
cutting-edge, innovative, unique
destroy, eliminate, epidemic, eradicate, infest, invade, taking over, war
epic, legendary
horrifying, terrifying

report explained that the body's decomposed condition would make it difficult for her to establish the cause of death. It was a surprise to everyone." In this passage, what is "it": the autopsy report or the decomposed condition of the body? Relative pronouns—that, what, which, who, and whom—create similar problems. For example, "The victim had called the police and then tried to drive to the police station, which is how the victim's body came to be found in the garage." To what, exactly, does "which" refer: the victim calling the police or the victim trying to drive to the police station? The longer the sentence and the greater the distance between noun and pronoun, the likelier it is that readers will be confused. Because pronouns can cause confusion, the safest approach is to avoid using pronouns as much as possible. Instead, use the noun or phrase to which they refer. Do not worry about being repetitive if the alternative is sacrificing clarity.

Avoid Equivocating

Equivocating means deliberately being ambiguous and evasive in an effort to avoid telling the truth, alienating audiences, making a commitment, and/or eliciting censure. Another word for equivocating is *doublespeak*. When we equivocate, there is not a single, clear interpretation of what we say. Instead, there are at least two interpretations. Equivocating introduces confusion and uncertainty into a communication in an attempt to mislead. Using abstract, vague terms is one method of equivocation. This can be an effective strategy to avoid alienating people on one side of a controversial issue. "Pro-justice" sounds like a good thing, which naturally is appealing. But it is an example of a problematically vague term. Someone could claim they are pro-justice in an argument for increasing punishment for convicted criminals and then later use the term in an argument for limiting the power of police. In one context, pro-justice refers to justice for victims, which is accomplished by punishing criminals. In the other context, pro-justice refers to justice for crime suspects, who are presumed innocent until proven guilty. Thus, in this example, the use of the broad, abstract term "pro-justice" allows the speaker to take two different positions, thus appealing to two separate sides of a controversial issue.

Not only can vague terms create problems when they are used differently in different contexts, but also, they can create problems when they are defined too narrowly or too broadly. Take, for instance, the statement that "I didn't lie; I just didn't tell the whole truth." Here, the speaker uses a narrow definition of "lie" so that not telling the truth does not qualify as lying. Similarly, someone who steals might rationalize, "But I didn't hurt anyone." The truth of this statement depends on an especially narrow definition of "hurt" that excludes emotional, psychological, and financial harms. Here, an unreasonably fine line is being drawn, which legitimizes telling half-truths and causing non-physical suffering.

Alternatively, one might use an unreasonably broad definition to blur a legitimate line between a broad category and a particular instance and, in doing so, endow the particular instance with the positive or negative quality associated with the broad category. Take, for example, the term "leech." Leeches are worms, many of which suck blood. But this term is often used more loosely to describe certain types of people, such as people on welfare and who are homeless. Such use of the term leech casts a negative, even predatory, light on the people it is used to described.

Including unnecessary qualifiers is another method of equivocation. Where **hedging** is the appropriate use of qualifiers to denote legitimate uncertainty, equivocating is the inappropriate use of qualifiers to create wiggle room by introducing an element of uncertainty where there actually is none. Perhaps we are in a courtroom, for instance, and we hear the defense attorney object to a question asked by the prosecutor. We would be equivocating if we described what happened as, "The defense attorney appeared to have objected to the prosecution's question." The terms "appear" and "seem" communicate some degree of uncertainty. As another example, suppose a police officer is accused of violating a suspect's right to have his attorney present during interrogation, and the suspect really had asked for his attorney. Perhaps the officer would say something like, "Sure, he might have asked for his attorney." But there is no *might* about it; the suspect did *in fact* ask for his attorney.

To be clear, it is absolutely appropriate to use qualifiers when uncertainty does exist, such as when we have incomplete and/or flawed evidence to support a conclusion. Such appropriate use of qualifiers constitutes hedging. But when some fact is readily observable and no uncertainty exists, we should refrain from using such equivocating qualifiers as allegedly, appears, could, might, may, possibly, perhaps, and seems.

Use Plain Language

If you want your audience to understand you, then use words they know. In other words, use plain language. **Plain language** involves words that just about anyone should be able to understand. As such, plain language is accessible. Do not make the mistake, however, of confusing "plain" with "common." Where plain language is easy to understand but can be formal, common language—while familiar—is informal and sometimes unsophisticated. Because criminal justice communications are formal communications, criminal justice communicators should use language that just about anyone should understand without resorting to being informal. As such, follow two rules to achieve plain language: (1) favor simple to fancy terms, and (2) avoid specialized language.

Favor Simple to Fancy Terms

Some people, who speak quite plainly in conversations, become afflicted with "thesauritis" when they write. **Thesauritis** is when novice writers replace simple terms with fancier terms—often using a thesaurus to identify synonyms for short terms—in an effort to impress their audience (Harris, 2017). The common result, unfortunately, is that the new word is less effective than the old word. First, more people know short, simple words than longer, fancier terms. This means that we facilitate effective communication by using simple terms. Suppose someone reported the whereabouts of an escaped prisoner, for which there was a $500 reward. Upon calling the police department to ask how to claim the reward, he is told he can "procure remuneration by effectuating an avouchment" at city hall. The average person is unlikely to know all of these words. Not understanding the response, moreover, this person most certainly would not be impressed with the fancy words.

Second, different terms often have different meaning, and the new word might not be as good a fit in the sentence as the word being replaced. Thus, we might be incorrect when we use a fancier term that has a different meaning than the simple term with which we began. Here is an example. Suppose students in a gun control class are assigned to write a paper. One student decides to compare gun control laws in two states, and this student wants to express the thought that one state has more lenient laws than another state. Thinking the simple word "lax" was not impressive enough, the student replaces "lax" with the similar-looking, longer term "laxative." The first word, however, means lenient, while the second word refers to a bowel movement stimulant.

"Big words" are not the best words unless they truly express the idea better than any smaller words. Sometimes, long words are unavoidable, such as when there really is not plainer word to express the same idea. But most times, as shown in Table 9.4, a simpler term is better than its fancier equivalent. The bottom line is, "Avoid fancy words," Strunk and White (1935/2000) explain; "Do not be tempted by a twenty-dollar word when there is a ten-center handy, ready and able" (p. 76).

Having established that fancy terms are inferior to simpler terms, let us look at the different approaches for preferring simple to fancy terms. First, if using big terms is an intentional effort to make the writer look smart and impress the reader, then the solution is to resist any urge to replace simple terms with fancy words. In other words, do not succumb to thesauritis. Second, if using big terms is an intentional effort to avoid using a particular word too frequently, then do some thinking. If the simple word in question is a key word, then repeating it often is probably a good thing. If the simple word in question is not a key word, then take steps to find alternative words that really have the same meaning. Looking up synonyms in a thesaurus is a good start, but do not stop there. Rather, after finding a word in a thesaurus, look it up in a dictionary to ensure that it really has the same meaning. Third, if using big words is unintentional, then the solution is to review our work with special attention to each word, considering whether a different, simpler term would be more effective. Sometimes, we pick up fancy words like dogs pick up ticks. We hear a word a few times, and then it becomes part of our regular

TABLE 9.4   Common Fancy Terms and Their Simpler Equivalents

Fancy Term	Simpler Equivalent(s)	Fancy Term	Simpler Equivalent(s)
ascertain	find out, learn	furnish	give, provide
attempt (verb)	try	herein	here
commence	begin, start	impact (verb)	affect
demonstrate	show	initiate	begin
employ (verb)	use	perform	do
endeavor (verb)	try	procure	buy, get
eventuate	happen	terminate	end, stop
finalize	agree, end, finish, settle	utilize	use

Source: Markel (2012, p. 249)

vocabulary. This tendency probably explains why "literally" is (mis)used so frequently. In this case, reviewing our draft with particular attention to long words and word choice can be helpful. For each long word, ask if there is a shorter, simpler term that means the same thing. For any word, consider whether there might be a different term that more clearly conveys your meaning.

Avoid Specialized Language

Specialized language is understood by members of groups but not by people outside of those groups. Here, we look at three categories of specialized language: (1) slang, (2) texting slang, and (3) jargon.

SLANG. **Slang** is an informal way of saying something, which is known to and used by members of broad groups (e.g., teenagers and drug users). Here are some of the many slang, or street names, for drugs (Drug Enforcement Agency Houston Division, 2017):

- Amphetamine: Amy, b-bombs, dolls, footballs, jolly beans, speed, bennies, uppers
- Cocaine: angel powder, Angie, candy, coke, cola, Florida snow, powder, White Lady
- Crack cocaine: 51s, bings, cookies, freebase, geek, ice, moon rock, sleet, white ball
- Heroin: Black Bitch, brown, Charlie, downtown, fairy dust, hard candy, smack
- LSD: acid, dots, Lucy in the Sky with Diamonds, mellow yellow, microdot, sugar cubes
- Marijuana: bud, chronic, grass, ganja, kiff, Mary Jane, mowing the lawn, pot, weed
- MDMA: bean, dancing shoes, E, E-bomb, Eve, Molly, Scooby snacks, Vitamin E
- Methamphetamine: beers, bump, Christine, clear, crank, fire, ice, shatter, Tina, zip
- Opium: Aunt Emma, big O, China, dreams, gum, incense, midnight oil, zero
- PCP: ace, angel dust, Crazy Eddie, purple rain, red devil, taking a cruise, zombie
- Xanax®: bars, footballs, Xanies, Zanbars, zanies, Z-bars

Over time, slang use spreads and sometimes makes its way into popular usage. This does not, however, make slang acceptable for *professional* communications.

TEXTING SLANG. **Texting slang** consists of abbreviated forms of expressions used in text messaging. Often expressed as initialisms ("OMG" for "Oh my God"), texting slang can include images called emoticons (e.g., smiley face, thumbs up). Texting itself has become common, with 81 percent of Americans sending and receiving text messages (Burke, 2016). But texting is less common among older age groups (Burke, 2016), and texting slang in particular seems to be a practice used mostly by teenagers (Birdsong, 2018). Here are some examples of texting slang (Birdsong, 2018):

- 121 = Let's chat privately
- IKR = I know, right?
- IMO = In my opinion
- MOS, POS = Mom/parents over shoulder
- SUS = Suspicious
- TBH = To be honest
- WRU = Where are you?

Both because it is informal and because it might not be understood across demographic groups, texting slang generally has no place in criminal justice communications. One possible exception is for comic effect in non-emergency tweeting (see Chapter 10).

JARGON. **Jargon** is highly specialized language, such as that used in a particular discipline or profession. Jargon is understood by members of the group, and thus serves as informal code language between group members. A widely used expression in the restaurant industry, for example, is "86," meaning leave off (e.g., onions on a burger). Examples of jargon in policing from just the beginning of the alphabet include the following (Hall, 2017):

- "924" = girlfriend or boyfriend on the side
- "A car" = two-person patrol unit
- "Adam Henry" = asshole
- "airmail" = something thrown from above (e.g., rooftop) down on police officers
- "ambulance monkey" = paramedic
- "aqua pig" = marine patrol officer
- "ATL" = attempt to locate
- "B girl" = prostitute
- "birthing" = pulling someone out of a car window
- "BOLO" = be on the look out
- "bottom feeder" = defense attorney
- "bus" = ambulance
- "caught a day" = getting a one-day suspension
- "CI" = confidential informant
- "collar" = arrest
- "CYOA" = cover your own ass

Like slang in general, some jargon has made its way into everyday use, such as "10-4" to mean "affirmative." But regular citizens, officials in other areas of government, victims and witnesses, and so on are unlikely to be familiar with most jargon. Thus, while jargon has its place in informal communications, it does not have an appropriate role in formal criminal justice communications.

Be Literal

Write so that your audience can take you literally. **Literal** means according to the exact meaning of words. **Figurative**, by way of contrast, means metaphorical, or departing from literal. When we use figurative language, the words take on a meaning different than we would find for them in a dictionary. Figurative language is perfectly appropriate for some types of communication—such as narrative writing (e.g., novels, poetry)—but it has no place in technical communication. Not only can figurative language be difficult to translate across cultures and languages, but also figurative language can be used to disguise, inflate, or trivialize the reality of a situation and true meaning of a communication.

Avoid Euphemisms

A **euphemism** is a delicate way to express something. It is a way of saying something without actually having to come right out and say it. Euphemisms are used to make something that could be unpleasant more palatable.

The criminal justice field is rife with euphemisms: We do not punish "criminals" in prisons; "offenders" are "rehabilitated" in "correctional facilities." Suspects are not "held captive"; they are "detained." And "prisoners" are not held in "cages" to "punish"; "inmates" are held in "cells" to "reform" or "protect the community." Juvenile lawbreakers certainly are not "convicted" and sent to "prisons"; their cases are "adjudicated" and they are sent to "detention centers" or "residential facilities." It is not just crime, criminals, and the criminal justice system that are cloaked in euphemisms. So are other controversial and sensitive topics such as death and dying, poverty and unemployment, and sex and reproduction. Table 9.5 presents some other euphemisms used in the contemporary United States.

Avoid Irony, Exaggeration, and Understatement

When we are **ironic**, we intend to mean something other than—perhaps opposite to—what we actually say. Some examples are

- When capital punishment was pronounced, a defendant saying, "Perfect." (Here, the defendant does not really mean execution is perfect for him. Really, he means execution is as far from perfect for him as a sentence could be.)
- When a wife comes home early to catch her husband in bed with another woman, the wife says, "Well, isn't this a pretty picture?" (Unless she was looking for a threesome or a hefty alimony, she probably meant this was an "ugly" picture.)

A **hyperbole** is an exaggeration intended to emphasize and/or be funny. Hyperbole is a common strategy for demonizing one's opponent or alternative perspectives:

- "He was behaving like a wild animal." (Probably not. He might have been yelling, spitting, and punching walls, but he was not walking around on all fours and eating raw meat.)

TABLE 9.5 Euphemistic Terms

Euphemism	Translation
passed away, no longer with us, at peace now, departed, go to a better place, breathe one's last breath	died/dead
put to sleep, quality-of-life death, ease suffering, aid in dying, end-of-life decision-making	euthanize
pregnancy termination, interrupt a pregnancy, emergency contraception, family planning	abortion
economically disadvantaged, temporary negative cash flow, unable to make ends meet, underprivileged	poor
personnel realignment, surplus reduction in personnel, workforce imbalance correction, dispense with services	termination/firing
economical with the truth, tall story, misspeak, credibility gap, stranger to the truth, ethically challenged, relayed misinformation	lie, to lie, liar
adult beverage, a drink, spirits, cocktail, the juice	alcohol
adult entertainment, adult content, mature content, explicit images	pornography
sleep together/sleep with, go to bed with/take to bed, make love/lovemaking, have relations, have an affair, be intimate	have sex
in the family way, expectant/expecting, with child, eating for two, in delicate condition	pregnant

- "If you support gun control, then you don't care about the Second Amendment." Or, "If you don't support gun control, then you don't care about children." (Both of these are false dilemmas, which is a form of logical fallacy [see Chapter 5] that reflects black-or-white thinking. But believing the "if" does not necessitate believing the "then." There are many shades of gray.)

A **litotes** is an understatement intended to emphasize and/or be funny. Like hyperbole, litotes can be used to demonize opponents or opposing viewpoints. They are often sarcastic:

- "He is no lover of freedom." (Here, meaning he routinely strongly advocates limiting personal freedoms ostensibly to protect society from realistic harms.)
- "Prison is no vacation." (Obviously: It is punishment; it is not meant to be relaxing and enjoyable.)

Avoid Idioms

An **idiom** is a collection of words that, taken together, has come to mean something other than what the individual words mean. Idioms rarely are understandable beyond their originating language or dialect. The saying, "let the cat out of the bag," for example, arises from older times when pigs were considered far more valuable than cats. A shrewd seller might put cats in a bag along with pigs, so the bag would weigh more and thus drive up the price. Letting the cat out of the bag exposed something hidden. In the criminal justice system, we often hear the expression "put teeth into," as in a new law putting teeth into an existing law. Here, the speaker does not mean to suggest that the new law installs dentures in a law. Instead, the point is that the new law empowers the existing law. A law prohibiting marijuana use, for example, might have "no teeth" until there is a budget for enforcing it. Table 9.6 presents some other examples of idioms in everyday use.

Like euphemisms, ironies, hyperboles, and litotes, idioms cannot be understood literally. Although these manners of speech can be perfectly appropriate in creative and fictional writing, they impede rather than facilitate effective technical communication.

TABLE 9.6   Idiomatic Expressions

Idiom	Meaning
at the drop of a hat	immediately, right away
burning the midnight oil	working late into the night
cry over spilled milk	lamenting something that has already happened
hot potato	controversial, sensitive issue
jump on the bandwagon	follow what others are doing
kill two birds with one stone	accomplish two things at once or with one action
miss the boat	miss a chance or opportunity
once in a blue moon	rarely
piece of cake	easy, not a problem at all
on the fence	undecided on an issue, refusing to commit to a side
under the weather	sick, ill
take with a grain of salt	don't interpret something too strictly or take something too seriously

Source: "Famous idioms: Meaning" (n.d.)

Prefer Positive to Negative Constructions

Where a **positive construction** is used to express some fact, a **negative construction** expresses something contrary to fact. Negative words and phrases include "no," "nobody," "none," "not," "nothing," "never," "nowhere," "neither … nor," and "no one." There are appropriate situations for using negative terms. For example, the Question, "Did you see the full moon last night?"; and the Answer, "No, I was already asleep." Or, "No one volunteered for neighborhood watch." Yet, there are many occasions when negative terms are inappropriate because they are indirect or, even worse, confusing. This is especially true in questions and when two negative terms are used in the same sentence. Here are some examples of indirect and confusing uses of negative terms, with the negative terms underlined:

1. "Do not leave your car unlocked." (negative statement)
2. "Didn't you see that car?" (negative question)
3. "There is no way the police will do nothing about this." (double negative statement)
4. "Isn't it true you didn't see the car?" (double negative question)

The first example illustrates how a negative construction can be indirect, or a roundabout way of making a point. It is both clearer and more concise to say, "Lock your car." A similar example is, "The house was not occupied." A more direct way to express this fact is, "The house was vacant." As shown in this example with underlining, we often can replace a negative phrase (d with a positive word.

With the questions, the person being asked the question might be unsure how to respond, and the person asking the question might be unsure what the response means. If someone answered simply "yes" or "no" in the second example, then it would be unclear whether they meant yes, they had not seen the car; yes, they had seen the car; no, they had not seen the car; or no, they had seen the car. The solution in the second example is to phrase the question positively rather than negatively: "Did you see the car?"

The third and fourth examples both involve a **double negative**—two negative terms in the same sentence. The solution in both examples is to treat the two negatives as cancelling each other out. Thus, the third example becomes: "The police will do something about this." Likewise, in the fourth example, we can solve the problem by using the two negatives to cancel each other out: "Is it true that you saw the car?" Once we make these adjustments, both the question and answer become easily decipherable.

Avoid Double-Barreled Questions

Another time questions can be confusing is when we ask two questions at the same time, which is called a **double-barreled question**. Here are some examples:

1. "Do you plan to vote for Candidate X because he's tough on crime?"
2. "Do you agree that the public defender was prompt and polite?"
3. "Did your son or daughter hear anything?"

The problem is when there are different answers to the two questions. Looking at the first example, suppose someone was going to vote for Candidate X (an answer of "yes" to the first question) because Candidate X supports lower taxes (an answer of "no" to the second question). In the second example, how should someone respond if they agree that the public defender was prompt but not that the person was polite? The third example is a little different. Here, a "no" would seem to indicate that neither the son nor the daughter heard anything, but would a "yes" refer to the son, the daughter, or both the son and the daughter?

Usually, the best solution is to separate the two questions, such as, "Do you plan to vote for Candidate X?" (If the response is yes); "Are you voting for Candidate X because he's tough on crime?" And with the second example, "Do you agree that the public defender was prompt?" And then, "Do you agree that the public defender was polite?" The third example could be improved by asking first, "Did your son hear anything?" and second, "Did your daughter hear anything?"

APPLICATIONS

Two communications that exemplify the importance of clarity are discussion posts and expert witness testimony.

Discussion Posts

A discussion forum is a common part of online (i.e., distance) courses, and some campus-based (i.e., face-to-face) courses with an online component might use them as well. Also known as discussion boards or online forums, **discussion forums** are a virtual message board where users can submit (i.e., post) a message and read and reply to other peoples' messages. As a class assignment, they begin with a discussion prompt, and then students are given some period of time (usually a week) to engage in a meaningful discussion on the prompt. Table 9.7 presents examples of discussion prompts related to crime theory, policy, and research.

Some classes take an informal approach to discussion forums, where students are asked to reflect on some reading, make connections between course materials and their own personal or professional experiences, or share their progress on and troubleshoot problems with course assignments (e.g., a term paper,). Other classes take a more formal

TABLE 9.7   Sample Discussion Forum Prompts

Compare and contrast different criminological theories in terms of crime's causes and control. Pick some specific form of crime, and decide which criminological theory best explains your selected form of crime. Then decide which criminological theory does the worst job explaining your selected form of crime.

Locate an empirical research article from a peer-reviewed criminology journal. Identify the research question, theoretical framework, and hypotheses. Next, outline its research methodology in terms of research design, sampling, and variable measurement. Finally, present its main findings.

Pick a criminological theory and propose a hypothesis derived from it. Then describe how you would design a study to test the hypothesis, focusing on how you would establish the three criteria of nomothetic causality.

Compare and contrast probability and nonprobability sampling methods. Consider their purposes, strengths, and weaknesses. Give at least one example of a research question suited to nonprobability sampling and at least one example of a research question suited to probability sampling.

Select a specific crime problem. Drawing from criminological theory, find a specific crime policy to propose as a possible solution for your selected crime problem. Explicitly identify the theory and link it to the crime policy.

approach, where students are prompted to summarize some reading; make connections between materials in one course with lessons from other courses or the real world; or otherwise engage in substantive, academic discussions. Here, the focus is on the latter: formal discussion forums.

Effective discussion posts are directly responsive to both the prompt and to the ongoing conversation. They also meet all assignment requirements. An example of requirements (with point values) for a weeklong discussion forum, which opens on a Monday and ends on a Sunday, is

- Post at least 5 times, writing 100 to 500 words. At least one post should be an original post. (20 pts)
- Submit posts on at least 3 separate days. The first post should be submitted by 11:59 p.m. on Tuesday. (10 pts)
- Ensure that all posts are unique, substantive, directly responsive to the assignment, and reflective of the ongoing discussion. Material that duplicates an earlier post is not unique. "Me too" is not substantive. (30 pts)
- Draw explicitly from the textbook and use your own words to summarize required readings and link them to the current discussion. Do not merely quote. (20 pts)
- Be professional, positive, and polite at all times. Do not attack your peers. (10pts)
- Edit for proper grammar, spelling, and punctuation. (10 pts)

Types

There are two types of posts: (1) original and (2) reply. An **original post** responds directly to a discussion forum assignment prompt without drawing from or referencing any other posts. A **reply post**, on the other hand, is a response to a post. A reply could be someone asking you a question in one of their posts, or you could post a reply that builds off or questions another post. In most cases, you should directly and thoroughly address all parts of the discussion forum prompt in original posts.

Best Practices

As usual, the best way to approach a graded class assignment is to read the instructions carefully, ask any questions about the instructions, and then adhere to the instructions. Beyond that, here are some best practices for formal discussion forum posts:

- **Give yourself time.** Begin as soon as possible, and then stay engaged throughout the duration of the discussion. Do not wait until a deadline to review the prompt, do any readings, or construct your posts. You might need some time to process readings and the prompt, to ask the professor for clarification, to handle unexpected events in your personal life, or to troubleshoot technical problems.

| BOX 9.3 | Plagiarism Pointer |

Plagiarism is but one form of unethical writing. Another form of unethical writing is presenting source material out of context such that we give our audience the wrong impression of the point being made in the source. Whether intentional or unintentional, both of these unethical writing practices have the effect of deceiving our audience.

- **Complete all of the relevant readings before you start the assignment.** Take notes. For this purpose (as opposed to quizzes and exams), your notes need not be detailed. Use your response as an occasion to demonstrate that you have completed the required readings.
- **Read the prompt, and then plan your approach.** If there are multiple parts to the prompt, decide which components to address in which posts. Dividing up the prompt's components can help you reach the minimum required number of posts without being redundant. Also, mapping out the prompt's components and your plan for addressing them can help ensure that you directly address all prompt components.
- **Explicitly address each component of the prompt.** Make it as easy as possible for your professor to see where you have addressed all parts of the prompt. Do not dodge challenging questions by providing abstract, tangential responses. And do not post superficial comments as a way around reading. Consider using informative subject lines (or titles) for the posts as well as sections and section headings within a post for the various prompt components.
- **Read all posts before submitting your own.** Doing so is essential to posting unique content. You are responsible for keeping abreast of and being responsive to the unfolding discussion. "Unique" is not limited to you not repeating yourself; you also should not repeat your classmates, even in your own words
- **Refrain from pointless and excessive quoting.** Some people resort to quoting as a way to avoid thinking deeply or to meet minimum word requirements. Yet rarely is there a valid reason for quoting in discussion forums: You usually do not need to quote the part of the peer's post you are commenting on because your entire class can read your peer's post themselves—and the same goes for assigned readings. Instead of quoting, show you understand the material by using your own words.
- **Identify sources.** When you use ideas from a source, provide an in-text citation, and then include a full Reference-list entry at the end of your post. This is part of being an ethical writer. Do not expect this material to contribute to your word count, however.
- **Type your posts in Word, and then copy and paste them into the discussion forum.** Sometimes, learning management systems will time out if you do not submit in a certain time period. Keeping your responses in a separate document can guard against that problem as well as other technical problems that are more common with learning management systems than with more established programs like Microsoft Office.
- **Proofread and edit before you post.** Check grammar, spelling, and punctuation as well as writing style. Even if your peers submit informal posts, you should remain professional, positive, and polite. For example, do not engage in petty squabbles, criticize unfairly, or attack people. While you may disagree with a peer's perspective, you should do so politely, explaining why you hold a different perspective. Stay professional.

Expert Witness Testimony

Expert witness testimony is the courtroom testimony of an expert witness. Expert testimony is perhaps where science and the law intersect most vividly. Experts are involved in the analysis and presentation of various forms of criminal evidence, including ballistics, biology and human anatomy, bite marks, blood and DNA, computers and digital forensics, drugs, engineering, finances, fingerprints, handwriting, psychology, shoeprints, statistics, and toxicology. According to the Federal Rules of Evidence 702 (https://www.law.cornell.edu/rules/fre/rule_702)

> A witness who is qualified as an expert by knowledge, skill, experience, training, or education may testify in the form of an opinion or otherwise if:
>
> (a) the expert's scientific, technical, or other specialized knowledge will help the trier of fact to understand the evidence or to determine a fact in issue;
>
> (b) the testimony is based on sufficient facts or data;
>
> (c) the testimony is the product of reliable principles and methods; and
>
> (d) the expert has reliably applied the principles and methods to the facts of the case.

Both the prosecution and the defense can use expert witnesses. The expert's testimony must be relevant to some material fact (see Chapter 6), and the expert must be qualified in the subject matter about which s/he will testify. Education and professional experience are typical measures of qualification.

Balancing Concerns

The point of an expert witness is that the evidence in question is complicated, thus requiring someone with specialized knowledge to analyze and interpret it properly. Thus, there is an inherent challenge to clear communication when dealing with expert witnesses. Rather than ignoring the challenge, however, it is vital to communicate complicated material in a way that is accessible to average adults. To be effective, the expert witness must bridge the gap between that expert's expertise and the jury's much more limited knowledge. Bridging this gap requires a delicate balance between too much and not enough technical information.

On the one hand, we do not want to be so technical that the jury loses interest or cannot understand us. There can be a motivation toward *oversharing*—to show how smart we are or to demonstrate that we earned our fee—but doing so can bore jurors and cause them to tune us out (Montiel, 2013). Do not try to show off or impress people with your advanced vocabulary or expansive knowledge. It is only natural, moreover, to talk about complicated topics using the specialized language we are accustomed to with such topics. But jurors could have little more than a high school education. So that our audience can understand us and realize the import of what we are saying, then, we should avoid jargon and specialized terms as well as providing—and spending lots of time presenting—unnecessary details. Thus, if you have to use a specialized term, define it. If you have to discuss a complex concept, break it down as simply as possible. Use graphics whenever possible to illustrate complicated processes and points.

On the other hand, however, we do not want to talk down to jurors or be not technical enough to convey the scientific rigor of our analysis and resulting conclusions. *Oversimplifying*, such as warning the jury they are about to hear "a bunch of mumbo jumbo," can lead to jurors tuning out expert testimony.

Best Practices

What follows is a list of best practices for giving expert witness testimony (Babitsky, 2013; Cappellino, 2017; Carner, 2012):

- **Be prepared.** Review all case materials closely. Avoid tunnel vision: Reaching a premature conclusion, and then dismissing alternative perspectives and contradictory evidence.
- **Understand the process.** First, you will be questioned directly by the lawyer who solicited your testimony (i.e., direct examination). Next, you will be questioned by the lawyer on the opposing side (i.e., cross-examination). After that, you might be called again on recross and redirect. Additionally, you could be recalled to the stand after having been dismissed, and the judge even might ask you questions. Do not expect the lawyer who solicited your testimony to object to everything objectionable, which could appear overly defensive. Instead, be prepared to hold your own.
- **Understand the question.** Listen closely, and make sure you understand exactly what the lawyer is asking. Ask the lawyer to clarify or rephrase if you are unsure exactly what the question is, such as with double-barreled questions and questions containing double negatives.
- **Answer the question that was asked.** Take the lawyer literally, and then do not go beyond the question when you answer. The question, "Have you examined the blood spatter patterns in this case?," for example, has a yes or no answer. This question is not actually asking for a description of the case's blood spatter patterns.
- **Tell the truth.** Do not guess or speculate without sound basis. Say "I don't know" if you do not know the answer to a question. If you realize you made a mistake, then own up to it immediately. Do not say things only to please the lawyer who solicited your testimony.
- **Choose your words and phrase your responses wisely.** Words such as "always" and "never" can come back to haunt you. If the answer is a qualified yes (or no), lead with the qualification so you are not interrupted after saying only "yes" or "no."
- **Take your time.** Do not be scared to stop and think. Do you recall something? Are there other possible explanations? If asked if you have analyzed a particular document, take the time to review the document in question. Do not assume the document the lawyer is holding is the one you analyzed. Take time to plan and deliver each response.
- **Make your testimony accessible to laypeople.** Simplify complex problems into discernible steps, present graphics wherever possible, put big numbers into perspective, and try to be as brief yet compelling as possible. Keep in mind that most people are uncomfortable with large numbers, and so buttress them with explanation and analogy. Take neither too long nor to too little time to present information accurately.
- **Be sensitive to body language.** Maintain eye contact with the lawyer questioning you, sometimes looking to the jury when your answer is long. Avoid fidgeting, scowling, crossing arms, or displaying other hostile or nervous mannerisms that might call into question your credibility.
- **Stick to the facts.** Remain professional and impartial. Your job is to weigh the evidence objectively, using your relevant expertise, and then to draw the most logical conclusion. Do not assume the role of victim advocate.
- **Remain calm.** Keep in mind that the cross-examining lawyer is supposed to try to fluster and undermine you. So, when this happens, do not take it personally or get defensive. Avoid arguing with the lawyer on cross-examination.

Note that these best practices do not address the analysis of scientific evidence or selection of expert witnesses. The focus here is on expert witness testimony in a courtroom as part of a jury trial.

EXERCISES
Matching
These exercises are designed to assess Chapter 9 Learning Objective 1 (see Box 9.1). Match each numbered statement to the lowercase letter corresponding to the key word it defines. Each key word will be used only once.

1. An informal way of saying something that is known to and used by members of broad groups
2. Using qualifiers in an appropriate way to indicate uncertainty
3. A question containing two separate questions
4. Exact
5. Abbreviated forms of expressions used in text messaging
6. An understatement intended to emphasize and/or be funny
7. The courtroom testimony of an expert witness
8. Replacing simple terms with fancy terms in an effort to impress the audience
9. A virtual (Internet) message board, where users can submit a message and read and reply to other people's messages
10. A sentence structure that expresses some fact
11. An exaggeration intended to emphasize and/or be funny
12. A discussion forum post that responds to or builds off of another discussion forum post
13. To the point
14. Words that just about anyone familiar with the language should know
15. A collection of words that, taken together, means something other than what the individual words mean
16. Showing consideration for others and their situations
17. The characteristic of a communication that is straightforward, unambiguous, and therefore able to be understood
18. According to the exact meaning of words
19. A sentence structure that expresses something contrary to fact
20. A delicate way of expressing something; a way of saying something without actually having to come right out and say it
21. Highly specialized language, such as that used in a particular discipline or profession
22. Deliberately being ambiguous and evasive in an effort to avoid telling the truth, alienating audiences, making a commitment, and/or eliciting censure
23. A discussion forum post that responds directly to the assignment prompt without drawing from or referencing any other posts
24. Metaphorical, or departing from literal, such that the words used take on a meaning other than their literal definition
25. Using words that mean something other than, perhaps even opposite to, what we actually say

26. Two negative terms in the same sentence

a. clarity
b. direct
c. discussion forum
d. double-barreled question
e. double negative
f. equivocating
g. euphemism
h. expert witness testimony
i. figurative
j. hedging
k. hyperbole
l. idiom
m. ironic

n. jargon
o. literal
p. litotes
q. negative construction
r. original post
s. plain language
t. positive construction
u. precise
v. reply post
w. slang
x. tact
y. texting slang
z. thesauritis

Multiple Choice

These exercises are designed to assess Chapter 9 Learning Objective 4 (see Box 9.1). Indicate the single most appropriate response to each item below.

1. Is the following statement clear or unclear? "Rather than answering the detective's questions, the witness kept beating around the bush."
a. clear
b. unclear

2. Is the following statement clear or unclear? "The defendant admitted his guilt when he learned that his mother would testify against him."
a. clear
b. unclear

3. Is the following statement clear or unclear? "The mother told her daughter that no one would take her away."
a. clear
b. unclear

4. Is the following statement clear or unclear? "The witness thought no one would believe her testimony because she works at a house of ill repute."
a. clear
b. unclear

5. Is the following statement clear or unclear? "We plan to commence transmitting the transcript as soon as we ascertain the client's facsimile number."
a. clear
b. unclear

6. Is the following question clear or unclear? "Did you report the break-in to the police? Yes or no?"
a. clear
b. unclear

7. Is the following question clear or unclear? "Did you call the police before or after you went outside? Yes or no?"
   a. clear
   b. unclear

8. Is the following question clear or unclear? "Did you report the break-in to the police and to your insurance? Yes or no?"
   a. clear
   b. unclear

9. Is the following question clear or unclear? "Did you not hear the glass shatter last night? Yes or no?"
   a. clear
   b. unclear

10. Is the following question clear or unclear? "Do you deny seeing the man enter the building? Yes or no?"
    a. clear
    b. unclear

11. Is the following answer clear or unclear? Question: "What did you do when you first arrived at the scene?" Answer: "The first thing I did when I arrived at the scene was taped off the crime scene."
    a. clear
    b. unclear

12. Is the following answer clear or unclear? Question: "What reason did you have for stopping the defendant?" Answer: "I got a call about a DIP."
    a. clear
    b. unclear

13. Is the following passage clear or unclear? Question: "What is your stance on lethal injection?" Answer: "For criminals sentenced to capital punishment, I support lethal injection."
    a. clear
    b. unclear

14. Is the following passage clear or unclear? Question: "What is the government's plan for dealing with meth labs?" Answer: "We are officially launching a war on meth labs."
    a. clear
    b. unclear

15. Is the following passage clear or unclear? Question: "How did you learn about the location of the meth lab?" Answer: "We got an anonymous tip that a meth lab was operating at that location."
    a. clear
    b. unclear

Editing
These editing exercises are designed to assess Chapter 9 Learning Objective 5 (see Box 9.1). Rewrite each of the following passages, editing them as needed to achieve clarity.

1. After they took the bloody sock out of the car, the couple hid it.
2. Do you think you could take the evidence to the lab?
3. Take this advice with a grain of salt: Always carry a loaded gun.
4. Isn't there a better way to handle this burglary case?
5. My boss is on the fence about how to handle juveniles who burglarize?
6. Their goal was to effectuate an expeditious arrest.
7. It can't be the case that no one was at home when the burglary happened.
8. They needed money because his mom was between jobs.
9. It is possible that the police might be interested in investigating the child's background.
10. Is the child attending school or is he employed?
11. He said he wasn't stealing because he never intended not to return the money.
12. Subsequent to breaking the window, the boy entered the home.

Writing
These writing exercises are designed to assess Chapter 9 Learning Objectives 2, 3, 6, and 7 (see Box 9.1).

1. Argue for the importance of clarity in criminal justice communications.
2. Outline strategies for achieving clarity in communications.
3. Suppose you have a discussion forum assignment. The discussion forum prompt is as follows: "What is America's most serious crime problem?" One of your classmates identified drugs as the most serious crime, explaining that drugs ruin communities and peoples' health as well as lead to more serious crimes like property and violent crime. Another classmate identified murder, saying that murder takes human lives, causes extreme suffering among friends and family members, and makes people fearful to walk the streets at night. Your assignment is to submit a total of three posts, one an original post and the other two reply posts, that are between 75 and 150 words each. In addition to being clear and responsive to the assignment, remember to be tactful in your reply posts.
4. Suppose you are the prosecutor in a case involving DNA evidence, and you are preparing a DNA expert to give expert witness testimony. It is a murder case in a small town with approximately 8,000 residents. The defendant's blood type is O Negative, and the DNA expert determined that the sample of blood collected at the scene also is O Negative. You want to ensure that the jury will understand the expert's testimony. So, you give the expert three examples of questions you intend to ask in the courtroom, requesting that the expert practice the responses. Your questions are

   - "How can you be sure the evidence has not been contaminated?"
   - "How likely is it that someone else in this town also has O Negative blood?"
   - "How confident are you that the blood found at the scene belongs to the defendant?"

Do some research on DNA evidence, such as by using the *Reference Manual on Scientific Evidence* (Federal Judicial Center and National Research Council, 2011). Construct model responses that use clear, plain language.

REFERENCES

Babitsky, Steven. (2013, January 24). *25 tips for expert witnesses.* Seak: The Expert Witness Training Company. Retrieved from https://www.testifyingtraining.com/25-tips-for-expert-witnesses/

Birdsong, Toni. (2018, January 13). 2018 texting slang update: How to decode what your teen is saying online. *McAfee: Securing Tomorrow, Today.* Retrieved from https://securingtomorrow.mcafee.com/consumer/family-safety/2018-texting-slang-update-decode-teen-saying-online/

Burke, Kenneth. (2016, May 24). 73 texting statistics that answer all your questions. *Text Request.* Retrieved from https://www.textrequest.com/blog/texting-statistics-answer-questions/

Cappellino, Anjelica. (2017, June 16). Top 15 tips for testifying as an expert witness. Retrieved from *The Expert Institute* website: https://www.theexpertinstitute.com/top-15-tips-testifying-expert-witness/

Carner, Doug. (2012, May 29). Turning an expert witness into a great witness. The Jury Expert website. Retrieved from http://www.thejuryexpert.com/2012/05/turning-an-expert-witness-into-a-great-witness/

Drug Enforcement Agency Houston Division. (2017, May 17). *Drug slang code words.* Intelligence Report (DEA-HOU-DIR-020-17). Retrieved from https://ndews.umd.edu/sites/ndews.umd.edu/files/dea-drug-slang-code-words-may2017.pdf

Famous idioms: Meaning. (n.d.) *English language smart words.* Retrieved from English Language Smart Words website: http://www.smart-words.org/quotes-sayings/idioms-meaning.html

Federal Judicial Center and National Research Council. (2011). *Reference manual on scientific evidence* (3rd ed.). Washington, DC: The National Academies Press.

Hall, Allen E. (2017, January 24). *What are some slang terms used among police officers?* Retrieved from Quora website: https://www.quora.com/What-are-some-slang-terms-used-among-police-officers

Harris, Robert A. (2017). *Using sources effectively: Strengthening your writing and avoiding plagiarism* (5th ed.). New York: Routledge.

Markel, Mike. (2012). *Technical communication* (10th ed.). Boston, MA: Bedford/St. Martin's.

Montiel, Denise. (2013, March 5). Effective communication in expert testimony. *American Bar Association: Trial Practice.* Retrieved from http://apps.americanbar.org/litigation/committees/trialpractice/articles/winter2013-0313-expert-witness-communication.html

Principle 9: Conciseness

A man who uses a great many words to express his meaning is like a bad marksman who instead of aiming a single stone at an object takes up a handful and throws at it in hopes he may hit.

—SAMUEL JOHNSON

People weed flower gardens because weeds do not belong in flower gardens. Weeds make it harder to see and appreciate the flowers in the gardens. We can liken the flowers to the main ideas that serve as the purpose for the communication and that we intend for the audience to understand and remember. Just as weeds detract from the beauty of a garden and pull focus away from the flowers, unnecessary words and clunky phrases weaken the flow of a communication and reduce the likelihood that the communication will achieve its purpose. Just as we weed gardens, then, we should weed our writing. Doing so will allow the audience to focus on the key points without having to do extra work or invest more time than is necessary. In other words, we can achieve a more effective and efficient communication process by being concise.

Concise writing involves using as few simple words as possible to make a point. It is vital in the world of criminal justice policy and practice for communications to be concise for at least two reasons. First, concise writing draws the focus to the communication's real purpose. It takes less cognitive effort for the audience to understand if they do not have to do the work of sifting out unnecessary verbiage. Second, many criminal justice decision makers simply do not have the time for longer communications (Jensen, McElreath, & Graves, 2013). Even when they have the time, most people are not going to pay attention long. On the one hand, audience members might not be *willing* to attend closely to a lengthy communication—especially one that is perceived as being overrun with weeds. On the other hand, even with the best of intentions, people generally do not seem *capable* of paying attention long. For these reasons, we need to make our point as clearly and quickly as possible.

This does not mean we "skimp" on important details or fail to develop pertinent facts, any more than weeding a garden means we pull out the flowers along with the weeds. No, we must recognize the difference between flowers and weeds so that we remove only the weeds and not the flowers. Accordingly, this chapter presents seven guidelines for removing the weeds while retaining the flowers in our communications. It then turns to two forms of criminal justice communications that highlight the need for conciseness: article abstracts and tweets. By the end of this chapter, readers should appreciate the importance of conciseness and be armed with several concrete strategies for achieving conciseness.

GUIDELINES

The foundation of conciseness is focus. To remove the weeds but keep the flowers, we first must know the difference between weeds and flowers. In a communication, this distinction revolves around our objective. The flowers are that which helps us meet our objective. The weeds, in contrast, are that which is not needed to meet our objective. Being aware of our objective, we then can follow seven guidelines to arrive at concise writing:

1. Eliminate "filler."
2. Exclude trite, meaningless statements.
3. Omit rhetorical questions.
4. Reword clunky prepositional phrases.
5. Refrain from redundancy.
6. Avoid obvious statements.
7. Prefer summaries to paraphrases and quotations.

Eliminate Filler

Filler is any word or group of words in a communication that has no meaning. They do not add information or advance our objective. Such words take up physical space in a writing and time in a briefing, but they do not in any way advance the purpose of the communication. Filler can take many forms. In Table 10.1, we see one form of filler common in written communication: unnecessarily wordy phrases.

BOX 10.2	Credibility Connection

Being concise and to the point shows your audience that you value their attention and respect their time. Your apparent concern fosters trust.

TABLE 10.1   Common Wordy Phrases

Wordy	Concise
Due to the fact that, considering that fact that, in view of the fact that	Because
Despite the fact that	Although
In addition to	Also, besides, too
In an effort to, in order to	To
In the event that, in the event of	If
In a situation in which	When
It is requested that you	Please
Prior to	Before
Provide guidance for/to	Guides
Subsequent to	After
Until such time as	Until
With the exception of	Except
With regard to	About

Sources: Nichol (2014); The University of Wisconsin–Madison Writing Center (2016)

Another form of filler is "fluff" or "bullshit." These terms are used to describe filler that is intentionally added to increase the length of a communication or disguise a lack of knowledge on the subject. On the one hand, effective communication demands that we know what we are talking about. Our credibility depends to a large degree on our subject-matter competence. On the other hand, fluff and bullshit are easier than we might think for our audience to detect, which means we are not fooling people when we go this route. Beyond not fooling our audience, we might irritate or offend our audience in addition to making ourselves and our agency look bad.

Regardless of its form, filler needs to be excised from our communications. The following subsections suggest some strategies for avoiding filler in written and oral communications. Although these strategies are covered one at a time, it is probably the case that a combination of these strategies is more effective in reducing filler than any single approach by itself.

Written Filler

One strategy for avoiding filler is by not intentionally inserting any in the first place. Developing an outline before we write is one way to guard against inserting unnecessary material (see Chapter 4). Using standard outline format forces us to think about how parts fit into the whole. We can also diagram an argument, which involves mapping out the argument's components and their connection with each other (see Chapter 5). Looking at our diagram, we should reconsider any unconnected components, asking whether they actually contribute to the argument.

Beyond that, there are two approaches for "weeding" the filler out of a communication we already have written. First, we can look at chunks of information and their relevance to the argument as a whole. Editing (see Appendix C) and reverse outlining are effective methods for removing unnecessary material we already have written. Reverse outlining is when we take a finished (or nearly finished) communication and put it into outline form. When we use a reverse outline, we can identify the primary objective of the communication, each main point, and how each main point is developed. Material that does not articulate or develop our objective and points should be reconsidered. It is possible that material that, upon first review, appears unnecessary actually was intended to serve a purpose. In this case, rather than eliminating the text, we need to rephrase or reposition it so that it can achieve the purpose for which it was intended.

Second, looking at a communication on a word-by-word basis, pretending that each word costs us $1 to use can be a helpful exercise in eliminating unnecessary words such as filler: Words that do not help us make our point are not worth the cost—especially when we consider how that costs add up for each nonessential word. Adjectives that add no information about the thing they are modifying belong in this category of filler. These pointless words can be used so poorly that they actually can detract from rather than add to meaning. Take, for example, the following situation in which an author interprets a statistic: "The table indicates that roughly 46.5% of the same engaged in the deceptive business practices." The word "roughly" implies that approximation is involved, which makes no sense when we are given a precise quantity.

Oral Filler

In an oral communication, we probably will need to address filler differently. In speeches, presentations, and other oral communications, filler can take the form of expressions such as "umm," "ah," "like," "I mean," "so," "you know," and "Like I said" (Dziedzic, 2011). Filler of this nature is often an unintentional product of nervousness. Even if our presentation is entirely scripted, we probably cannot weed it all out. To catch and avoid filler in public speaking, we can try these three strategies (Dziedzic, 2011):

1. Record ourselves so we can identify the filler we tend to use.
2. Try using informative transitions (e.g., "next," "for example") in places where we tend to use filler.
3. Slow down our speaking so that we can exercise greater control over the words we use.

Exclude Trite, Meaningless Statements

Trite expressions are overused, unoriginal, and generally meaningless. Beyond that, they can trivialize a communication, making the speaker look ignorant and/or insincere. These include adages, clichés, maxims, mottos, proverbs, puns, slogans, and witticisms. Sometimes used for dramatic effect, other times as filler, and yet other times as an appeal to traditionalism or popular belief, such sayings do not have an appropriate role in technical communication. Refrain from such uninformative, banal expressions as, for instance, "The early bird catches the worm" and "Make love, not war." Take one of the following approaches to ensure that your communications are devoid of these expressions:

1. If you are using one of these sayings to make a point or share pertinent information, then replace it with more formal, direct language; or
2. If you are using one of these sayings for a reason other than to make a point or share pertinent information (e.g., as filler), then simply delete it.

Omit Rhetorical Questions

A **rhetorical question** is a question asked when no answer is sought. Rhetorical questions tend to be used for dramatic effects or as filler. Here are some examples of rhetorical questions:

- "Have you ever been the victim of identity theft? Well, if you have, then. . . ."
- "What are some of the consequences of identify theft? First. . . . Second. . . ."
- "Why do identity theft victims not call the police? There are several reasons. . . ."
- "Can you blame them for not calling the police? Victims. . . ."
- "But why not give the police a chance? How could the police solve a crime if there is no report? These are some legitimate questions. . . ."

In these examples, notice how a question is asked, and then the communicator continues without giving the audience a chance to answer the question, either answering the question or moving on to the next point. Rhetorical questions are thus different from genuine questions, which we ask because we want to know the answer and when the person being asked has an opportunity to respond (e.g., witness interviews, courtroom testimony). Genuine questions can be appropriate in some circumstances, but rhetorical questions do not have an appropriate role in technical communications.

We should answer questions, not ask them, in technical communications. Rather than asking and answering our own questions, then, we should be straightforward and to the point. Here is an example of a rhetorical question (underlined), which is answered in the sentence that follows it: "How should the arresting officer handle a suspect who physically resists? Well, that officer should. . . ." Instead, just describe how an arresting officer should handle a suspect who physically rests, such as, "Options for responding to a resisting suspect include. . . ." In sum, formal, criminal justice communications are presentations; save questions for conversations. Thus, rather than asking a rhetorical question, take one of the following two approaches:

1. If your purpose in using the rhetorical question is to make a point or share pertinent information, then replace the rhetorical question with a clear and concise statement; or
2. If you are using the rhetorical question for a reason other than to make a point or share pertinent information (e.g., as filler), then simply delete it.

Reword Clunky Prepositional Phrases

A **prepositional phrase** is a set of words, beginning with a preposition and ending with a noun or pronoun (called the *object of the preposition*), that modify some other part of the sentence. Sometimes, prepositional phrases are needlessly clunky. Here are some examples of prepositional phrases wherein the prepositional phrase is enclosed in brackets, the preposition is underlined once, and the object of the preposition is underlined twice:

- "He examined the witness [in the interviewing room]."
- "She walked [around the table]."
- "[For several hours], the detective questioned the suspect."
- "[Throughout the United States], it is illegal to leave suspects [for so many hours] [in interrogation rooms]."
- "He turned on the light, and then he put the evidence [on the table]."

These examples show that not only can prepositional phrases appear anywhere in a sentence, but also there can be more than one prepositional phrase in a single sentence.

Notice the use of strikethrough in the fourth and fifth examples above, which draws attention to how "to" (in the fourth example) and "on" (in the fifth example), are being used as a particle. A *particle* is a word that can be used as a preposition but instead is being used as part of a verb: "to leave" (in the fourth example) and "turned on" (in the fifth example).

The reason prepositional phrases are covered in this chapter on concise writing is that some prepositional phrases are appropriate and necessary, but many are not. When they are not necessary, prepositional phrases make the sentence clunky—they are weeds in a flower garden. To rid a communication of any unnecessary prepositional phrases, follow these two steps:

1. **Identify any prepositional phrases.** Table 10.2 lists many commonly used prepositions. For each possible preposition, we need to determine whether it is a preposition or a particle.
   a. **Test A.** If you can identify the object of a preposition, then the word is being used as a preposition.
   b. **Test B.** Move the phrase in question to the beginning of the sentence. If the sentence retains the same meaning when we move the phrase to the beginning, then the phrase is a prepositional phrase. Test B is not always necessary, but can be helpful if you have doubts about Test A.
2. **Consider ways to reword the sentence without the prepositional phrase.** The question here is whether the sentence can be more concise and yet remain clear and informative if we remove the prepositional phrase.
   a. **Solution A.** If the prepositional phrase modifies a noun or pronoun, try replacing the prepositional phrase with a possessive construction.
   b. **Solution B.** If the prepositional phrase modifies a verb and the sentence is in passive voice (i.e., where the verb acts upon the subject), try switching to active voice (i.e., where the subject does the action). If Solution A works, then you do not need Solution B.

TABLE 10.2   Common Prepositions

Prepositions Indicating Time		Prepositions Indicating Space		Other Prepositions
after	throughout	about	near	at
before	since	above	off	by
during	until	across	on	for
past	within	behind	outside	of
		below	over	to
		beneath	past	with
		beside	through	
		between	toward	
		in	up	

Here are two examples of how to identify and weed out unnecessary prepositional phrases using the steps outlined above:

- **Example 1: She wanted to leave as soon as possible.**
  - Step 1: The word "to" could be a preposition.
    - Test A: There does not seem to be a noun or pronoun acting as the object of the preposition. Although the "to" has not passed Test A, we will double check using Test B.
    - Test B: Revising the sentence to "To leave she wanted as soon as possible" does not make sense. We can conclude that "to" is not a preposition, and so there is no prepositional phrase in this sentence. We do not need to proceed to Step 2.
- **Example 2: The man used force to take the purse of the woman.**
  - Step 1: There are two possible prepositions: "to" and "of." We need to investigate each of these possibilities separately.
    - "to"
      - Test A: There does not seem to be a noun or pronoun acting as the object of the preposition. We will try Test B just to be sure.
      - Test B: Revising the sentence to "To take the man used force the purpose of the woman" makes no sense. We can conclude that "to" is not a preposition.
    - "of"
      - Test A: There is a noun acting as the object of the preposition: "woman." We can skip Text B and move to Step 2.
  - Step 2 with "of": Can the sentence be improved by editing out the prepositional phrase?
    - Solution A: Does the prepositional phrase modify a noun? Yes, it modifies "purse," so we can eliminate the prepositional phrase by switching to possessive form: "The man used force to take the woman's purse." Having solved the problem of an unnecessary prepositional phrase, we do not need to continue to Solution B.

Refrain from Redundancy

A **redundant** word or collection of words is superfluous in that it is merely repeating information that appears elsewhere in the communication. While repetition of key words can be a helpful way of highlighting certain information and helping the audience follow and remember important parts of our argument, repetition of unimportant material has no benefit for audience. What follows is a list of phrases that can be indicative of redundancy in written and oral communications:

- Like I said (before [or already]) . . .
- To repeat (myself) . . .
- As previously stated . . .
- Again . . .

The words listed serve to announce that redundant information is being presented. Both the listed words and the redundant information following them usually can be deleted without losing any information, clarity, or flow.

TABLE 10.3   Common Redundant Wordings

Absolutely certain	Estimated at about	Past history
Actual experience	Few in number	Protest against
Added bonus	Foreign imports	Repeat again
Basic fundamentals	Forever and ever	Same identical
Collaborate together	Free gift	Still remains
Completely finished	Invited guest	Unexpected surprise
End result	A.M. in the morning	Usual custom
Enter in	P.M. in the evening/at night	Written down

Source: Nichol (2014)

Another type of redundancy occurs when words with similar meanings are used together, such as the phrase "unintended mistake." By definition, however, a "mistake" is accidental, or unintended. Table 10.3 catalogues common redundant wordings that should be omitted from our criminal justice communications. To spot this type of redundant wording in a sentence, review each sentence closely, considering each word and whether it adds information or meaning. Words that do not add meaning, clarify material, or otherwise advance the communication's objective have no place in compelling criminal justice writings or presentations.

Avoid Obvious Statements

We all have probably have encountered the phrase "needless to say" at least once in our readings—perhaps we have used that phrase in our own writings and presentations. This phrase acts as a red flag for unnecessary text: If something truly is "needless to say," then it should not be said. If, however, something should be said, it then is not "needless to say." The phrase "needless to say" is, therefore, pointless to include in any communication. Rarely does a technical writer intend to insult his or her audience, yet this can happen when the audience is told that something is "obvious." Similar to the case of the phrase "needless to say," if something is "obvious," then there is a good chance is need not be said. For the same reason, we should avoid using the phrase "of course" in criminal justice communications.

Table 10.4 lists some obvious statements to avoid in any formal communication. To avoid such unnecessary language, we need to be aware that such phrases are undesirable, and we must take the time to look for and delete them from the communication we are preparing. Keep in mind, however, that, as the writer, we are expected to be the expert on the material. Thus, what might seem "obvious" to us might not be at all obvious to

TABLE 10.4   Common Obvious Statements

Needless to say	Of course	As everyone knows
Obviously	As plainly seen	Everybody knows that
To state the obvious	It goes without saying that	As we know

our audience. Either way, it is safest to avoid the possibility of insulting our audience by telling them something is "obvious" or known by "everyone."

Prefer Summaries to Paraphrases and Quotations

There are good reasons for including quotations and paraphrases of source material, but communications usually are more effective the less material we use from sources and the more we rely on our own ideas and words. In addition to helping us achieve brevity, limited use of quotations and paraphrases can push us to express our unique ideas clearly using our own words. Rarely do two communications have identical objectives, parameters, and audiences. Consequently, different communications generally are unable to use exactly the same ideas, words, and sentence structure to make their points and develop an original argument effectively.

Quotation

A **quotation** is source material repeated verbatim, using the exact same words and sentence structure to express the exact same idea as the source. We indicate quotations by including an in-text citation and by using quotation marks or by using block quotations. Direct quotes can be a bit like spices. A little bit of the right spice can make a delicious meal, but using too much spice, or using the wrong spice, can ruin the dish. In fact, some dishes are best with no spices at all, and the stronger the spice, the less of it we should use. As such, direct quotations should be used sparingly and only with good reason in any technical communication. The longer the quotation, furthermore, the more compelling should be the reason for including it.

To justify inclusion in a technical writing, the source material should contribute directly to the point you are trying to make. Direct quotations never should be used intentionally to fill space or because you do not fully understand what the source is saying. Indeed, it can be considered unethical writing to cite sources and include source material if the source has not been read completely and understood (Roig, 2015). In general, quotations are effective when the source being quoted meets one or more of the following criteria (Harris, 2011, pp. 41–42):

- The source's exact words are more powerful or eloquently written than any summary or paraphrase could be;
- Using the source's exact words confirms or "serves as a second voice" for the point you are making, which can enhance credibility;
- The source's writing style and/or vocabulary add appropriate "historical flavor";
- The source makes a controversial statement, which can ensure that readers do not mistake you for the author of that statement; and
- When your communication will interpret or analyze the source, and you want the reader to have an exact understanding of what the source said and in what context.

When we directly quote a source—regardless of the length of the quote—we must distinguish between the verbatim source text and our own writing as well as properly cite the source of the text (see Appendix B).

Paraphrase

A **paraphrase** is source material relayed in our own words and sentence structure, using approximately the same amount of space to convey the source's idea accurately (Harris, 2011). More specifically, a proper paraphrase has the following features (KU Writing Center, n.d.):

- "Alters the wording of the passage without changing its meaning.
- Retains the basic logic of the argument.
- Retains the basic sequence of ideas.
- Retain[s] the basic examples used in the passage.
- Accurately conveys the author's meaning and opinion."

We indicate paraphrases by including an in-text citation (or other appropriate style of source attribution, e.g., footnote, endnote). Sometimes, it makes sense to insert some direct quotations in a paraphrase. If we do this, then we need to be sure that we distinguish between verbatim source text and our own writing using quotation marks (see Appendix B).

Paraphrasing is an effective way to relay a short amount of complicated material (Harris, 2011). While we can retain the same level of detail and line of reasoning as the source we are consulting, we can adapt the language to our particular purpose and audience. We could leave out some source material, for example, that is not relevant to our communication. Some examples of situations where paraphrases are appropriate are outlining sequential steps in a process or methods used and breaking down a complicated passage to make it easier for your audience to understand. Properly used, paraphrasing can be a particularly effective way to demonstrate knowledge of the source material without disrupting the flow and tone of the communication.

Summary

A **summary** is source material relayed using not only our own words and sentence structure but also in substantially less space to convey the source's idea accurately. When we summarize, we take a relatively big chunk of information and boil it down to its essence or main point. Material suitable for summaries includes statements of a person's main argument or position on an issue, overviews of theories, and conclusions reached in court cases and research studies. Like a paraphrase, with a summary, we are using source material but in our own words. Also, as with a paraphrase, we indicate summaries by including an in-text citation (or footnote or endnote). Unlike paraphrasing, however, we summarize by leaving out most details, such as the reasoning process or exact steps. Further, because they are briefer and more succinct than quotations and paraphrases, summaries are the most helpful in terms of achieving concise writing.

Table 10.5 shows an example of a direct quotation, paraphrase, and summary, while Table 10.6 delineates the key considerations that should govern the decision of which method to use when incorporating source material. While quoting and paraphrasing do have their purposes, the bottom line is that because effective criminal justice communications need to be concise, we should summarize unless we have a compelling reason to quote or paraphrase.

TABLE 10.5 Example of a Quotation, Paraphrase, and Summary

Quotation	"Under any of the standards of scrutiny the Court has applied to enumerated constitutional rights, this prohibition—in the place where the importance of the lawful defense of self-family, and property is most acute—would fail constitutional muster" (*District of Columbia v. Heller*, 2008).
Paraphrase	In *District of Columbia v. Heller* (2008), the Supreme Court began by noting that the Second Amendment protects individuals' rights to own a gun for self-protection, and that this right is not limited to individuals serving in the military. Second, the Court explained, however, that this right can be limited, such as by regulations on the sale of guns, locations where guns cannot be carried, and conditions disqualifying people from owning guns. And third, the Court ruled that Washington, DC's, requirement that all handguns owned in the home must be kept in a disabled state, such as by a trigger lock, violates the Second Amendment.
Summary	The Supreme Court ruled that citizens have a constitutional right to have a gun at home for the purpose of self-defense (*District of Columbia v. Heller*, 2008).

Source: District of Columbia v. Heller, 554 U.S. 570 (2008)

TABLE 10.6 Decision Matrix for Quoting, Paraphrasing, or Summarizing

		Quotation	Paraphrase	Summary
Importance	*Low*	No	No	Yes
	High	Yes	Yes	Yes
Complexity	*Low*	Yes	No	Yes
	High	No	Yes	Yes
Clarity	*Low*	No	Yes	Yes
	High	Yes	No	Yes
Length	*Short*	Yes	Yes	NA
	Long	No	No	Yes
Overall		Quoting is warranted when the material is not only important but also is clear, fairly short, and not too complex. Quoting should be done sparingly, with especially strong justification for long and/ or many quotes.	Paraphrasing is warranted when the material is important and fairly short but yet also rather complex and/or unclear. Paraphrasing is an effective way to simplify and clarify, and can include some short quotes.	Summarizing is warranted in most cases when the material is important and fairly long, regardless of complexity or clarity. Summarizing should be treated as the default method for incorporating source material.

Note: This table starts from the assumption that the information is pertinent to the communication. That is, we know we want to include the information, and the question this table helps us answer is *how* to include that information. These are general guidelines—not strict rules—to which there may be exceptions. "No" means not appropriate.

Source: Harris (2017).

BOX 10.3 **Plagiarism Pointer**

Remember that plagiarism involves words, ideas, and information. Regardless of whether you quote, paraphrase, or summarize, you must give credit to the source.

APPLICATIONS

Although all forms of criminal justice communication should strive for conciseness, there are times when we will have no choice but to be brief. Two such situations are abstracts and tweets.

Abstracts

Scholarly research reports—whether of primary or secondary research—usually contain an "abstract." An **abstract** is a concise summary of an article's purpose, methods, and conclusion. Even if you are unfamiliar with abstracts, you might be familiar with executive summaries. Abstracts are similar to executive summaries in their purpose, but abstracts are shorter and used with different types of writings. Both abstracts and executive summaries appear toward the beginning of a written communication, between the title page and text. Executive summaries are common in longer documents (e.g., government reports, graduate-level capstone papers), while abstracts are typically found in shorter documents (e.g., journal articles, conference programs). Reflecting these length differences, executive summaries tend to be longer ($\approx$ 1–3 pages) than abstracts ($\approx$ 1 paragraph).

Abstracts give people an idea of what the paper is about. Potential readers use an article's abstract to help them determine whether a given article is relevant to their research and worth reading in its entirety. For this reason, the abstract often gives people their first impressions of an article. As such, the quality of an abstract can make the difference between whether a potential reader chooses to read or ignore the report. Without being boring, confusing, or overly detailed, the abstract should give potential readers an accurate "snapshot" of the information contained in the article.

Contents and Organization

Most article abstracts range from 150 to 250 words, which corresponds roughly to a third or half page of double-spaced, 12-point, Times New Roman text. The word limit is set by editors, publishers, or others; and then authors have to comply with the word limit for their article to be published. Just because they are short does not mean they are easy to write. Indeed, many writers find it difficult to summarize a 25-page paper in 200 words. Here, we will look one strategy for developing an effective abstract, and then we will look note some things that we should not do in our abstract.

Because the job of the abstract is to summarize the paper, a fruitful starting point is to identify the paper's major parts. Along these lines, Table 10.7 illustrates how a hypothetical research report's main sections can be used to structure the report's abstract in a paper investigating whether wealthy defendants receive more lenient sentences than poor defendants. What is happening in this abstract is that each of the paper's major sections is being summarized in one sentence, with the result being a summary of the entire paper. The first sentence relates the research topic to a significant real-world controversy, the second sentence contextualizes the study in terms of the existing research on the topic, the third section explains how the study was conducted, the fourth sentence summarizes the findings, and the fifth sentence considers the implications of the findings.

The example provided in Table 10.7 is certainly not the only way to construct an abstract, and there are sure to be occasions when it makes sense to deviate from this

TABLE 10.7   Structure of an Empirical Research Article Abstract

Paper Section	Abstract Sentence (and Word Count)
Introduction	The United States claims to be a country where "justice is blind," but many contend that the criminal justice system routinely allows widespread exceptions to this ideal. (27 words)
Literature Review	Existing research indicates that, for a variety of crime types and spanning various jurisdictions within the United States, there is a gap between the severity of sentences meted out to wealthy versus poor defendants. (34 words)
Methodology	The present study uses federal sentencing data for property offenders from 2000 to 2010 and logistic regression to determine whether wealthy defendants are less likely to be incarcerated than poor defendants when offense seriousness and strength of evidence are considered. (40 words)
Results	Although preliminary models reveal sentencing disparities based on defendant income, multivariate models suggest that—once offense seriousness and strength of incriminating evidence are controlled—wealthy and poor defendants are equally likely to be incarcerated. (34 words)
Conclusion	These results suggest that earlier studies reporting income-based sentencing disparities are based on incomplete models of how sentences are determined and that future research might want to consider additional variables influencing sentencing decisions. (33 words)
Total: 168 words	

example. Sometimes, it might make sense to use two sentences to summarize a section, or to summarize two sections in one sentence. It makes sense to think about the article's strengths, and then to emphasize those strengths in the abstract.

It does not make sense, however, to put any of the following in our abstract: quotations and citations, digressions and definitions, or examples and minor details. Except in very rare circumstances, the abstract is not the place to discuss other studies. Instead, we want to keep the focus on our article, to provide an accurate preview of the article, and to motivate people to read our article.

Best Practices

Here are some general best practices for writing abstracts:

1. **Provide a succinct overview of the paper:** Be concise yet thorough and accurate. Consider writing the abstract last so you can be sure it accurately covers the paper. Present material in the abstract in the same order as the material appears in the paper.

2. **Summarize each major section:** Capture the essence of each major section— Introduction, Literature Review, Methodology, Findings, and Discussion—in one (or perhaps two) sentence(s). In addition, if your paper involves theory (e.g., testing a theory, integrating or modifying existing theories, proposing a theory), include a sentence on theory.

3. **Use your own words, sentence structure, and thoughts:** Do not quote or otherwise include source materials in the abstract. The abstract should be you telling your audience what your paper is about.

4. **Save details for the paper itself:** Focus on the main points and sections of the paper, saving details, explanations, interpretations, qualifications, and so on for the paper itself.

5. **Use one tense consistently:** Pick a logical tense, and then use it consistently.

Tweets

Social media provides an immediate way to communicate directly with millions of people throughout the world. Unlike watching the news on TV or reading newspapers (online or hard copy), moreover, information shared via social media is not filtered by major media corporations. Just about anyone can post just about anything any time.

Twitter is one particularly popular social media platform, with 330,000,000 monthly active users (Newberry, 2018). By 2017, Twitter had eclipsed Facebook, reddit, and all other major social media platforms in terms of how social media users get their news (Newberry, 2018). Twitter is a way to receive and spread news. On Twitter, an original post is called a **tweet**, while reposting or forwarding a post is called a **retweet**. Tweets can be text, pictures, videos, GIFs, links, and/or emojis. The challenge is that a tweet cannot exceed 280 characters of text, including spaces. (Note: Until recently, the character limit for tweets was 140.) As such, public relations tweeting exemplifies the need for concise communications.

Law-Enforcement Use of Social Media

More than 553 law-enforcement agencies from 44 states participated in the 2015 International Association of Chiefs of Police (IACP) sixth annual survey about police use of social media, indicating that 96.4 percent of agencies use social media (IACP, 2015). At the time, Facebook was by far the most popular social media platform used (94.2 percent), followed by Twitter (71.2 percent), and then YouTube (40.0 percent). These survey results indicated that it is most common for a public information officer to manage the agency's social media presence (47.0 percent); but 32.6 percent of agencies' social media accounts are managed by command staff and 28.1 percent by a chief executive, 25.9 percent by a civilian employee, 16.7 percent by an officer, 13.4 percent by a crime prevention officer, 11.6 percent by a community policing officer, and 8.4 percent by some other person. While 77.8 percent of agencies have a written social media policy, another 11.7 percent said they were in the process of developing a social media policy (IACP, 2015).

As shown in Figure 10.1, there are a variety of reasons why law-enforcement agencies use social media: gathering information about crime, notifying the public about crime and other emergencies, engaging the community and managing reputations, and hiring and training. Social media use is regarded as effective in achieving all of these purposes: 85.5 percent of agencies believe it helps them solve crimes, and 83.5 percent believe it has improved policy–community relations (IACP, 2015).

Here, we focus on public communication, looking at how Twitter can be used as a way for criminal justice system agencies to connect with citizens. Compared with the traditional press release, Twitter (and other social media platforms) facilitate a more widespread and interactive form of citizen and community engagement. On the one hand, Twitter allows the police to improve the accuracy of crime news reporting. Law-enforcement use of social media is not filtered by the media, which can select and skew

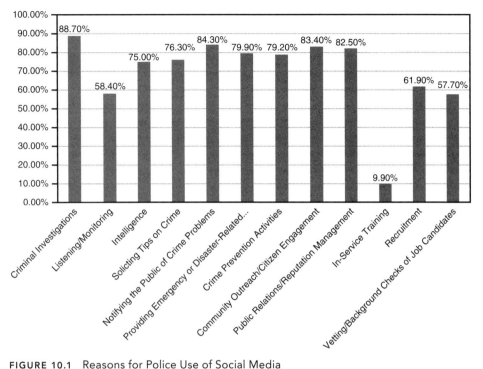

FIGURE 10.1 Reasons for Police Use of Social Media
Source: IACP (2015)

information in addition to slow down the dissemination of information (Davis, Alves, & Sklansky, 2014). On the other hand, Twitter (as with other social media outlets) allows the police to reach a wide audience and, in turn, gives members of the audience a quick and convenient forum to communicate directly with the police (Davis et al., 2014). The use of social media combined with a witty writing style seems to make Twitter a particularly effective means of communicating with and making a positive impact on community members—many of whom otherwise might have had a negative impression of law enforcement.

There appear to be two general styles of law-enforcement communications via social media: serious and humorous. The first is appropriate when communicating about an actual crime problem or other emergency situation, while the second is appropriate in non-emergency situations to foster police–community relations. Illustrative of the first style, the Boston Police Department famously used Twitter to control the flow of information and publicize pictures of the suspects in the 5 days following the Boston Marathon bombing, including advising citizens to avoid large crowds, correcting mistaken news reports that a suspect was in custody, and keeping citizens apprised on the progress of the investigation (Swann, 2013). In line with the second style, the Riley County Police Department is one of many law-enforcement agencies that uses a sense of humor to give law enforcement a friendly and approachable persona (Coppola, 2013). Table 10.8 shares examples of police tweets. Notice how the tweets in the top half reflect the serious style, while the tweets in the bottom half reflect the humorous style.

TABLE 10.8   Tweets Posted by Police Departments

Tweet (Character Count)	Police Department (Source)
Serious Tweets	
Despite reports to the contrary there has not been an arrest in the Marathon attack. (84)	Boston Police Department (Bindley, 2013)
#WANTED: Updated photo of 19 year-old Dzhokhar Tsarnaev released. Suspect considered armed & dangerous. [Photo of Tsarnaev] (104 plus image)	
#MediaAlert: WARNING – Do Not Compromise Officer Safety/Tactics by Broadcasting Live Video of Officers While Approaching Search Locations (136)	
CAPTURED!!! The hunt is over. The search is done. The terror is over. And justice has won. Suspect in custody. (110)	
Now through June 2nd our Officers will be out in force for compliance to wearing your seat belt in the Click It or Ticket campaign. In 2017, nationwide the rate of seatbelt use was 89%. They save over 14,000 lives each year & reduce injury & death by 50%. Buckle Up for Safety!! (278)	Madison Police Department, Alabama (Madison Police Department, n.d.)
Humorous Tweets	
Instead of smoking weed today, eat a donut. Even better . . . have two! #GlazeItDontBlazeIt #420 [Image of Glazed Donut] (91 plus image)	Iowa State University Police Department (FAIL Blog, n.d.)
We have not yet declared a State of Emergency despite #TheBachelor being off air around EC. @WQOW assures us they will fix it. (126)	Eau Claire Police Department, Wisconsin (Heynen, 2018)
Trying to broker this deal now: If we get 10,000 followers by April, we want a police cat. If you support this important public safety initiative, follow us % RT #BigGoals #PoliceCatAssociationofAmerica (203)	Troy Police Department, Alabama (Siacon, 2018)
MSP K9s "not amused" by cats in law enforcement. Too bad, so sad. The cats are coming! twitter.com/mspmetrodet/status/972084625718824960 (137)	
TPD has now switched to an all cats, all the time format. JK We still handle crimes, traffic & general shenanigans. Call us. (125 plus emoji)	
Now that we have some time to kill, anyone get ripped off by their drug dealer and wanna report them? (102)	Lawrence Police Department, Kansas (Geers, 2017)

Best Practices

Some best practices for law-enforcement tweeting are

1. **For your department, have a social media presence and policy.**
   - Have a written social media policy for your agency that reflects best practices for community policing and professional use of social media. Provide training on agency social media policy.
   - Assign at least one person to be in charge of social media. The bigger your department, the more people that might be needed to monitor and maintain active and positive social media presence.
   - Develop an emergency management social media protocol, and include training regarding departmental policies, best practices, and emergency management using social media.

2. **In non-emergency times, maintain a consistent and visible presence via humorous and/or advisory tweets.**
   o You do not need to post every day, but post frequently enough to develop and then sustain rapport with community members.
   o Try to be helpful (without being "preachy"), not limiting yourself to traditionally defined police matters.
   o Achieve humor without being politically incorrect or otherwise in poor taste. Making fun of "dumb criminals" and being sarcastic can alienate people.
3. **In emergency times, manage the situation with frequent, informative, and serious tweets.**
   o Without providing too much details (or details related to the ongoing investigation), keep people informed about the unfolding event, posting every hour or so. Even when there has not been a development, consider posting just for reassurance.
   o Correct, or at least warn about, mistaken reports about the event.
   o Do not try to be funny or witty.
   o At the end of major emergency situations, it might be helpful to debrief. This could be accomplished with a link to detailed information reviewing what happened, what steps will be taken in the future, and where people who need help can go.
4. **In general, include photos, videos, and other engaging items to attract attention and enhance memory.** Photos of wanted suspects, missing children, and stolen property are more effective than text descriptions when you are looking for someone or something.
   o Respond to questions in a reasonable timeframe.
   o Remember that you are representing a professional law-enforcement agency to the community, and avoid jargon (which the general public might not understand; Grubb & Hemby, 2019).
   o If you exceed 280 characters, your message will be split into multiple tweets. Thus, err on the side of caution and (a) limit your message to 280 characters, or (b) place the key material in the first 280 characters.

EXERCISES
Matching
These exercises are designed to assess Chapter 10 Learning Objective 1 (see Box 10.1). Match each numbered statement to the lowercase letter corresponding to the key word it defines. Each key word will be used only once.

1. A question asked for which no answer is sought
2. Any word or group of words that has no real meaning; they take up space without adding any information
3. A reposting or forwarding of a post on Twitter
4. Source material relayed using not only our own words and sentence structure but also in substantially less space to convey the source's main idea accurately
5. Using as few simple words as possible to make a point

6. Source material relayed in our own words and sentence structure, using approximately the same amount of space to convey the source's idea accurately
7. Overused, unoriginal, and generally meaningless statements
8. A set of words, beginning with a preposition and ending with a noun or pronoun (called the object of the preposition), that modify some other part of the sentence
9. A concise summary of an article's purpose, methods, and conclusion
10. Source material repeated verbatim—using the exact same words and sentence structure to express the exact same idea as the source
11. An original post on Twitter
12. The quality of a word or collection of words that is superfluous because it merely repeats information that appears elsewhere in the communication

a. abstract	g. redundant
b. concise	h. retweet
c. quotation	i. rhetorical question
d. filler	j. summary
e. paraphrase	k. trite expressions
f. prepositional phrase	l. tweet

Multiple Choice

These exercises are designed to assess Chapter 10 Learning Objective 4 (see Box 10.1). Indicate the single most appropriate response(s) to each item below.

1. Which of the following statements exhibits the principle of concise writing?
   a. More men than women are incarcerated in U.S. prisons and jails.
   b. In U.S. prisons and jails, one can find more men than women incarcerated.

2. Which of the following statements exhibits the principle of concise writing?
   a. Regarding the issue of men and women incarcerated in U.S. prisons today, there are more men than there are women.
   b. U.S. prisons and jails house more male than female inmates.

3. Which of the following statements exhibits the principle of concise writing?
   a. Obviously, bad economic conditions cause crime rates to increase.
   b. Bad economic conditions cause crime rates to increase.

4. Which of the following statements exhibits the principle of concise writing?
   a. Crime rates increase when economic conditions deteriorate.
   b. Under circumstances in which economic conditions deteriorate, crime rates tend to be high.

5. Which of the following statements exhibits the principle of concise writing?
   a. As we all know, men are more violent than women are.
   b. Although they both witness violence, men tend to be more violent than women.

6. Which of the following statements exhibits the principle of concise writing?
   a. Men exhibit more violence than women do.
   b. Notwithstanding the fact that they both witness violence, men tend to be more violent than women.

7. Which of the following statements exhibits the principle of concise writing?
   a. Infanticide is defined as the killing of a person under 12 months of age.
   b. Infanticide is the killing of a person under 12 months of age.

8. Which of the following statements exhibits the principle of concise writing?
   a. Infanticide is a situation in which a mother kills her baby before it reaches the age of 12 months.
   b. Infanticide is when a parent kills his or her baby before the baby reaches the age of 12 months.

9. Suppose the audience needs to know which costs more: executing homicide offenders or incarcerating them for life. Which of the following statements exhibits the principle of concise writing?
   a. Life imprisonment costs more than executing homicide offenders.
   b. Considering dollars and cents, it costs more to incarcerate offenders for life than to execute them.

10. Suppose the audience needs to know which costs more: executing homicide offenders or incarcerating them for life. Which of the following statements exhibits the principle of concise writing?
    a. Concerning the matter of cost, life imprisonment is more expensive than execution.
    b. Execution is less expensive than is life imprisonment.

Editing

These writing/editing exercises are designed to assess Chapter 10 Learning Objective 5 (see Box 10.1). Rewrite each of the following passages, editing them as needed to achieve concise writing.

1. Each and every prisoner was issued a change of clothes.
2. The patrol unit was scheduled to commence at 5:00 a.m.
3. The reason for the failure of the diversion policy for juvenile offenders is that it was used as a supplement instead of as an alternative to formal criminal justice intervention.
4. In the event that chain of custody is violated, then the evidence will be inadmissible in court.
5. It has been reported by the probation officer that several technical violations occurred.
6. The results indicate that approximately 68.25 percent of the sample admitted to speeding at least once within the past week.
7. Despite the fact that the job candidate failed the psychological background test, the agency hired that person.

8. Stress is associated in a causative way to aggressive behavior among adolescents and adults.
9. The original plan was for the judge to monitor the offenders sentenced to drug courts. The original plan was not followed.
10. It is possible that DNA evidence for some cases has been lost.
11. The presentence investigation report summarized the defendant's past criminal history.
12. The officers voted in favor of utilizing pepper spray.

Writing

These discussion items are designed to assess Chapter 10 Learning Objectives 2, 3, 6, and 7 (see Box 10.1).

1. Why is being concise important in both academic and professional criminal justice communications?
2. Outline strategies for achieving concise communication.
3. Locate an article in an academic peer-reviewed journal. *Do not read its abstract.* Read the article, and then reverse outline it. Summarize each of the article's main sections in one sentence. Use your summaries to construct a concise abstract for the article. Edit your first draft in terms of the five guidelines for concise writing as well as other principles of effective criminal justice communications. Then compare your abstract with the article's abstract in terms of concise writing and the other effective communication principles.
4. Suppose you are the officer charged with your police department's Twitter account. Thus, you need to be professional—and clever. Create a series of four Twitter posts that blend humor with anti-crime messages (e.g., drunk driving, drugs). Each post should be limited to 280 characters (including spaces) and should include one or more of the following items: image, video, GIF, link, emoji. For each item included from the list, reduce your maximum character count by 25 (e.g., if you include a picture, then your post should have no more than 255 characters).

REFERENCES

Bindley, Katherine. (2013, April 26). Boston Police Twitter: How cop team tweets led city from terror to joy. *Huffington Post.* Retrieved from https://www.huffingtonpost.com/2013/04/26/boston-police-twitter-marathon_n_3157472.html

Coppola, Michele. (2013, Summer). Tweeting your way to better community relations. *TechBeat.* National Law Enforcement and Corrections Technology Center, National Institute of Justice. Retrieved from http://www.rileycountypolice.org/sites/default/files/tweeting-your-way_article_0.pdf

Davis, Edward F. III, Alves, Alejandro A., & Sklansky, David Alan. (2014, March). Social media and police leadership: Lessons from Boston. *New Perspectives in Policing Bulletin* (NCJ 244760). Washington, DC: U.S. Department of Justice, National Institute of Justice. Retrieved from https://www.ncjrs.gov/pdffiles1/nij/244760.pdf

District of Columbia v. Heller, 554 U.S. 570 (2008).

Dziedzic, Sylwia. (2011). "6 filler words that, like, won't get you hired, you know?" Retrieved from *BrandYourself* website: http://

blog.brandyourself.com/product-tutorials/ 6-filler-words-that-wont-get-you-hired/

FAIL Blog. (n.d.). *Iowa State University Police Department's Twitter account is a treasure trove of hilarious tweets.* Retrieved from CHEEZburger website:http://cheezburger.com/1403141/iowa-state-university-has-treasure-trove-of-hilarious-tweets

Geers, Jacob. (2017, January 31). This police department has the most hilarious Twitter game ever and you won't stop laughing. *Thought Catalog.* Retrieved from https:// thoughtcatalog.com/jacob-geers/2017/01/ this-police-department-has-the-most-hilarious-twitter-game-ever-and-you-wont-stop-laughing/

Grubb, Robert E., & Hemby, K. Virginia. (2019). *Effective communication in criminal justice.* Thousand Oaks, CA: Sage Publications.

Harris, Robert A. (2011). *Using sources effectively: Strengthening your writing and avoiding plagiarism* (3rd ed.). Glendale, CA: Pyrczak Publishing.

Heynen, Nick. (2018, January 15). S12 times the Eau Claire Police Department's Twitter game was ♦♦♦. *Wisconsin State Journal.* Retrieved from http://host.madison.com/wsj/ entertainment/times-the-eau-claire-police-department-s-twitter-game-was/collection_ ec51b9d0-c1ca-5c71-bcc0-5411a11296a6. html#1

International Association of Chiefs of Police (IACP). (2015). *2015 social media survey results.* Retrieved from http://www.iacpsocialmedia.org/wp-content/uploads/2017/01/ FULL-2015-Social-Media-Survey-Results .compressed.pdf

KU Writing Center. (n.d.). *Paraphrase and summary.* The University of Kansas Writing Center. Retrieved from https://writing.ku .edu/paraphrase-and-summary

Madison Police Department. (n.d.). *Tweets.* Retrieved from https://twitter.com/madison policeal?lang=en

Newberry, Christina. (2018, January 17). 28 Twitter statistics all marketers need to know in 2018. *Hootsuite.* Retrieved from https:// blog.hootsuite.com/twitter-statistics/

Nichol, Mark. (2014). "50 redundant phrases to avoid." *Daily Writing Tips.* Retrieved from http://www.dailywritingtips.com/50-redundant-phrases-to-avoid/

Roig, Miguel. (2015). *Avoiding plagiarism, self-plagiarism, and other questionable writing practices: A guide to ethical writing.* Retrieved from https://ori.hhs.gov/avoiding-plagiarism-self-plagiarism-and-other-questionable-writing-practices-guide-ethical-writing

Siacon, Aleanna. (2018, March 11). Troy Police Department launches Twitter campaign to get a #policecat. *WZZM13.* Retrieved from https://www.wzzm13.com/article/news/ local/michigan/troy-police-department-launches-twitter-campaign-to-get-a-police-cat/69-527635382

Swann, Patricia. (2013, May 24). How the Boston police used Twitter during a time of terror. *Public Relations Tactics,* June. Retrieved from http://apps.prsa.org/Intelligence/Tactics/Articles/view/10197/1078/ How_the_Boston_Police_Used_Twitter_ During_a_Time_o#.WwmHT0gvyUk

The University of Wisconsin–Madison Writing Center. (n.d.). *The writer's handbook.* Retrieved from http://writing.wisc.edu/Handbook/CCS_wordyphrases.html

CHAPTER 11

Presentation

BOX 11.1	Learning Objectives

After reading this chapter, students are able to

1. Recognize terminology relevant to effective PowerPoint presentations.
2. Argue for the importance of effective PowerPoint presentations.
3. Outline methods for preparing and delivering effective PowerPoint presentations.
4. Distinguish between effective and ineffective ways to design, structure, and present content in PowerPoint.
5. Prepare an effective PowerPoint presentation.
6. Deliver an effective PowerPoint presentation.

Only the prepared speaker deserves to be confident.

—DALE CARNEGIE

If you dread public speaking, it might help to know that you are not alone: A fifth of Americans (20 percent) report a fear of public speaking (Chapman University Survey of American Fears, 2017). Not only are public speaking nerves normal, but also they are not entirely bad. First, fear of public speaking can be beneficial. On the one hand, what you are experiencing is the very natural fight or flight reaction to perceived threat, which pumps your body full of adrenaline and energy with which to confront the threat (Correctional Services Canada, 2008; Grubb & Hemby, 2019). On the other hand, your stress can motivate you to take preparation seriously so that you are able to approach your presentation with confidence and do your best. Second, your audience might not even notice your anxiety, and it is only in very rare situations that nervousness causes someone to completely "choke"—that is, be so overcome by stage fright that that person cannot finish the presentation (Grubb & Hemby, 2019). And third, even if some members of your audience can tell you are nervous, the odds are pretty good that because many audience members likely also dread public speaking, they will empathize with you rather than think less of you.

This point of this discussion is that feeling nervous is okay. It does not make you inferior or incapable, nor does it present an insurmountable obstacle to academic and professional success. It is true that some people experience more nervousness than others—just like some athletes experience more pregame jitters than others. The challenge is to recognize how your body responds to a public speaking situation and then to take any necessary steps to ensure that your nerves do not diminish the effectiveness of your communication. Ultimately, the key is preparation: The more prepared you are, the more knowledgeable you will be. And the more knowledgeable you are, the more confident you will be. When you are confident, you can master your fear and deliver a compelling presentation.

The best presenters engage their audience. An engaged audience, in turn, is more likely to pay attention, understand, and recall our message. Because research shows that we learn and remember more with our eyes than with our ears (Collins, 2004; Evergreen, 2017), this chapter considers visual aids to be a crucial element in a successful presentation. Further, although there are many types of visual aids (e.g., videos, posters), Microsoft PowerPoint presentations remain the most standard form of visual aid used in professional presentations (Lens, McCallister, Luks, Le, & Fessler, 2015). Not only do visual aids illustrate and reinforce our message, but also, returning to the problem of public speaking nerves, visual aids can calm us down some by deflecting some of the audience's attention from us (Grubb & Hemby, 2019).

Accordingly, this chapter is mostly about how to prepare and deliver compelling PowerPoint presentations. This chapter builds off the previous 10 chapters because much of the work that goes into preparing a PowerPoint presentation is the same as for papers. Chapter 1 outlined the six stages involved in producing criminal justice communications, for example, and a solid presentation will involve those six stages. Chapter 2 was about professionalism, which is equally important in oral as in written communications. Likewise, as discussed in Chapter 3, we need to identify our objective and parameters as well as learn about our audience; and as presented in Chapter 4, we will need to choose and use the most effective organizational structure for our presentation. The next six chapters addressed logic (Chapter 5), evidence (Chapter 6), completeness (Chapter 7), correctness (Chapter 8), clarity (Chapter 9), and conciseness (Chapter 10)—all of which are relevant to presentations. Rather than repeating material presented in these earlier chapters, this chapter covers additional considerations in the preparation and delivery of criminal justice presentations: design, structure, contents, handouts, practice, and delivery.

DESIGN

One of the first decisions when we begin working in PowerPoint is our design. **Design** refers to the way we make some object appear in an attempt to make it more appealing or useful. In this section, we look at PowerPoint's design options, noting, however, that there is much more to design, which we will cover in subsequent sections.

PowerPoint comes with many design options. That said, you should not use them (Reynolds, 2016; see also Friend, 2017; Schmaltz & Enström, 2014). First, PowerPoint templates may look impressive, but they can give a "prepackaged" feel to your presentation. Second, many PowerPoint templates have design elements that interfere with your goal of facilitating your audience's attention and ability to understand and remember your message. Make it as easy as possible for your audience to follow along with your presentation. This means you want to eliminate any distractions (e.g., artsy fonts, decorative images) and to present material in as clear and straightforward a manner as possible.

So, instead of using one of PowerPoint's designs, create your own. Simplicity and consistency are the two overarching design principles in creating a PowerPoint theme. You want a simple, consistent theme that will not distract your audience from your message (Friend, 2017; Reynolds, 2016). Flashy design elements can pull your audience's attention away from you and your message, and inconsistent design can confuse your audience and/or make you look careless. Our audience should not have to do more work than is absolutely necessary to see the point of a slide, understand the material, or recall the point at a later date. We do not want our audience to have to turn their head to read a title that starts at the bottom and goes up, for example, nor do we want them to have to reorient themselves as we move from slide to slide because we have varied our alignment.

Colors

Start with PowerPoint's basic black and white template, and work from there, starting with choosing your colors. There are two basic color themes: (1) light text on a dark background and (2) dark text on a light background. Either way, pick colors that are high in contrast, and then be consistent with your use of color throughout the presentation. **High contrast** means that the light color is very light, while the dark color is very dark. High-contrast colors are easily distinguished and do not blend together, even if we print in black and white or in grayscale. Table 11.1 is a decision grid you can use to select your colors. You might not know the presentation room's lighting, in which case you definitely want to be sure to select high-contrast colors (Lens et al., 2015) and probably should err on the side of using light text on a dark background because research has identified it as the single most effective PowerPoint color scheme (Grubb & Hemby, 2019).

If you use the color combinations in Table 11.1, you will be safe. Be sure to use solid colors rather than, for example, patterned (e.g., polka dots, checkerboard) backgrounds (Collins, 2004). If you choose to use different colors than in Table 11.1, however, you would want to consider some additional issues. First, avoid color combinations that can be hard for people with color-blindness to see, such as red and green (Lens et al., 2015). Second, recognize that different colors have different connections to our emotions: Cool colors (e.g., green, blue) are more calming, while warm colors (e.g., red, orange) are livelier (Friend, 2017). Sometimes, we want to avoid evoking—or we want to evoke—certain emotional reactions, and our choice of color should reflect such a goal. Third, there are divided opinions on using black and white, and so the safest choice might be to refrain from using black and white. Certainly do not use the plain white background in PowerPoint's most basic template (Ravilious, 2016).

TABLE 11.1   Decision Grid for Choosing a PowerPoint Color Scheme

Dark Room	Light Room
Light text with dark background	Dark text with light background
Ideal: Light yellow on dark blue	Ideal: Dark blue on light yellow

Sources: American Society of Human Genetics (2013), Grubb and Hemby (2019), Reynolds (2016)

Logo

You might want to add your organization's logo and name. This can be a particularly nice touch at conferences, where presenters represent multiple organizations. There is no problem with doing so, but you would need to be careful. These items should appear only on the very first and very last slides (American Society of Human Genetics, 2013). Make it small and in a corner as opposed to large and overwhelming. If you can find only a blurry, watermarked, or outdated image of your logo, then do not use it. Using a poor-quality logo would detract from, not add to, the professionalism of your presentation.

Font

As with colors, you want to choose a simple font or font set, and then use it consistently. Use either: (a) a single sans serif font, or (b) a single sans serif font for text combined with a single serif font for headings. **Sans serif** refers to fonts with letters that have no little feet (e.g., Arial, Calibri), while **serif** refers to fonts with letters having little feet (e.g., Times New Roman, Cambria). Table 11.2 shows some appropriate fonts for professional PowerPoint presentations. Sans serif fonts are recommended for the text because, unlike on a printed page, sans serif fonts are easier to read on a projected screen (de Wet, 2006; Evergreen, 2017).

Do not use all caps, small caps, or all lowercase letters. Instead, use a logical combination of uppercase and lowercase letters (de Wet, 2006). It makes sense to put titles in title case and statements and phrases in sentence case (see Chapter 4). In terms of font, you also might need a system for how you will emphasize key words. Text is harder to read when it is in all caps (American Society of Human Genetics, 2013; de Wet, 2006; Evergreen, 2017). Underlining also can be hard to read (Schwartz, n.d.), and so it seems that the safest way to emphasize certain text is to use italics or extra bold and light weights (Friend, 2017).

Alignment

Text should be displayed from top to bottom and left to right. Slide titles should appear at the top, therefore, and the content below them. Alternatively, you might put the title in a smaller box to the left and the content in a larger box to the right. Because centered

TABLE 11.2   Recommended Fonts for PowerPoint Presentations

Sans Serif	Serif
Arial	Cambria
Calibri	Constantia
Candara	Garamond
Corbel	Rockwell
Futura	
Gills Sans	
Helvetica	
Tahoma	
Verdana	

text is more difficult to read than left-aligned text (Evergreen, 2017), left align all text (i.e., make sure each line of text starts at the left side of the slides rather than using centered, justified, or right alignment).

STRUCTURE

Now, we need to think about how best to put our outline into PowerPoint slides. We are still not worried about how to make each of the individual slides look, but we do need to carve up the substance of our presentation into a logical PowerPoint format.

Components

Start by dividing your outline into its three major components: (1) introduction, (2) the body, and (3) the conclusion. The introduction should be no more than 10 percent of the presentation. Likewise, the conclusion should not exceed 10 percent of the presentation (Grubb & Hemby, 2019, pp. 100–101). Thus, 80 percent of the presentation should be the body. The introduction starts with your first word to the audience. It continues as you introduce yourself and your topic, and it ends once you have told your audience what the rest of the presentation entails. The conclusion begins after you have made your last point and have begun to summarize the main parts of the presentation. It ends when you have spoken your last word to your audience. The body is all the material in between the introduction and conclusion.

Next, think about how long your presentation will be. For each minute in your presentation, you want no more than one content slide (National Conference of State Legislatures, 2017). Some slides contain real, substantive content (e.g., steps in a process, a pie chart). These are content slides, and they are the ones that need 1 minute. Other slides are more like section headings in a paper. Unless you have a lot to say when you show them, you need not allot these slides 1 minute. You might be able to move a little faster when you cover simpler points, and you might need to move a little slower when you cover more complicated points.

Using this formula, a 10-minute presentation would give you 1 minute (i.e., 1 slide) for the introduction, 8 minutes (i.e., up to 8 slides) for the body, and 1 minute (i.e., 1 slide for the conclusion. Given these restrictions, you can only cover so much in a single presentation. Also, keep in mind that the typical audience can only handle so much information in a given time period. Somewhere between two and six points is recommended (Friend, 2017; Grubb & Hemby, 2019). Shorter presentations (e.g., less than 10–15 minutes) should try to stick to two or three points, while longer presentations can probably cover up to six points.

Layout

By this point, you have an idea of how many slides you will have, so this is a good time to create the individual slides. PowerPoint offers a variety of slide layouts, as shown in Figure 11.1. We should use a combination of layouts in a presentation. But we should not use variety just to "spice things up." Instead, for any given slide, we should choose the most appropriate slide layout.

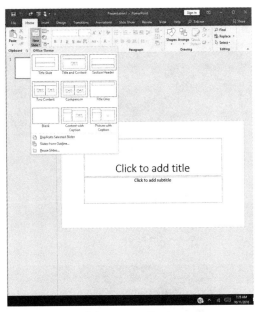

FIGURE 11.1   Slide Layout Options

Title Slide

First, we need a "Title Slide" (the first one in Figure 11.1) for our first slide, which will contain the title of the presentation; our full name, title/position, and organizational information; and the name, date, and location of the conference (when applicable). Figure 11.2 is an example of a title slide. Notice how all text is left aligned, the slide is clean and uncluttered, and there is a single large sans serif font.

Overview Slide

Second, we need a "Title and Content" slide (the second one in Figure 11.1) for our second slide, which is the Overview slide. The Overview slide is to a PowerPoint presentation what a Table of Contents is to a paper: It lists the major parts of the communication so that the audience knows what material will be covered and in what order.

There are multiple ways to format an Overview slide. When we are deciding on format, we should be influenced by two considerations. First, we want to give our audience a clear and accurate idea of what our presentation will cover and in what order. Second, throughout our presentation, we want our audience to be able to recall this slide so they understand where we are and how much of the presentation is left. Any time and as often as they like, people reading a document can physically see how much of the document is left simply by turning back to the table of contents. But a presentation audience does not have these options, and so we need to take multiple steps to help bring them along with us.

Figures 11.3 and 11.6 provide two methods for formatting an Overview slide. In Figure 11.3, Method A involves a simple numbered list. In Figure 11.6, Method B involves a more sophisticated progress circle along with section numbering. Both methods are clear that the presentation consists of three parts. The **progress circle** indicates how far

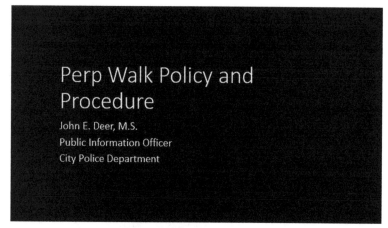

FIGURE 11.2   Example of a Title Slide

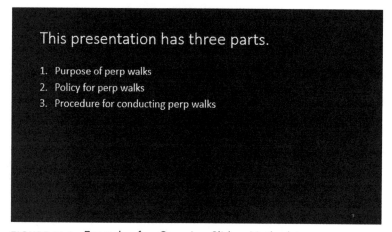

FIGURE 11.3   Example of an Overview Slide—Method A

into the presentation we are. When the circle is a third of the way full, for example, the presentation is a third of the way through.

Section Slides

Third, we will need a series of "Section Header" slides (option 3 in Figure 11.1) to divide the presentation up into major sections. The text on these section header slides should correspond with the text listed in our Overview slide, and any mapping devices that appeared in the Overview slide should appear as appropriate on the section slides. It is critical that the section slides mirror the Overview slide, both in order and in wording. Otherwise, the audience might get confused.

Figures 11.4 and 11.5 show section slides corresponding to Figure 11.3, which was the first method (Method A) shown for Overview slides. This is a relatively straightforward way to help the audience follow along, which relies exclusively on text. Notice

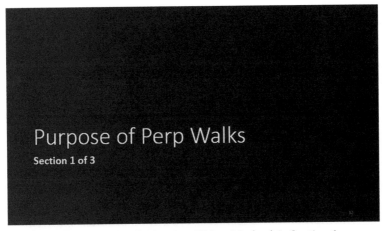

FIGURE 11.4   Example of a Section Slide—Method A, Section 1

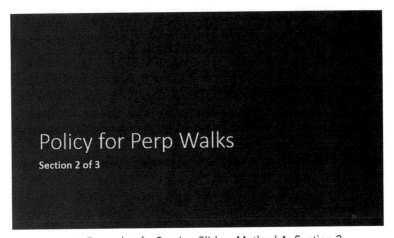

FIGURE 11.5   Example of a Section Slide—Method A, Section 2

how the subheading goes a step beyond identifying the section's number by reminding the audience of how many sections there are in the presentation. Figures 11.7 and 11.8, on the other hand, correspond to the second method (Method B), as shown in Figure 11.6. Here, the section number and section heading are supplemented by the progress circle, which is larger but otherwise identical to the title slide. The progress circle gives the audience an immediate visual of how much of the presentation has been covered and is left.

Content Slides

Fourth, we will need a series of content slides to go between the section slides. We will use some combination of the following layouts: "Title and Content" (option 2 in Figure 11.1), "Two Content" (option 4 in Figure 11.1), "Comparison" (option 5 in Figure 11.1), "Content with Caption" (option 8 in Figure 11.1), and "Picture with

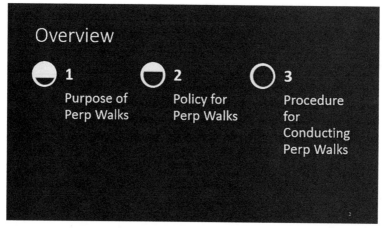

FIGURE 11.6   Example of an Overview Slide—Method B

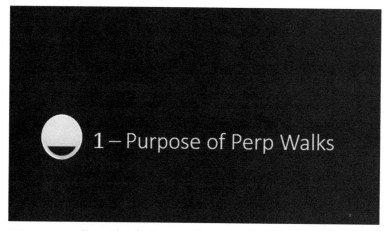

FIGURE 11.7   Example of a Section Slide—Method B, Section 1

Caption" (option 9 in Figure 11.1). (Some versions of PowerPoint have more than these options.) These content slides will be the "meat" of our PowerPoint. In them, we will present our data and evidence. For each content slide, our choice of layout should be dictated by the point we are making: We want to choose the layout that will best help the audience understand our message. We will return to this topic in the following section.

The "Title and Content" slide (see Figure 11.9) is probably the most useful, because it gives the most room to present your content. But the "Two Content" slide and the "Comparison" slide (see Figure 11.10) can be especially effective when your point is to show similarity or difference, such as before-and-after images.

References Slide

Fifth, we may need a References slide, which works best on a "Title and Content" slide. Just like in a paper, it is imperative that you properly credit the sources of your information. But unless you are required to use a particular documentation style, there is more

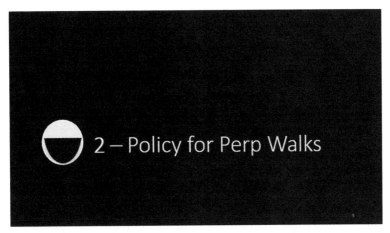

FIGURE 11.8 Example of a Section Slide—Method B, Section 2

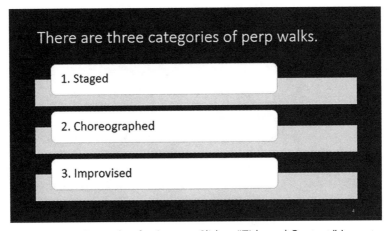

FIGURE 11.9 Example of a Content Slide—"Title and Content" Layout

flexibility in presentations. You could follow APA format (see Appendix B), you could use endnotes, and/or you could put your References in a handout. Figure 11.11 is an example of a References slide. This format makes sense if you used in-text citations throughout your content slides (see Figure 11.10). If you use endnotes, however, then you would need to number your sources and arrange them in numerical rather than alphabetical order in the References slide. If you put your References in a handout, remember that you still should properly credit your sources where they are used in your PowerPoint slides (e.g., in-text citations).

Closing Slide

And sixth, our final slide will announce the end of our presentation and may invite questions and/or provide our contact information. We can use a "Title Slide" or a "Section Header" slide layout. Figure 11.12 is an example of a closing slide using the "Title Slide"

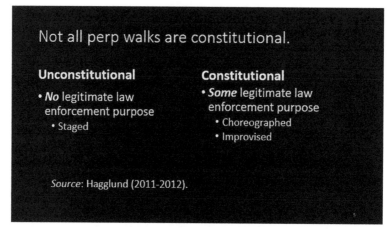

FIGURE 11.10   Example of a Content Slide—"Comparison" Layout

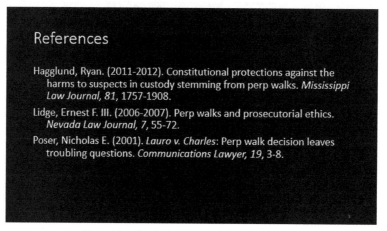

FIGURE 11.11   Example of a References Slide

layout. If you are distributing your business cards and/or a handout with your contact information, then you might prefer to put something along the lines of "Thank you" or "Questions?" on your closing slide.

FIGURE 11.12   Example of a Closing Slide

CONTENT

This section is about content slides—not title or other slides. There are different ways to present the same information, some of which are more effective than others. This section begins by presenting two different slide styles. Next, it outlines how to achieve simplicity in each slide; and then it presents methods of data visualization.

Style

There are two basic styles of content slide: (1) traditional and (2) assertion–evidence. Figure 11.13 illustrates the former, while Figure 11.14 illustrates the latter.

Traditional

The **traditional style** is what most people envision when they think of PowerPoint. As illustrated in Figure 11.13, there is a title at the top, which can be a word or a phrase, and then the rest of the slide contains content, which is usually in the form of a bullet or numbered list but can also be in graphic form (e.g., table, chart, image). Key considerations in designing effective traditional-style slides are text amount, text format, text size, and presentation consistency.

First, limit both the number of rows of text and the number of words in each row. Some rules for determining the appropriate number of rows and words are

- **Rule of 5:** Put a maximum of five words in a line, with no more than five lines on a slide and no more than five text-heavy slides in a row (GCF Global, n.d.; see also de Wet, 2006).
- **Rule of 6:** Put a maximum of six words in a line, with no more than six lines of text on a slide (American Society of Human Genetics, 2013; Collins, 2004). The longer the words, the fewer words that should appear in a line (Collins, 2004).

Pick and follow one of these rules for the amount on text in traditional-style content slides.

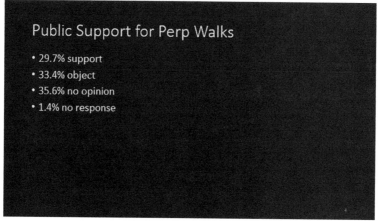

FIGURE 11.13   Example of a Traditional Slide
Source: Van Slyke, Benson, and Virkler (2018)

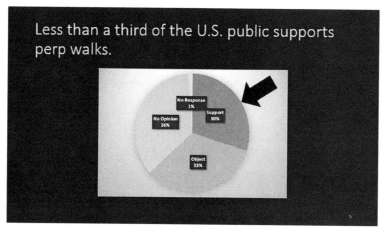

FIGURE 11.14   Example of an Assertion–Evidence Slide
Source: Van Slyke, Benson, and Virkler (2018)

Second, do not write in full sentences or paragraphs. Instead, use as little text as possible to convey your message (Friend, 2017; Reynolds, 2016). Key words and phrases are best (Grubb & Hemby, 2019; National Conference of State Legislatures, 2017). Not only should you use few words, but also you should use the simplest words possible (National Conference of State Legislatures, 2017).

Third, keep the font large. Never shrink the font to make more text fit into a slide. Instead, split multiple points into multiple slides and/or trim down the text to the key words. The font needs to be large enough that people in the back of the room can read it (National Conference of State Legislatures, 2017; Reynolds, 2016). In general, avoid going below 28-point font (de Wet, 2006; Schwartz, n.d.). If you are presenting in a large room, use at least 40-point font (Schwartz, n.d.).

And fourth, be consistent with how you present information both within a single slide and across multiple slides. Within a single slide, this guideline applies to aspects of writing mechanics such as capitalization, hyphenation, punctuation, and spelling as well as to phrasing. Table 11.3 compares lists, one lacking consistency and the other exhibiting consistency. Two corrections are shown for each inconsistent list. The first inconsistent list fails to use parallel structure (consistent phrasing). The first way this phrasing failure is corrected is by starting each listed item with an adjective and ending it with a noun. The second way it is corrected is by starting each listed item with an action verb and ending it with a noun. The second inconsistent list exhibits haphazard punctuation at the end of the listed items. The first way this punctuation failure is corrected is simply by removing the punctuation from the end of each listed item, and the second way it is corrected is by both removing the punctuation at the end and condensing each listed item to a single noun.

Across multiple slides, pay attention to writing mechanics such as which words are capitalized to reflect that they are proper nouns, where you use hyphens to connect words, when you use an abbreviation, and how you spell terms. Different usage can confuse the audience, who might think you are referring to different things. Referring to a court case, for example, be consistent with "court" or "Court." Inconsistency might imply that you are talking about different courts, such as a lower "court" and the Supreme "Court."

Assertion–Evidence
While the **assertion–evidence style**, shown in Figure 11.14, starts with a title at the top similar to traditional style, the assertion–evidence title is in the form of a claim (or assertion). The rest of the slide contains evidence for that assertion, which is in graphic form.

TABLE 11.3   Consistency in Lists

Not Consistent	Consistent
The police have several duties: • Enforcing the law • Solve crimes • Protection of the public • Assistance during emergencies	The police have several duties: • Law enforcement • Crime solving • Public protection • Emergency assistance
	The police have several duties: • Enforcing the law • Solving crimes • Protecting the public • Assisting during emergencies
People commit crime for many reasons: • They need money. • They are angry. • They are frustrated, • They do it for fun	People commit crime for many reasons: • They need money • They are angry • They are frustrated • They do it for fun
	People commit crime for many reasons: • Money • Anger • Frustration • Amusement

Sources: American Society of Human Genetics (2013); de Wet (2006); Presentitude (2016); Schmaltz and Enström (2014); Vjestica (2012)

Follow these guidelines to construct effective assertion–evidence slides (Carnegie Mellon University, n.d.; "How to Create an Assertion–Evidence Presentation," n.d.):

1. Give the slide a title that clearly states the assertion in no more than two lines.
2. Make the body of the slide a visual that serves as evidence of the assertion.
3. Only use words when absolutely necessary in the body of the slide, never exceeding four lines of text.

The assertion–evidence style may require more up-front work than traditional style, but there are several benefits to expending the extra effort to use it. First, research indicates that audiences remember material better when it is presented in assertion–evidence style compared with traditional style (Lens et al., 2015). This effectiveness could be explained by the relatively more straightforward message in assertion–evidence slides and/or the use of graphics. On the one hand, compare the slide titles in Figure 11.13 and 11.14. Figure 11.13's title contains no real information beyond announcing the subject matter, whereas Figure 11.14's title explicitly states the slide's message. On the other hand, graphics are superior ways of communicating compared to words, "allow[ing] us to move information along the memory continuum to catch the reader's eye, focus the reader's attention, and affix in the reader's memory" (Evergreen, 2017). A second benefit of this style is that it forces us to determine and articulate the single point we will make for each slide—that it is the point that we state as the slide's title. And a third benefit is the lack of text, which means we are in no danger of falling into the trap of reading off our slides. The superiority of the assertion–evidence style leads to the conclusion that, whenever possible, we should use it rather than the traditional style.

Simplicity

Regardless of which style we choose, the following guidelines will help us achieve simplicity in each of our slides (American Society of Human Genetics, 2013; Carnegie Mellon University, n.d.; Collins, 2004; Feloni, 2015; Friend, 2017; RAND, 1996; Wax, n.d.):

1. **Make one point per slide.** You should be able to summarize each slide by completing this one simple sentence: "The point of this slide is that ___." If you need more than one sentence (or if you need a complex sentence) to summarize a slide, then the slide covers too much. In this case, break up the material into multiple slides or, if some of the material is not essential to your objective, delete it.
2. **Give each slide a unique title that conveys the one point being made.** Do not give multiple slides the same title. Instead, either condense all that material onto one slide, or give more specific titles to the different slides.
3. **Use as little text as possible on each slide.** The more text you put on your slides, the more you force your audience to choose between listening to you or reading your slides. When this happens, your PowerPoint transforms from helping to hindering communication. Use key words and phrases instead of complete sentences and paragraphs in the body of content slides.
4. **Prefer graphics to text.** Text is the least powerful way to communicate, and so it should be used in the body of content slides only as a last resort. We return to this guideline in the following subsection.

5. **Put only material that is essential on your slides.** Avoid clutter—text, pictures, clipart, transitions, builds, animation, or anything else that takes up space without helping you make your point. Empty space is a good thing because it allows the audience's attention to focus on the important information that does appear on your slide.

Remember that criminal justice communications are not supposed to be entertaining, which means there is no reason to add in clipart, sounds, or other effects simply to "jazz up" your PowerPoint. These features detract from the professionalism of the presentation and redirect the focus of the audience. Likewise, a PowerPoint is a visual aid for your audience, not a teleprompter for you. It is not a script, it should not be a series of sentences copied and pasted from a paper, and it definitely should not display your narrative. Keep your audience focused on you and your message.

Visualization

Communication is best facilitated by a combination of hearing words and seeing images associated with those words (Collins, 2004; Schmaltz & Enström, 2014; see also Lens et al., 2015; RAND, 1996). From this it follows that graphics are more effective than text in our PowerPoint slides, and we should therefore replace text with graphics wherever possible. Thus, this subsection is about **data visualization**, a term that refers to a "representation and presentation of data that exploits our visual perception abilities in order to amplify cognition" (Kirk, 2012).

Once we know what point we will be making with a given slide, the first step in data visualization is to ask ourselves how best to represent that point. A bullet list is rarely the answer. Sometimes, a bullet list can be acceptable, such as in the Overview slide or in a slide summarizing our major points. Table 11.4 outlines different methods of data visualization according to our purpose.

After selecting the most appropriate graphic given our purpose, our second step is to ensure that we prepare it in a clear and understandable way. PowerPoint has many options for graphics: Click "Insert," and then select "Chart." Pick the simplest version of the graphic you have chosen, and input your data. In preparing your graphic, avoid the following practices (Lens et al., 2015; Reynolds, 2016):

1. Picking a fancier form of the appropriate graphic, such as three-dimensional, patterned, or shadowed;
2. Crowding the graphic with too much data or more detail than necessary; and
3. Using poor-quality, watermarked, and/or low-resolution images.

Ensure that the important information stands out. Try not to rely too heavily on color distinctions. Instead, show percentages and labels on the pie chart pieces. If one part of the graphic is the key part, then highlight it, such as making the pie chart slice pop out or inserting an arrow pointing to it. You can add shapes, such as arrows, boxes, and circles, and you can include text boxes to help you make your point.

Finally, we should be careful not to confuse data visualization with decoration. All of the data visualization methods presented in Table 11.4 have a particular informational purpose, which is why we use them. Do not use other graphics or features that have no informational purpose, such as

1. Clipart;
2. Cartoons;
3. Pictures;
4. Transitions between slides;
5. Builds within slides (i.e., showing one bullet at a time);
6. Sound effects; or
7. Audio or video clips.

TABLE 11.4   Options for Displaying Data Visually

Purpose	Appropriate Graphic	Best When ...	Avoid When ...
Presenting numerical information	Table	You have data on many variables	You want to highlight differences
	Bar graph	You want to highlight differences across a few groups	There are no real differences or are more than eight groups
	Line graph	You want to show change over time or demonstrate trend	You have categorical rather than continuous data
	Pie chart	You want to show the relative size of parts of a whole or how a whole is distributed	There are more than six parts of the whole
	Pictograph (or infographic)	You want to stimulate interest or facilitate memory	The situation is very serious or material is complex
Presenting logical relationships	Diagram	You want to show how items are related	There is no relationship among the items
	Organization chart	You want to show positions and hierarchy within an organization	The organization and/or its hierarchy are irrelevant to the point you are making
Presenting a process or instructions	Checklist	You want to list steps to follow or items that are needed	When the exact steps or items are unknown or not necessary
	Flow chart	You want to show the stages in a process	The process does not involve a single set of clear and consistent stages
	Logic (or decision) tree	You want to show how different choices lead to different outcomes	There are not clear and consistent paths from early choices to later outcomes
Presenting pictorial or spatial characteristics	Photograph	You want to show an exact image of an object, place, or person	The image is of poor quality or obscures the point you are trying to make
	Screenshot	You want to show what appears on a computer screen	There may be a need to alter the image
	Line drawing	You want to show a simplified or focused image of an object, place, or person	You cannot produce a, accurate, professional, high-quality drawing
	Map	You want to give directions or show a geographic area	The map is outdated

The rule of thumb is, unless it directly advances, highlights, reinforces, or clarifies the single point being made in the slide, leave it out. Do not try to be cute, funny, or entertaining. Unless the presentation is actually about technical features that make PowerPoints livelier, there is not a good reason to include pictures, animation, or the other features listed above. Not only are these features unprofessional, but some of them also slow down presentations, particularly transitions and builds.

This is not to say that there is never a good reason to include any these features. On the contrary, there are some excellent reasons for using them. In a presentation about how to deal with a resisting suspect, for example, a video clip of a police officer subduing an uncooperative citizen could be perfectly appropriate. Such a video would be a clearer and more powerful way of teaching people how to handle the situation than a verbal description or even a verbal description coupled with a graphic.

HANDOUTS

In many situations, it can be helpful to provide a handout for the audience (de Wet, 2006; Friend, 2017). Handouts give them something to take away, and they give you a way to provide more details than were appropriate in your presentation. Information suitable for a handout includes references/sources, main points, contact information, graphics, and URLs (Evergreen, 2017). If your presentation is based on a paper, you could give out the paper. If you choose to distribute handouts, however, you need to do it right. This means the following:

1. **Exhibit all nine principles of effective criminal justice communication laid out in previous chapters of this text.** The handout should not be a hastily prepared afterthought, or it can do more harm than good.
2. **Get an estimate of how many people will be in your audience** so that you know how many copies to make (Grubb & Hemby, 2019).
3. **In most cases, wait to distribute the handout until after your presentation** (Friend, 2017; Grubb & Hemby, 2019; Reynolds, 2016). Tell your audience before you start your presentation if you will be doing this, so that they do not needlessly work to take notes (Evergreen, 2017). If you distribute your handout before your presentation, the audience will tend to read it instead of listen to you, and you might become distracted by their reading and page turning (Grubb & Hemby, 2019).
4. **In the case of an instructional or tutorial presentation, consider leaving blanks throughout the handout and distributing it prior to your presentation** (Evergreen, 2017). Then, the audience can fill in the blanks as you go through the presentation, which can help keep their attention as well as give them something to do.

PRACTICE

Once you have a full, complete draft of your PowerPoint, which you have revised and edited, you are ready to start practicing your delivery. We are unlikely to deliver a successful presentation without having rehearsed multiple times. Here are some suggestions for practicing your presentation in the days leading up to it (Correctional Services Canada, 2008; de Wet, 2006; Grubb & Hemby, 2019; National Conference of State Legislatures, 2017; Ravilious, 2016):

- **Know your material.** Do your research, and become an expert on the subject matter. This will give you confidence, and it will enhance your credibility. Mastery of the material also frees you from being dependent on notecards and being tempted to read your presentation to the audience.
- **Practice with your PowerPoint.** Coordinate your narrative with the progression of the slides. Make sure you know what order your slides are in and how to move backward.
- **Time yourself.** Adjust as needed your narrative and/or PowerPoint so that your presentation is neither too short nor too long.
- **Record yourself and/or practice with an audience.** Look for areas for improvement, and then work on them. Pay attention to factors such as readability of the PowerPoint, how fast you speak, oral filler (e.g., "um"), and eye contact.
- **Figure out how to pronounce all words.** If there is any word in your presentation with which you are unfamiliar, make sure you know how it should be pronounced. Mispronouncing words—especially key words—calls your competence and credibility into question. Do not assume you know how to pronounce an unfamiliar word. You can type words into an Internet search engine to learn (or confirm) their proper pronunciation.
- **Wean yourself off of a word-for-word script.** If you have written a script for yourself, gradually move away from using it. The more you practice, the less you will need it. Before you present, convert the script to brief notecards.
- **Simulate the actual presentation conditions.** If you will be using notecards when you present, then use notecards when you rehearse. If you will be using a microphone to deliver your presentation, then try to use a microphone during your rehearsals. Whenever possible, rehearse in the presentation room using the same technology that you will use to deliver. Make sure your PowerPoint is readable from the back of the room.
- **Take your rehearsals seriously.** Try to practice exactly how you intend to deliver. Work on not reading your presentation and on using appropriate body language. Rehearse again and again until you perfect your delivery.
- **Anticipate questions from the audience.** Try to think of what questions the audience might ask, and prepare and rehearse responses to them.
- **Have a backup plan.** Save your presentation in more than one place (e.g., flash drive and email it to yourself). Be prepared for technology failures in the presentation room (e.g., having to present without your PowerPoint). You might want to try rehearsing without your PowerPoint, just in case.

There is a good chance that you will be nervous about your presentation; after all, 1 in 5 American adults are. But try to keep in mind that the best way to cure your nerves is preparation and practice. Even if you are not nervous, practice is as vital to a successful presenter as it is to a successful athlete.

DELIVERY

Delivery occurs in three phases: (1) your approach to the front of the room and technical setup, (2) your prepared speech and PowerPoint presentation, and (3) a question-and-answer (Q&A) session.

Approach

Whenever possible, try to do the following before you start speaking (Grubb & Hemby, 2019; National Conference of State Legislatures, 2017; Ravilious, 2016):

- **Walk calmly to the front of the room.** Avoid walking too fast or dragging your feet. Try your best to control your anxiety.
- **Make sure the screensaver is off.** Otherwise, it might interrupt your presentation.
- **Upload your presentation to the hard drive.** Disks tend to be slower. You can also go ahead and put your flash drive back in your pocket so you do not leave it behind.
- **Wait until your PowerPoint and presentation equipment are ready.** Unless you have no choice, wait to begin until everything (e.g., microphone, projector) is ready.

If there is an awkward delay, such as happens with technology problems or a key audience member has not arrived, you might want to leave the room (which can be a good idea if you are especially anxious). If you need a reason to leave the room, consider using the restroom or getting something to drink. If you are not too nervous, you could use this time to engage in light conversation with audience members, which can help build rapport.

Speech

Your presentation begins with an introduction. If you are not introduced to the audience, then you need to introduce yourself. This should be brief and is an ideal opportunity to establish your expertise and credibility. The audience should know the following about you before you launch into your presentation: (a) your name and position/title, (b) your academic and professional qualifications, and (c) any other relevant qualifications (Correctional Services Canada, 2008). After you have introduced yourself, you are ready to begin with your presentation introduction.

Throughout your presentation, the single most important rule is this: **Do *not* read to the audience** (de Wet, 2006; GCF Global, n.d.; Grubb and Hemby, 2019; National Conference of State Legislatures, 2017; RAND, 1996; Ravilious, 2016; Reynolds, 2016). Why? Consider these quotes:

- "Adults dislike nothing more than having an entire speech read to them" (Grubb & Hemby, 2019, p. 97).
- "Nothing is deadlier than a briefing in which the briefer reads the charts" (RAND, 1996, p. 13).
- "Reading from the screen with your back to the audience is both lazy and boring to watch" (Ravilious, 2016).

In sum, your presentation will be a failure if you read to your audience—whether you are reading a paper, notecards, your phone, or text-heavy slides.

BOX 11.3 | Credibility Connection

Maintaining a professional communication style and demeanor will foster trust. If you want your audience to believe what you say or do what you recommend, then you need them to believe you are credible. Being prepared, knowing about the subject matter, acting confident, maintaining eye contact, and meeting the audience's expectations are ways to build your credibility.

The second most important rule, closely related to the first is ***Never* turn your back on your audience** (American Society of Human Genetics, 2013; Grubb & Hemby, 2019; Reynolds, 2016). Do *not* talk to your PowerPoint with your back to your audience. On occasion, you might briefly look and gesture at your presentation, but your body and face should face the audience just about the entire time.

In addition to these two rules are the following guidelines (American Society of Human Genetics, 2013; Grubb & Hemby, 2019; National Conference of State Legislatures, 2017; Ravilious, 2016):

- **Maintain eye contact with people around the room.** Avoid looking at no one as well as looking at just one or two people. You do not need to make eye contact with every audience member, but do make eye contact with several people throughout the room. When you meet someone's eyes, maintain that eye contact for a few seconds before moving your eyes to another audience member.
- **Speak slowly and loudly.** Without speaking unnaturally slow or yelling, speak slowly enough that you can enunciate and your audience can digest what you say and loud enough that people in the back can hear you without straining. Occasional pauses, such as between slides, can help the audience follow along and give you a chance to think and catch your breath.
- **Incorporate some reviews and previews.** **Reviews** remind your audience of material already presented, linking present information with past information. **Previews** give your audience a glimpse of information to come, showing how present information will relate to future information. These devices, some examples of which are listed in Table 11.5, can help your audience integrate and appreciate the importance of material as you move through your presentation.

TABLE 11.5   Reviews and Previews

Reviews	Previews
As I said earlier …	I'll return to this later …
As you will recall …	Keep this in mind …
Earlier, I noted that …	Remember this point when I get to …
Remember from earlier how …	This information will become important later when …
This relates to the previous point …	This will be an important point when we return to the idea of …
To reiterate …	We'll get back to this idea later when we cover …

Sources: Markel (2012); see also Friend (2017), Reynolds (2016)

- **Be lively.** Avoid speaking in a monotone. Move around the front of the room. Use body language to emphasize or reinforce points. But do not force it by being overly enthusiastic or repeatedly using the same, perhaps unnatural, hand motion. Be professional, but vary your speech and motion to keep the audience engaged.
- **Avoid verbal filler.** We sound unprofessional when we repeatedly say words such as "like," "um" and "you know." It is better to pause in silence while you think of your next words than to litter your narrative with filler. Likewise, refrain from asking rhetorical questions.
- **Pay attention to the time.** Pace yourself, keeping to a schedule of roughly one slide per minute. Avoid moving too quickly through slides. If you notice that you are running out of time, then speed up. If you notice that you are nearing the end sooner than expected, then you can use the leftover time for a **question-and-answer (Q&A) session**, when members of the audience can ask the presenter questions.
- **Look for signals from the audience.** The audience's nonverbal communication can give you clues as to whether they understand you, are getting restless, might be offended, or like what they hear (see Table 11.6). If, for example, you see a lot of tightly crossed arms and raised eyebrows across the audience, then you might reasonably infer that your audience is skeptical and will need more convincing.

TABLE 11.6   Nonverbal Communication Signals

Behavior/Mannerism	Possible Meaning
Positive Signs	
Eye contact	Sincerity, interest, respect
Nodding head	Approval, understanding, encouragement
Arms loosely folded across chest	Relaxation
Back straight, shoulders back	Confidence
Negative Signs	
Slow blink	Disinterest, perceived superiority
Eye dart	Disinterest, dishonesty
Eye roll	Sarcasm
Looking away	Impatience, distraction, disinterest
Raised eyebrow	Disbelief, skepticism, surprise
Chin jutting out	Obstinance
Slouched/slumped shoulders	Fatigue, lack of enthusiasm, discouragement
Arms tightly folded across chest	Defiance, refusal
Arms akimbo	Arrogance
Fidgeting hands	Anxiety, boredom
Drumming/tapping fingers	Nervousness, deception
Bouncing/shaking leg(s)	Impatience, urgency, disinterest, anxiety, irritation
Tightly crossed legs	Closed off
Tapping toes	Anxious, urgency, disinterest

Sources: Grubb and Hemby (2019), Whitbourne (2012)

- **Do not apologize.** You do not need to apologize for situations that are beyond your control, such as a technical failure. And if something is in your control, then take the steps necessary to prevent problems. Do not, for example, apologize for not knowing how to pronounce a word—get the pronunciation right. If you lose your train of thought, just take a pause, and move on. Apologizing for mistakes can draw unnecessary attention to them.
- **Keep your promises.** The beginning of your presentation announces what you will be covering, so make sure that you cover everything you said you would. When you say you are wrapping up, wrap up—do not keep going for several more minutes.
- **End on a strong note.** Do not make your last words weak. Grubb and Hemby (2019) give this example of a horrible way to end a presentation: "I guess that's all I have" (p. 101). You want to leave a positive impression, which you can do by summarizing your main points, thanking your audience, and inviting questions.

Question-and-Answer Session

Once we have concluded, there will often be a short question-and-answer (Q&A) session. The Q&A period might directly follow our presentation, or it might occur after a series of presentations so that the audience can ask questions of several presenters. There might be someone who directs the Q&A session, such as a panel moderator, but it might be you who calls on people and keeps an eye on the time. Here are some suggestions for effectively handling a post-presentation Q&A session (Correctional Services Canada, 2008; Grubb & Hemby, 2019):

- **Invite questions.** Offer to answer questions when you are done presenting. Acting open to questions shows confidence, gives the impression that you have a strong command of the material, and suggests that you truly care about the audience's experience.
- **Maintain composure.** Do not act like you face a firing squad, and try not to show that you are offended, irritated, flustered, or embarrassed.
- **Repeat each question before you respond.** This gives you an opportunity to ensure that you understand the question in addition to time to think of your answer, and it ensures that people in the back of the room heard the question.
- **Answer questions directly and honestly.** Do not dodge particular people or evade answering certain questions.
- **Respect the person asking the question.** Treat each question as though it is an excellent one. Do not treat questions as silly or unimportant, and do not chide people for asking questions that you already addressed.
- **Be honest.** Admit when you do not know the answer. If this happens, offer to contact the person at a later date with the answer (and be sure to get his/her contact information so you can make good on your offer).

How you handle the Q&A session can be a decisive factor in the overall impression you make on your audience. It will likely be their last interaction with you, and you do not want to undo your hard work on preparing, rehearsing, and delivering by becoming defensive or "bullshitting" during Q&A.

EXERCISES
Matching
These exercises are designed to assess Chapter 11 Learning Objective 1 (see Box 11.1). Match each numbered statement to the lowercase letter corresponding to the key word it defines. Each key word will be used only once.

1. Easily distinguished because the light color is very light and the dark color is very dark
2. The content slide style wherein the title is a word or phrase and the content is usually in a bullet/numbered list
3. A visual indicator of how far into the presentation we are
4. Fonts with letters that do not have little "feet," such as Arial and Calibri
5. A way of presenting data visually that maximizes audience cognition
6. Language that reminds the audience of material already presenting as a way of linking present information with past information
7. The content slide style wherein the title is an assertion and the content is (usually graphic) evidence supporting that assertion
8. The period after one or more presentations when the audience can ask the presenter(s) questions
9. The way we make some object appear in an attempt to make it more appealing or effective
10. Fonts with letters that do have little "feet," such as Times New Roman and Cambria
11. Language that gives the audience a glimpse of information to come as a way of linking present information to future information

a. assertion–evidence style
b. data visualization
c. design
d. high contrast
e. previews
f. progress circle
g. Q&A session
h. reviews
i. sans serif
j. serif
k. traditional style

Multiple Choice
These exercises are designed to assess Chapter 11 Learning Objective 4 (see Box 11.1). Indicate the single most appropriate response to each item below.

1. Which of the following is an effective way to design a PowerPoint presentation?
   a. Use one of PowerPoints template designs.
   b. Create your own PowerPoint design.

2. Which of the following is an effective way to design a PowerPoint presentation?
   a. Use low-contrast colors.
   b. Use high-contrast colors.

3. Which of the following is an effective way to design a PowerPoint presentation?
   a. Use light yellow text on a dark blue background.
   b. Use red text on a green background.

4. Which of the following is an effective way to design a PowerPoint presentation with your organization's logo?
   a. Put the logo on each slide.
   b. Put the logo on the first and last slide.

5. It is best to use what type of font for the text of a PowerPoint presentation?
   a. sans serif (e.g., Arial)
   b. serif (e.g., Times New Roman)

6. Which of the following is an effective way to design a PowerPoint presentation?
   a. Use all caps.
   b. Use all lowercase.
   c. Use small caps.
   d. Use a combination of uppercase and lowercase letters.

7. How should text be aligned in a PowerPoint presentation?
   a. left-aligned
   b. right-aligned
   c. centered
   d. justified

8. Which of the following is true regarding the three major components of a PowerPoint presentation?
   a. The introduction should account for 33 percent, the body should account for 34 percent, and the conclusion should account for 33 percent of the presentation.
   b. The introduction should account for 25 percent, the body should account for 50 percent, and the conclusion should account for 25 percent of the presentation.
   c. The introduction should account for 10 percent, the body should account for 80 percent, and the conclusion should account for 10 percent of the presentation.
   d. The introduction should account for 5 percent, the body should account for 90 percent, and the conclusion should account for 5 percent of the presentation.

7. For _____ in your presentation, you should have no more than one content slide.
   a. every 30 seconds
   b. every 1 minute
   c. every 2 minutes
   d. every 5 minutes

8. The second slide in a PowerPoint presentation should be the …
   a. title slide
   b. Overview slide
   c. first section slide
   d. first content slide
   e. References slide

9. Which style of content slide is the more effective way to communicate in a PowerPoint presentation?
   a. assertion–evidence
   b. traditional

10. Which of the following is *not* advised when designing effective traditional-style PowerPoint slides?
   a. Put as much text as possible in each row of text.
   b. Limit the number of rows of text.
   c. Keep the font large, not going below 28-point font for the text.
   d. Use parallel structure within lists.

11. Which of the following is *not* true about assertion–evidence style PowerPoint slides?
   a. The title should be a word or phrase.
   b. The title should be a sentence.
   c. The title should not exceed two lines.
   d. Graphics should be preferred to text in the body of the slide.

12. Which of the following is an effective way to design a PowerPoint content slide?
   a. Make one point per slide.
   b. Make between two and six points per slide.

13. Which of the following is an effective way to design a PowerPoint content slide?
   a. Use as little text as possible on each slide.
   b. Give each slide a unique title.
   c. Prefer text to graphics.
   d. Put only material that is essential on your slides.

14. Which of the following is an effective way to achieve data visualization in a PowerPoint slide?
   a. Pick the fanciest version of the graphic you choose.
   b. Use watermarked images.
   c. Include as much data and detail as possible.
   d. Select the simplest version of the graphic you choose.

15. Which of the following graphics is most appropriate when you want to show lines of authority in a police department?
   a. bar graph
   b. flowchart
   c. table
   d. organization chart

16. Which of the following graphics is most appropriate when you want to show that crime has declined during the past 12 months?
   a. table
   b. line graph
   c. diagram
   d. map

17. Which of the following graphics is most appropriate when you want to show the factors that determine whether to arrest or warn a suspect?
    a. pie chart
    b. screenshot
    c. logic tree
    d. pictograph

18. Which of the following graphics is most appropriate when you want to show how three different neighborhoods have different homicide rates?
    a. bar graph
    b. organization chart
    c. checklist
    d. line drawing

19. Which of the following belongs in a professional PowerPoint presentation?
    a. clipart
    b. cartoons
    c. transitions between slides
    d. sound effects
    e. long video clips
    f. none of the above

20. In general, handouts should be distributed …
    a. before your presentation
    b. during your presentation
    c. after your presentation

21. Which of the following is recommended as you practice your PowerPoint presentation?
    a. Time yourself.
    b. Practice in front of a mirror.
    c. Use a word-for-word script each time to memorize your presentation.
    d. Do not over-practice.

22. What is the single most important rule for delivering a presentation?
    a. Periodically make jokes.
    b. Wear patriotic colors.
    c. Do not read to the audience.
    d. Use exaggerated hand gestures.

23. Which of the following is recommended for the delivery of PowerPoint presentations?
    a. Pick one person in the audience with whom to maintain eye contact.
    b. Speak slowly and loudly.
    c. Apologize if you make a mistake.
    d. Try to ignore the audience's nonverbal communication behaviors.

24. Which of the following forms of nonverbal communication suggests that the audience might *not* be receptive to your presentation?

   a. nodding heads
   b. arms loosely folded across the chest
   c. raised eyebrow
   d. ankles crossed

25. Which of the following is *not* recommended for Q&A sessions?
   a. Repeat each question before you respond.
   b. Make up an answer if you do not know the answer.
   c. Respect the person answering the question.
   d. Invite questions.

Writing

These discussion items are designed to assess Chapter 11 Learning Objectives 2, 3, 6, and 7 (see Box 11.1).

1. Argue for the importance of effective PowerPoint presentations.
2. Outline methods for preparing effective presentations (Hint: Cover design, structure, and content).
3. Outline methods for delivering effective presentations (Hint: Cover handouts, practice, and delivery).
4. Prepare an effective PowerPoint presentation. Pick some area directly relevant to crime and/or its control, and prepare a 10-minute PowerPoint presentation.
5. Deliver an effective PowerPoint presentation. Share your 10-minute presentation with an audience.

REFERENCES

Chapman University Survey of American Fears. (2017). *America's top fears 2017*. Retrieved from https://blogs.chapman.edu/wilkinson/2017/10/11/americas-top-fears-2017/

American Society of Human Genetics. (2013). *Suggestions for preparing effective PowerPoint presentations*. Retrieved from http://www.ashg.org/2013meeting/pages/abstract_powerpoint.shtml

Carnegie Mellon University, Global Communication Center. (n.d.). *Designing effective PowerPoint presentations*. Retrieved from https://www.cmu.edu/gcc/handouts/powerpoint-handout-pdf

Collins, Jannette. (2004). Education techniques for lifelong learning: Making a PowerPoint Presentation. *RadioGraphics*, 24, 1177–1183.

Correctional Services Canada. (2008). Section 1: Tips for effective presentations. *Speakers Binder*. Retrieved from http://www.csc-scc.gc.ca/text/pblct/sb-go/01-eng.shtml

de Wet, Catharina F. (2006). Beyond presentations: Using PowerPoint as an effective instructional tool. *Gifted Child Today*, 29(4), 29–39.

Evergreen, Stephanie D. H. (2017). *Presenting data effectively: Communicating your findings for maximum impact* (2nd ed.). Thousand Oaks, CA: Sage Publications.

Feloni, Richard. (2015, January 30). 8 insights that will change the way you give PowerPoint presentations. *Business Insider*. Retrieved from http://www.businessinsider.com/8-tips-for-great-powerpoint-presentations-2015-1

Friend, Kristen. (2017, March 2). *8 tips for creating effective PowerPoint presentations*. Custom Legal Marketing. Retrieved from https://www.customlegalmarketing.com/2017/03/8-tips-for-creating-effective-powerpoint-presentations/

GCF Global. (n.d.). *PowerPoint tips: Simple rules for better PowerPoint presentations.* Goodwill Community Foundation, Inc. Retrieved from https://www.gcflearnfree.org/powerpoint-tips/simple-rules-for-better-powerpoint-presentations/1/

Grubb, Robert E., & Hemby, K. Virginia. (2019). *Effective communication in criminal justice.* Thousand Oaks, California: Sage Publications.

How to create an assertion-evidence presentation. (n.d.). Retrieved from http://sites.psu.edu/202cjaenicke/wp-content/uploads/sites/13153/2008/10/Assertion-Evidence-Slides-Instruction_Set.pdf

Kirk, Andy. (2012). *Data visualization: A successful design process.* Birmingham, UK: Packt Publishing Ltd.

Lens, Peter H., McCalister, Jennifer W., Luks, Andrew M., Le, Tao T., & Fessler, Henry E. (2015). Practical strategies for effective lectures. *Annals of the American Thoracic Society,* 12(4), 561–566.

Markel, Mike. (2012). *Technical communication* (10th ed.). Boston, MA: Bedford St. Martin's.

National Conference of State Legislatures. (2017, August 8). *Tips for making effective PowerPoint presentations.* Retrieved from http://www.ncsl.org/legislators-staff/legislative-staff/legislative-staff-coordinating-committee/tips-for-making-effective-powerpoint-presentations.aspx

Presentitude. (2016, April 11). Six safe fonts to use in your next presentation. *Presentitude.* Retrieved from http://presentitude.com/c-fonts/

RAND. (1996). *Guidelines for preparing briefings.* Communications Consulting Group and Publications Department. Santa Monica, CA: Author. Retrieved from http://www.dtic.mil/dtic/tr/fulltext/u2/a317235.pdf

Ravilious, Ben. (2016, September 16). 28 great PowerPoint presentation tips. *ParticiPoll.* Retrieved from https://www.participoll.com/powerpoint-presentation-tips/

Reynolds, Garr. (2016) *Top ten slide tips.* Retrieved from http://www.garrreynolds.com/preso-tips/design/

Schmaltz, Rodney M., & Enström, Rickard. (2014, October 8). Death to weak Power-Point: Strategies to create effective visual presentations. *Frontiers in Psychology,* 5, 1138. doi:10.3389/fpsyg.2014.01138

Schwartz, Michelle. (n.d.). *Creating an effective PowerPoint presentation.* Learning and Teaching Office, Ryerson University. Retrieved from https://www.ryerson.ca/content/dam/lt/resources/handouts/EffectivelyPresentingContent.pdf

Van, Slyke, Shanna, Benson, Michael L., & Virkler, William M. (2018). Confidence in the police, due process, and perp walks: Public opinion on the pretrial shaming of criminal suspects. *Criminology & Public Policy,* 17(3), 605–634.

Vjestica, Illiya. (2012, September 10). 5 classic presentation fonts. *Presentation Design.* Retrieved from https://thepresentationdesigner.co.uk/5-classic-presentation-fonts/

Wax, Dustin. (n.d.). 10 tips for more effective PowerPoint presentations. Retrieved from *Lifehack* website: https://www.lifehack.org/articles/featured/10-tips-for-more-effective-powerpoint-presentations.html

Whitbourne, Susan Krauss. (2012, June 30). The ultimate guide to body language: From your head to your toes, how to code and decode unconscious cues. *Psychology Today.* Retrieved from https://www.psychologytoday.com/us/blog/fulfillment-any-age/201206/the-ultimate-guide-body-language

Researching

> Research is formalized curiosity. It is poking and prying with a purpose.
>
> —ZORA NEALE HURSTON

Recall from Chapter 6 that **research** is a purposeful, systematic investigation designed to increase knowledge. Research is covered in this textbook because evidence is such an important component in compelling criminal justice communications, and research is a process for locating and producing evidence. Weak evidence will lead to a weak communication, while strong evidence is a necessary but not sufficient component of a strong communication.

How we approach the task of researching depends on why we are researching, and so this appendix begins by distinguishing between three different research motives. We then take a brief look at the different ways research is presented, with emphasis on secondary research. The rest of this appendix looks at strategies for organizing, conducting, and tracking the secondary research process.

RESEARCH MOTIVES

There are three broad motives for conducting research: (1) substantiating claims, (2) documenting knowledge, and (3) advancing knowledge. All else equal, as we move from the first to the second and then the third motive, our task becomes increasingly challenging, and the product becomes increasingly valuable.

Substantiating Claims

Chapters 5 and 6 discussed the role of evidence: Evidence is needed to substantiate claims. Thus, one motive for conducting research is to find proof. Just as a prosecutor who needs evidence to prove that a murder defendant caused the death of the victim, researchers will need proof for each claim they assert in their papers. As researchers and writers, we cannot expect our audience to believe something just because we say it. Instead, we need to offer proof that what we say is true. Where in the field, such proof is gathered in the criminal investigation process, in academia, such proof is gathered in the research process. We look to books, government documents, scholarly journals, and so on to find evidence supporting our claims.

This is the most common research motive. This motive characterizes papers written by students in grade school and many undergraduate student papers. Persuasive papers, debates, and term papers exemplify this research motive, as in these situations, we really just need some evidence to support what we say. As a result, while these papers do use evidence, they usually are not replete with evidence the way papers are that stem from the second and third research motives. In other words, most people who engage in research are not looking to gain as thorough as possible an understanding on a topic, which is the common foundation for the second and third research motives.

Documenting Knowledge

The second motive for research is to document what is known about a particular topic. For example, we might want to know about trends in school shootings, the demographic profile of school shooters, or the relationship between social media and school shootings. To learn what is known about any of these topics, we would identify, collect, and synthesize the existing relevant research. To synthesize means to combine multiple studies into one new study. In doing so, we would be conducting nonempirical, secondary research. (For more on nonempirical and secondary research, see Chapter 6). The resulting paper would present and describe the research others have conducted on the topic, and our conclusions would be based on our analysis of the already existing research.

To a limited extent, this research motive characterizes most student research papers for classes. For these papers, students select or are assigned a topic, and then their job is to locate and synthesize credible, relevant research. To a greater extent, many journal articles reflect this approach, particularly studies that synthesize the existing research on a phenomenon as the basis for suggesting directions for theory and research or for policy and practice. An important difference between papers for courses and papers for publication is in their thoroughness. When writing research papers for classes, students generally have the goal of locating sufficient sources so that they meet the instructor's minimum resource requirement (e.g., citing at least 5 sources). When writing papers for publication, however, researchers have a much loftier goal: locating every possible source so that they produce as comprehensive as possible a paper.

Advancing Knowledge

The third motive for research is to advance what is known about a particular topic. To advance what is known, the researcher must first establish what is known and then push that knowledge further. In other words, the first step in advancing knowledge is to document the existing knowledge, as described above. Once we have established what we already know, then we will be in a position to extend that knowledge further with our own primary research. Some primary research is empirical, which means it involves the collection and analysis of data from the real world, such as sentencing statistics from the United States Sentencing Commission, interviews with judges in federal district courts, surveys of citizens or students, analysis of news reports about arrests, and our own observations of trials. (Again, see Chapter 6 for more on primary research).

This research motive characterizes many scholarly journal articles as well as graduate theses and doctoral dissertations. Researchers who want to advance knowledge can do so in such ways as collecting and analyzing empirical data to present original findings, collecting and analyzing empirical data to replicate an existing study, and analyzing another researcher's empirical data to test a new theory.

RESEARCH PRODUCTS

It might be helpful to have a clear idea of the end product of research before we delve into how to conduct research. The product differs to some extent across research motives, especially between the first motive and the second and third motives.

Research Papers

A term paper is a popular type of student paper that requires the writer to do some research. Evidence is not the sole focus of such papers, although instructors will judge whether critical thinking is evident in the selection of credible and relevant evidence as well as if evidence was incorporated effectively into the paper. Reflecting the role of evidence in these writings to substantiate claims, the critical issue is whether appropriate evidence was provided to substantiate each claim in the paper. Because most claims will be made in the paper's body, most of the evidence will appear in the body. Some claims will be made in the introduction, which will require evidence. Most of the claims made in the conclusion will reflect evidence already presented in the paper, and so there may be few or no studies cited in the conclusion.

Literature Review Papers

A **literature review** presents the existing research on a phenomenon in a logical way so as to demonstrate patterns in findings, theory, and/or methods. When our motive is to document knowledge, the research paper we ultimately produce is a literature review. The conclusions we reach in such a paper are based on our reading and synthesis of the research studies we have presented. We might conclude, for example, that school shootings have increased over the past two decades. Except in research methods courses, undergraduate student papers typically focus on findings—what past researchers have found out about the phenomenon. Higher level literature reviews, in contrast, tend to identify theoretical approaches and whether those approaches have been supported by empirical research as well as methodological approaches for collecting and analyzing empirical data on the phenomenon.

Literature Review Sections

When our motive in to advance knowledge, then the literature review is one section in our research paper. There is a critical difference between the role of the literature review in documenting versus advancing knowledge. In the latter, in addition to documenting patterns in findings, theory, and/or methods, the literature review justifies our approach for advancing knowledge. It substantiates our claim that we are indeed advancing the literature. Through a careful and complete literature review, we can show that our study is indeed contributing to existing knowledge. For instance, the literature review might demonstrate a flaw in the methods used in prior research, or perhaps it would suggest a theory to explain the phenomenon. In the first scenario, you could advance knowledge by correcting for the methodological flaw; and in the second scenario, you could advance knowledge by testing the suggested theory's ability to explain the phenomenon.

Problem Formulation Section

Across the three research motives, the paper should begin with a problem formulation, which defines and establishes the significance of the topic. The problem formulation should set the stage for the rest of the paper, and so we articulate our problem formulation in the introduction section of the paper. Do not skip this task simply because you are assigned to write a paper—or even if you are assigned the topic. Instead, show that you understand the phenomenon and its importance. The last question you want your audience asking as they move from your introduction to your literature review is, "Who cares?" If your research motive is to substantiate claims, then your introduction's purpose is to argue for the importance of the issue under investigation. If your research motive is to document knowledge, then your introduction's purpose is to show why it is important for someone to document knowledge on the phenomenon. Likewise, if your research motive is to advance knowledge, then your introduction's purpose is to show why it is important for someone to advance knowledge on the phenomenon the way you do in the pages that follow.

Establishing the significance of a topic requires some evidence, which means you need to do some research to find evidence of something indicative of a problem, such as the following:

- It is prevalent (e.g., high crime and/or victimization rates are indicative of a problem that affects many people).
- It is increasing (e.g., rising crime and/or victimization rates suggest that a problem is becoming more serious and may continue to grow unless something is done about it).
- It is expensive (e.g., even if a crime problem is not particularly prevalent, it might be incredibly costly and, thus, be prudent to address).
- It causes other problems (e.g., something that by itself seems innocuous or irrelevant to criminal justice could have harmful, crime-related effects, such as sugar consumption and lead exposure).
- It has generated widespread public concern or fear (e.g., some crime might not be prevalent or increasing, but if people are panicked about it, then that panic might detract from real problems and/or affect behavior).

Without sensationalizing the issue (see Chapter 2 on professionalism), you want to find and use some evidence to demonstrate that the topic is (or should be) of concern to criminal justice academics and/or practitioners.

PRELIMINARY RESEARCH

The first step most of us need to take after we have our topic in mind is preliminary research. **Preliminary research** is different from (purposeful) research in that it is more exploratory. The less familiar with our topic we are, the more important preliminary research is and the more of it we likely will need to do. We want to get an idea of how our topic has already been handled by previous researchers. Use preliminary research to inform, organize, and guide the rest of your research.

First, see how others define your topic. Suppose, for example, our paper topic is "consumer fraud." We might first look through several sources to see how "consumer fraud" is defined. Some studies might use a broad definition of consumer fraud, one that encompasses criminal and noncriminal forms of fraudulent and misleading sales practices. Others might use a more limited definition, one that is restricted to violations of criminal law. Knowing that such distinctions exist, you can pay attention to them as you move forward in your research and the eventual writing of your paper. Different definitions might lead to different conclusions.

Second, see if you can identify different forms of your topic. Although consumer fraud is just one form of white-collar crime, there are many different forms of consumer fraud (e.g., advance-fee fraud, mortgage fraud, investment fraud, online purchase fraud, home repair fraud). Try to make a list of forms. Like definitions, researchers who look at different forms might reach different conclusions about, say, the demographic profile of perpetrators or estimates of financial losses. Awareness of these differences can help you show your knowledge of the subject matter as well as make sense of differences in findings. Additionally, the different forms might be helpful later when you use search terms to locate studies.

Third, see if you can distinguish between separate subtopics. A little preliminary research would reveal that different researchers have approached consumer fraud from different angles. Perhaps some people looked at consumer fraud trends over time, others have distinguished between different forms of consumer fraud, others have described the demographic characteristics of consumer fraud offenders, others have identified predictors of consumer fraud victimization, and still others have examined whether consumer fraud offenders have been deterred by criminal punishments. At this point, we might realize our topic is actually quite broad—perhaps unmanageably so. If we have the choice, in this case, we might want to narrow down our topic to one of these areas (e.g., predictors of consumer fraud victimization). If we do not have the choice, we will have a good idea of the different categories of information that we will need to research and cover in our paper.

RESEARCH QUESTIONS

We have completed our preliminary research when we are able to articulate one or more research questions. A **research question** is a specific question that can be answered by conducting research. Research questions are the key to a successful research process. Recall that the first part of the definition of research is that it is *purposeful*. Successful research requires that, from the outset, we have a clear, specific idea of what we are looking for. Research without research questions would be like a scavenger hunt without a list of items. If you do not know exactly what you are looking for, then you are unlikely to know (a) when you have found it or (b) when you are done looking.

Research questions are (a) in question form, (b) specific, and (c) verifiable through research. In Chapter 5, we learned about claims of fact. A research question asks a specific

TABLE A-A.1 Research Questions

Not a (Good) Research Question	A Good Research Question
"white-collar crime" *The problem*: This is not a question, and it is vague.	"When was the phrase 'white-collar crime' first used?"
"What is white-collar crime?" *The problem*: Although a question, this is vague.	What are the different ways to define white-collar crime?
"Should white-collar crime be punished more harshly than street crime?" *The problem*: Although a question, this is a matter of opinion rather than of research (i.e., it reflects a claim of value rather than of fact).	Is white-collar crime punished more harshly than street crime?
"Are white-collar offenders more likely to go to hell than street offenders?" *The problem*: This is a philosophical or supernatural question—not a question that can be answered by conducting research.	"Do religious authorities consider white-collar crime to be more serious than street crime?"

question of fact, and its answer is a claim of fact. Table A-A.1 distinguishes between research questions and other expressions. Here are some more examples of research questions:

- How has white-collar crime been defined?
- What are the different forms of white-collar crime?
- What are the demographic characteristics of white-collar criminals?
- What are the demographic characteristics of white-collar-crime victims?
- Which results in greater financial losses: white-collar or street crime?
- What are the different sanctions given to convicted white-collar criminals?
- Are white-collar criminals less likely to be incarcerated than street criminals?
- Do white-collar criminals have a harder time than street criminals getting a job following criminal conviction?

Research, then, becomes the search for a credible answer to your research question(s). Your research—that is, your systematic search for evidence—is complete once you have convincingly answered your research question(s).

Substantiating Claims

When our motive for research is to substantiate claims, we will need a research question for each claim of fact. If we have any claims of value or policy, then we will need to derive from them claims of fact before we can research them. (Review Chapter 6's discussion of proof requirements to see how to go about deriving fact claims from policy and value claims.)

For example, perhaps our task is to write a persuasive paper, and our thesis is that white-collar crime is more serious than street crime. This is a claim of value, which cannot be converted into a research question. So, we need to break our thesis down into claims of fact, and then convert each claim of fact into one or more research questions. One claim of fact could be that white-collar crime victimizes more people than does street crime. The research question to substantiate this claim of fact would be, "Are more people victimized by white-collar crime than by street crime?" We might be able to find a single study to answer this question, which means that a single study would have to report victimization for both white-collar and street crimes and show that the white-collar crime victimization rate is higher than the street crime victimization rate. Or we might have to find two different studies, one reporting white-collar crime victimization rates and the other reporting street crime victimization rates, and then compare those victimization rates to reach our own conclusion about white-collar crime victimization being higher than street crime victimization.

When we write to substantiate claims, our paper is organized around our claims, each of which should have supporting evidence. Substantiating claims can involve one or more pieces of evidence. The more contentious the claim, the more pieces of evidence we should offer. Likewise, the weaker the evidence, the more pieces of evidence we should provide so that the strengths of one piece compensate for the weaknesses of another piece. In sum, we need to

1. Identify each of our claims,
2. Translate any value or policy claims into fact claims,
3. Convert each fact claim into a research question,
4. Locate relevant and credible evidence to answer each research question, and
5. Repeat this process until each claim has been convincingly supported.

Documenting Knowledge

When our research motive is to document knowledge, our goal is to provide a representative and accurate portrait of the existing research on our topic. Our entire paper will be a literature review, and it will be organized around the different definitions, forms, and/or subtopics that we identified in our preliminary research. We might choose to narrow down our topic, and/or we might choose to focus on a particular definition, form, or subtopic. We may limit our literature review to empirical research, or perhaps we also would want to include nonempirical research that has proposed theoretical approaches to understanding our topic. If we do, then a coverage statement would play an important role in our introduction (see Chapter 3). We might, for instance, tell readers early on that our study is limited to empirical consumer fraud research that looks at victimization of individuals, excluding nonempirical research and research on organizations as victims.

Our job in our literature review is to document what is known about the topic in a clear and logical way. Our paper should be organized around each issue we intend to cover, with a research question for each of these issues. Keeping with the same example of empirical research on the victimization of individuals by consumer fraud, we might organize our paper around findings regarding (a) victimization rates over time and space, (b) demographic characteristics of victims, (c) behavioral characteristics of victims, and (d) reporting behavior of victims. Alternatively, perhaps we have a narrower focus: reporting behavior of individual consumer fraud victims. In this case, we might go into more detail, such as presenting (a) theoretical approaches, (b) research designs, and (c) main findings.

Once we determine the breadth and depth of our coverage of the topic, then we are ready to articulate research questions and outline our literature review paper. The body of the paper would have sections representing each subtopic, and we would need at least one research question for each subtopic. Our research process would then involve collecting the existing research that directly addresses each of our research questions. Our primary concern is gaining an accurate understanding of the current state of knowledge on the topic. This concern has an important implication for how we go about locating studies: We need to make sure our way of picking and choosing studies does not give us an inaccurate, or biased, understanding. The obvious way to nullify this concern would be to include every single relevant study, but this would require a lot of time and effort. The next best approach, then, is to include an adequate amount of studies while taking steps to avoid obtaining a biased subset of all possible studies.

We need to be reasonably thorough in our inclusion of the existing research, but we probably do not need to be completely thorough (as is true when we seek to advance knowledge; see the next section). A reasonable guide for determining when we can stop trying to locate additional research to answer a given research question is **diminishing returns**. This is the point we reach when each additional study both requires more effort to locate and adds little or no new knowledge. Overall, then, the following steps can be used when conducting research to document knowledge:

1. Carve our topic into subtopics,
2. Articulate one or more research questions for each subtopic,
3. Locate enough sources for each research questions until we reach the point of diminishing returns, and
4. Repeat this process for each research question.

Advancing Knowledge

When our research motive is to advance knowledge, our goal is to provide a thorough portrait of the existing research on our topic. Because our goal is to contribute to, or advance in a meaningful way, what is known about the topic, we will have a literature review section in our paper that presents what already is known. Our literature review should also suggest and justify the approach we are taking in our contribution. Thus, for each issue we want to investigate in our own study, we should have a research question.

If we have federal sentencing data, for example, and we want to do primary, empirical research on sentencing of white-collar criminals, we need to consider what it is about white-collar crime sentencing that we are going to investigate in our analysis. For example, if we want to use the federal sentencing data to determine if white-collar criminals are sentenced more leniently than street criminals, then our literature review needs to document how existing research has gone about answering that question. Perhaps all of the existing research on this issue is old. One way for us to advance that literature could be to update it.

Unlike researching to substantiate a claim, it is critical for us to be thorough when we are doing research to advance knowledge. This distinction has an important implication: We must locate and obtain every available piece of evidence when we are seeking to advance knowledge. We cannot skip relevant studies that are hard to obtain in full text, for example. We have to look at the total evidence—not some subset of the total evidence. Otherwise, our contention that we are advancing knowledge is fallacious because it is based on an incomplete review of existing knowledge. Consequently, when we are advancing knowledge, the research process is much more onerous than when we are merely substantiating a claim.

That said, articulating specific research questions can narrow down what is relevant or not, thus reducing the body of total evidence to a manageable size. Plus, we can usually limit our literature review to empirical research, ignoring studies that relate to our topic but do not present findings based on analysis of data. And we can ignore studies that, while empirical, do not present original results. When the same authors produce multiple studies analyzing the same data (e.g., a preliminary report and a final report, or a journal article and then a book), we can prefer the first or most complete publication. This is not to say that we want our research questions to be so narrow that answers to them would be meaningless. But we do want to be very clear and purposeful in each step we take in our endeavor to advance knowledge, following these steps:

1. Identify each issue we want to investigate in our empirical analysis,
2. Articulate a research question for each issue we intend to investigate,
3. Locate every single relevant and original existing study that answers our research question, and
4. Repeat this process until we have identified all existing research for each research question.

SEARCH TERMS

Here, we pick up at the point where we have articulated our research questions and are ready to start searching for relevant sources. Research questions can be used as search terms themselves or to arrive at search terms. **Search terms** are words typed into a search engine to generate results. Because your research question is an exact expression of what you want to find, start with it rather than with key words and phrases taken from it. To start with the research question itself, type (or copy and paste) it into a search engine as the search term without quotation marks. To move from the research question to search terms, you will need to identify your search terms. The best search terms are the key words in your research question and any variants of them. The key words convey the essence of your topic.

Suppose our topic is "preventing cyberbullying," and we are writing a research paper for a course. Thus, we do not need an exhaustive (or even thorough) review of the research; we just need enough relevant and credible evidence to substantiate any claims in our paper about how to prevent cyberbullying. At minimum, we know we will need an introduction, a body, and a conclusion. Starting with the introduction, we need to define our topic and establish its significance. We might choose to cite evidence that cyberbullying is a problem that affects lots of people (claim 1) and that cyberbullying has negative consequences (claim 2). Our research question for claim 1 is could be, "How prevalent is cyberbullying?" And our research question for claim 2 could be, "What are the effects of cyberbullying on the victims?"

Taking this one research question at a time, the key words in the first research question are "cyberbullying" and "prevalence." Thus, for each of these terms, we would think about alternative words that have a similar meaning. If we get stumped, we might do some preliminary research to see what terms are used to describe cyberbullying, we could look in a thesaurus to see what synonyms are listed for "cyberbully," and/or we could do a basic Google search for something along the lines of "other words for cyberbullying"

TABLE A-A.2   Search Term Possibilities for Cyberbullying Prevalence

Cyberbully	Prevalence
troll	estimate
bully online	statistic
cyberharassment	frequency
online harassment	rate

(without quotation marks). Based on some brainstorming, preliminary research, and/or searches for similar terms, we can create a table (or lists—whatever works best for us) of possible search terms and combinations, such as Table A-A.2. Taking our lists of words in Table A-A.2, we can create various combinations of search terms by matching each term in the first column with each term in the second column, such as

- cyberbully prevalence;
- cyberbully estimate;
- cyberbully statistic;
- cyberbully frequency;
- cyberbully rate;
- bully online prevalence;
- bully online estimate;
- bully online statistic;
- bully online frequency;
- bully online rate;

and so on, until we have matched each word in the first column with each term in the second column.

If the first search term we use gives us the evidence we need from a credible source, then we can move on. If not and the problem is that the results do not seem relevant, we would want to use a different search term. If not and the problem is that we cannot establish the source's credibility, then we would need to look for a different source that is credible, but we would not need to change search terms.

Rarely will our first search give us everything we need to know, so we need to look at how to troubleshoot imperfect search results.

Too Many Results

One problem we might encounter is too many results. Here are some suggestions for a search that returns too many results to use:

1. **Add quotation marks to narrow the results down to those with the greatest potential for relevancy.** You could enclose your entire research question in quotes, or you could enclose one or more parts of your research question in quotes. Either way, doing so will exclude any source that does not contain exactly the same question or phrase as yours.

2. **Sort the results by most recent first.** Generally speaking, the more recent results are better than older results. First, they tell us what is currently happening,

whereas older results tell us what did happen. Second, their literature review can give us a summary of the past research, and their References can be used to locate older studies.

3. **Use more specific variants of words in your research question.** To narrow down a search, we need a term that is more specific (e.g., from "dog" to "poodle" or from "weapon" to "gun"). These are not equivalent terms, as we discussed earlier, where we can use a thesaurus. Instead, we start with the broad term and then try to break that broad term apart into categories, dimensions, types, or forms.

Figure A-A.1 illustrates a word family tree, which is one way of identifying search term variants that are not synonyms. In Figure A-A.1, moving from left to right leads to progressively more specific terms. It illustrates how a broad word can be broken down into more specific categories: "Bullying" can be classified either as "traditional bullying" or as "cyberbullying." Here, traditional bullying and cyberbullying both are forms of bullying, but cyberbullying is not traditional bullying. Thus, the lines connect terms to their more or less specific variants.

When using a search term family tree to generate fewer results—that is, when using a more specific version of a general term (e.g., using "outing" instead of "cyberbullying" as your search term), realize that your results may not generalize back to the broader term. In other words, results pertaining to outing specifically might not be true for the entire category of cyberbullying. What we know about "physical" bullying, likewise,

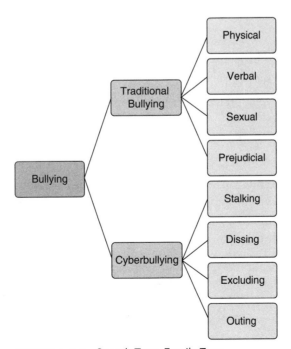

FIGURE A-A.1   Search Term Family Tree

might not be the same as what we know about "verbal" bullying, "sexual" bullying, or "prejudicial" bullying. We can address this situation in one of two ways:

1. Specify in our own paper when a source looked at a more specific phenomenon rather than the more general phenomenon in our research question.
2. Rephrase our own research question to be about the more specific phenomenon than about the more general phenomenon.

Too Few Results

Another problem we might encounter is too few results. In this case, consider these suggestions:

1. **Remove any quotation marks.** Whether the quotes enclose the entire research question or some part of it, removing them should generate more results.
2. **Strip your research question down to key words.** For example, shave "How prevalent is cyberbullying?" down to "prevalence cyberbullying."
3. **Replace some of the words with synonyms and/or broader terms.** You could go from specific terms to more general terms (e.g., from "poodle to dog" or from "gun" to "weapon"). Looking at Figure A-A.1, this involves moving left in the search term family tree. Another strategy is to use similar terms, which might be more popular than your original search terms, in the literature on your topic (see Table A-A.2 and its discussion).

Whether the problem is too many or too few results, modifying search terms is one approach to obtaining different search results. Another approach is switching search tools.

SEARCH TOOLS

This section presents and distinguishes between three search tools: Internet search engines, library databases, and Google Scholar. This material is intended to help you choose and use an appropriate search tool. Students should note, however, that their instructor might have certain requirements or expectations for search tools, which of course would need to be followed.

Search Engines

A **search engine** is an Internet program or website that allows users to input a search term to obtain information sources matching the search term. Popular search engines include Google, Yahoo, and Bing. A broad range of information can be found using Internet search engines: commercial (.com), organizational (.org), governmental (.gov), and educational/scholarly (.edu). Anyone can use these search engines, and much information found using them is free. Also, anyone can post anything on the Internet, which contributes to the diversity of information that can be accessed.

Search engines have their limitations. One set of limitations concerns access limits and fees. A fee may be required to view the full text of some sources. Similarly, some websites, such as the *New York Times*, allow a user to access a limited number of articles before having to pay to view more. A second limitation is a byproduct of the fact that anyone can post material on the Internet: The results we obtain using Internet search engines are of uncertain credibility. This is a serious limitation when our goal is to produce credible, compelling communications. Despite looking professional, sources can be biased, inaccurate, or otherwise untrustworthy. Thus, we often have to spend some time and effort evaluating the credibility of a result before we are prepared to believe and cite it.

If you find a relevant source but have doubts about its credibility, try one or more of these strategies:

1. **Open another browser window and learn what you can about the author and/or publisher.** All else equal, authors with educational or practical expertise are generally more credible than those without, and publishers that use some level of scrutiny (e.g., peer review) can be considered more credible than other publishers.
2. **Search for another version of the information,** such as an official one with all bibliographic information present.
3. **Examine the source carefully,** asking if its conclusions are objective, logical, and evidence-based.
4. **Compare the source with other sources.** Corroboration, or agreement across different sources, can be a sign of credibility.

If none of these strategies work, then the safest assumption to make is that the source is not credible. If you are just looking for a single piece of evidence to substantiate a point, you should move on to a different source. But if you are trying to collect as many sources as possible, hang on to it.

When you are hunting for a topic, doing preliminary research, looking for cases or examples of some phenomenon, then a search engine can be a good choice. Search engines like Google and Yahoo are great places to type in broad inquiries like "controversial issues in criminal justice" to get ideas for topics. You also can find trial transcripts, the full text of Supreme Court decisions, and reports and statistics from a wide variety of government agencies in these search engines. And, in these search engines, you can input terms (alone or along with the word "synonym" or "thesaurus") to help identify alternative search terms. So, there are many good reasons for using search engines. But quality research does not stop here. Instead, once you begin your real research—that is, tracking down credible research evidence—you will need to move on to library databases and/or Google Scholar.

Library Databases

A library database is a library's electronic collection of information that allows users to input a search term to obtain information sources matching the search term. Compared with Internet search engines, library database results are narrower. Some databases contain research publications within a particular discipline (e.g., PsycINFO for psychology, LexisNexis for law), others contain research publications from a range of academic disciplines (e.g., ProQuest Social Science Databases for the social sciences, ScienceDirect for the natural sciences and technology), and still others are multidisciplinary (e.g., JSTOR, Academic Search). Unlike most Internet search engines, some process was used to regulate the contents of library databases, with the result being that library database results tend to be more trustworthy than Internet search engine results. Another advantage to using library databases is their options for refining your search. You can conduct an advanced search to limit your results to those that are, for example, in full text, research reports, peer reviewed, or in a particular academic discipline.

As an example, Figure A-A.2 shows ProQuest search results using the same research question as earlier in this chapter: "What is the prevalence of cyberbullying?" (with no quotation marks). This initial search yielded 333 results, but we can narrow this down to full-text and peer-reviewed results, as shown in Figure A-A.3. Now, we have 227 results, all of which should be full-text and peer-reviewed sources, which means that all of these sources are easily accessible as well as trustworthy.

Like Internet search engines, library databases have their limitations. First, there is less information in these databases than is accessible using Internet search engines. For example, a law database might not include every legal journal; thus, the search results might be incomplete. Second, not everyone can access library databases; rather, students, faculty, and staff belonging to the library's institution can use these databases. Third, library databases can foster overconfidence. For example, we might check the box to limit our results to those that are peer-reviewed and still get some results that are not peer reviewed. When a journal that uses peer review also publishes other types of contributions, such as essays

FIGURE A-A.2   Unfiltered ProQuest Search Results

FIGURE A-A.3   Filtered ProQuest Search Results

and book reviews, this can happen. Thus, when it comes to evaluating the credibility of sources, while library databases do most of this work for us, we still should exercise some caution and confirm that each result we intend to use matches our criteria.

Google Scholar

Like library databases, Google Scholar is an effective way to identify quality sources of information. Google Scholar results include journal articles, books, and government and technical documents. It does not include many of the questionable results we see in Google, such as Wikipedia, advocacy websites, commercial advertisements, and blogs.

Where Google Scholar is superior to library databases is in its coverage: It has access to more sources, which means it is more comprehensive. Figure A-A.4 shows the Google Scholar results for the same search question about prevalence of cyberbullying. Compared with the few hundred results obtained using ProQuest, Google Scholar yields more than 12,000 results. Second, library databases simply might not be an option, such as is true for people who are unaffiliated with a library.

But there are two important limitations to Google Scholar. First, it does not have most of the filters that library databases do, such as peer review and full text. This

FIGURE A-A.4   Google Scholar Search Results

means you have to do more work accessing full-text sources and judging the credibility of each potential source. Second, you might have to pay to access the full text directly through Google. In Figure A-A.4, you can see that some results have a .pdf or .doc link off to the right. These are the results that can be accessed in full text for free in Google Scholar (although not all of these links work). Thus, it can take some more effort to get a full-text copy for free using Google Scholar compared with library databases. Still, there are ways to avoid having to pay to access full-text articles located using Google Scholar:

- **Do a Google search for the article,** using the article's title (without quotation-marks). There might be a free, full-text version available.
- **Log into your institution's library website,** looking to see if your library has the article. You might be able to find an electronic copy of the article in full text after logging in as a user. If your library does not carry the article, then you can try requesting an interlibrary loan, which is when another library provides the source. Check with a librarian about your options for locating articles.
- **Email the author of the article,** asking if that author would provide you with a full-text copy. Some authors are happy to share their research.

If we are in a hurry (such as happens, e.g., when we procrastinate on starting a paper and have only a day or two to complete it), we have fewer options for obtaining full-text articles for free. This fact should serve as incentive to start the research process as soon as possible.

Given the strengths and weaknesses of Google Scholar, many people prefer library databases for academic research and writing. Especially if you do not feel comfortable distinguishing between credible and non-credible sources, then library databases are your ideal search tool. But if you keep running into the problem of too few sources, and switching search terms and library databases does not solve your problem, then you might want to give Google Scholar a try.

SEARCH RECORDS

When you conduct multiple searches, using different search terms and search tools, it is easy to lose track of what you have tried. Duplicating efforts can be time-consuming and frustrating. Mistakenly thinking you have searched somewhere you have not searched, on the other hand, can lead to the exclusion of relevant sources. Having a search strategy and recording your steps, moreover, is an important aspect of engaging in a *systematic* investigation—that is, of conducting research. Thus, an efficient practice is to record the following details for each of your searches:

1. **Search date.** The search results might change as new sources are added. This becomes especially important when you conduct a search over a period of time, such as collecting empirical research over the course of several months or collecting news reports over a period of days or weeks.
2. **Search tool.** Keep track of each Internet search engine and library database you use.
3. **Search term.** Record precisely what you enter as your search terms, specifying when you use quotation marks. Consider using multiple search terms in one search tool before moving on to another search tool.
4. **Search refinements.** Make note of any specifications to your search, such as whether the results are restricted to certain years, to research articles, or to peer-reviewed sources. Also note if the results are sorted in a way other than by most relevant first.
5. **Search progress.** Often, you will not have time to conduct a thorough search within a search tool in one sitting. If you have to stop searching before you finish a given search, then record where you left off so that you know where to pick your search back up later.
6. **Sources you rule out.** Each time you locate a source, review it; and if you determine that it is not appropriate to include in your research, make a note of it. Record its bibliographic details so you will recognize it if you come across it later, and also note your reason for excluding it (e.g., not relevant, not credible).
7. **Sources you need to find in full text.** Each time you locate a source that looks appropriate to include but is not immediately accessible in full text, make a note of it. Compile these notes in a single document—a "Hit List" of sorts—so you

have a record of all the sources you will need to find in full text to determine whether they should be included in your research.

8. **Sources you found in full text and rule in.** Each time you locate a full-text source and conclude that it is appropriate for inclusion in your research, then save a copy of it and record its full bibliographic information. This document serves as your "Working References" list and can be used as the foundation for the References section that will ultimately be in your final paper.

Large research projects, long research projects, and multiple research projects can make it challenging to keep track mentally of what you have tried and what you have not tried. Recording this information as you go, then, can save time and energy in the long run while also yielding as comprehensive a research project as possible.

Formatting

The proper words in the proper places are the true definition of style.

—JONATHAN SWIFT

When we talk about publication styles, we are talking about formal rules that achieve consistency. These formal rules are presented in books called style guides. There are multiple styles guides, such as APA (American Psychological Association), Chicago (or Turabian), MLA (Modern Language Association), and Bluebook. Publishers and others seek consistency when they use style guides: consistency regarding what information goes where and how the final product should look.

Think of what a journal is, and you can begin to appreciate the importance of a style guide. In a given journal issue, multiple articles (perhaps 10) will have been written, each by different authors. Different authors often have different ways of formatting their documents (e.g., some use Times New Roman, while others use Calibri; some double space, while others single space; some set section headings in all caps, and others use different-colored fonts to format section headings). The journal, however, needs a consistent look across articles within an issue. Style guides are a way of achieving a uniform look and feel within a publication when there are multiple people contributing to that publication.

Style guides address writing mechanics (e.g., grammar, spelling, and punctuation), paper layout (e.g., title page, section headings, page numbers), and ways of crediting source material (e.g., in-text citations, footnotes, references). We learned about different communication styles in Chapter 2, considering topics such as tone and diction. In this chapter, we are going to concentrate on the layout of written communications and how to format in-text citations and references in APA style. The *Publication Manual of the American Psychological Association* is now in its sixth edition (APA, 2010).

LAYOUT

The main parts of an APA-style paper are presented in Table A-B.1. The entire document should be double spaced, with 1-inch margins on all four sides, left-aligned text, and zero spacing before and after paragraphs. Your software might automatically add space between paragraphs, so you need to check this while you are adjusting all the rest of your settings when you first open a blank document to get started. In Microsoft Word, click Home → Paragraph, and then ensure that spacing is set to 0 both before and after paragraphs

In addition to the main parts shown in Table A-B.1, all pages should have a running head and page numbers. A **running head** is an abbreviated form of the paper's title, which should be placed in the upper left-hand corner and be set in all caps. The running head looks a little different on the title page than in the rest of the document: On the title page only, it is prefaced with the phrase "Running head:" (which is not in all caps). Page numbering should begin on the title page, appear in the upper right-hand corner, and run through the last page of the paper. Like all other text in an APA-style paper, the running head and page numbers should be set in 12-point Times New Roman font.

Title Page

Figure A-B.1 is an example of an APA-style title page. The paper's title should be a clear and concise summary of the paper's main idea expressed in 12 or fewer words. In papers written for classes, students often do not need to include an author note. When an author note is needed, it consists of the following:

- First paragraph: Complete departmental affiliation
- Second paragraph: Any change in affiliation since the study was completed
- Third paragraph: Any acknowledgments and special circumstances
- Fourth paragraph: Name and complete contact information

Notice how there is no bold in the title page, and how the running head is a shortened version of the paper's title. The running head certainly should not exceed one line, nor should it be longer than the paper title. Use the key words from the paper title to create the running head.

TABLE A-B.1 Main Parts of an APA-Style Paper

Part	Contents
Title Page	Paper title Author name Institutional affiliation Author note
Abstract Page	"Abstract" heading Abstract paragraph Keywords list
Text	Paper title Body of paper, with sections and section headings and in-text citations
References Page(s)	"References" heading Complete bibliographic information for all sources cited in the text
Footnotes*	Any footnotes to the text
Tables and Figures*	Any tables or figures mentioned in the text

*These parts are optional; not all APA-style papers have them. We will not cover them in this chapter.

Long-Term Effects of Drug Courts on Recidivism

Jane E. Doe

Utica College

Author Note

Jane E. Doe, Department of Criminal Justice, University of Lakes, Ponds, Streams, and Rivers.

Jane E. Doe is now at the Department of Criminal Justice, Criminology, and Sociology, Beach University.

This research was supported by a grant from the University of Lakes, Ponds, Streams, and Rivers.

Address correspondence to Jane E. Doe, 555 Sandy Road, Beach University, Gorgeousville, MY, 55555-5555 (email: jedoe@beachu.edu).

FIGURE A-B.1   Sample APA-Style Title Page

Abstract Page

Figure A-B.2 is an example of an APA-style abstract page. The page has the word "Abstract" at the top, which is centered but not in bold. APA does not specify minimum or maximum lengths for abstracts, instead directing writers to follow the abstract length requirements set by their publisher. However, APA does say that most abstracts are 150–250 words. The abstract is a paragraph—which is not indented—that gives a succinct yet complete overview of the paper. Chapter 10 of this textbook provides guidance on how to write an abstract. Under the abstract, the word "Keywords" is indented, italicized, and immediately followed by a colon. The keywords listed should reflect the paper's major ideas, such as theoretical framework, key variables, special statistical techniques, and relevant criminal justice policies and practices.

Text

The text, or body, of the paper begins after the abstract page. The paper's title is repeated at the top (centered and not in bold), and then the text begins. The paper's title should be identical to the paper title presented on the title page. Notice how there is no "Introduction" section heading between the paper's title and the start of the text. Each new

Abstract

Drug offenders constitute a significant portion of the U.S. correctional population. While accumulating evidence points to the ineffectiveness of incarceration in deterring future offending, drug courts have proliferated to address the continuing problem of high recidivism rates and associated correctional costs posed by drug offenders. The proposed study would advance the existing research by evaluating the effectiveness of drug courts on reducing recidivism using a classical experimental design with not only random assignment to treatment and control groups but also a 5-year follow-up period. The lengthy follow-up period is particularly important, as drug court treatment typically lasts for 12–18 months and past research tended to use 1- and 2-year follow-up periods, which provided little data on recidivism rates following program completion. Recidivism reductions immediately following program completion have been noted, yet for drug courts to substantially impact correctional costs and truly rehabilitate drug offenders, evidence is needed that they produce longer term, lasting effects.

Keywords: drug court, recidivism, program evaluation, outcome assessment, experiment

FIGURE A-B.2   Sample APA-style Abstract Page

paragraph is indented ½ inch. Press enter once to start a new paragraph. Your software might automatically indent the next paragraph for you; if not, use the tab key instead of the space bar to indent. Do not put a blank line space between paragraphs. Figure A-B.3 shows an example of APA style for the first page of text.

Figures A-B.4 and A-B.5 show the formatting of sections and section headings in APA style. Notice how there are no blank line spaces between sections or surrounding section headings. APA provides for up to five levels of heading, with each level having its own format. A fundamental rule regarding use of level headings is that no paper should have only one section for a heading level. For example, no paper should have only one level-1 section and section heading. Within any level-1 section, no paper should have only one level-2 section and section heading. Within any level-2 section, no paper should have only one level-3 section and section heading, and so on.

Table A-B.2 provides further details on the formatting of the five possible levels of heading. Some of these formatting specifications merit further attention. The first is capitalization. Levels 1 and 2 are set in "Title Case," while levels 3, 4, and 5 are set in "Sentence case." **Title case** means capitalizing (a) the first word, (b) all major words, (c) any other word four or more letters, and (d) words connected to a capitalized word via hyphen. Major words are nouns, verbs, pronouns, adjectives, and adverbs. Even short

DRUG COURTS AND RECIDIVISM   3

Long-Term Effects of Drug Courts on Recidivism

Judges have a range of options from which to choose when sentencing convicted offenders. This decision is influenced by factors such as the seriousness of the crime, the danger the offender presents to the community, and the likelihood of recidivism (Steffensmeier, Ulmer, & Kramer, 1998). Drug courts are a relatively recent approach to reducing recidivism among drug offenders, which became popular in the United States starting in the 1990s (Goldkamp, White, & Robinson, 2001; Spohn, Piper, Martin, & Frenzel, 2001; Wilson, Mitchell, & MacKenzie, 2006). Key components of drug courts include treatment for drug abuse/addition and monitoring by specially trained judges (Mitchell, Wilson, Eggers, & MacKenzie, 2012).

Nonviolent drug offenders comprise approximately 16% of state and 50% of federal prison populations (Mitchell, Cochran, Mears, & Bales, 2017). While repeat offenders comprise the bulk of the U.S. prison population, drug offenders are among the most likely to return to crime after serving their sentences (Gottfredson, Najaka, & Kearley, 2003; Spohn et al., 2001; Wilson et al., 2006). The recidivism of drug offenders therefore presents a significant financial problem.

Given a lack of evidence that prison deters repeat offending by drug offenders (Mitchell et al., 2017), the proposed study asks if drug courts affect recidivism among drug offenders. The hypothesis is that drug courts reduce recidivism among drug offenders. To test this hypothesis, the proposed study would employ an experimental research design to determine whether drug offenders sentenced to drug court are less likely to recidivate than are drug offenders not sentenced to drug courts. Extending previous research, the proposed study would involve random

FIGURE A-B.3   Sample APA Style Text

verbs (e.g., "is" and "are") should be capitalized. Non-major words include articles, conjunctions, and prepositions. Longer prepositions—such as "before" and "around"—also are capitalized. Words following a hyphen, such as "Meta-Analysis," are capitalized when using title case. **Sentence case**, in contrast, means capitalizing only (a) the first word and (b) any proper nouns. Table A-B.3 distinguishes further between title case and sentence case.

The second formatting specification that needs additional attention is the lead-in paragraph headings for levels 3, 4, and 5. Like a new paragraph, these headings are indented. They are set in sentence case and end with a period, but they are not complete sentences. There are two spaces after these headings. And the section starts on the same line as these headings, with a complete sentence. Table A-B.4 provides more examples of these headings.

References

Figure A-B.6 shows how to format the References. We will get into more detail about what bibliographic information to include and how to format it shortly. For now, notice how this part of the APA-style paper is formatted. The References start on the page after the last page

The next section reviews the existing evaluation research on the effectiveness of drug courts in terms of reducing recidivism, and the section after that presents the proposed study's research design. This research proposal ends with a discussion of the potential strengths and weaknesses of the proposed study.

Literature Review

This section reviews the existing empirical research on the impact of drug courts on recidivism by drug offenders. First, the studies will be analyzed in terms of their research question/hypothesis, theoretical framework/orientation, research design, sampling, dependent and independent variable measurement, and key findings. Second, patterns in the existing research will be identified with regard to methodology and results.

Existing Research

Research question/hypothesis. In general, the existing literature has asked if drug courts affect recidivism, hypothesizing that drug court participation decreases recidivism. Goldkamp et al. (2001) hypothesized that drug court would decrease recidivism, but that drug courts would only have this effect among those who completed drug court treatment. Spohn et al. (2001) asked if drug court participants would exhibit less recidivism than would comparison drug offenders across a variety of measures of recidivism. Gottfredson et al. (2003) hypothesized drug offenders sentenced to drug court would exhibit less criminal behavior than drug offenders not sentenced to drug court regardless of the way recidivism was measured. Wilson et al. (2006) asked if there is evidence that drug courts reduce recidivism when using a rigorous evaluation research design. Mitchell et al. (2012) asked if there is evidence that drug courts reduce recidivism when looking

FIGURE A-B.4   Sample APA-Style Sections and Section Headings–Part A

of text; the References do not begin on the same page as the end of the text, nor should there be a blank page between the last page of text and the start of the References. Like the rest of the paper, it is double-spaced and set in 12-point Times New Roman font. The page numbers continue from the text, and the running head is also at the top of the References. The References is titled "References"—not "Works Cited," "Sources," "Bibliography" or "Reference." The heading is centered, but it is not in bold. The References list uses a **hanging indent**, which means subsequent lines (i.e., all lines but the first line for each source listed) are indented.

DOCUMENTATION

Documentation refers mostly to in-text citations and References; as such, documentation deals with how to identify the sources of ideas, words, and other information (e.g., images, computer code). The goal in this chapter is to provide a basic guide to proper APA format, but this chapter will not attempt to cover APA Style for every type of source. Should you need further details on APA formatting of in-text citations and References, you are encouraged to consult the most recent edition of the APA Manual itself—do not rely on sources other than APA when it comes to proper APA style, and do not rely on an older edition of the APA Manual.

DRUG COURTS AND RECIDIVISM   5

Theoretical framework/orientation. Most of the existing research has not incorporated a theoretical framework or orientation. Goldkamp et al. (2001), Spohn et al. (2001), Wilson et al. (2006), and Mitchell et al. (2012) did not use a theoretical framework. Gottfredson et al. (2003), in contrast, used deterrence theory as their theoretical framework.

Research design. The existing research is divided in terms of the type of research design used to examine the effectiveness of drug courts on recidivism. Goldkamp et al. (2001), Spohn et al. (2001), and Gottfredson et al. (2003) used an experimental research design. Wilson et al. (2006) and Mitchell et al. (2012) used meta-analysis as their research design.

Sampling. Treating individual drug offenders as the unit of analysis, experimental drug court evaluations generally examine one or two jurisdictions, while meta-analytical drug court evaluations encompass more jurisdictions.

Experimental studies. Because the experimental studies looked at few jurisdictions, the sampling method focused on selection of individual drug offenders.

Goldkamp et al. (2001). Goldkamp et al. (2001) used stratified sampling to obtain a sample of 1,083 drug offenders in Portland, Oregon, and of 979 drug offenders in Las Vegas, Nevada, between the years 1991 and 1997.

Spohn et al. (2001). Spohn et al.'s (2001) began with all felony drug offenders sentenced in Douglas County, Omaha, Nebraska, between January 1997 and March 1998. All drug court participants for whom complete information could be collected, and then drug offenders in the comparison groups were selected by matching them to drug court participants in terms of most serious offense and age, race/ethnicity, and sex. The final sample consisted of 285 drug court

FIGURE A-B.5   Sample APA-Style Sections and Section Headings—Part B

TABLE A-B.2   APA-Style Heading Format

Level	Format	Examples from Figures A-B.4 and A-B.5
1	Centered, Bold, Headline Case	**Literature Review**
2	Left-Aligned, Bold, Headline Case	**Existing Research**
3	Indented, bold, sentence case, ending with a period.	**Research question/hypothesis.**
		Theoretical framework/orientation.
		Research design.
		Sampling.
4	Indented, bold, italics, sentence case, ending with a period.	*Experimental studies.*
5	Indented, italics, sentence case, ending with a period.	*Goldkamp et al. (2001).*
		Spohn et al. (2001).

In-Text Citations

Table A-B.5 provides a quick overview of when to cite information sources and how to indicate a source's exact words. We are going to cover each of these situations, one at a time, and then we will look at the special case of citing statistics.

TABLE A-B.3   Title Case Versus Sentence Case

Title Case	Sentence Case
Recidivism Results	Recidivism results
Florida and Minnesota Drug Courts	Florida and Minnesota drug courts
Findings on Rearrest Versus Reconviction	Findings on rearrest versus reconviction
Attitudinal Differences Before Treatment	Attitudinal differences before treatment
Records Provided by the FBI	Records provided by the FBI

TABLE A-B.4   Lead-In Paragraph Headings

Level	Example
3	**Comparison of adults and juveniles.** The drug court effect was more pronounced for adult than for juvenile drug offenders. The adults appear to have taken the treatment more seriously.
4	***Experimental and comparison groups.*** Participants were assigned randomly to either the experimental or control group. Because of random assignment, selection effects should not be problematic.
5	*Length of follow-up period.* Most participants who completed the treatment and had not reoffended within 6 months remained crime-free throughout the entire 2-year follow-up period. These data suggest that the first 6 months are critical for successful community reintegration.

DRUG COURTS AND RECIDIVISM   12

References

Babbie, E. (2013). *The practice of social research* (13th ed.). Belmont, CA: Wadsworth, Cengage
    Learning.

Goldkamp, J. S., White, M. D., & Robinson, J. B. (2001). Do drug courts work? Getting inside
    the drug court black box. *Journal of Drug Issues, 31*(1), 27–72. doi:
    10.1177/002204260103100104

Gottfredson, D. C., Najaka, S. C., & Kearley, B. (2003). Effectiveness of drug treatment courts:
    Evidence from a randomized trial. *Criminology & Public Policy, 2*(2), 171–196. doi:
    10.1111/j.1745-9133.2003.tb00117.x

Mitchell, O., Cochran, J. C., Mears, D. P., & Bales, W. D. (2017). The effectiveness of prison for
    reducing drug offender recidivism: A regression discontinuity analysis. *Journal of
    Experimental Criminology, 13*(1), 1–27. doi: 10.1007/s11292-017-9282-6

Mitchell, O., Wilson, D. B., Eggers, A., & MacKenzie, D. L. (2012). Assessing the effectiveness
    of drug courts on recidivism: A meta-analytic review of traditional and non-traditional
    drug courts. *Journal of Criminal Justice, 40*(1), 60–71. doi:
    10.1016/j.jcrimjus.2011.11.009

Spohn, C., Piper, R. K., Martin, T., & Frenzel, E. D. (2001). Drug courts and recidivism: The
    results of an evaluation using two comparison groups and multiple indicators of
    recidivism. *Journal of Drug Issues, 31*(1), 149–176.

Steffensmeier, D., Ulmer, J., & Kramer, J. (1998). The interaction of race, gender, and age in
    criminal sentencing: The punishment cost of being young, black, and male. *Criminology,*

FIGURE A-B.6   Sample APA-Style References Page

TABLE A-B.5 Basic Rules of Citation

Source Material	In-Text Citation	Quotation Marks	Block Quotation
Any idea or other information that comes from outside your own head, which is expressed entirely in your own words and sentence structure	X		
Any idea or other information that comes from outside your own head, which is expressed partially or entirely in the source's own words and sentence structure—the quoted language is fewer than 40 words	X	X	
Any idea or other information that comes from outside your own head, which is expressed partially or entirely in the source's own words and sentence structure—the quoted language is 40 or more words	X		X

Citing When Writing in Your Own Words

Most of the time, student writers are citing one source at a time. The required elements of such a citation are the author's last names and source's publication year. When the author is a group or organization instead of individuals, then the group name replaces author last names. The in-text citation is part of the sentence, which means the period goes after the in-text citation. Table A-B.6 provides examples.

TABLE A-B.6 APA-Style In-Text Citations—Single Source

Situation	In the Text		In Parentheses	
	First Mention	*Subsequent Mentions*	*First Mention*	*Subsequent Mentions*
One author	Shaffer (2011) . . .	Shaffer (2011) . . .	. . . (Shaffer, 2011).	. . . (Shaffer, 2011).
Two authors	Hartley and Phillips (2001) . . .	Hartley and Phillips (2001) . . .	. . . (Hartley & Phillips, 2001).	. . . (Hartley & Phillips, 2001).
Three to five authors	Spohn, Piper, Martin, and Frenzel (2001) . . .	Spohn et al. (2001) . . .	. . . (Spohn, Piper, Martin, & Frenzel, 2001).	. . . (Spohn et al., 2001).
Six or more authors	Green et al. (2007) . . .	Green et al. (2007) . . .	. . . (Green et al., 2007).	. . . (Green et al., 2007).
Group author— Common abbreviation for the group	Office of Juvenile Justice and Delinquency Prevention (OJJDP, 2008) . . .	OJJDP (2008) . . .	. . . (Office of Juvenile Justice and Delinquency Prevention [OJJDP], 2008).	. . . (OJJDP, 2008).
Group author— No common abbreviation for the group	The Sentencing Project (2005) . . .	The Sentencing Project (2005) . . .	. . . (The Sentencing Project, 2005).	. . . (The Sentencing Project, 2005).
No author identified*	The article, "State Drug Court Conference" (2017), . . .	The article, "State Drug Court Conference" (2017), . . .	. . . ("State Drug Court Conference," 2017).	. . . ("State Drug Court Conference," 2017).

*"State Drug Court Conference" is a shortened version of an article appearing in a newsletter for which no author was identified.

TABLE A-B.7   APA-Style In-Text Citations—Multiple Sources

Situation	In the Text	In Parentheses
Same author(s), different publication year	Belenko (1998, 2011) . . .	. . . (Belenko, 1998, 2011).
Same author(s), same publication year	Belenko (2002a, 2002b) . . .	. . . (Belenko, 2002a, 2002b).
Different authors	Belenko (1998) and Wolfe (2004) . . .	. . . (Belenko, 1998; Wolfe, 2004).

Where Table A-B.6 shows how to cite a single source, Table A-B.7 shows how to cite multiple sources at the same time. Citing multiple sources is an effective way to demonstrate agreement on some point. The rules for first mention versus subsequent mentions are the same as with one author, so I will not continue to distinguish between these situations. More important to the issue of multiple sources in one citation, however, is whether the sources are by the same or different authors and the order in which to list the sources.

When you have more than one work by the same author published in the same year, determine which one is "a," which one is "b," and so on by using alphabetical order with the title of the work. The source labeled "a" is the one that comes before the source labeled "b" when using alphabetical order. It will be important to use this same system in the References list. Likewise, when citing more than one work by different authors, list the sources in alphabetical order according to the first authors' last names.

Citing When Quoting Fewer Than 40 Source Words

The key difference in APA formatting for a direct quote versus when you write in your own words and sentence structure is the addition of page numbers for direct quotes. If the page number is not available, try to cite some other indicator of the quoted material's location (e.g., paragraph or chapter number). Exact language from a source must be enclosed in *double* quotation marks. Use *single* quotation marks to indicate a quote within a quote. Providing only an in-text citation when you use a source's exact words is plagiarism because an in-text citation identifies the source of information; quotation marks indicate the source's language. Thus, failing to enclose the quote in quotation marks means you are claiming to be the author of those words. Table A-B.8 provides examples of in-text citations for direct quotations.

Citing When Quoting 40 or More Source Words

Longer quotes—quotes of 40 or more words—are formatted differently than shorter quotes. First, shorter quotes are placed within double quotation marks, while longer quotes are set off in block quotation format. As illustrated in Figure A-B.7, block quotation format means creating a new paragraph for the quote and indenting the quoted paragraph

TABLE A-B.8   APA-Style In-Text Citations—Short Quotes

In the Text	In Parentheses
Mitchell, Wilson, Eggers, and MacKenzie (2012) asked, "Why are juvenile drug courts less effective than other kinds of drug courts?" (p. 60).	Previous researchers have asked, "Why are juvenile drug courts less effective than other kinds of drug courts?" (Mitchell, Wilson, Eggers, & MacKenzie, 2012, p. 60).

Ultimately, Lowenkamp, Holsinger, and Latessa (2005) determined:

> Overall, this research indicates that drug courts provide a very modest reduction in recidivism at present. This reduction is compromised by programs that fail to target high-risk offenders.... These conclusions must be tempered by the small number of analyses included in this research and the fact that the quality of the research on drug court programs is, overall, of poor methodological quality. (p. 11)

FIGURE A-B.7 APA-Style In-text Citation–Long Quotes

½ inch on both the right and the left side. Second, where single quotation marks are used to indicate a quote within a quote for shorter quotations, double quotation marks are used to indicate a quote within a quote for longer quotations. And third, in shorter quotes, the in-text citation is treated as part of the sentence, and thus the period or other terminal point goes *after* the in-text citation. But in longer quotes, the in-text citation is not part of the sentence, and therefore the ending mark goes *before* the in-text citation.

Citing Statistics
Statistics are a special circumstance that requires treatment somewhere between how you cite source material expressed in your own words and how you cite quoted material. If a study documents a precise quantity—say, 62 percent of parolees or 20 percent of defendants—and you want to include that statistic in your paper, then you must provide the page number for the statistic (or some other indicator of the statistic's location in the source, such as paragraph or table number). Do not use quotation marks when it is only the statistic you are including in your paper.

References
Other than personal communications, every source cited in the text must have a corresponding Reference list entry. In-text citations should provide the same information as the References: author name(s) and publication year. The information provided for each source must not only be complete, but it should be consistently formatted using correct APA style. If you cannot find all the information necessary to make an entry complete, then you probably do not have enough information to determine that the source is credible; in this case, reconsider using the source. Especially if you can identify neither the author nor the publisher, you are unlikely to have sufficient information by which to verify that a source is credible.

Note from the outset that no less bibliographic information should be provided for sources found online than for sources found in hard copy. If anything, more information should be provided for sources located online: URL or digital object identifier (doi). This is true for all types of sources: journal articles, books, government reports, newspaper and magazine articles, and so on.

An important step in proper APA formatting of the References is recognizing the type of source you are citing. This is because different formats are used for different types of sources. Thus, after addressing the overall structure of an APA-style References list, the remainder of this chapter covers how to format entries for the types of information sources commonly used in criminal justice communications.

Overall Structure

Sources should be listed in alphabetical order according to the last name of the first author. If the same author(s) has multiple sources published in different years, then list them from the earliest to the most recent publication year. If the same author(s) has multiple sources published in the same year, assign each of these sources a lowercase letter (i.e., "a" for the first source, "b" for the second source), placing the letter directly after the publication year, and then arrange these sources in alphabetical order according to the title of the work; for example, 2007a, 2007b, and so on. Use the same lettering system for the in-text citations as in the References list.

Remember to use a hanging indent for all Reference-list entries, such that the first line for each entry is flush left, while each subsequent line for an entry is indented ½ inch. Also keep in mind that everything in the References should be in 12-point, black, Times New Roman font. Thus, whenever you enter a URL or doi, you will need to remove any hyperlink formatting (i.e., color and underlining).

Journal Articles

The required bibliographic elements for a journal article are

1. Author name(s)
2. Publication year
3. Article title
4. Journal title
5. Volume number
6. Issue number (only for journals that are newly paginated for each issue)
7. Page range
8. doi or URL (unless hard copy)

Table A-B.9 shows proper APA-style formatting of journal articles. If the author is an organization rather than an individual (or set of individuals), then use the organization's full name similar to how it is used in the in-text citation.

Sometimes, the version of a journal article you are looking at will not contain all the required bibliographic information. When this happens, conduct an Internet search to look up the rest of the information. One of the best places to find this information is the journal's website. Copy and paste the journal name into your browser. Once you are at the journal's homepage, you can usually search by year/volume and then issue number to find a particular article. You should be able to see the full bibliographic information even if the article itself is not available (for free) on the journal website. This is probably the most effective and efficient option, but it might not always work. Do not just give up and report

TABLE A-B.9   **APA-Style References—Journal Articles**

Situation	Example of Proper Formatting
Single author	Shaffer, D. K. (2011). Looking inside the black box of drug courts: A meta-analytic review. *Justice Quarterly, 28*(3), 493–521. doi:10.1080/07418825.2010.525222
Two authors	Hartley, R. E., & Phillips, R. C. (2001). Who graduates from drug courts? Correlates of client success. *American Journal of Criminal Justice, 26*(1), 107–119. doi:10.1007/BF02886860
Three to seven authors	Gottfredson, D. C., Najaka, S. C., & Kearley, B. (2003). Effectiveness of drug treatment courts: Evidence from a randomized trial. *Criminology & Public Policy, 2*(2), 171–196. doi:10.1111/j.1745-9133.2003.tb00117.x
Eight or more authors	Matusow, H., Dickman, S. L., Rich, J. D., Fong, C., Dumont, D. M., Hardin, C., . . . Rosenblum, A. (2013). Medication-assisted treatment in U.S. drug courts: Results from a nationwide survey of availability, barriers, and attitudes. *Journal of Substance Abuse Treatment, 44*(5), 473–480. doi:10.1016/j.jsat.2012.10.004

incomplete bibliographic information; instead, keep trying. You could use a library database, such as ProQuest or Academic Search Premier, to try looking up the article. Journal articles downloaded from these library databases often have a cover sheet with full bibliographic information. Another strategy is to copy and paste the journal article title into your web browser, and try to find another publication that cites it so you can get the information from that source's References. This last strategy should be used as a last resort, because it is possible for this material to be incorrectly cited in another source.

Books and Book Chapters

We will need to treat separately entire books versus edited books. With an *entire book*, there is one author (or one set of authors): One person (or one set of people) wrote all of the book's chapters. The required bibliographic elements for an entire book written by one author or set of authors are

1. Author name(s)
2. Publication year
3. Book title
4. Edition number and/or volume number (as applicable)
5. Publisher location: City, State
6. Publisher name

But with an *edited book*, there are different authors: Different people wrote different chapters in the book. The required bibliographic elements for an edited book with chapters written by different authors are

1. Chapter author name(s)
2. Publication year
3. Chapter title
4. Book editors' name(s)
5. Boot title
6. Edition number and/or volume number (as applicable)
7. Page range
8. Publisher location: City, State
9. Publisher name

TABLE A-B.10   APA-Style References—Books and Chapters in Books

Situation	Example of Proper Formatting
Book written entirely by one set of authors	Inciardi, J. A., McBride, D. C., & Rivers, J. E. (1996). *Drug control and the courts.* Thousand Oaks, CA: Sage Publications, Inc.
Chapter in an edited book	McColl, W. D. (2002). Theory and practice in the Baltimore City Drug Treatment Court. In J. L. Nolan Jr. (Ed.), *Drug courts: In theory and in practice* (pp. 3–26). Hawthorne, NY: Aldine de Gruyter.
Book with multiple editions	Melton, G. B., Petrila, J., Poythress, N. G., & Slobogin, C. (2007). *Psychological evaluations for the courts: A handbook for mental health professionals and lawyers* (3rd ed.). New York, NY: The Guilford Press.
Book with separate volumes	Petko, J. T. (2017). The professionals and procedures involved in drug courts. In P. S. Lassiter & T. J. Buser (Eds.), *Annual review of addictions and offender counseling: Best practices* (Vol. 3, pp. 79–96). Eugene, OR: Resource Publications.

Table A-B.10 provides some examples of how to format books and book chapters.

Government Reports

The general rule is to provide the same bibliographic elements in the same order for government reports as for hard copies of entire books, with the addition of any number assigned to the report. In practice, however, formatting of government reports differs widely. For example, we usually access government reports online, which means we will need to add the URL. Government reports often have organizations as authors, which means we do not need to list the publisher toward the end of the entry if it is already been listed as the author (see this difference in Table A-B.11). The required bibliographic elements for government reports are

1. Author name
2. Publication year (and month if an issue brief)
3. Report title
4. Report number (if one has been assigned)
5. Publisher name (unless listed as the author)
6. URL

TABLE A-B.11   APA-Style References—Government Reports

Situation	Example of Proper Formatting
People as authors	Morgan, R. E., & Kena, G. (2017). *Criminal victimization, 2016* (NCJ 251150). Retrieved from Bureau of Justice Statistics website: http://www.bjs.gov/index.cfm?ty=pbdetail&iid=6166
Organization as authors	U.S. Department of Justice, Office of Justice Programs, Office of Juvenile Justice and Delinquency Prevention. (2016). *Juvenile drug treatment court guidelines* (NCJ 250368). Retrieved from https://www.ojjdp.gov/pubs/250368.pdf
Issue brief	U.S. Executive Office of the President, Council of Economic Advisers. (2015, December). *Fines, fees, and bail: Payments in the criminal justice system that disproportionately impact the poor* (Issue Brief No. 031394). Retrieved from https://obamawhitehouse.archives.gov/sites/default/files/page/files/1215_cea_fine_fee_bail_issue_brief.pdf

TABLE A-B.12   APA-Style References—Newspaper and Magazine Articles

Situation	Example of Proper Formatting
Newspaper article	Hoffman, J. (2018, June 4). She went to jail for a drug relapse. Tough love or too harsh? *New York Times*. Retrieved from https://www.nytimes.com/2018/06/04/health/drug-addict-relapse-opioids.html
Newsletter article	State drug court conference held in Little Rock. (2017, July). *The Line*. Retrieved from https://courts.arkansas.gov/sites/default/files/tree/The%20Line%20Summer2017.pdf

News Articles
For online newspaper articles, the required bibliographic elements are

1. Author name(s)
2. Publication year, month, and date
3. Article title
4. Newspaper title
5. URL

If your source is a *hard copy* newspaper article, then you would replace the URL with the page number(s). Table A-B.12 shows how to format these entries both when an author is identified and when no author is identified for the article.

Legal Documents
Legal documents are addressed separately from other information sources because APA style follows *Bluebook* style for the citation of legal materials. More specifically, the *APA Manual* advises its writers to consult the latest edition of *The Bluebook: A Uniform System of Citation* for guidance on how to cite court decisions (*Bluebook* Rule 10), statutes (*Bluebook* Rule 12), legislative materials (*Bluebook* Rule 13), and administrative and executive materials (*Bluebook* Rule 14). Table A-B.13 therefore provides just a few examples of proper formatting for some common types of legal documents.

CLOSING APA ADVICE
Here are some things to keep in mind if you are assigned to write an APA-style paper:

- Buy a copy of the APA Manual. And if you cite many legal documents, then also buy a copy of the *Bluebook*. Keep these books at least throughout your college career.
- Read the paper instructions carefully, noting any deviations from APA style your professor requires. Some professors, for example, might tell you to omit an author note on the first page or to add a table of contents after the abstract page.
- Before you use any programs, websites, or settings to do your APA formatting for you, ask your professor if that is acceptable. If part of your assignment is to learn APA style and demonstrate that you can use it correctly and consistently, then it might be considered cheating if you do not do all your own APA formatting.
- Collect full bibliographic information for each source as you go. Do not wait until your paper is completely written to start looking for the required bibliographic

TABLE A-B.13 APA-Style In-Text Citations and References—Legal Documents

Situation	Example of Proper Formatting	
	In the Text	*In the References*
Court decision	*Lessard v. Schmidt* (1972) . . . . . . (*Lessard v. Schmidt*, 1972).	Lessard v. Schmidt, 349 F. Supp. 1078 (E.D. Wis. 1972).
Court decision, appealed case	*Durflinger v. Artiles* (1981/1984) . . . . . . (*Durflinger v. Artiles*, 1981/1984).	Durflinger v. Artiles, 563 F. Supp. 322 (D. Kan. 1981), *aff'd*, 727 F.2d 888 (10th Cir. 1984).
Statute	Mental Health Systems Act (1988) . . . Mental Health Systems Act of 1988 . . . . . . (Mental Health Systems Act, 1988).	Mental Health Systems Act, 42 U.S.C. § 9401 (1988).
Enacted federal bill or resolution	Senate Resolution 107 (1993) . . . (S. Res. 107, 1993).	S. Res. 107, 103d Cong., 139 Cong. Rec. 5826 (1993) (enacted).
Federal report or document	Senate Report No. 102-114 (1991) . . . . . . (S. Rep. No. 102-114, 1991).	S. Rep. No. 102-114, at 7 (1991).
Federal regulation	FDA Prescription Drug Advertising Rule (2006) . . . . . . (FDA Prescription Drug Advertising Rule, 2006).	FDA Prescription Drug Advertising Rule, 21 C.F.R. § 202.1 (2006).
Executive order	Executive Order No. 11,609 (1994) . . . . . . (Executive Order No. 11,609, 1994).	Exec. Order No. 11,609, 3 C.F.R. 586 (1971–1975), *reprinted as amended in* 3 U.S.C. 301 app. at 404-07 (1994).

Source: APA (2010, Appendix 7.1)

elements. This means you need to pay attention to each type of source you are using so that you know what bibliographic information you will need to include.

- Do not trust other sources to tell you what proper APA style is. Sources other than the APA manual itself might be wrong; therefore, using them could lead to you having incorrect APA-style formatting in your paper.
- Give yourself time to proofread and edit for correct and consistent APA style. Keep in mind that APA style concerns both the contents of a paper (e.g., abstract, running head) and how that content is formatted (e.g., spacing, heading structure).
- Do not assume that because you think APA formatting is unimportant, your professor thinks APA formatting is trivial. Some professors take APA formatting more seriously than others. Publishers also take APA seriously. Publication may be delayed, for example, until APA formatting is correct.

REFERENCES

American Psychological Association (APA). (2010). *Publication manual of the American Psychological Association* (6th ed.). Washington, DC: Author.

Editing

I've found the best way to revise your own work is to pretend that somebody else wrote it and then to rip the living shit out of it.

—DON RUFF

This chapter presents methods for effectively and efficiently editing criminal justice communications. In its broadest sense, **editing** is the process of reviewing, revising, and refining information to enhance its understandability and impact. In criminal justice and other technical communications, editing often revolves around enhancing clarity, condensing material, and ensuring correctness. Overall, this means that, when we edit, we are maximizing the comprehensibility and credibility of our communications—we are moving beyond acceptable to compelling.

Editing does not always receive the attention it deserves. Some people believe they are strong enough writers without needing to edit. Other people simply run out of time and do not have the opportunity to edit. While time constraints are a real challenge, this textbook takes the firm position that there is no such thing as writing that is so strong that it could not possibly be improved by editing. The mere idea that a communication is perfect prior to editing might be as ludicrous as the notion that an athlete is so good that s/he could not possibly benefit from any more practice prior to the next tournament. Like athletes, writers can always become better. Editing, then, is as vital to successful communication as practice is to successful competition.

The rest of this chapter will present approaches and stages for editing effectively and efficiently. The strategies covered here primarily pertain to written communications, particularly various types of research papers written for courses and/or publication. That said, much of this chapter's contents apply to oral communications and PowerPoint presentations as well.

STRATEGIES

Here are some ways to maximize the effectiveness and efficiency of editing:

- **Give yourself time.** Editing takes time. Do not assume you are such a good writer that your work cannot be improved with editing. Professional writers take editing and revisions seriously.

- **Sleep on it.** Wait at least until the day after you have finished writing to start editing. Things that made sense when you wrote them might make less sense later. If you have written something over a period of time, you might not realize when you were being repetitious. Step back from your writing, and then reassess it with an open and fresh frame of mind.
- **Concentrate.** Pick a quiet place, minimizing distractions. Turn off the television, for example. Focus on editing; do not try to multitask while editing.
- **Read aloud.** Reading aloud forces you to read slower, which helps you catch smaller errors that you might otherwise miss, such as the wrong word or a missing punctuation mark.
- **Solicit feedback from others.** Ask others to review your drafts. What might seem clear and complete to you could seem unclear and/or incomplete to others who are less involved and/or who have more expertise on the topic. When you get feedback, address it—do not fight it. You are not your audience, so if someone tells you they do not understand, then you have some work to do. You might be wrong, or you might only need to clarify your meaning. But do not ignore or argue with feedback.
- **Do not be afraid to get some critical feedback—and try not to get offended.** Keep in mind that your ultimate goal is to deliver the best possible communication. Others will be impressed that you cared enough to solicit feedback and then took the feedback seriously.
- **Do not resist change.** Try not to become too attached to early drafts or parts of them. You might think a particular sentence sounds particularly eloquent, but perhaps that sentence is more fancy sounding than it is clear or informative. Be open-minded, and approach editing with a dedication to the best product possible instead of making less work for yourself.
- **Edit in stages.** (See below.)

STAGES

Edit in stages, focusing on one issue at a time, rather than by trying to catch and fix everything in a single read-through. Start with the big picture: substantive content. Changes in substance will have a ripple effect, often changing smaller aspects such as writing mechanics and layout. If, for example, you decide that a paragraph does not belong in the paper, then it would have been a waste of time to have edited that paragraph for writing mechanics. Likewise, if the deleted paragraphs had some in-text citations that did not appear elsewhere in the paper, you would have wasted your time formatting those in-text citations and their corresponding References list entries. Thus, efficient editing begins with what the communication says, moves to how the message is said, and ends with how the communication looks.

Stage 1: Purpose and Substance

The primary concerns at this stage of editing are that the communication is responsive to its objective, parameters, and audience and that the substantive content is evidence-based, logical, complete, and correct. Be prepared to make major revisions during this stage, such as conducting additional research to locate more and better sources of evidence, deleting and rewriting entire paragraphs, and adding sections addressing alternative perspectives and contradictory evidence.

Table A-C.1 provides a checklist to use during the first stage of editing. Answer each question truthfully; you would only be wasting your time if you were to answer untruthfully. Avoid glibly answering yes, and—instead—be critical, and take this process seriously. Ask yourself if there is any chance that a reasonable person might answer "no" to any of these questions. Once you have truthfully answered "yes" to these questions, then you will be ready to begin Stage 2.

TABLE A-C.1   Questions to Ask Yourself While Editing—Stage 1

	Responsiveness
1	Does the communication's purpose reflect the purpose of the assignment?
2	Do all of the contents of the communication reflect the purpose?
3	Does the introduction clearly introduce the purpose?
4	Does the introduction describe how the communication will achieve its purpose?
5	Does the middle develop and achieve the purpose?
6	Does the end summarize how the purpose was achieved?
7	Does the communication clearly meet all assignment requirements?
8	Has the communication been tailored to the intended audience(s) in terms of its needs, expectations, knowledge, experience, and uses for the communication?
	Organization
9	Does the communication have a beginning, a middle, and an end?
10	Does the communication have a readily discernible organizational structure?
11	Is the organizational structure the organizational structure that is best suited to achieving the communication's purpose?
	Evidence
12	Is evidence offered to support each claim of fact?
13	Have objective criteria been identified so that each claim of value can be assessed in terms of the evidence offered to support it?
14	Have alternatives and objective criteria been identified so that each claim of policy can be assessed in terms of the evidence offered to support it?
15	Has each piece of evidence been acquired ethically/legally?
16	Is each piece of evidence logically connected to the claim for which it is offered as proof?
17	Is the claim for which each piece of evidence is offered as proof logically connected to the purpose of the communication?
18	Is the source of the evidence competent?
19	Is the evidence believable?
20	Is the evidence really what it is said to be?
21	Is the evidence the best evidence to support the claim?
22	Have primary sources been preferred to secondary sources?
23	Have empirical sources been preferred to nonempirical sources?
24	Have professional and substantive sources been preferred to popular and sensational sources?
25	Has each piece of evidence been introduced?
26	Has any contradictory evidence or claims been addressed?

(Continued)

TABLE A-C.1 *(Continued)*

27	Are acknowledgments made for any limitations associated with pieces of evidence or the total body of evidence?
28	Is there a summary of the evidence and how it supports the communication's main purpose claim?
29	Does the total evidence adequately support the communication's main purpose/claim?
30	On the basis of all the information provided, is the information believable?
	Logic
31	Is there clear coherence across all parts of the communication?
32	Does the paper's title accurately capture the essence of the communication?
33	Does each section's title accurately capture the essence of the section?
34	Are claims logically consistent with other claims, including the purpose and conclusion?
35	Are claims logically consistent with any (explicit or implicit) assumptions?
	Completeness
36	Is all of the relevant information present?
37	Are any gaps in information provided avoided?
38	Have alternative perspectives been identified?
39	Have both sides of controversial issues been presented?
40	Is there balanced coverage of material, including alternative perspectives and opposing sides to controversial issues?
41	Have any constraints in coverage been identified and justified?
42	Are any coverage constraints reasonable?
	Correctness
43	Is all of the information true?
44	Does the communication avoid withholding any true and relevant information?
	Professionalism
45	Is the communication ethical in all regards?
46	Has the communication been produced and presented with integrity?
47	Is it open and honest?
48	Are all sources properly credited?
49	Does it foster a sense of legitimacy?
50	Does it inspire trust?

Stage 2: Fit and Flow

At this stage, the communication's content is pretty well set, but you will consider whether adjustments need to be made to how the information is arranged and how each part of the communication connects to the material before and after it. Table A-C.2 presents a series of questions to guide you through the second stage of editing. As with Stage 1, the goal is to answer "yes" truthfully to each of these questions.

If the communication includes an abstract, keywords, executive summary, and/or table of contents, once you have completed Stage 2 is a good time to make sure these components (a) are present and (b) accurately reflect the purpose, contents, and organizational structure of the communication. When these components are written earlier in the process, they might be vague or inaccurate reflections of the communication as it now stands—especially if you made major revisions during Stage 1 of editing.

TABLE A-C.2 Questions to Ask Yourself While Editing—Stage 2

	Organization
1	Are organizational devices used to help the audience follow along and understand how parts are related to the whole?
2	Is there a clear and logical progression of ideas from beginning to end?
3	Are sections and section headings used effectively to separate major ideas and parts of the communication?
4	If level-1 headings are used, are there at least two level-1 headings (in the paper)?
5	If level-2 headings are used within any level-1 section, are there are least two level-2 headings (in each section with a level-2 heading)?
6	If level-3 headings are used within any level-2 section, are there at least two level-3 headings (in each section with a level-3 heading)?
7	If level-4 headings are used within any level-3 section, are there at least two level-4 headings (in each section with a level-4 heading)?
8	If level-5 headings re used within any level-4 section, are there at least two level-5 headings (in each section with a level-5 heading)?
9	Is each section heading unique?
10	Does each paragraph express one clear idea?
11	Is there a topic sentence for each paragraph that reflects the paragraph's main idea?
12	Are transitions used to connect ideas from paragraph to paragraph and section to section?

Stage 3: Language and Mechanics

Stages 1 and 2 reviewed and revised the entire communication and how each of its parts fits and flows into the rest of the communication. Once the substance and structure of your communication is set, it is time to look at smaller parts of the communication: sentences, phrases, and words. The goal of Stage 3 is to ensure that the language is as professional, correct, clear, and concise as can be. Accordingly, Table A-C.3 presents questions to ask yourself about writing mechanics and style. Once you have truthfully answered "yes" to all questions in Table A-C.3, it will be time to move on to the fourth and final stage of editing.

It can be difficult to remember and apply consistently all the rules regarding proper grammar, spelling, and punctuation. Rules on when to capitalize or to write out numbers are not always intuitive. To refresh your memory, try to review Chapter 8 in this book, the relevant chapters in the American Psychological Association manual (APA, 2010), or some other authoritative text on writing mechanics before you begin Stage 3 of editing. As you edit, whenever you encounter a situation where the rule is unclear, consult the chosen text, and then make a note of how you handled the situation. Should you encounter the same or a similar situation later in your editing, you will be able to look back on your notes and repeat what you did before, thereby ensuring consistency within the communication.

Stage 4: Layout and Documentation

The last editing stage is when we apply the finishing touches—making sure the communication has the right look and conforms to any style/formatting requirements. In this section as elsewhere in this text, we will follow APA style. Table A-C.4 presents the last

TABLE A-C.3 Questions to Ask Yourself While Editing—Stage 3

	Correctness
1	Are all sentences complete?
2	Is there subject–verb agreement?
3	Are verb tenses logical and consistent?
4	Are modifiers placed as close as possible to the term they modify?
5	Is there parallel construction?
6	Are words properly and consistently capitalized?
7	Are words properly and consistently italicized?
8	Are numbers presented properly and consistently?
9	Has the right word been used in every occasion?
10	Have hyphens and en dashes been used properly and consistently?
11	Have plural and possessive forms of nouns and pronouns been presented properly and consistently?
12	Has each abbreviation been defined upon its first use?
13	Have abbreviations been introduced only for terms used at least three times?
14	Once defined, has each abbreviation been used consistently thereafter?
15	Have terminal points—periods, question marks, and exclamation points—been used properly and consistently?
16	Have pausing points—commas, semicolons, colons, and em dashes—been used properly and consistently?
17	Have quotation points—double quotation marks, single quotation marks, ellipses, and brackets—been used properly and consistently?
18	Have other punctuation points—parentheses, brackets, and slashes—been used properly and consistently?
19	Are there two spaces between sentences (per APA)?
20	Is there one space between words and initials?
	Clarity
21	Is the language direct and to the point?
22	Is the word choice precise and concrete rather than vague and abstract?
23	Does the communication avoid ambiguity and equivocation?
24	Is plain language used throughout?
25	Are simple terms used instead of fancy terms?
26	Is specialized language—slang, texting slang—and jargon—avoided?
27	Have outdated expressions been avoided?
28	Do the words and sentences say exactly what you mean?
29	Have euphemisms ben avoided?
30	Have irony, exaggerations, and understatements been avoided?
31	Have idioms been avoided?
	Conciseness
32	Has text been eliminated unless it adds information?
33	Have trite and meaningless statements been avoided?
34	Have rhetorical questions been avoided?
35	Have redundant statements been omitted?

36	Have prepositional phrases been reworded to avoid unnecessary text?
37	Are summaries and paraphrases preferred to direct quotations?
	Professionalism
38	Does the communication exhibit an assertive communication style?
39	Does the communication maintain a professional tone?
40	Is it objective rather than subjective?
41	Is it logical rather than emotional?
42	Is it serious rather than humorous?
43	Is it impersonal rather than intimate?
44	Does the communication maintain professional diction?
45	Does it avoid personal words?
46	Does it write out words instead of using contractions?
47	Does it avoid colloquialisms?
48	Does it avoid loaded terms?

TABLE A-C.4   Questions to Ask Yourself While Editing—Stage 4

	Layout
1	Is the entire document double-spaced, with 1-inch margins on all four sides, left-aligned text, and 0 spacing before and after paragraphs?
2	Is the entire document in 12-point Times New Roman font?
3	Are there page numbers on all pages, beginning with "1" on the title page?
4	Is there a running head on all pages, beginning on the title page?
5	Is the running head set in all caps?
6	Is the running head an abbreviated version of the paper's title?
7	Does the title page contain the paper's title, centered?
8	Does the title page contain the author name(s), centered, directly under the paper's title?
9	Does the title page contain the author affiliation(s), centered, under the author name(s)?
10	Does the title page contain an author note?
11	Is the title page devoid of any other text?
12	Are all contents of the title page in regular font (e.g., no bold)?
13	Does the abstract page follow the title page?
14	Is the abstract page numbered "2"?
15	Does the word "Abstract" appear on the first line, centered, and not on bold?
16	Is the abstract a single paragraph that is not indented?
17	Does a list of keywords appear on the line directly below the abstract?
18	Is the keywords list indented?
19	Is the word "Keywords" capitalized, italicized, and followed by a colon?
20	Does the text begin on the page following the abstract page?
21	Is the first page of text numbered "3"?
22	Does the paper's title appear on the first line of the first page of text, centered, in title case, and not in bold?

(Continued)

TABLE A-C.4 *(Continued)*

23	Does the paper's title on the first page of text repeat exactly the paper's title as presented on the title page?
24	Does the first paragraph of text begin directly under the paper's title on the first page of text, without the section heading "Introduction"?
25	Is each new paragraph indented ½ inch?
26	Are blank line spaces omitted between paragraphs and sections?
27	If level-1 headings are used, are they centered, bold, and in title case?
28	If level-2 headings are used, are they left-aligned, bold, and in title case?
29	If level-3 headings are used, are they indented, bold, in sentence case, ended with a period, and followed directly (on the same line) with the start of paragraph text?
30	If level-4 headings are used, are they indented, bold, italicized, in sentence case, ended with a period, and followed directly (on the same line) with the start of paragraph text?
31	If level-5 headings are used, are they indented, italicized, in sentence case, ended with a period, and followed directly (on the same line) with the start of paragraph text?
32	Does the References page begin on the page following the last page of text?
33	Do the page numbers continue from the last page of text through the References?
34	Does the word "References" appear at the top of the References page, centered, and not in bold?
35	Is there still double-spacing and 0 spacing before and after paragraphs throughout the References?
36	Has a hanging indent been used for every Reference-list entry?
37	Has hyperlink formatting been removed throughout the References?
	Documentation
38	Are all sources of ideas/information accompanied by an in-text citation?
39	Are all quotes of less than 40 words enclosed in quotation marks and accompanied by an in-text citation that includes the page number(s) of the quote and is followed by a period?
40	Are all quotes of 40 or more words set off in block quotation format and accompanied by an in-text citation that includes the page number(s) of the quote and is preceded by a period?
41	Are in-text citations correctly and consistently formatted?
42	Is there a Reference-list entry for every in-text citation?
43	Are the References devoid of any entries that are not cited in the text?
44	Is the information provided in the References consistent with the information provided in the in-text citations (e.g., spelling of names, publication year)?
45	Does each Reference list entry contain all the required bibliographic elements?
46	Are the Reference list entries correctly and consistently formatted?

set of questions to ask yourself while editing. Once you have truthfully answered "yes" to all of these questions, then you are done and ready to deliver.

As with Stage 3, APA format is detailed and not easy for most people to remember. It is unlikely that anyone whose job is not copyediting would be able to complete Stage 4 properly without consulting the APA manual. Thus, when you check the paper's layout, have an APA template directly in front of you so you can compare your paper to the template. Proceed one page at a time, beginning with the title page and ending with the References page. In addition to confirming that the required parts are all present and in the right places, look at elements like spacing, font, capitalization, italics, and bold.

Likewise, when you review in-text citations, have examples of proper APA formatting in front of you. Compare the examples side by side with your in-text citations, looking not only at whether all the required information is there and in the right places, but also elements like spacing, punctuation, and abbreviations (esp. "et al." and "&" versus "and"). Look at one type of source at a time rather than reviewing the sources in the order in which they appear; for example, check all the in-text citations for journal articles first, book chapters second, and so forth. And then do the same with the References as with the in-text citations: Use a template, and then review your work one type of source at a time. Pay attention to what information is provided, what order that information appears, and how that information is formatted (e.g., capitalization, italics, spacing, punctuation).

REFERENCES

American Psychological Association (APA). (2010). *Publication manual of the American Psychological Association* (6th ed.). Washington, DC: Author.

GLOSSARY

5WH QUESTIONS Questions that ask a person what, when, where, who, why, and how. (Chapter 1)

A

ABSTRACT A concise summary of an article's purpose, methods, and conclusion. (Chapter 10)

AFFIDAVIT A written statement of facts made under oath. (Chapter 6)

ANNOTATED BIBLIOGRAPHY A References list with a brief summary for each source. (Chapter 1)

ARGUMENT The fusion of claims, evidence, and inference used to reach a conclusion. (Chapter 5)

ARREST REPORT A police officer's official documentation of an arrest. (Chapter 8)

ASSERTION–EVIDENCE STYLE With PowerPoint, the content slide style wherein the title is an assertion and the content (usually graphic) is evidence supporting that assertion. (Chapter 11)

ASSERTIVE COMMUNICATION STYLE The communication style that involves being forthright about your purpose without being antagonistic or evasive. (Chapter 2)

ASSUMPTIONS Beliefs taken to be true that can influence an argument but often remain unstated. (Chapter 5)

B

BLUF The format of a communication that is arranged with the "bottom line up front." (Chapter 4)

BREADTH In communication, the range or extent of a topic. (Chapter 7)

BURDEN OF PROOF The obligation to provide evidence to prove (substantiate) what is being asserted. (Chapter 6)

C

CHEATING As it pertains to academic dishonesty, the giving or getting of unauthorized assistance in the completion of graded work. (Chapter 2)

CIRCUMSTANTIAL EVIDENCE Evidence (proof) that substantiates some fact indirectly. (Chapter 6)

CLAIM A contention; an arguable assertion of fact (this is), value (this is better), or policy (this is what we should do). (Chapter 5)

CLAIM OF FACT An assertion that a condition has (or has not) existed, exists (or does not exist), or will exist (or will not exist). (Chapter 6)

CLAIM OF POLICY An assertion that some condition should (or should not) exist. (Chapter 6)

CLAIM OF VALUE An assertion that one condition is better than another (or other) conditions. (Chapter 6)

CLARITY The characteristic of a communication that is straightforward, unambiguous, and therefore able to be understood. (Chapters 1 and 9)

COLLOQUIALISMS Informal expressions, such as "have a good one" and "no problem." (Chapter 2)

COMPELLING Powerful. (Chapter 1)

COMPETENCE Substantive knowledge and technical skills necessary for doing well what needs to be done. (Chapter 5)

COMPLETENESS The characteristic of a communication that is thorough, containing all pertinent parts and information. (Chapters 1 and 7)

COMPLETE SENTENCE A statement that expresses one complete thought and has a subject and verb. (Chapter 8)

COMPOUND TRANSITION A combination of two or more transitional (idea-linking) terms to create a single transitional phrase. (Chapter 4)

CONCISENESS The characteristic of a communication that uses as few simple words as possible to make a point. (Chapters 1 and 10)

CONTRACTIONS Multiple words joined together with an apostrophe and by abbreviating one of the words. (Chapter 2)

CORRECTNESS The characteristic of a communication that is free from error in terms of both the truth/accuracy of the information itself and the proper presentation of the information. (Chapters 1 and 8)

COVER LETTER A letter written by an applicant to the organization to which one is applying to, which expresses the applicant's interest in and suitability for a job. (Chapter 2)

COVERAGE STATEMENT A way of stating a communication's objective that identifies the topic and gives the audience a sense of the breadth or depth in which the topic will be covered. (Chapter 3)

CREDIBILITY Believability; inspiring trust and confidence. (Chapter 1)

CRIME SCENE REPORT A document describing a crime scene in detail. (Chapter 7)

CRIMINAL EVIDENCE Proof of or relating to law-breaking behavior. (Chapter 6)

CRITICAL THINKING Conscious reflection that leads us to base beliefs on a fair and logical assessment of available information. (Chapter 5)

CRITIQUE A critical analysis and assessment of a communication. (Chapter 8)

D

DATA VISUALIZATION A way of presenting data visually that maximizes audience cognition. (Chapter 11)

DEDUCTIVE LOGIC Reasoning from general principles (premises) to a more specific conclusion. (Chapter 5)

DEFINING CLAUSE An essential part of a sentence, such that removing it would alter the meaning of the sentence. (Chapter 8)

DEMONSTRATIVE EVIDENCE Evidence (proof) that serves as a substitute for real evidence; it is some representation of real evidence. (Chapter 6)

DEPTH In communication, level of detail and specificity. (Chapter 7)

DESIGN The way we make some object appear in an attempt to make it more appealing or effective (Chapter 11)

DICTION Word choice. (Chapter 2)

DIMINISHING RETURNS The point at which each additional study both requires more effort to locate and adds little or no new knowledge. (Appendix A)

DIRECT To the point. (Chapter 9)

DIRECT EVIDENCE Evidence (proof) that, on its own, substantiates some fact directly and with a great deal of confidence. (Chapter 6)

DISCUSSION FORUM A virtual (Internet) message board, where users can submit a message and read and reply to other peoples' messages. (Chapter 9)

DOCUMENTARY EVIDENCE Evidence (proof) written, typed, or otherwise compiled by people. (Chapter 6)

DOCUMENTATION The proper identification and formatting of the sources of ideas, words, and other information, especially as it concerns in-text citations and References. (Appendix B)

DOUBLE-BARRELED QUESTION A question containing two separate questions. (Chapter 9)

DOUBLE NEGATIVE Two negative terms in the same sentence. (Chapter 9)

E

EDITING Broadly, the process of reviewing, revising, and refining information to enhance its understandability and impact. (Appendix C)

EMPIRICAL RESEARCH Research (a purposeful, systematic investigation designed to increase knowledge) that is based on unique observations of the real world. (Chapter 6)

EQUIVOCATING Deliberately being ambiguous and evasive in an effort to avoid telling the truth, alienating audiences, making a commitment, and/or eliciting censure. (Chapter 9)

ESSAY TOPIC The general subject matter to which an essay question pertains. (Chapter 3)

ESSAY VERB The word or phrase in an essay question that specifies the objective in drafting the response. (Chapter 3)

ETHICAL CODES OF CONDUCT Rules for ethical decision-making and behavior prescribed by organizations for members to follow. (Chapter 2)

ETHICAL DILEMMA A choice between options having moral implications. (Chapter 2)

ETHICS Moral standards governing decisions and actions. (Chapter 2)

EUPHEMISM A delicate way of expressing something; a way of saying something without actually having to come right out and say it. (Chapter 9)

EVIDENCE Proof; that which is used to justify a claim. (Chapters 1, 5, and 6)

EXPERT WITNESSES People who have some professional, specialized knowledge relevant to the disposition of a case. (Chapter 6)

EXPERT WITNESS TESTIMONY The courtroom testimony of an expert witness. (Chapter 9)

F

FIGURATIVE Metaphorical, or departing from literal, such that the words used take on a meaning other than their literal definition. (Chapter 9)

FILLER Any word or group of words that has no real meaning; they take up space without adding any information. (Chapter 10)

H

HALF-TRUTH A statement known or believed to be only partially true or to be a combination of truth and falsehood. (Chapter 8)

HANGING INDENT A form of paragraph formatting that involves leaving the first line flush left and then indenting all subsequent lines. (Appendix B)

HEDGING Using qualifiers in an appropriate way to indicate uncertainty. (Chapter 9)

HIGH CONTRAST Easily distinguished because the light color is very light and the dark color is very dark. (Chapter 11)

HOMOPHONES Words that sound the same but have different spellings and meanings. (Chapter 8)

HYPERBOLE An exaggeration intended to emphasize and/or be funny. (Chapter 9)

I

IDIOM A collection of words that, taken together, means something other than what the individual words mean. (Chapter 9)

INAPPROPRIATE PARAPHRASING Making only superficial alterations—substituting some words for others, reorganizing the order of words in a sentence, or putting sentences in a different order than the source text—and then giving the source credit for the idea by including a citation but claiming the words as your own by omitting quotation marks. (Chapter 2).

INDUCTIVE LOGIC Reasoning from specific observations (evidence) to a more general conclusion. (Chapter 5)

INFERENCE The logical connection between the different pieces of an argument; the reasoning we do to get from one piece of the argument to the next piece. (Chapter 5)

INFORMATIVE COMMUNICATIONS A purpose of communication that imparts information with the main goal of rendering the audience (more) knowledgeable about the topic. (Chapter 3)

INTELLIGENCE BRIEFING A formal written or oral communication that suggests a specific course of action based on the analysis of data. (Chapter 4)

INTERROGATION The police questioning of a crime suspect. (Chapter 1)

INTERVIEW The police questioning of a person who is not a crime suspect. (Chapter 1)

IRONIC Using words that mean something other than, perhaps even opposite to, what we actually say. (Chapter 9)

INTEGRITY The characteristic of people who hold moral principles that are reflected in their words and behavior. (Chapter 2)

J

JARGON Highly specialized language, such as that used in a particular discipline or profession. (Chapter 9)

JUDICIAL NOTICE A conclusion reached on some basis other than the formal, legal evidentiary process. (Chapter 6)

K

KNOWLEDGE A justified true belief. (Chapter 8)

L

LAB REPORT A formal account of an experiment or some other procedure used to obtain results. (Chapter 7)

LAY WITNESSES People who have some personal knowledge relevant to a case. (Chapter 6)

LAYERED TRANSITIONING A combination of two or more transitional (idea-linking) structures to distinguish between lines of thought or between major and minor elements. (Chapter 4)

LITERAL According to the exact meaning of words. (Chapter 9)

LITERATURE REVIEW A presentation of the existing research on a phenomenon so as to demonstrate logically patterns in findings, theory, and/or methods. (Appendix A)

LITOTES An understatement intended to emphasize and/or be funny. (Chapter 9)

LOADED TERMS Words or phrases with a positive or negative connotation. (Chapter 2)

LOGIC The reasoning process used to reach a conclusion. (Chapters 1 and 5)

LOGICAL FALLACY An error in reasoning. (Chapter 5)

LOGICAL PARADOX An irrational situation involving contradictory, or logically incompatible, beliefs. (Chapter 5)

LYING Fabrications, misrepresentations, and omissions of material facts. (Chapter 2)

M

MODULAR DESIGN A way of formatting a communication that breaks down the communication into separate parts tailored to different audiences. (Chapter 3)

MOSAIC PLAGIARISM Making only superficial alterations—substituting some words for others, reorganizing the order of words in a sentence, or putting sentences in a different order than the source text—and then claiming both the idea and the words as your own by omitting a citation. (Chapter 2)

N

NEGATIVE CONSTRUCTION A sentence structure that expresses something contrary to fact. (Chapter 9)

NONDEFINING CLAUSE Information that is not essential to a sentence, such that removing it would not alter the meaning of the sentence. (Chapter 8)

NONEMPIRICAL RESEARCH Research (a purposeful, systematic investigation designed to increase knowledge) that is *not* based on unique observations of the real world; it is based on information that already exists. (Chapter 6)

O

ORGANIZATION The characteristic of a communication that has been arranged in the manner most likely to achieve its objective; the process of planning and arranging information in the manner most likely to achieve our objective. (Chapters 1 and 4)

ORGANIZATIONAL DEVICE A signal to the audience about how some information fits into, or advances, the overall communication. (Chapter 4)

ORGANIZATIONAL STRUCTURE A method for arranging information in a communication. (Chapter 4)

ORIGINAL POST A discussion forum post that responds directly to the assignment prompt without drawing from or referencing any other posts. (Chapter 9)

P

PARAPHRASE Source material relayed in our own words and sentence structure, using approximately the same amount of space to convey the source's idea accurately. (Chapter 10)

PAUSING POINTS Punctuation marks that go in the middle of a sentence to signal a halt and achieve clarity: comma, semicolon, colon, and em dash. (Chapter 8)

PEER REVIEW The process whereby subject matter and/or methodological experts in the field review a paper for strengths and weaknesses, screening out flawed studies so that only the strongest studies are published. (Chapter 6)

PERFORMANCE REVIEWS Written assessments, often conducted annually, by supervisors of an employee's performance in meeting job expectations. (Chapter 2)

PERSONAL WORDS Personal pronouns, such as I, me, you, we, and ours. (Chapter 2)

PERSUASIVE COMMUNICATIONS A purpose of communication that imparts information with the main goal of influencing the audience's beliefs, attitudes, and/or actions. (Chapter 3)

PERSUASIVE PAPER A formal written communication that addresses a controversial topic and argues for a particular position on that topic by providing reasons that support the position taken on the issue. (Chapter 4)

PERTINENT Relevant and important. (Chapter 7)

PLAGIARISM Failing to acknowledge properly the source of information—whether intentional or unintentional. (Chapter 2)

PLAIN LANGUAGE Words that just about anyone familiar with the language should know. (Chapter 9)

POLICY ANALYSIS An applied research product that examines the effectiveness of some policy in achieving its stated goal(s). (Chapter 5)

POLICY PROPOSAL An applied research product that assesses some phenomenon and proposes a plan for addressing it. (Chapter 5)

POSITIVE CONSTRUCTION A sentence structure that expressed some fact. (Chapter 9)

PRESENTENCE INVESTIGATION REPORT (PSI) A written report of an investigation into a defendant's life that will assist the judge in making an informed sentencing decision. (Chapter 5)

PRECISE Exact. (Chapter 9)

PRELIMINARY RESEARCH   Research undertaken for the purpose of exploring a topic, which can be used to inform, organize, and guide the rest of your research. (Appendix A)

PREMISE   A claim offered to support some other claim or from which a conclusion is derived. (Chapter 5)

PREPOSITIONAL PHRASE   A set of words, beginning with a preposition and ending with a noun or pronoun (called the object of the preposition), that modifies some other part of the sentence. (Chapter 10)

PRESUMPTION   A conclusion reached on the basis of established or accepted facts and does not require evidence. (Chapter 6)

PREVIEWS   Language that gives the audience a glimpse of information to come as a way of linking present information to future information. (Chapter 11)

PRIMACY EFFECT   The phenomenon whereby an audience is strongly affected by the material encountered first. (Chapter 4)

PRIMARY AUDIENCE   The key person or group for whom a communication is intended, who will use the communication to guide decisions and/or actions. (Chapter 3)

PRIMARY SOURCE   The original source of some piece of information. (Chapter 6)

PROBATIVE VALUE   Usefulness is proving the truth or falsity of the proposition to which it is legally connected. (Chapter 6)

PROFESSIONALISM   The consistent exhibiting of certain personal characteristics in addition to technical competence that inspires trust. (Chapters 1 and 2)

PROGRESS CIRCLE   A visual indicator of how far into the presentation we are. (Chapter 11)

PROPER   Conforming to accepted standards. (Chapter 8)

PURPOSE STATEMENT   A way of stating a communication's objective that, in a single, succinct sentence, tells the audience both the topic and purpose of the communication. (Chapter 3)

Q

Q&A SESSION   The period after one or more presentations when the audience can ask the presenter(s) questions. (Chapter 11)

QUOTATION   Source material repeated verbatim—using the exact same words and sentence structure to express the exact same idea as the source. (Chapter 10)

R

REAL EVIDENCE   Tangible evidence (proof) that can be observed in a courtroom using the five senses. (Chapter 6)

RECENCY EFFECT   The phenomenon whereby an audience is strongly affected by the last material encountered. (Chapter 4)

REDUNDANT   The quality of a word or collection of words that is superfluous because it merely repeats information that appears elsewhere in the communication. (Chapter 10)

REPLICATION   Occurs when documented steps can be followed to achieve the same results. (Chapter 7)

REPLY POST   A discussion forum post that responds to or builds off of another discussion forum post. (Chapter 9)

RESEARCH   A purposeful, systematic investigation designed to increase knowledge. (Chapter 6)

RESEARCH PAPER   A formal document that communicates the results of the author's purposeful, systematic investigation of a topic. (Chapter 6)

RESEARCH QUESTION   A specific question that can be answered by conducting research. (Appendix A)

RESOLUTION   In an argument, the one main conclusion that must be resolved to end the argument; the heart of the argument. (Chapter 5)

RESPONSIVENESS   A characteristic of a communication that directly and thoroughly reflects, or reacts to, the situation at hand; directly addressing the objective, adhering to all parameters, and being tailored to the audience(s). (Chapter 1, Chapter 3)

RÉSUMÉ   A document listing a job applicant's education, skills, and employment history. (Chapter 2)

RETWEET   A reposting or forwarding of a post on Twitter. (Chapter 10)

REVIEWS   Language that reminds the audience of material already presented as a way of linking present information with past information. (Chapter 11)

RHETORICAL QUESTION   A question asked for which no answer is sought. (Chapter 10)

RUN-ON SENTENCE   A statement that expresses more than one complete thought and has two or more sets of subjects and verbs. (Chapter 8)

RUNNING HEAD   An abbreviated form of the paper's title, which (according to APA style) should be placed in the upper left-hand corner of the page and be set in all caps. (Appendix B)

S

SANS SERIF Fonts with letters that do not have little "feet," such as Arial and Calibri. (Chapter 11)

SEARCH ENGINE An Internet program or website that allows users to input search terms to obtain information sources matching the search term. (Appendix A)

SEARCH TERMS Words typed into a search engine to generate results. (Appendix A)

SEARCH WARRANT AFFIDAVIT An affidavit (written statement of facts made under oath) submitted by a police officer to a judge to request a search warrant. (Chapter 6)

SECONDARY AUDIENCE The person or people who will read/listen to a communication and whose decisions/actions may be influenced but will not be directly dictated by the communication. (Chapter 3)

SECONDARY SOURCE A source other than the primary source of some information. (Chapter 6)

SELF-PLAGIARISM Reusing your own work, either in part or in whole—such as submitting the same paper in two courses or using a part of a paper written in one course for a discussion post in another course—without the express permission of both instructors. (Chapter 2)

SENTENCE CASE A way of formatting that means capitalizing only the first word and any proper nouns. (Appendix B)

SENTENCE FRAGMENT A statement that lacks a subject and/or verb and does not express a complete thought. (Chapter 8)

SENTENCE OUTLINE The blueprint for a communication that arranges complete sentences along with key words and phrases (for section headings) in a way that conveys what information will be presented in what order. (Chapter 4)

SERIF Fonts with letters that do have little "feet," such as Times New Roman and Cambria. (Chapter 11)

SLANG An informal way of saying something that is known to and used by members of broad groups. (Chapter 9)

SKEPTICAL The characteristic of a person who doubts rather than automatically believes. (Chapter 5)

SOURCE The origin of some information. (Chapter 6)

SOURCE EVIDENCE Proof that originates outside of the communication offering it as substantiation of some claim. (Chapter 6)

STANDARD OF PROOF The level of probability necessary to conclude that enough evidence has been presented to prove (substantiate) a claim. (Chapter 6)

SUMMARY Source material relayed using not only our own words and sentence structure but also in substantially less space to convey the source's main idea accurately. (Chapter 10)

T

TACT Showing consideration for others and their situations. (Chapter 9)

TECHNICAL COMMUNICATION The process of finding, using, and sharing information. (Chapter 1)

TED QUESTIONS Questions that ask a person to tell, explain, and describe something. (Chapter 1)

TERMINAL POINTS Punctuation marks at the end of a sentence: period, question mark, exclamation point. (Chapter 8)

TERTIARY AUDIENCE People or groups who might be interested in a communication and whose decisions/actions may be influenced by the communication although they are remote from the communication in terms of time and space. (Chapter 3)

TESTIMONIAL EVIDENCE Evidence (proof) that people say. (Chapter 6)

TEXTING SLANG Abbreviated forms of expressions used in text messaging. (Chapter 9)

THESAURITIS Replacing simple terms with fancy terms in an effort to impress the audience. (Chapter 9)

THESIS STATEMENT A way of stating a communication's objective that identifies the topic as well as the communicator's stance on that topic. (Chapter 3)

TITLE CASE A way of formatting that means capitalizing the first word, all major words, any word that is four or more letters, and words connected to a capitalized word via hyphen. (Appendix B)

TONE Attitude toward the subject and the communication task itself. (Chapter 2)

TOPIC OUTLINE The blueprint for a communication that arranges key words and phrases in a way that conveys what information will be presented in what order without going into detail. (Chapter 4)

TOPIC SENTENCE A clear statement of what a paragraph is about. (Chapter 4)

TOTAL EVIDENCE All available relevant evidence. (Chapter 6)

TRADITIONAL STYLE With PowerPoint, the content slide style wherein the title is a word or phrase and the content is usually in a bullet/numbered list. (Chapter 11)

TRANSITION   A word or collection of words that connects ideas within a communication. (Chapter 4)

TRITE EXPRESSIONS   Overused, unoriginal, and generally meaningless statements. (Chapter 10)

TRUTH   An accurate reflection of reality. (Chapter 8)

TWEET   An original post on Twitter. (Chapter 10)

U

UNTRUTH   A statement that is known or believed to be false. (Chapter 8)

V

VOLUME EFFECT   The phenomenon whereby an audience is strongly affected by the material encountered the most. (Chapter 4)

ANSWERS TO END-OF-CHAPTER EXERCISES

CHAPTER 1 – INTRODUCTION

Matching

1. n. professionalism
2. k. interview
3. l. logic
4. d. compelling
5. g. correctness
6. m. organization
7. o. technical communication
8. p. TED questions
9. j. interrogation
10. c. clarity
11. b. annotated bibliography
12. f. conciseness
13. h. credibility
14. e. completeness
15. a. 5WH questions
16. i. evidence

Writing

Note: Answers will vary, but some suggestions are provided here.

1. For students, effective communication skills are necessary for earning good grades, a high GPA, and graduation. As they transition into the workforce, students (and others) will need effective communication skills to get recommendation letters, prepare job application materials, and participate in job interviews. Beyond college, employers are looking for strong communication skills, then they make hiring decisions. Not only will practitioners spend a lot of time writing and speaking, but also effective communication fosters credibility, trust, and confidence; makes them more successful at their job; helps their agency's

reputation; and facilitates the effective and efficient operation of the criminal justice system. This is true for police officers, crime analysts, lawyers, and correctional officers.

2. Criminal justice communications are one form of technical communication. Technical communication is the process of finding, using, and sharing information; and it is different from other forms of communication, most notably those communications that are opinionated and/or sensationalized. Where opinionated communications often involve the communicator sharing personal information and using personal language, technical communications are objective and impersonal. Unlike criminal justice communications, opinionated communications thus may include the communicator's experiences, feelings, intuitions, passions, preferences, and attitudes. While sensationalized communications are developed for dramatic or entertainment purposes, criminal justice communications are serious. Sensationalized communications may try to frighten or trick, use emotional appeals, or inspire fear or other emotions. But criminal justice communications either present information in a nonjudgmental, purely descriptive manner, or they seek to persuade using logic and evidence.

3. Criminal justice communications involve multiple special challenges: (1) consequences, (2) conflicts of interest, (3) sensitivity, (4) urgency, and (5) complexity. First, for both students and practitioners, communications are high-stakes endeavors. For practitioners, communications can have serious consequences that extend beyond the communicator. Second, for both students and practitioners, communications can involve conflicts of interests, where the communicator has to choose between competing concerns. Third, criminal justice communications often involve sensitive topics and situations, which can be controversial and emotional. Fourth, criminal justice communications can involve urgency, which is a combination of time sensitivity, seriousness, and pressure. And fifth, criminal justice communications can be complex, requiring communicators to address highly complicated, nuanced material perhaps from multiple fields of study.

4. The nine principles of compelling criminal justice communication are (1) professionalism, (2) responsiveness, (3) organization, (4) logic, (5) evidence, (6) completeness, (7) correctness, (8) clarity, and (9) conciseness. First, professionalism refers to the consistent exhibiting of certain personal characteristics in addition to technical competence that inspires trust. Second, responsiveness means directly addressing the objective, adhering to all parameters, and being tailored to the audience(s). Third, organization involves the arrangement of information in a manner that will best help the communication achieve its purpose. Fourth, logic refers to the reasoning used to support a belief or reach a conclusion. Fifth, evidence is proof of a claim, grounds for belief, or that which justifies belief. Sixth, completeness refers to thoroughness—containing all pertinent parts and information. Seventh, correctness means free from error in terms of both the truth/accuracy of the information itself and the proper presentation of that information. Eighth, clarity means straightforward, unambiguous, and therefore able to be

understood. And ninth, conciseness means using as few simple words as possible to make a point.

5. The six stages of the communication process are (1) planning, (2) collecting information, (3) synthesizing information, (4) drafting, (5) improving and finalizing, and (6) delivering. First, planning involves determining and clarifying the communication's objective(s), parameters, and audience(s). It also involves laying out exactly how we will proceed through the rest of the process of producing the communication, such as setting milestones with deadlines. Second, collecting information involves deciding what information is needed and where, and then making and executing a plan for acquiring the needed information. Also, it involves critically evaluating evidence, avoiding sources of dubious credibility, and compensating for flawed sources by using multiple sources. It might involve building an annotated bibliography. Third, synthesizing information involves studying and making sense of all the collected information and then figuring out how to put together all the pieces of information to form a coherent whole. After reading the sources, this stage involves organizing and outlining the communication. Fourth, drafting means creating the first full iteration of the communication. This stage involves getting all the material down on paper, but not a concern with writing quality. Fifth, improving and finalizing involves critically evaluating our drafts and then modifying them until we have done the best we can do. We start with the big issues and then move on to the smaller issues only after we have addressed the big issues. And sixth, delivering involves submitting the final paper or giving the presentation.

6. Answers will vary.

7. Answers will vary.

CHAPTER 2 – PRINCIPLE 1: PROFESSIONALISM
Matching

1. i. ethics
2. d. contractions
3. m. lying
4. t. self-plagiarism
5. a. assertive communication style
6. o. performance reviews
7. h. ethical dilemma
8. p. personal words
9. b. cheating
10. s. résumé
11. n. mosaic plagiarism
12. c. colloquialisms
13. q. plagiarism
14. u. tone
15. g. ethical codes of conduct

16. e. cover letter
17. l. loaded terms
18. r. professionalism
19. f. diction
20. k. integrity
21. j. inappropriate paraphrasing

Multiple Choice

1. b
2. a
3. a
4. b
5. c
6. a
7. b
8. d
9. a
10. b
11. a
12. d
13. a
14. c
15. c
16. d
17. c
18. c
19. a
20. b

Editing

Note: Answers may vary, but some suggestions are provided here.

1. This paper presents the major categories of terrorism, comparing and contrasting the different types of terrorism in terms of goals, tactics, targets, and consequences. The goal of this paper is to facilitate a better understanding of what terrorism is and of its many forms.
2. Terrorists believe that by frightening people, they can achieve change.
3. Terrorism is a popular topic in the news and entertainment media.
4. There are many ways for governments to guard against terrorism. (Then list ways rather than making a tasteless joke that trivializes the issue.)
5. Many people, fearing terrorism and worrying about the next terrorist, wonder what can be done to prevent terrorism.
6. This paper is about terrorism. Or, This paper is about the crime of terrorism.
7. Having a stable job can serve as a buffer between having extreme political view and violent behavior (LaFree, Jensen, James, & Safer-Lichtenstein, 2018). Or, Employed people with extreme political views are less likely than unemployed

people with extreme political views to go on to commit violent crime (LaFree, Jensen, James, & Safer-Lichtenstein, 2018).

8. Criminology "has paid insufficient attention" to violent political extremism (LaFree, Jensen, James, & Safer-Lichtenstein, 2018, p. 258).

Writing

Note: Answers will vary, but some suggestions are provided here.

1. Professionalism is important for both students and practitioners of criminal justice. Students should learn to make professionalism a habit, so that maintaining professionalism comes natural to them once they embark on a criminal justice career. Additionally, academic integrity is a form of professionalism. Students need to be sure to avoid lying, cheating, and plagiarizing. Not only do these actions speak poorly of their integrity and professionalism, but they also can result in penalties that can reduce the chance of successful employment, such as a lower GPA (due to failing the assignment or course) and an "F for cheating" on the transcript. For practitioners, professionalism correlates with success. On the one hand, professionals are good workers who can be counted on to get the job done despite challenges that may arise. These are the people who are most likely to get jobs and promotions. On the other hand, professionalism instills trust, giving professional people and their organization legitimacy, which makes people more likely to cooperate and obey laws and agents of the criminal justice system. People who are unprofessional can tarnish the reputation of their agency or even the entire criminal justice system.

2. The first guideline for professionalism is to adopt an assertive communication style. The assertive communication style is the middle ground between aggressiveness and passivity. Assertive communicators are goal-oriented and straightforward, open and honest, and respectful of and attentive to others. The second guideline is to adhere to the strictest standards of integrity and ethics, which involves having high personal standards of morality and consistently using those standards to make decisions and guide action. And the third guideline is to maintain an appropriate level of formality, which relates to both tone and diction. In terms of tone, we should maintain a formal to moderately formal communication style, which is achieved by being objective instead of subjective, logical instead of emotional, serious instead of humorous, and impersonal instead of intimate. In terms of diction, we should avoid personal words, contractions, colloquialisms, and loaded terms.

3. Answers will vary.

4. Answers will vary.

CHAPTER 3 – PRINCIPLE 2: RESPONSIVENESS

Matching

1. d. informative communications
2. j. secondary audience
3. l. thesis statement

4. e. modular design
5. c. essay verb
6. a. coverage statement
7. k. tertiary audience
8. i. responsiveness
9. b. essay topic
10. h. purpose statement
11. f. persuasive communications
12. g. primary audience

Multiple Choice
1. b
2. c
3. a
4. a
5. d
6. b
7. a
8. c
9. d
10. c
11. b
12. a
13. a

Editing
Note: Answers may vary, but some suggestions are provided here.

1. Shaming should be used as a sanction for convicted white-collar criminals. Or, Shaming would be an effective sanction to use for convicted white-collar criminals.
2. Home confinement with electronic monitoring is a cost-effective alternative to pretrial detention as well as to post-conviction sanctioning.
3. Over time, felon disenfranchisement has shifted to being a punishment against the wealthy to becoming a method of controlling the poor. Or, The disenfranchisement of felons and ex-felons impacted the results of the 2000 presidential election.
4. This paper argues against the decriminalization of marijuana. Or, This paper will argue that marijuana use should be decriminalized.
5. Incarceration is the least effective method for deterring crime and rehabilitating criminals. Or, Compared with alternative sanctions such as fines, home confinement with electronic monitoring, and drug courts, incarceration costs more money and yet prevents less crime.
6. Sex offender registration and community notification laws are ineffective in preventing sex offending. Or, Sex offender registration and community notification laws are overly broad and should only apply to people convicted of the most serious sex crimes. Or, Sex offender registration and community notification serve as barriers to effective community reintegration.

Writing

Note: Answers will vary, but some suggestions are provided here.

1. Both academic and professional criminal justice communications may be judged to be failures if they are not directly and fully responsive to their objective, requirements (parameters), and audience. In school, a nonresponsive communication will result in reduced or no credit. No credit might be the result if the communication departs substantially from its required objective and/or parameters. In the field, a nonresponsive communication might fail to meet a need, be useless to its audience, confuse the audience, be perceived as offensive, have immediate negative consequences (such as when opposing counsel rightfully objects to one of our questions), and/or give others an unfavorable impression of you and perhaps your agency. We need to know our audience so that we can use terms they understand, provide the appropriate level of background material, and avoid offending or alienating them. In both school and the field, communications that are too long might not be read/listened to in their entirety.

2. There are three guidelines for developing responsive criminal justice communications: (1) address the objective; (2) adhere to the parameters; and (3) target the audience. First, addressing the objective involves (a) understanding the objective, which involves recognizing the different objectives of communications and may involve asking questions about the assignment; (b) stating the objective clearly and up front in the form of a purpose, coverage, or thesis statement; and (c) achieving the objective by staying focused, providing necessary material, and omitting irrelevant material. Second, adhering to the parameters deals with following any and all requirements for the communication, such as length, resources, and format. And third, targeting the audience involves (a) identifying the audience(s), which might include primary, secondary, and tertiary audiences; (b) learning about the audience(s) in terms of their needs, expectations, knowledge, experiences, and use for the communication; and (c) customizing the communication for the audience(s).

3. A purpose statement is a single sentence that identifies the communication's topic and objective without taking a position on the topic or going into detail about how the topic will be handled. An example of a purpose statement is, "This paper's purpose is to outline different forms of animal cruelty." A coverage statement is a single sentence that identifies the topic and gives the audience a sense of the breadth or depth in which the topic will be covered. An example of a coverage statement is, "This paper will describe various forms of animal cruelty involving livestock." A thesis statement identifies the communication's topic and position on the issue. Where purpose and thesis statements are appropriate for informative communications, thesis statements are appropriate for persuasive communications. An example of a thesis statement is, "Given its extent, needlessness, and consequences to the harmed animals, cruelty to livestock should be felony-level crime."

4. The primary audience is the key person or group for whom the communication is intended and who will use the communication to determine their decisions and/or actions. There is always at least one primary audience. The secondary audience consists of people who will read/listen to the communication and may use the communication to determine their decisions and/or actions; however, they are more removed than the primary audience from the communication process. The tertiary audience consists of still other people who may be interested in the communication, and the communication might influence their decisions or actions. But the tertiary audience is the most removed from the communication process in terms of time and space. Thus, the communication is most relevant for the primary audience and least relevant for the tertiary audience; further, the primary audience is the smallest and least diverse, while the tertiary audience is the largest and most diverse. An example of primary, secondary, and tertiary audiences is a judge's instructions to the jury, where the jury is the primary audience, lawyers and other judges are the secondary audience (who may cite the instructions in their cases), and researchers and interested citizens are the tertiary audience (who may research the instructions for a paper and/or just be interested in legal matters).
5. Answers will vary.

CHAPTER 4 – PRINCIPLE 3: ORGANIZATION

Matching

1. h. persuasive paper
2. n. transition
3. a. BLUF
4. f. organizational device
5. o. volume effect
6. m. topic sentence
7. e. organization
8. j. recency effect
9. d. layered transitioning
10. l. topic outline
11. g. organizational structure
12. b. compound transition
13. c. intelligence briefing
14. i. primacy effect
15. k. sentence outline

Multiple Choice

1. d
2. b
3. d

4. c
5. b
6. a
7. d
8. c
9. a
10. b
11. d
12. b

Editing
Note: Answers may vary, but some suggestions are provided here.

1. There are two good reasons to report crime. First, reporting crime increases the odds that the perpetrator will be apprehended and punished. Second, reporting crime also increases the validity of crime statistics.

2. There are advantages and disadvantages to reporting crime. On the one hand, reporting crime increases the odds that the perpetrator will be apprehended and punished. Further, reporting crime increases the validity of crime statistics. On the other hand, reporting crime can expose the person to danger, such as if the perpetrator wants revenge for being reported. Additionally, reporting crime may lead to the person having to testify in court, which takes time and can be stressful.

3. Whether a crime is reported depends on a series of conditions. First, there needs to be a crime. Second, there needs to be some knowledge of the crime. Third, there needs to be some desire, or motivation, to report the crime. And fourth, there needs to be an ability for the crime to be reported.

4. Some crimes suffer more from under-reporting than other crimes. For example, more robberies than rapes are reported.

5. Crime reports can emerge in different ways. First, victims can report. Second, eyewitnesses can report. Third, people who overhear or find some evidence, like a diary, can report. Fourth, police officers can discover a crime and report, too.

6. People who are victimized by fraudsters sometimes don't report because they feel embarrassed that they fell for a scheme.

7. While many victims do not report their victimization, many other victims do report. The first reason some victims don't report is because they are not aware that they were victimized by a crime. The second reason is that some victims are embarrassed that they were victimized. The third reason is that some victims don't want to deal with the police. And the fourth reason is that some victims might think that reporting the crime will be a waste of time. In contrast, however, many victims do report their victimization. One reason is that they trust the police to do their best to apprehend the perpetrator. A second reason is that think they will get a sense of satisfaction if the perpetrator is

punished. And a third reason is that they think reporting is their duty as a U.S. citizen.

8. It is understandable that Andrew Smith did not report it when he saw someone steal cigarettes from a convenience store. To give a little context, Andrew had been victimized several times in the past and, each time, felt as though the police didn't take his victimizations seriously.

9. Blame and shame go a long way toward explaining under-reporting of crimes such as rape and fraud. Plainly put, people are unlikely to report if they will be blamed or shamed for being victimized.

10. There is a substantial "dark figure" of crime because of under-reporting. Regardless, crime statistics are not entirely useless. For instance, we can use crime statistics to identify trends over time and space.

Writing

Note: Answers will vary, but some suggestions are provided here.

1. The point of communication is to share information, and effective organization makes it easier for the audience to follow along and understand the information. Effective organization also can make a communication more interesting (which means it can make the audience more willing to pay attention) and easier to accept, such as when presenting to a hostile or skeptical audience. For the communicator, organization also can save resources like time and effort. Overall, the communicator can look like an expert as s/he guides her/his audience through a well-structured communication, which can boost her/his credibility.

2. There are five guidelines for developing a well-organized criminal justice communication. First, have a beginning (the introduction), a middle (the body), and an end (the conclusion). Second, outline before you write. There are topic outlines and there are sentence outlines, both of which show what information will be included and in what order. Third, adopt an appropriate organizational structure. There are numerous organizational structures, and the one chosen should be the one that best reflects the communication's objective. Fourth, employ organizational devices to highlight the organizational structure. Organizational devices include abstracts and executive summaries, a table of contents or overview slide, "road maps," transitions, lists, headings and subheadings, and reviews and previews. Fifth, use structural variation to distinguish between major and minor material. Each paragraph should express one idea, start with a transition, and contain a topic sentence. Each sentence should express one thought, with the most important information either at the beginning or end.

3. Answers will vary.

4. Answers will vary.

CHAPTER 5 – PRINCIPLE 4: LOGIC

Matching

1. l. logical fallacy
2. s. skeptical
3. b. assumptions
4. i. inductive logic
5. d. competence
6. h. evidence
7. f. critical thinking
8. o. policy proposal
9. g. deductive logic
10. p. premise
11. a. argument
12. m. logical paradox
13. n. policy analysis
14. e. conclusion
15. k. logic
16. r. resolution
17. c. claim
18. j. inference
19. q. presentence investigation report (PSI)

Multiple Choice

1. d
2. d
3. a
4. b
5. d
6. a
7. a
8. c
9. d
10. a
11. a
12. b
13. b
14. a
15. b
16. c
17. d
18. d
19. a
20. e

Editing

Note: Answers may vary somewhat.

1.

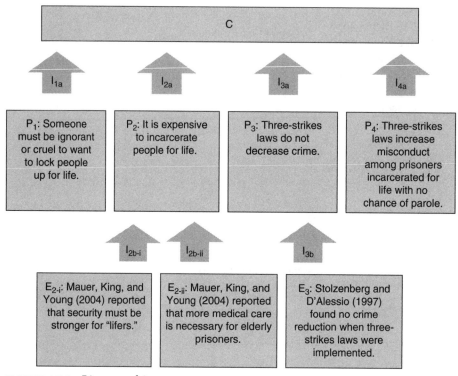

FIGURE AK.1 Diagram of Argument

2. Answers will vary, though the basic conclusion should be the same: The overall argument is adequate.
3. Answers will vary, though appropriate answers will (a) omit P_1 and (b) either omit P_4 or add supporting evidence for it.

Writing

Note: Answers will vary, but some suggestions are provided here.

1. Simply put, logic can protect us from accepting false or dubious claims, making bad decisions, advancing indefensible/inadequate conclusions, and taking ill-advised action.
2. To produce logical communications, we need to (1) be a habitual critical thinker, (2) be informed, (3) avoid logical fallacies, (4) diagram arguments, and (5) advance defensible claims. First, being a habitual critical thinker involves self-awareness, open-mindedness and objectivity, and skepticism. Second, being informed encompasses both the subject matter at hand and, more generally, how logic and argumentation work. Third, we need to avoid making logical fallacies such as fallacies of

inconsistency, irrelevance, vacuity, distortion, and mistaken relationship. Fourth, diagramming arguments helps us understand arguments as well as expose weaknesses in arguments. In doing so, it is important not only to map the argument itself but also to add relevant but absent elements and cross out any irrelevant but present elements. And fifth, advancing defensible claims boils down to ensuring that the claims we make are adequately justified and appropriately phrased. We need to have a solid reason for what we believe and do, in other words, and we need to state our conclusions in a manner that preserves their logic.

3. Answers will vary.
4. Answers will vary.
5. Answers will vary.

CHAPTER 6 – PRINCIPLE 5: EVIDENCE

Matching

1. k. empirical evidence
2. dd. total evidence
3. aa. source evidence
4. d. claim of fact
5. t. probative value
6. a. affidavit
7. p. nonempirical research
8. g. criminal evidence
9. u. real evidence
10. v. research
11. l. evidence
12. y. secondary evidence
13. o. lay witnesses
14. x. search warrant affidavit
15. e. claim of policy
16. bb. standard of proof
17. w. research paper
18. q. peer review
19. m. expert witness
20. z. source
21. f. claim of value
22. h. demonstrative evidence
23. c. circumstantial evidence
24. s. primary source
25. n. judicial notice
26. b. burden of proof
27. r. presumption
28. cc. testimonial evidence
29. i. direct evidence
30. j. documentary evidence

Multiple Choice

1. b
2. b
3. a
4. a
5. a
6. a
7. b
8. b
9. a
10. b
11. b
12. a
13. b
14. b
15. a
16. b
17. a
18. a
19. b
20. a
21. b
22. b
23. a
24. b
25. a

Editing

Note: Answers may vary somewhat (esp. exact language), but some suggestions are provided here.

1. There is no evidence to support this claim of fact. Evidence of cybercrime rates over time needs to be provided to support the claim that rates of cybercrime have been increasing for years.

2. There is no reason to believe that the source of this evidence is credible. "Hackers R Us" not only sounds like a popular/sensational source, but also it sounds less than objective. Empirical, preferably peer-reviewed, research is needed to determine whether one thing causes another thing. Alternatively, Hackers R Us could be used appropriately to substantiate a lesser claim such as, "It has been asserted that the leading cause of cybercrime victimization is low self-control."

3. The source of the evidence provided does seem credible, but there is no logical connection between the evidence and the claim of value. Because this is a claim of value, proving it should begin with identifying objective criteria on which to base a judgment regarding whether cybercrime is not viewed seriously enough. What do we consider "seriously enough?" For each criterion, there needs to be a

way to measure it, a fact claim, and evidence to support the fact claim. Only then can the value claim be judged.

4. Wikipedia is not a credible source of evidence to substantiate a fact claim of correlation. It is a secondary, nonempirical source. The source of this claim in Wikipedia should be consulted and then cited.

5. The source of the evidence provided does seem credible, but evidence from 2004 is not relevant to a fact claim about current (2018) conditions. Current evidence needs to be provided, or the claim should be edited to remove the phrase "At present."

6. The evidence does not provide certain knowledge of the fact claim. The claim should be revised to reflect what we actually do know based on the evidence: According to two eyewitnesses, the girl hit the boy and stole his lunch.

7. The video footage is circumstantial evidence, which does not allow us to be certain of the asserted claim. A good deal of inference is involved in using the video footage evidence to substantiate the claim. Other people, for example, wear red jackets and black pants. While the video footage has some probative value because it is logically consistent with the claim that Amy is the girl in the film, as she was wearing a red jacket and black pants, but additional evidence is needed to reasonably conclude that Amy is the girl in the film.

8. This is hearsay evidence. Instead of relying on a secondary source of the witness's statement about not having seen Amy hit the boy, we need to consult the primary source: the witness.

9. This is circumstantial evidence. While it is logically consistent with the claim, it does not with certainty prove the claim. Many people are left-handed. Had the evidence indicated that the assailant was right-handed where Amy is left-handed, then it would have been strong evidence that Amy was *not* the assailant. More evidence is needed to prove that Amy is the assailant.

10. This is circumstantial evidence. While logically consistent with the claim that Amy was on her computer 5 miles away at the time of the crime—and thus could not possibly have committed the crime—it does not by itself rule out the possibility that Amy committed the crime. Someone else could have been using Amy's computer.

Writing

Note: Answers will vary, but some suggestions are provided here.

1. Evidence plays a central role in the study and practice of criminal justice. Evidence is necessary to make rational, informed decisions and to guide action, and criminal justice students and professionals are expected to prove the assertions they make. Student research papers, for example, need to be based on evidence. Evidence is a key part of the day-to-day operation of the criminal justice system, from policing to courts to corrections. Moreover, scientific evidence is increasingly being used in courtrooms. And since 2000, the criminal justice system has embraced the evidence-based practice movement, meaning that decisions about crime-control policies are made on the basis of evidence about what works.

2. We need to evaluate each piece of evidence and then the total evidence. To evaluate a single piece of evidence, we should ask the following eight questions:
    1. Has the evidence been legally/ethically obtained?
    2. Is the evidence logically connected to the claim it seeks to prove?
    3. Is the claim to which the evidence relates logically connected to the ultimate issue to be decided?
    4. Does the probative value of evidence outweigh the risks of using the evidence?
    5. Does the person providing the evidence have the ability to narrate events and understand the duty to tell the truth?
    6. Should the person providing the evidence be believed?
    7. Is the evidence what it is claimed to be?
    8. Is the evidence the original source/version?

    Total evidence refers to all available evidence. A case/argument should be decided based on the total evidence—not a single piece or some subset of the total evidence. The person who initiated the argument generally has the burden of proving his or her case so as to meet some standard of proof. The more serious the consequences, the higher the standard of proof.

3. Answers will vary.
4. Answers will vary.

CHAPTER 7 – PRINCIPLE 6: COMPLETENESS
Matching
1. b. crime scene report
2. d. depth
3. f. pertinent
4. a. breadth
5. g. replication
6. e. lab report
7. c. complete

Multiple Choice
1. a
2. b (arson is missing)
3. b (judges are missing)
4. b (stage 1: plan is missing)
5. a
6. b (German legal system description is missing)
7. b (there are no reasons for to support the thesis/ultimate claim)
8. a
9. a
10. b (include graphics is missing)
11. b (oddities is missing)

Editing
Note: Answers may vary, but some suggestions are provided here.

1. history of policing in the United States, major phases of policing in China, key developments in Anglo-American law enforcement
2. identifying words for police used in England and perhaps some other countries, identifying words for police, lawyers, and judges used in England
3. coercive methods of crime control, liberal approaches to crime control, non-incarcerative methods of crime control, new and emerging methods of crime control, effective methods of crime control
4. wrongful convictions in the midwestern United States, wrongful convictions in the United States, miscarriages of justice in Oklahoma
5. enumerating and describing the different reasons for wrongful convictions, determining the frequency of the different reasons for wrongful convictions, comparing and contrasting the different reasons for wrongful convictions
6. major events in Watergate, turning points in Watergate, a month-by-month chronology of Watergate
7. chronicling wrongful convictions in the twenty-first century, focusing on the justice system process; chronicling wrongful convictions in the southern United States, examining the people involved
8. examining causes and ways to prevent property crime victims from lying to police, theory-based ways to prevent property crime victims from lying to police
9. examining reasons why elderly larceny-theft victims lie to police, and providing step-by-step instructions for ways to reduce lying; examining reasons why minority larceny-theft victims lie to police, including case studies for each reason

Writing
Note: Answers will vary, but some suggestions are provided here.

1. Complete communications are important for criminal justice students and professionals alike. Complete communications avoid the problems caused by incomplete communications. The first problem incomplete communications cause is implying that the person who created it does not care and didn't put enough thought and effort into the product's development to identify and include everything important. The second problem is implying that the person who created it is ignorant, not knowing the subject matter well enough to recognize what information that was pertinent was missing and should have been added. The first and second problems can reflect negatively on you, your boss, and even your entire organization. The third problem is that an incomplete communication might have to be redone until it is complete, which is an inefficient consumption of resources. Fourth, an incomplete communication can be difficult if not impossible to follow, and so the audience might not be able to understand or implement the message. Fifth, an incomplete communication can result in poor, ineffective, unsafe, and/or illegal actions. Missing information can cause significant problems. In sum, the field of criminal justice embraces the need for "the truth, the whole truth, and nothing but the truth."

2. There are two basic guidelines for producing complete communications. First, include all pertinent information. Pertinent information is both relevant and important. To include all pertinent information, (a) understand your objective, parameters, and audience; (b) do your research; (c) present both sides; (d) outline before you write; (e) deliver on promises; (f) present balanced coverage; (g) remember to cite the sources of all ideas, information, and words; (h) be your own critic; (i) get feedback; and (j) give yourself time. Second, address any coverage constraints. Coverage constraints can arise when there is too much information or when there is too little information. When there is too much information, try to strike an appropriate balance between breadth and depth, such as refining the topic to make it less broad and/or detailed. Too little information can stem from there being no information (such as on a new topic), flawed information, or loosely related information. When there is *no information*, use the following strategies: (a) acknowledge the lack of information on the topic; (b) try to draw on information that is loosely related (when appropriate); and (c) try to conduct research/investigation to produce pertinent information. When there is *flawed information*, use the following strategies: (a) acknowledge the limitations of existing information on the topic; (b) try to reach conclusions based on the flawed information, but then clearly articulate how those conclusions are tentative due to the flawed information on which they are based; and (c) try to conduct research/investigation to produce stronger information. When there is *loosely related information*, use these strategies: (a) acknowledge the loose connection between the topic and the available information; (b) try to reach conclusions based on the loosely related information, but then clearly articulate how those conclusions are tentative due to their loose connection with the information on which they are based; and (c) try to conduct research/investigation to produce more relevant information.

3. Answers will vary.

4. Answers will vary.

CHAPTER 8 – PRINCIPLE 7: CORRECTNESS
Matching

1. c. correct
2. j. pausing points
3. g. homophones
4. a. arrest report
5. p. untruth
6. d. critique
7. n. terminal point
8. i. nondefining clause
9. f. half-truth
10. l. run-on sentence
11. b. complete sentence
12. h. knowledge

13. e. defining clause
14. o. truth
15. k. proper
16. m. sentence fragment

Multiple Choice

1. a
2. a
3. b
4. b
5. b
6. b
7. a
8. a
9. a
10. a
11. a
12. b
13. a
14. b
15. b
16. b
17. a

Editing
The necessary edits are indicated by underlining.

1. Listening to the first witness's story might have had an <u>effect</u> on the second witness's story.
2. The male witness stood <u>beside</u> the female witness.
3. From the victim's account, the officer <u>inferred</u> that the victim felt responsible.
4. They suspect said he was innocent. <u>Regardless</u>, he was arrested.
5. The new evidence might <u>alter</u> the timeline of events leading up to the crime.
6. The investigating officer thought the DNA evidence would <u>complement</u> the video footage.
7. The interview served a <u>dual</u> purpose.
8. Because the child was a <u>minor</u>, the officer wanted the child's parent present for questioning.
9. The crime happened at work rather than at the victim's <u>residence</u>.
10. The <u>principal</u> investigator watched the video footage multiple times.
11. According to the witness, "The robber asked if I 'wanted to die today,' but I was too scared to say anything."
12. The store would not be open the next day because <u>its</u> windows were broken.
13. Under common law, "every final decision by a court creates a precedent" (Worrall, Hemmens, and Nored, 2010, p. 35).

Writing

Note: Answers will vary, but some suggestions are provided here.

1. Being incorrect can lead to confusion and be expensive, counterproductive, offensive, and even lethal. Wrongful convictions and executions exemplify the most obvious form of incorrectness: being wrong about the truth. Various problems can result from the improper presentation of information, such as typos in laws, books, and search warrants. Not telling the truth limits knowledge. Errors, including inconsistencies, in writing mechanics might cause your audience to winder if you are ignorant or just plain sloppy, which in turn can lead your audience to doubt the substance of your communication. The audience might wonder if you can be trusted to report facts accurately and interpret evidence correctly if you prove that you are unable (or unwilling) to use proper writing mechanics. In sum, improper writing mechanics can chip away at your credibility, thus jeopardizing the effectiveness of the communication as well as your reputation as a professional.

2. To develop correct communication, we need to (1) present only information that is true and (2) present information in proper form. The first, presenting only true information, involves (a) knowing the truth, (b) telling the truth, and (c) avoiding untruths and half-truths. The second, presenting information in its proper form, involves (a) learning the rules, (b) using proper grammar, (c) using proper spelling, (d) using proper punctuation, and (e) being consistent.

3. Answers will vary.

4. Answers will vary.

CHAPTER 9 – PRINCIPLE 8: CLARITY

Matching

1. w. slang
2. j. hedging
3. d. double-barreled question
4. u. precise
5. y. texting slang
6. p. litotes
7. h. expert witness testimony
8. z. thesauritis
9. c. discussion forum
10. t. positive construction
11. k. hyperbole
12. v. reply post
13. b. direct
14. s. plain language
15. l. idiom
16. x. tact
17. a. clarity

18. o. literal
19. q. negative construction
20. g. euphemism
21. n. jargon
22. f. equivocating
23. r. original post
24. i. figurative
25. m. ironic
26. e. double negative

Multiple Choice
1. b
2. a
3. b
4. b
5. b
6. a
7. a
8. b
9. b
10. a
11. a
12. b
13. a
14. b
15. a

Editing
Note: Answers may vary, but some suggestions are provided here.

1. After the couple took the bloody sock out of the car, they hid the sock. Or, The couple hid the bloody sock after they took it out of the car.
2. Would you take the evidence to the lab. Or, Please take the evidence to the lab.
3. You should carry a loaded gun. Or, My advice is to always carry a loaded gun.
4. Is there a better way to handle this burglary case?
5. My boss cannot decide how to handle juveniles who burglarize.
6. Their goal was to make a quick arrest.
7. Someone must have been at home when the burglary happened.
8. They needed money because his mom was unemployed.
9. The police might be interested in investigating the child's background. Or, The police might investigate the child's background.
10. Is the child attending school? Is the child employed?
11. He said he was not stealing because he always intended to return the money.
12. After breaking the window, the boy entered the home.

Writing

Note: Answers may vary, but some suggestions are provided here.

1. The success of a communication is determined by whether the receiver under-stands the message the way the sender intends, and clarity is a way of ensuring the success of communications. When messages are clear, they are as easy as possible for the receiver to understand. When messages are unclear, they might be hard to understand or cause misunderstanding. Unclear student communi-cations fail to demonstrate the student's substantive language and communica-tion skills. Unclear field communications might result in people not being able to make sense of them, which makes evidence less helpful in solving crimes and securing guilty convictions. When evidence is too vague, confusing, or unintel-ligible, the criminal justice system is less effective and efficient.

2. There are five guidelines for producing clear communications: (1) be explicit, (2) use plain language, (3) be literal, (4) prefer positive to negative construc-tions, and (5) avoid double-barreled questions. First, being explicit means being straightforward. When we are explicit, we are direct, precise, and unambiguous. Thus, we leave no room for doubt as to what we mean. Second, using plain lan-guage means we choose words that everyone in our audience should be able to understand. Plain language involves favoring simple terms to fancy terms as well as avoiding specialized language (e.g., jargon, slang). Third, being literal means using words according to their actual meaning as opposed to using words in a figurative sense. We are literal when we avoid euphemisms, irony, exaggera-tion, understatement, and idioms. Fourth, preferring positive to negative con-structions involves using negative terms only when doing so is the more direct and less confusing way to convey our meaning. We should always avoid double negatives. Fifth, avoiding double-barreled questions means we refrain from in-cluding two separate issues in a single question. We can avoid double-barreled questions by putting separate issues into separate questions.

3. Answers will vary.

4. Answers will vary.

CHAPTER 10 – PRINCIPLE 9: CONCISENESS

Matching

1. i. rhetorical question
2. d. filler
3. h. retweet
4. j. summary
5. b. concise
6. e. paraphrase
7. k. trite expressions
8. f. prepositional phrase

9. a. abstract
10. c. quotation
11. l. tweet
12. g. redundant

Multiple Choice

1. a
2. b
3. b
4. a
5. b
6. a
7. b
8. b
9. a
10. b

Editing

Note: Answers may vary somewhat, but some suggestions are provided here.

1. Every prisoner was issued a change of clothes.
2. The patrol unit was scheduled to begin at 5:00 a.m. Or, The patrol unit was scheduled to start at 5:00 a.m.
3. The juvenile offender diversion policy failed because it was used as a supplement instead of as an alternative to formal criminal justice intervention.
4. If the chain of custody is violated, then the evidence will be inadmissible in court.
5. The probation officer reported several technical violations.
6. The results indicate that 68.25 percent of the sample admitted speeding at least once within the past week. Or, Results indicate that 68.25 percent of the sample admitted speeding at least once within the past week.
7. The agency hired the job candidate even though that person failed the psychological background test. Or, Although the job candidate failed the psychological background test, the agency hired that person.
8. Stress causes aggressive behavior among adolescents and adults. Or, Stress causes adolescents and adults to behave aggressively.
9. The original plan for the judge to monitor the offenders sentenced to drug courts was not followed.
10. DNA evidence for some cases might have been lost. Or, DNA evidence for some cases might be lost.
11. The presentence investigation report summarized the defendant's criminal history.
12. The officers voted in favor of using pepper spray.

Writing
Note: Answers will vary, but some suggestions are provided here.

1. There are at least two reasons why concise writing is important: (1) it facilitates effective understanding and communication, and (2) there might not be time for more lengthy and detailed communications. First, writing concisely helps the reader focus on the important information. Filler and other unnecessary text can cloud your message and interfere with successful communication. Second, writing concisely makes for a brief communication. Abstracts in academia have upper (and lower) word limits, while intel reports given by professionals are designed to facilitate rapid decision-making for a busy audience.

2. The five guidelines for achieving concise writing are (1) eliminate filler, (2) reword unnecessary prepositional phrases, (3) refrain from redundancy, (4) avoid obvious statements, and (5) prefer summaries to paraphrases and quotations. First, eliminating filler is concerned with editing out words that add no meaning and do not help achieve the communication's purpose. Filler consumes time and space without providing information. Second, unnecessary prepositional phrases should be replaced with briefer wordings, such as substituting possessive constructions for clunky prepositional phrases. Third, redundant text repeats other text in the communication without adding any new information or clarity. Redundant text is superfluous and should be deleted. Fourth, obvious statements imply that the information is known to all and, hence, not necessary to impart. If the information truly is "obvious," then it that information should be deleted; if, however, the information is not "obvious" (considering the intended audience), then the word "obvious" (and other terms with similar meaning) should be deleted. Fifth, quotations and paraphrases should be used only in limited, justified circumstances. Usually, summaries of source material are most effective because they allow us to stay focused on achieving the purpose of our communication and maintaining our voice and flow.

3. Answers will vary.

4. Answers will vary.

CHAPTER 11 – PRESENTATION

Matching

1. d. high contrast
2. k. traditional style
3. f. progress circle
4. i. sans serif
5. b. data visualization
6. h. reviews
7. a. assertion–evidence style
8. g. Q&A session
9. c. design
10. j. serif
11. e. previews

Multiple Choice

1. b
2. b
3. a
4. b
5. b
6. d
7. a
8. c
9. b
10. a
11. a
12. a
13. a
14. d
15. d
16. b
17. c
18. a
19. f
20. c
21. a
22. c
23. b
24. c
25. b

Writing

Note: Answers will vary, but some suggestions are provided here.

1. Ineffective PowerPoint presentations can make us look unprofessional and cast doubt on our credibility as well as impede the audience's attention, comprehension, and memory/recall. Effective presentations, in contrast, not only make us look professional and boost our credibility but also help with audience attention, comprehension, and recall. Effective presentations make it as effortless as possible for the audience to receive and later recall our message.

2. The preparation of effective PowerPoint presentations involves (1) design, (2) structure, and (3) content.

   First, when designing a PowerPoint presentation, we should create our own design rather than using one of PowerPoint's design templates. Our design should use two high-contrast colors, preferably light yellow text on a blue background. If we want to show our organization's logo, we can put it on the first and last slides, small and in a corner. We should choose one or two basic fonts and use a logical combination of uppercase and lowercase letters. The main text should be in a sans serif font, while headings can be in a serif font. If we need to emphasize a word or phrase, we can use italics or extra bold or light weights.

Text should be presented from top and bottom and left to right, which means we should put slide titles at the top and then left-align all text.

Second, when structuring a PowerPoint presentation, we should divide the presentation into its three main components: (1) introduction, (2) body, and (3) conclusion. The introduction and the body should each comprise no more than 10 percent of our presentation, while the body should be 80 percent of our presentation. For each minute we have to present, we should have no more than one content slide. We should also not try to cover too many points: somewhere between two (for shorter presentations) and six (for longer presentations) is recommended. Structure also involves layout. We need to select suitable slide layouts for the different parts of our presentations. The title slide, for example, should use the "Title Slide" layout, while the second slides should use the "Section Header" layout. We need an Overview slide directly after the title slide, which should show the different sections of the presentation. We can then use organizational devices, such as section numbering and progress circles, on the Overview slide and section slides, to help the audience follow along and gauge progress.

Third, we need to use effective methods for presenting our material on the content slides. Whenever possible, we should use the assertion–evidence style instead of traditional-style slides. If we use traditional style, then we need to be sure to put only a limited amount of text on each slide (e.g., following the rule of 5 or rule of 6), to show key words and phrases rather than full sentences and paragraphs, to keep the font large (with body text no smaller than 28-point), and be consistent in the presentation of material (both within and across slides). It is especially important to use parallel structure in lists. If we use the assertion–evidence style, then we will make each content slide's title an assertion (or claim), and then show evidence proving that claim in the body of the slide. The title should not exceed two lines, and we should try to show evidence in graphic rather than text form, only using words where absolutely necessary.

Regardless of which style we choose for our content slides, we need to keep it simple, which involves making one point per slide, giving each slide a unique title, using as little text as possible, preferring graphics to text, and including only essential material on the slides. In choosing a graphic, we should be influenced by the point we seek to make because different graphics are appropriate for making different points. Once we have chosen a graphic, we should present it as simply as possible, avoiding fancy embellishments (e.g., three-dimension or shadow effects), unnecessary data and details, and poor-quality images. Further, to keep it simple, we need to leave out any elements that make us look unprofessional and/or do not help us make our point, such as clipart, cartoons, sound effects, and transitions between slides.

3. The delivery of effective PowerPoint presentations involves (1) handouts, (2) practice, and (3) the actual delivery. First, handouts are an effective complement to a professional PowerPoint presentation. Details that would crowd and complicate PowerPoint slides are appropriate in handouts, such as References and URLs. A good handout will exhibit all nine principles of effective criminal justice communication. In most cases, the handout should be distributed after the presentation so as not to be distracting.

Second, practice is a critical component of effective delivery. To maximize the benefits of practice, make sure you know your material, practice with your PowerPoint, time yourself, record yourself and/or practice with an audience, figure out how to pronounce all words, wean yourself off of a word-for-word script, simulate the actual presentation conditions as closely as possible, take your rehearsals seriously, anticipate questions from the audience, and have a backup plan.

Third, delivery occurs in three phases: (1) approach, (2) speech, and (3) Q&A. To begin, walk calmly to the front of the room. Upload your presentation to the hard drive, make sure the computer's screensaver is off, and then do not begin until all the presentation equipment (e.g., projector, microphone) is ready. Next is the speech. Start by introducing yourself and your topic, then begin your presentation. The most important rule for giving an effective presentation is not to read to the audience. The second most important rule is never to turn your back on the audience. Other guidelines are to maintain eye contact with people around the room, speak slowly and loudly, incorporate reviews and previous, be lively, avoid verbal filler, pay attention to the time, look for signals from the audience, do not apologize, keep your promises, and end on a strong note. Finally, Q&A starts after you have concluded your speech. Invite questions, and then maintain composure, repeat each question before you respond, answer questions directly and honestly, respect the person asking the question, and be honest.

4. Answers will vary.
5. Answers will vary.

INDEX